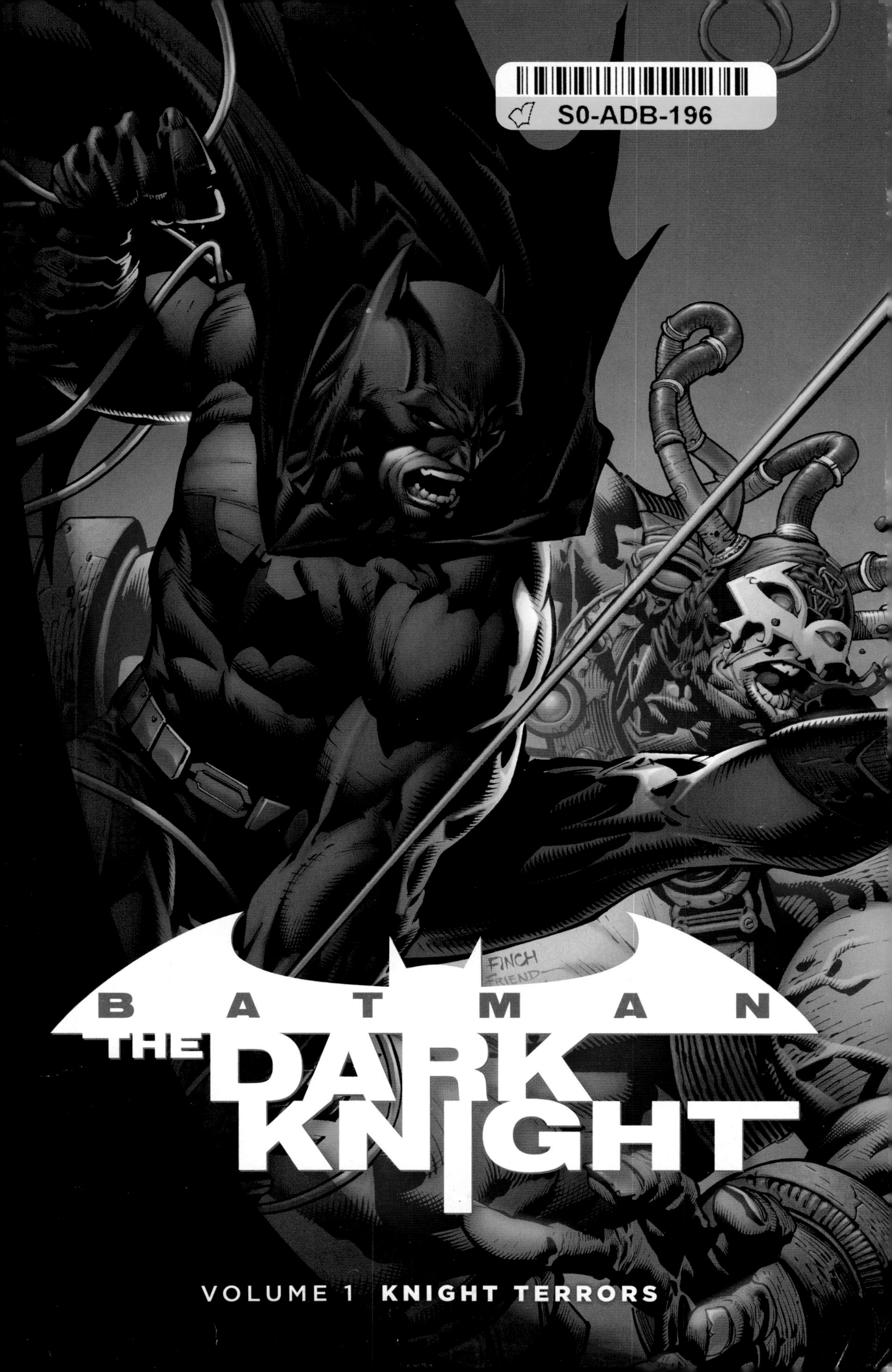
FINCH
FRIEND

BATMAN THE DARK KNIGHT

VOLUME 1 KNIGHT TERRORS

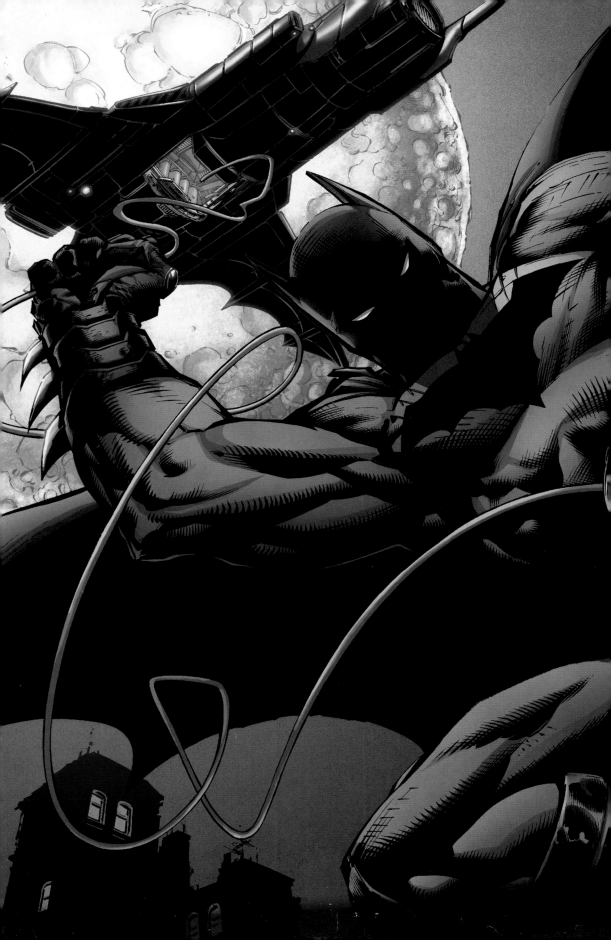

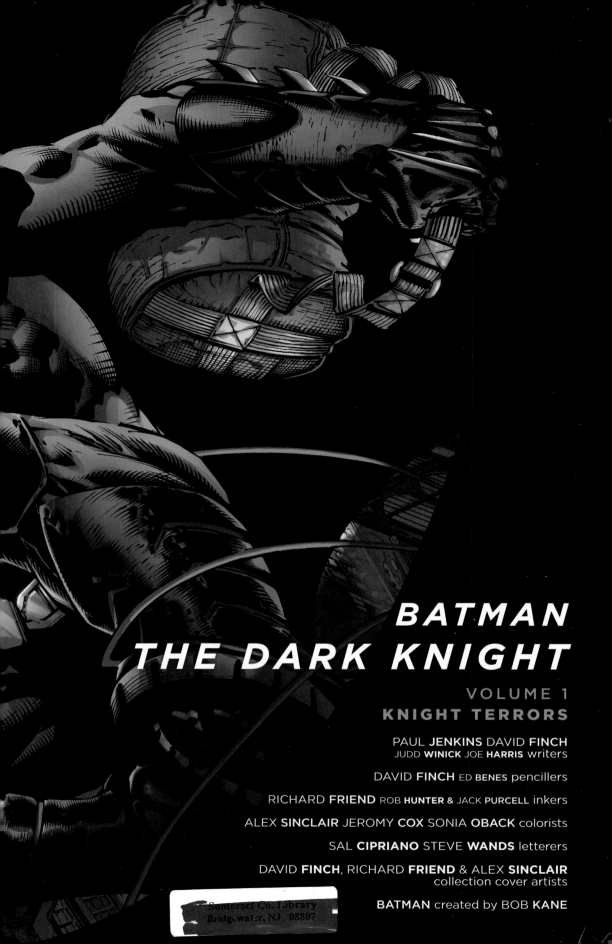

BATMAN
THE DARK KNIGHT

VOLUME 1
KNIGHT TERRORS

PAUL **JENKINS** DAVID **FINCH**
JUDD **WINICK** JOE **HARRIS** writers

DAVID **FINCH** ED BENES pencillers

RICHARD **FRIEND** ROB **HUNTER** & JACK **PURCELL** inkers

ALEX **SINCLAIR** JEROMY **COX** SONIA **OBACK** colorists

SAL **CIPRIANO** STEVE **WANDS** letterers

DAVID **FINCH**, RICHARD **FRIEND** & ALEX **SINCLAIR**
collection cover artists

BATMAN created by BOB **KANE**

MIKE MARTS Editor – Original Series RICKEY PURDIN Assistant Editor – Original Series ROWENA YOW Editor
ROBBIN BROSTERMAN Design Director – Books ROBBIE BIEDERMAN Publication Design

BOB HARRAS Senior VP – Editor-in-Chief, DC Comics

DIANE NELSON President DAN DIDIO and JIM LEE Co-Publishers
GEOFF JOHNS Chief Creative Officer
JOHN ROOD Executive VP – Sales, Marketing and Business Development
AMY GENKINS Senior VP – Business and Legal Affairs NAIRI GARDINER Senior VP – Finance
JEFF BOISON VP – Publishing Planning MARK CHIARELLO VP – Art Direction and Design
JOHN CUNNINGHAM VP – Marketing TERRI CUNNINGHAM VP – Editorial Administration
ALISON GILL Senior VP – Manufacturing and Operations HANK KANALZ Senior VP – Vertigo & Integrated Publishing
JAY KOGAN VP – Business and Legal Affairs, Publishing JACK MAHAN VP – Business Affairs, Talent
NICK NAPOLITANO VP – Manufacturing Administration SUE POHJA VP – Book Sales
COURTNEY SIMMONS Senior VP – Publicity BOB WAYNE Senior VP – Sales

BATMAN THE DARK KNIGHT VOLUME 1: KNIGHT TERRORS

DC Comics, 1700 Broadway, New York, NY 10019
A Warner Bros. Entertainment Company
Printed by RR Donnelley, Salem, VA, USA. 6/14/13. First Printing.

ISBN: 978-1-4012-3711-0

Library of Congress Cataloging-in-Publication Data

Finch, David, 1972-
Batman, the dark knight. Volume 1, Knight terrors / David Finch, Paul Jenkins, Richard Friend.
p. cm.
"Originally published in single magazine form in Batman: The Dark Knight 1-9."
ISBN 978-1-4012-3543-7
1. Graphic novels. I. Jenkins, Paul, 1965- II. Friend, Richard (Illustrator) III. Title. IV. Title: Knight terrors.
PN6728.B36F46 2012
741.5'973—dc23
2012022442

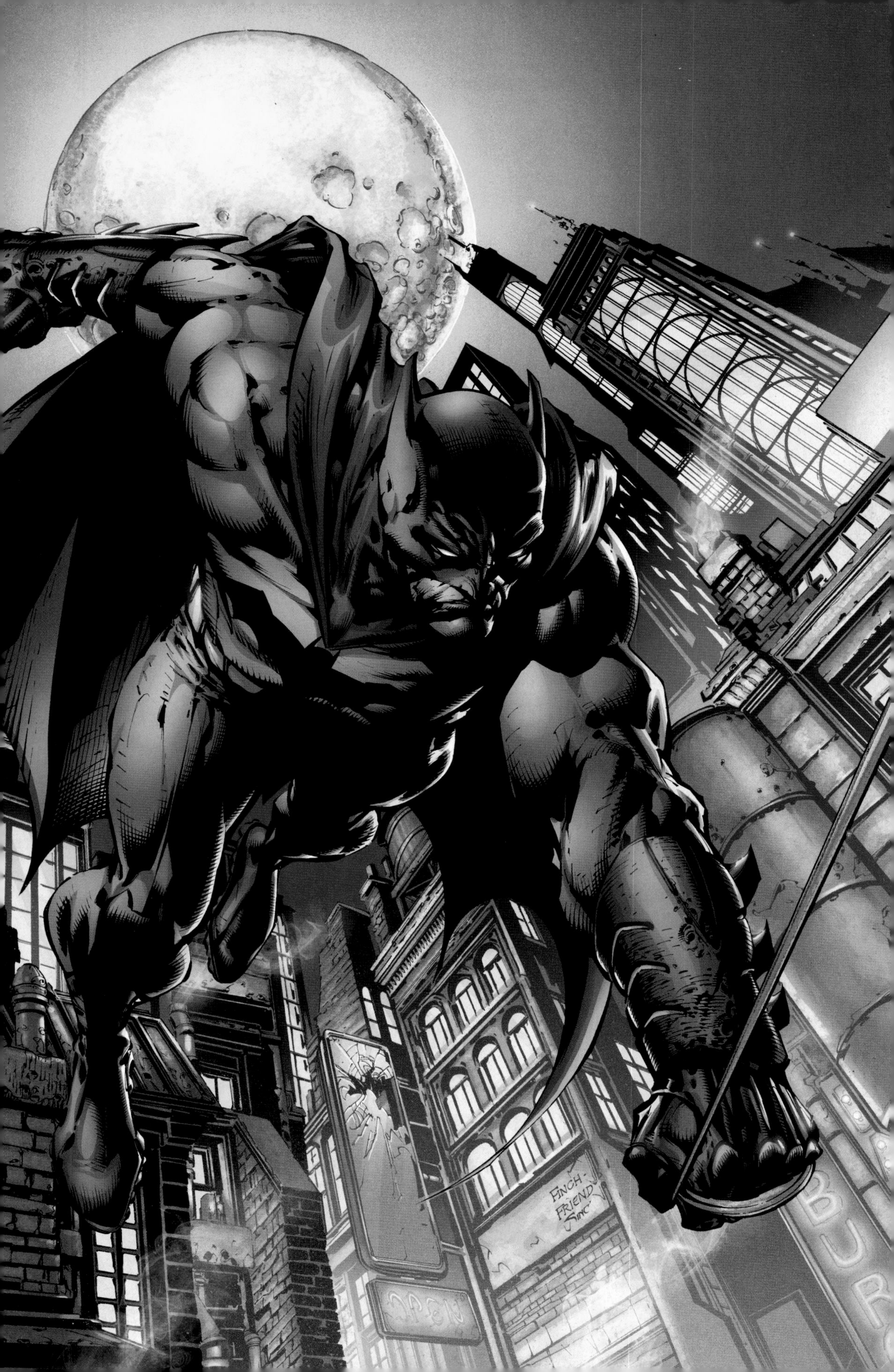
FINCH-
FRIEND
SINC

PAUL

END inker

cover art by DAVID FINCH, RICHARD FRIEND & ALEX SINCLAIR

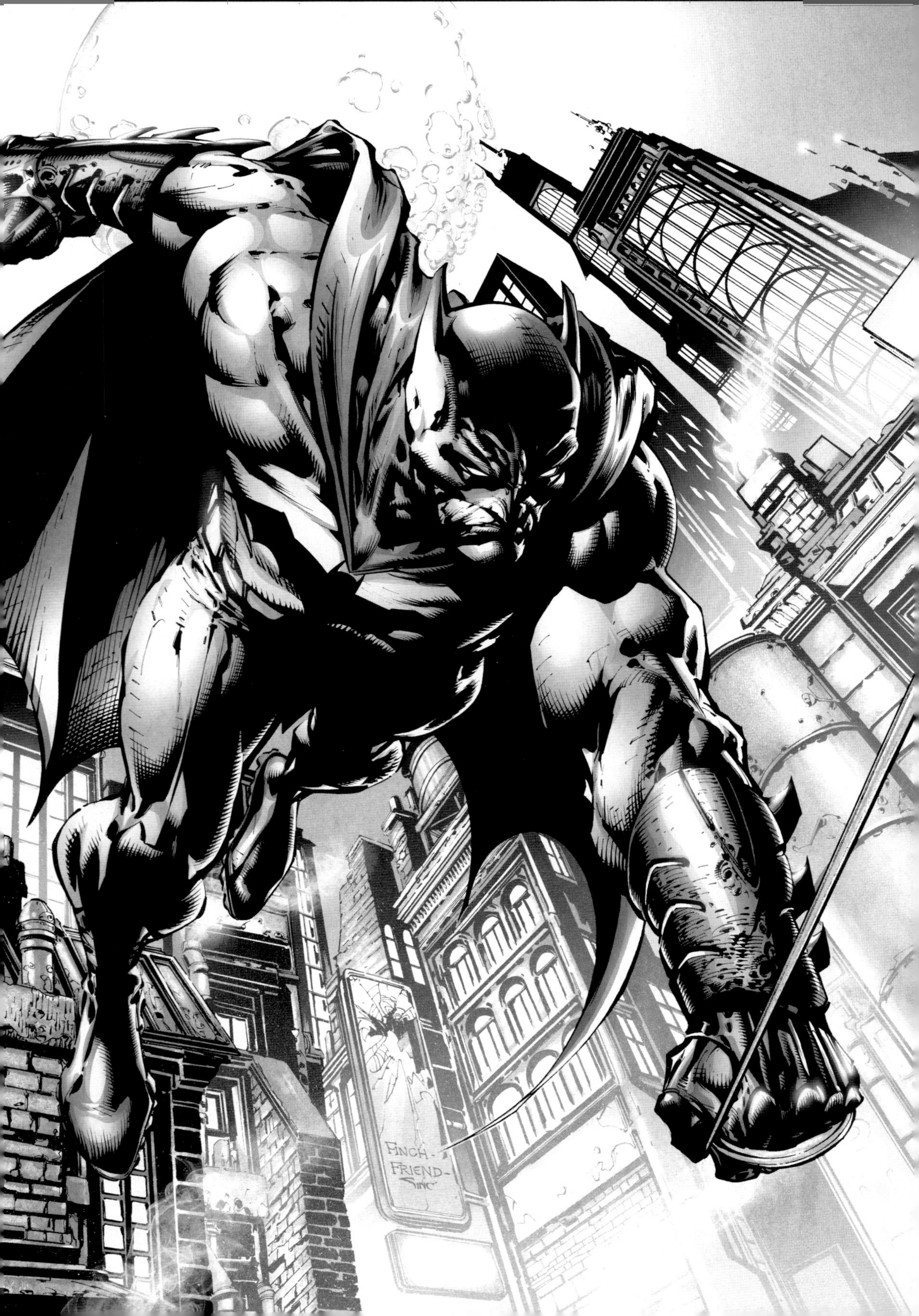
FINCH-
FRIEND-
SINC'

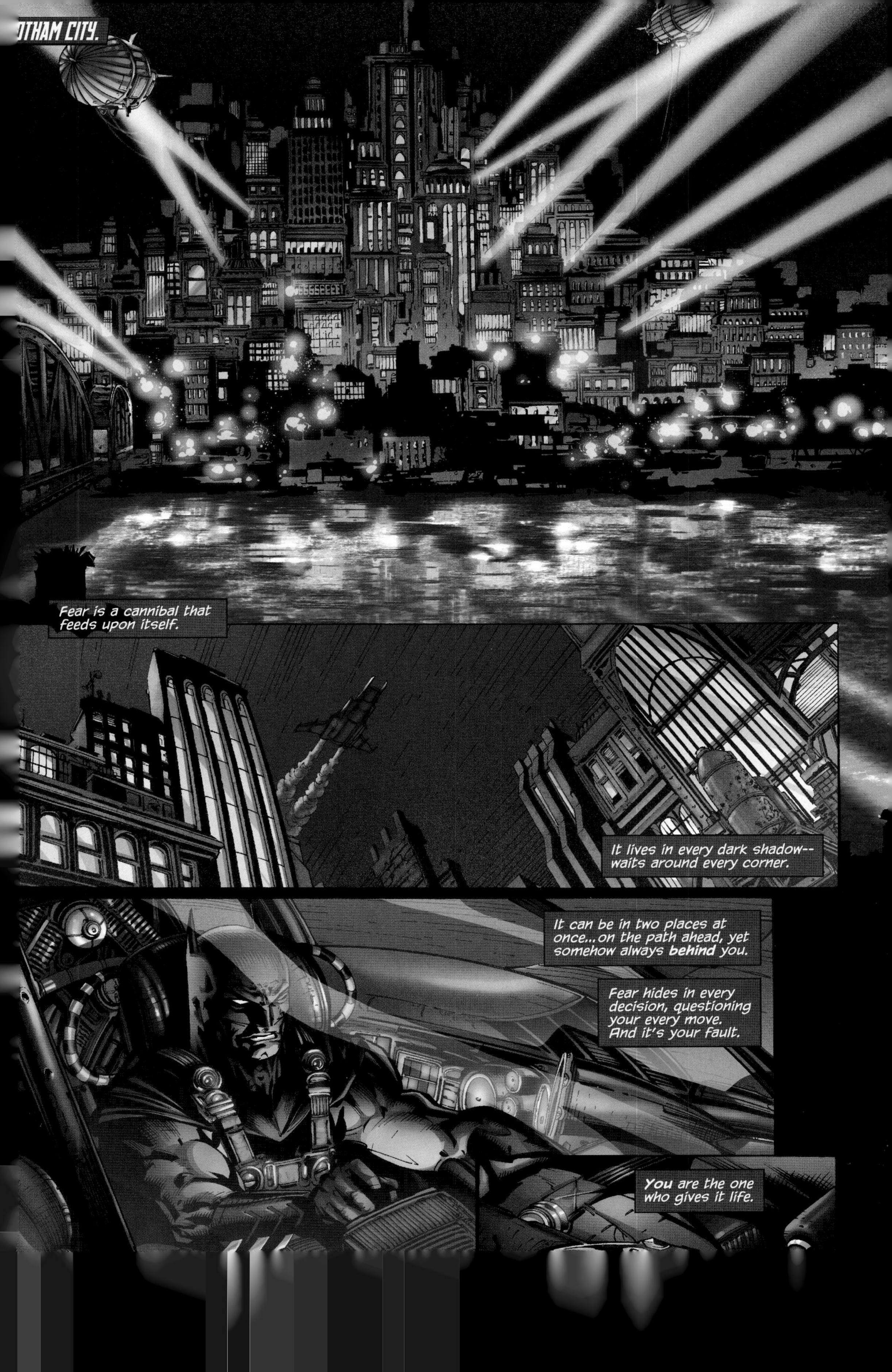
OTHAM CITY.
Fear is a cannibal that feeds upon itself.
It lives in every dark shadow--waits around every corner.
It can be in two places at once...on the path ahead, yet somehow always **behind** you.
Fear hides in every decision, questioning your every move. And it's your fault.
You are the one who gives it life.

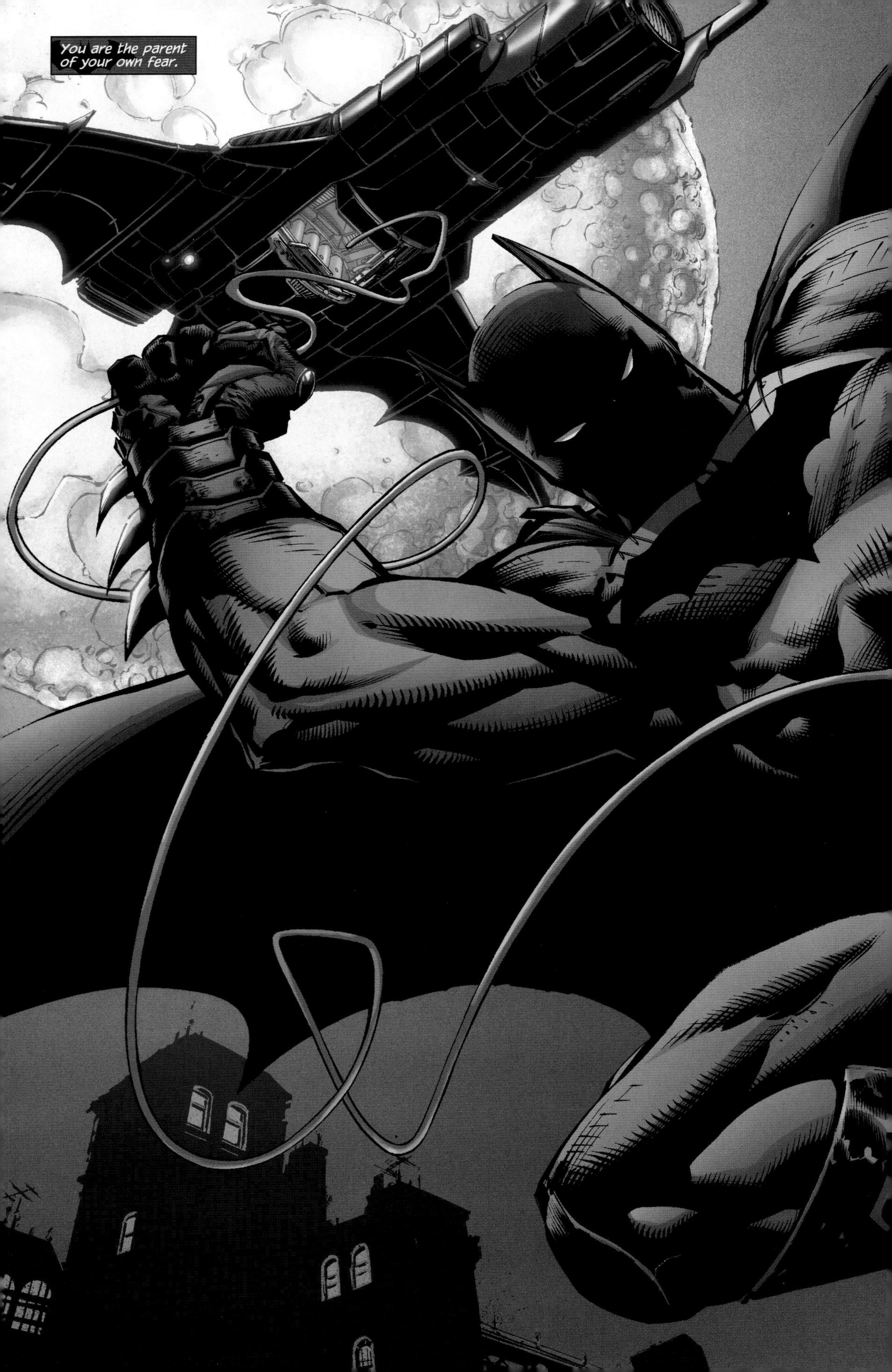
You are the parent
of your own fear.

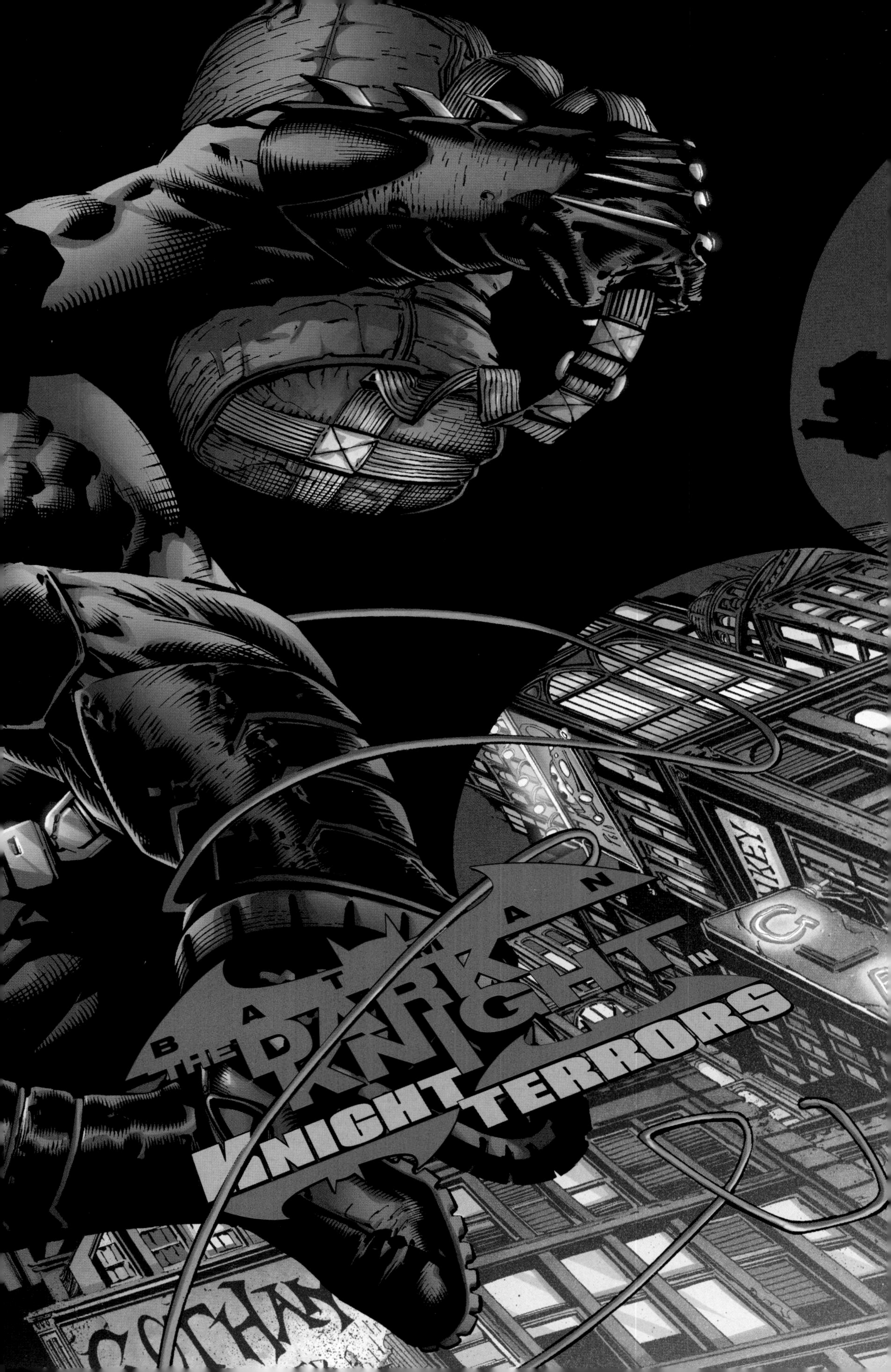
BATMAN
THE DARK KNIGHT
IN
KNIGHT TERRORS

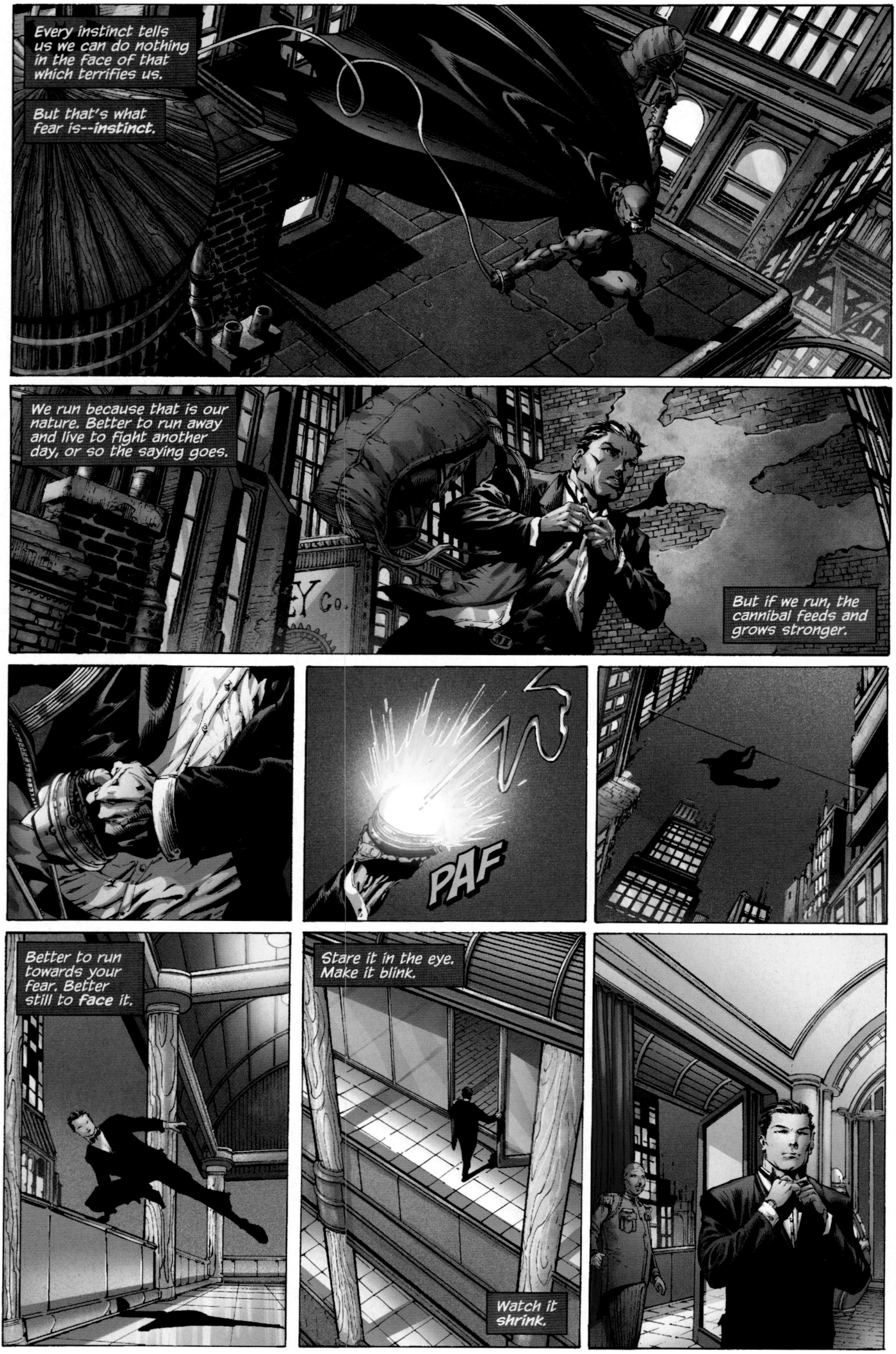
Every instinct tells us we can do nothing in the face of that which terrifies us.
But that's what fear is--instinct.
We run because that is our nature. Better to run away and live to fight another day, or so the saying goes.
But if we run, the cannibal feeds and grows stronger.
PAF
Better to run towards your fear. Better still to face it.
Stare it in the eye. Make it blink.
Watch it shrink.

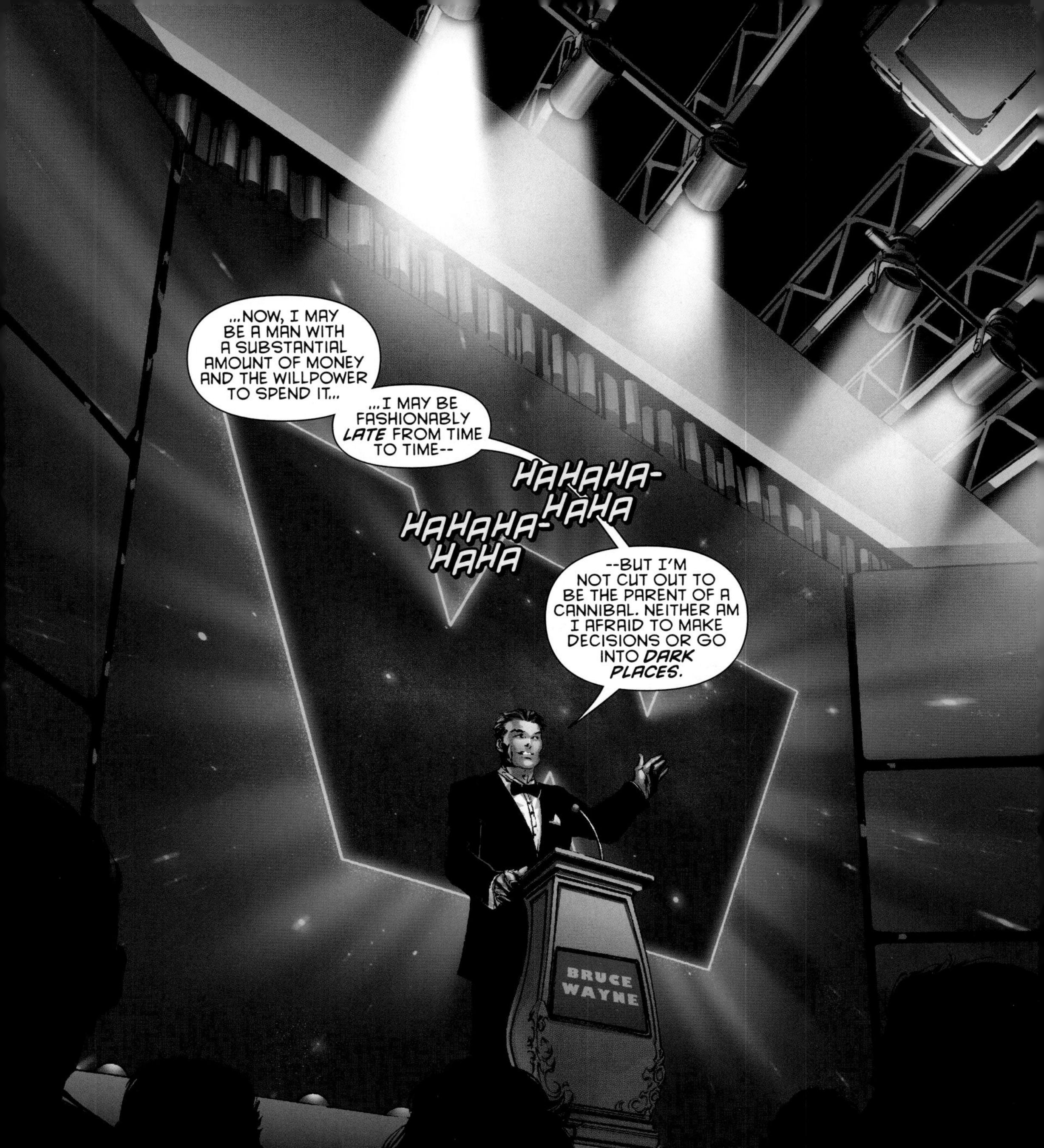
...NOW, I MAY BE A MAN WITH A SUBSTANTIAL AMOUNT OF MONEY AND THE WILLPOWER TO SPEND IT...
...I MAY BE FASHIONABLY *LATE* FROM TIME TO TIME--
HAHAHA-HAHA
HAHAHA-HAHA
--BUT I'M NOT CUT OUT TO BE THE PARENT OF A CANNIBAL. NEITHER AM I AFRAID TO MAKE DECISIONS OR GO INTO *DARK PLACES*.
BRUCE WAYNE
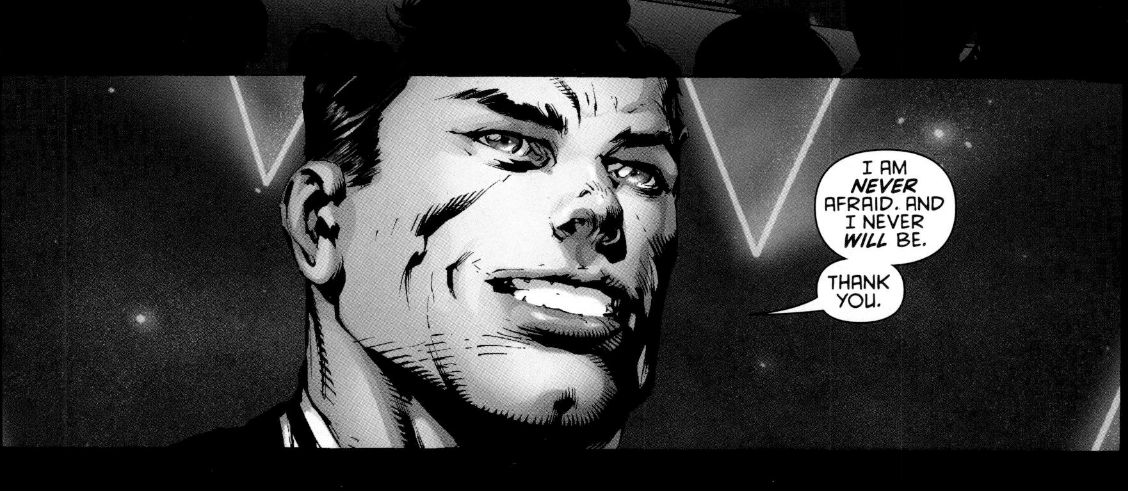
I AM *NEVER* AFRAID. AND I NEVER *WILL* BE.
THANK YOU.

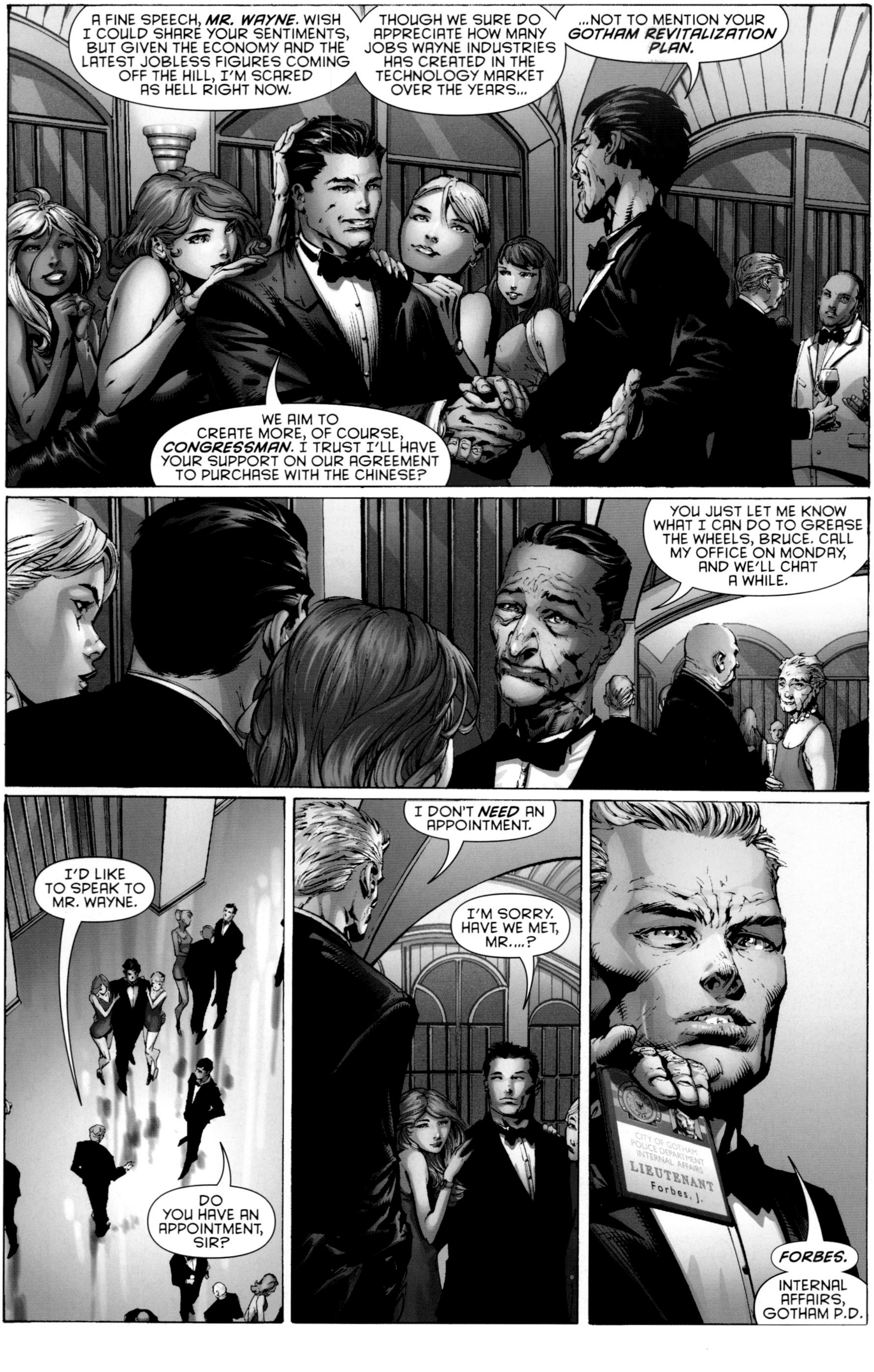
A FINE SPEECH, MR. WAYNE. WISH I COULD SHARE YOUR SENTIMENTS, BUT GIVEN THE ECONOMY AND THE LATEST JOBLESS FIGURES COMING OFF THE HILL, I'M SCARED AS HELL RIGHT NOW.
THOUGH WE SURE DO APPRECIATE HOW MANY JOBS WAYNE INDUSTRIES HAS CREATED IN THE TECHNOLOGY MARKET OVER THE YEARS...
...NOT TO MENTION YOUR GOTHAM REVITALIZATION PLAN.
WE AIM TO CREATE MORE, OF COURSE, CONGRESSMAN. I TRUST I'LL HAVE YOUR SUPPORT ON OUR AGREEMENT TO PURCHASE WITH THE CHINESE?
YOU JUST LET ME KNOW WHAT I CAN DO TO GREASE THE WHEELS, BRUCE. CALL MY OFFICE ON MONDAY, AND WE'LL CHAT A WHILE.
I'D LIKE TO SPEAK TO MR. WAYNE.
DO YOU HAVE AN APPOINTMENT, SIR?
I DON'T NEED AN APPOINTMENT.
I'M SORRY. HAVE WE MET, MR....?
CITY OF GOTHAM POLICE DEPARTMENT INTERNAL AFFAIRS
LIEUTENANT
Forbes, J.
FORBES.
INTERNAL AFFAIRS, GOTHAM P.D.

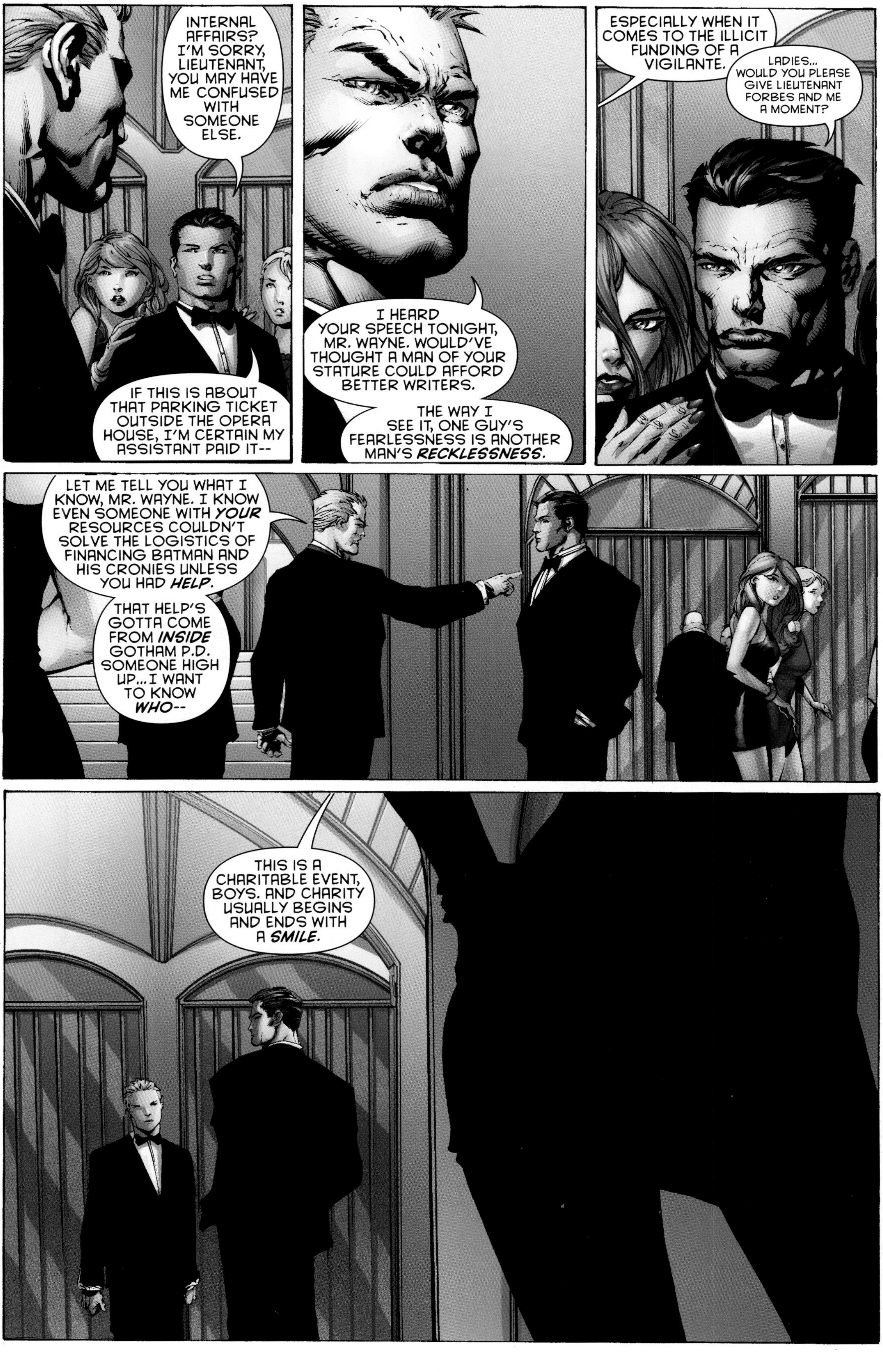
INTERNAL AFFAIRS? I'M SORRY, LIEUTENANT, YOU MAY HAVE ME CONFUSED WITH SOMEONE ELSE.
IF THIS IS ABOUT THAT PARKING TICKET OUTSIDE THE OPERA HOUSE, I'M CERTAIN MY ASSISTANT PAID IT--
I HEARD YOUR SPEECH TONIGHT, MR. WAYNE. WOULD'VE THOUGHT A MAN OF YOUR STATURE COULD AFFORD BETTER WRITERS.
THE WAY I SEE IT, ONE GUY'S FEARLESSNESS IS ANOTHER MAN'S *RECKLESSNESS*.
ESPECIALLY WHEN IT COMES TO THE ILLICIT FUNDING OF A VIGILANTE.
LADIES... WOULD YOU PLEASE GIVE LIEUTENANT FORBES AND ME A MOMENT?
LET ME TELL YOU WHAT I KNOW, MR. WAYNE. I KNOW EVEN SOMEONE WITH *YOUR* RESOURCES COULDN'T SOLVE THE LOGISTICS OF FINANCING BATMAN AND HIS CRONIES UNLESS YOU HAD *HELP*.
THAT HELP'S GOTTA COME FROM *INSIDE* GOTHAM P.D. SOMEONE HIGH UP... I WANT TO KNOW *WHO*--
THIS IS A CHARITABLE EVENT, BOYS. AND CHARITY USUALLY BEGINS AND ENDS WITH A *SMILE*.

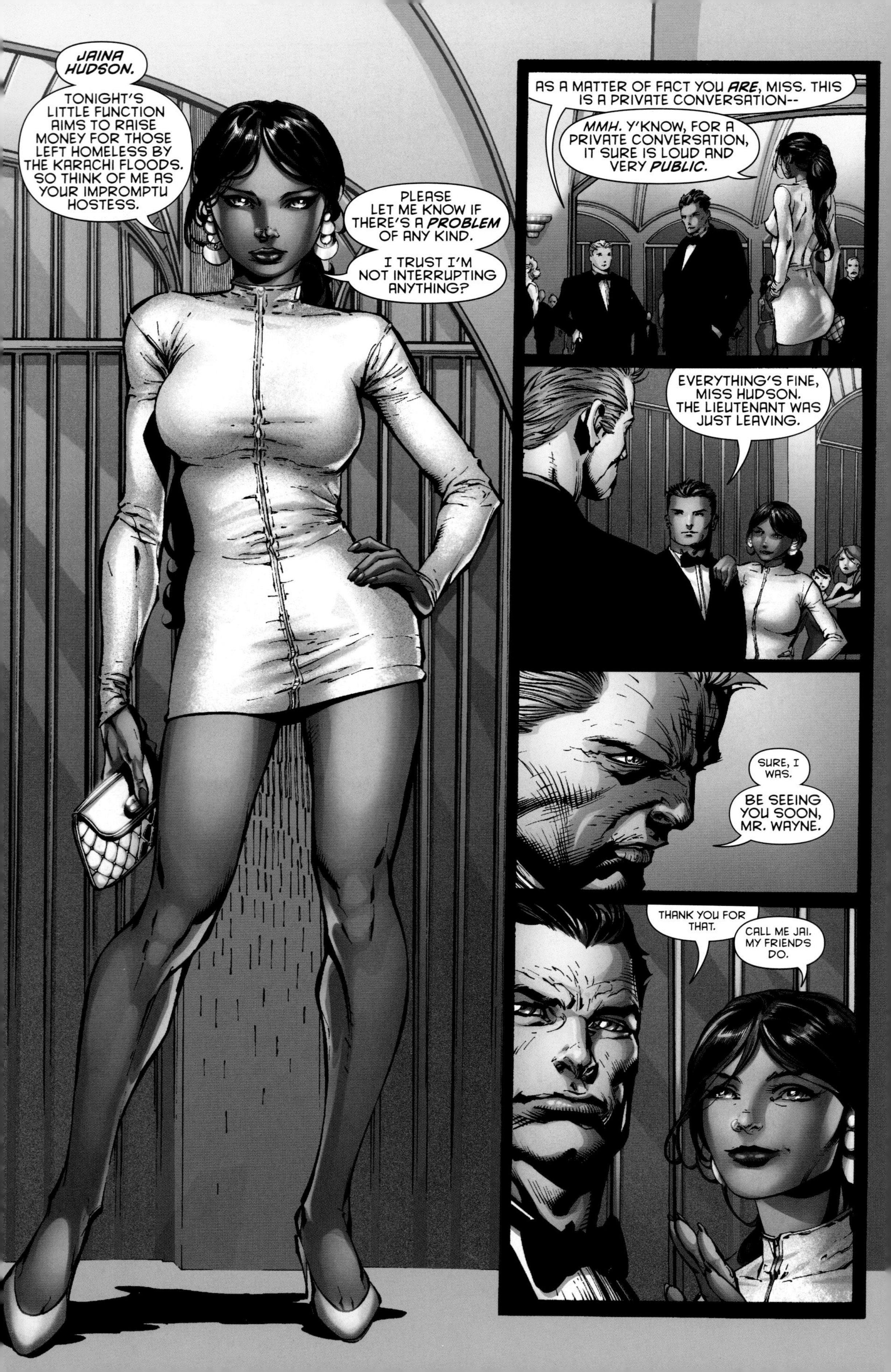
JAINA HUDSON.
TONIGHT'S LITTLE FUNCTION AIMS TO RAISE MONEY FOR THOSE LEFT HOMELESS BY THE KARACHI FLOODS. SO THINK OF ME AS YOUR IMPROMPTU HOSTESS.
PLEASE LET ME KNOW IF THERE'S A PROBLEM OF ANY KIND.
I TRUST I'M NOT INTERRUPTING ANYTHING?
AS A MATTER OF FACT YOU ARE, MISS. THIS IS A PRIVATE CONVERSATION--
MMH. Y'KNOW, FOR A PRIVATE CONVERSATION, IT SURE IS LOUD AND VERY PUBLIC.
EVERYTHING'S FINE, MISS HUDSON. THE LIEUTENANT WAS JUST LEAVING.
SURE, I WAS.
BE SEEING YOU SOON, MR. WAYNE.
THANK YOU FOR THAT.
CALL ME JAI. MY FRIENDS DO.

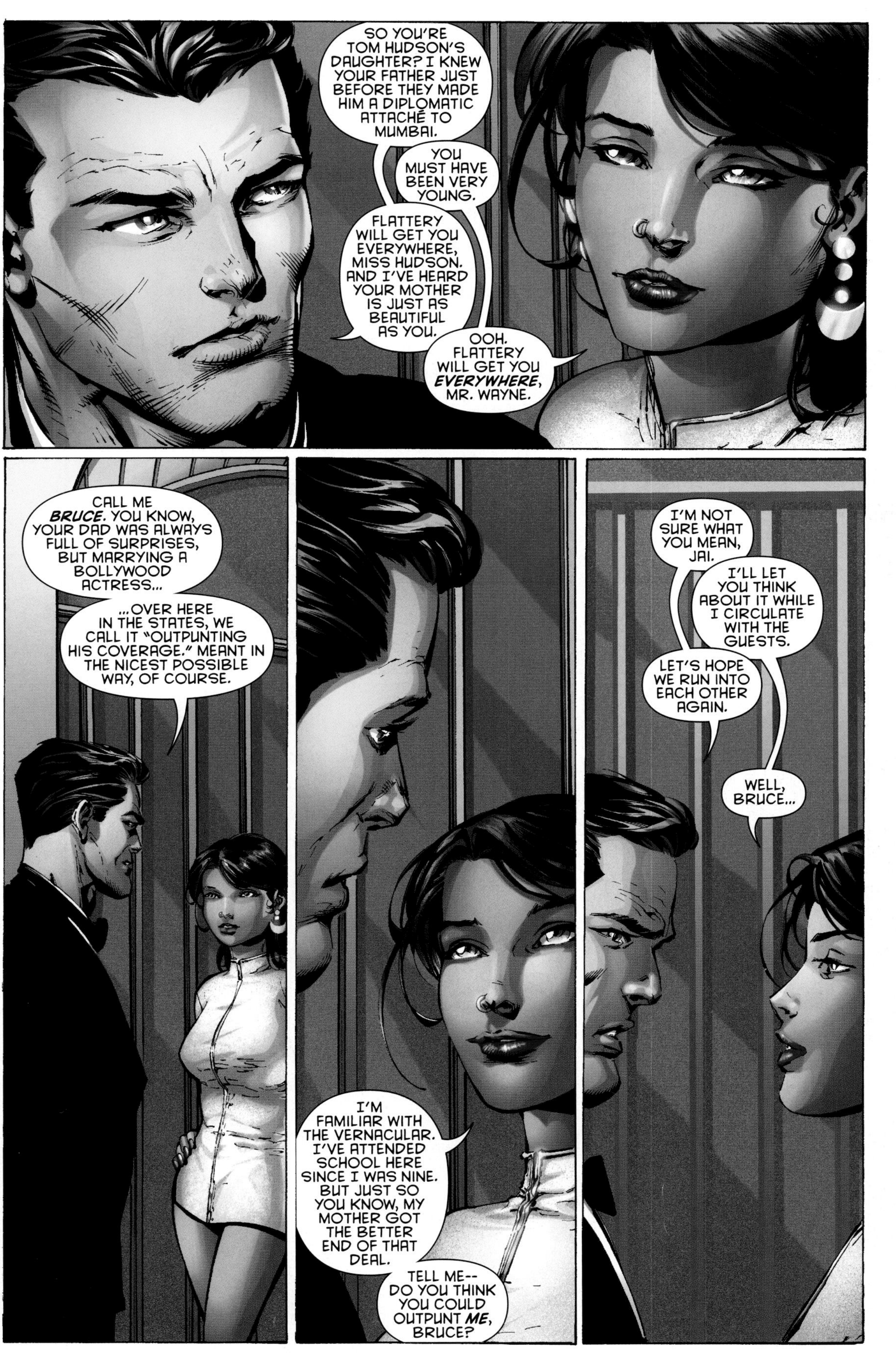
SO YOU'RE TOM HUDSON'S DAUGHTER? I KNEW YOUR FATHER JUST BEFORE THEY MADE HIM A DIPLOMATIC ATTACHÉ TO MUMBAI.
YOU MUST HAVE BEEN VERY YOUNG.
FLATTERY WILL GET YOU EVERYWHERE, MISS HUDSON. AND I'VE HEARD YOUR MOTHER IS JUST AS BEAUTIFUL AS YOU.
OOH. FLATTERY WILL GET YOU ***EVERYWHERE***, MR. WAYNE.
CALL ME ***BRUCE***. YOU KNOW, YOUR DAD WAS ALWAYS FULL OF SURPRISES, BUT MARRYING A BOLLYWOOD ACTRESS...
...OVER HERE IN THE STATES, WE CALL IT "OUTPUNTING HIS COVERAGE." MEANT IN THE NICEST POSSIBLE WAY, OF COURSE.
I'M FAMILIAR WITH THE VERNACULAR. I'VE ATTENDED SCHOOL HERE SINCE I WAS NINE. BUT JUST SO YOU KNOW, MY MOTHER GOT THE BETTER END OF THAT DEAL.
TELL ME-- DO YOU THINK YOU COULD OUTPUNT ***ME***, BRUCE?
I'M NOT SURE WHAT YOU MEAN, JAI.
I'LL LET YOU THINK ABOUT IT WHILE I CIRCULATE WITH THE GUESTS.
LET'S HOPE WE RUN INTO EACH OTHER AGAIN.
WELL, BRUCE...

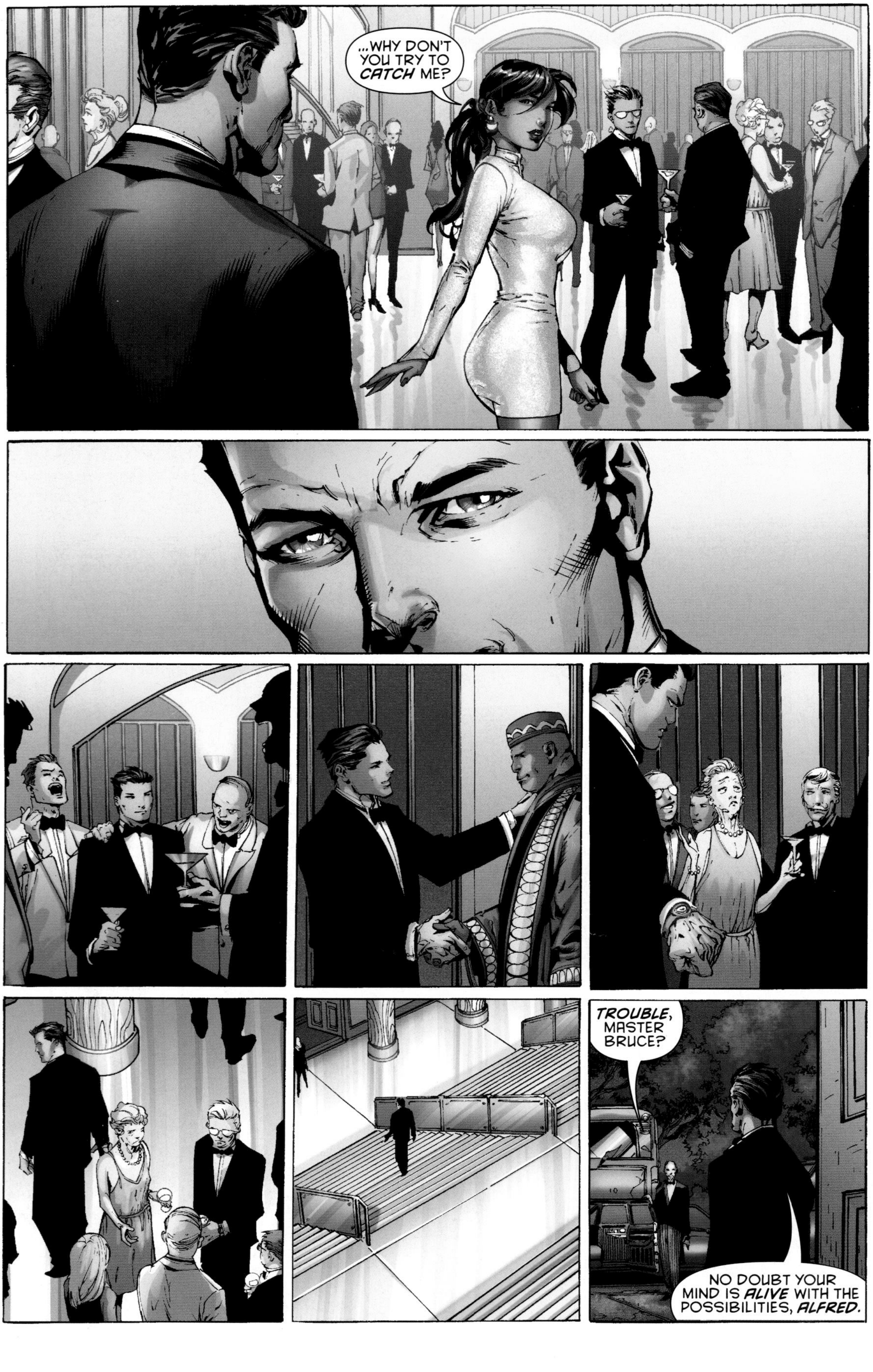
...WHY DON'T YOU TRY TO CATCH ME?
TROUBLE, MASTER BRUCE?
NO DOUBT YOUR MIND IS ALIVE WITH THE POSSIBILITIES, ALFRED.

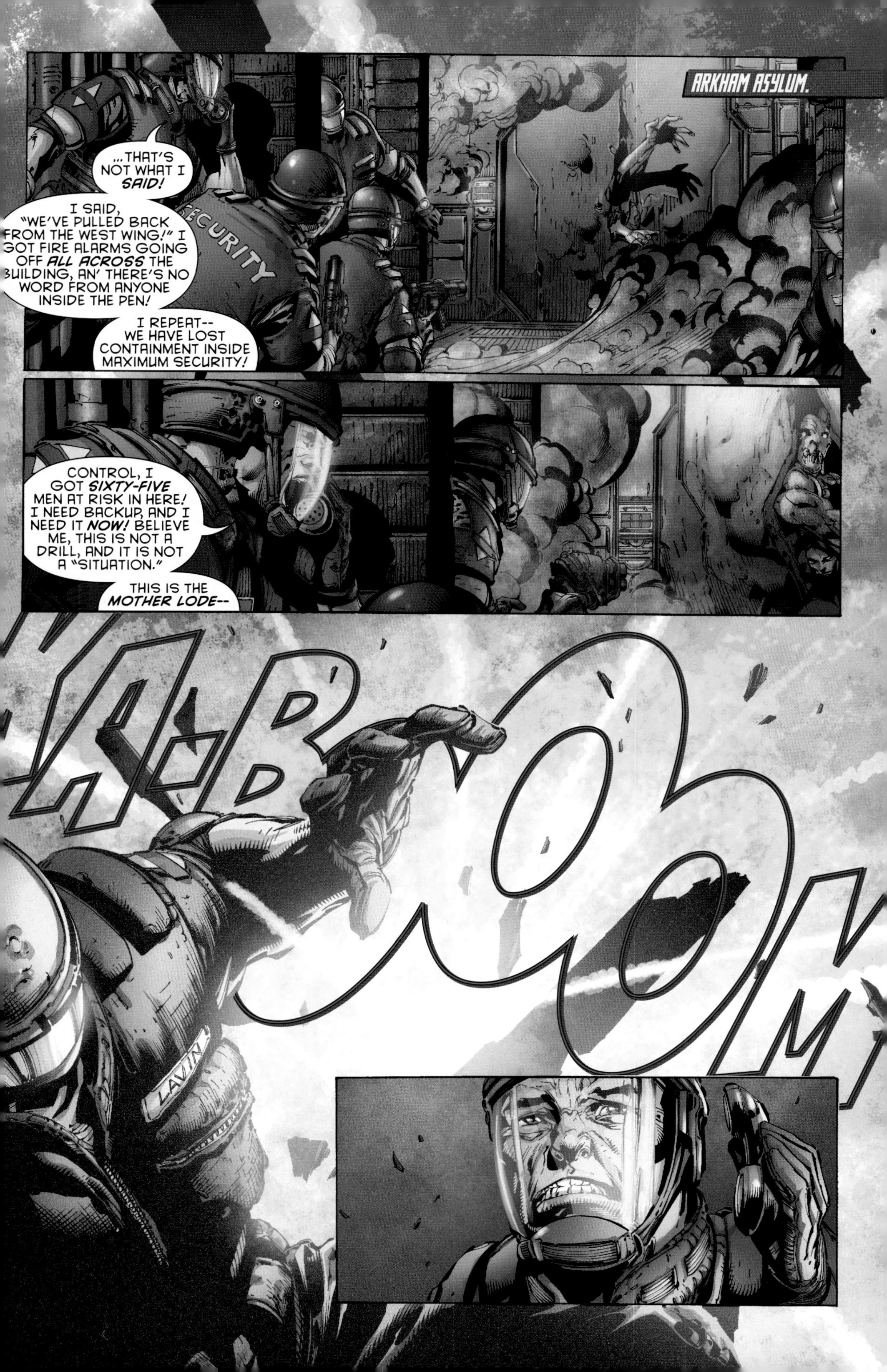
ARKHAM ASYLUM.
...THAT'S NOT WHAT I SAID!
I SAID, "WE'VE PULLED BACK FROM THE WEST WING!" I GOT FIRE ALARMS GOING OFF ALL ACROSS THE BUILDING, AN' THERE'S NO WORD FROM ANYONE INSIDE THE PEN!
I REPEAT-- WE HAVE LOST CONTAINMENT INSIDE MAXIMUM SECURITY!
SECURITY
CONTROL, I GOT SIXTY-FIVE MEN AT RISK IN HERE! I NEED BACKUP, AND I NEED IT NOW! BELIEVE ME, THIS IS NOT A DRILL, AND IT IS NOT A "SITUATION."
THIS IS THE MOTHER LODE--
LAVIN

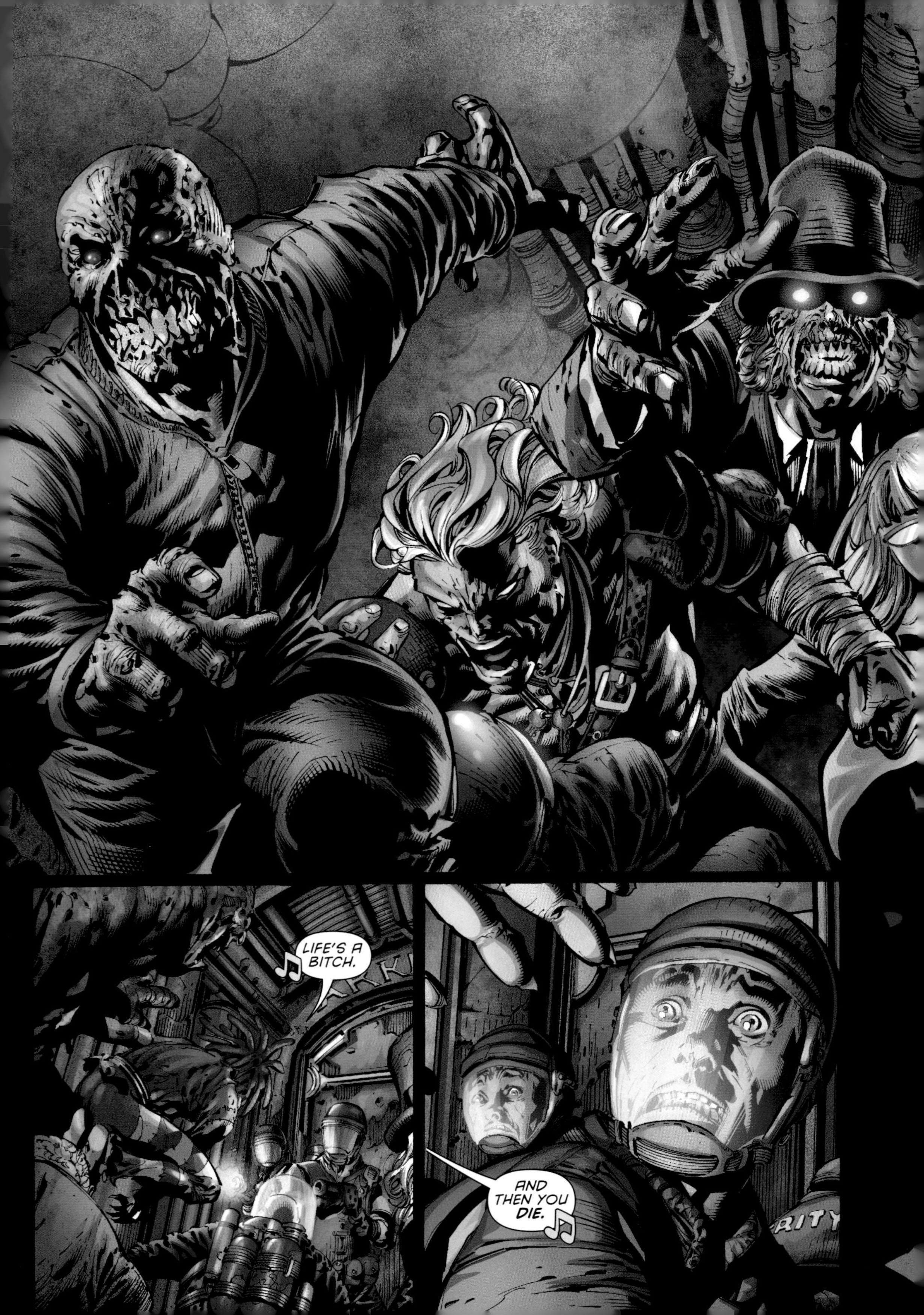
LIFE'S A BITCH.
AND THEN YOU DIE.

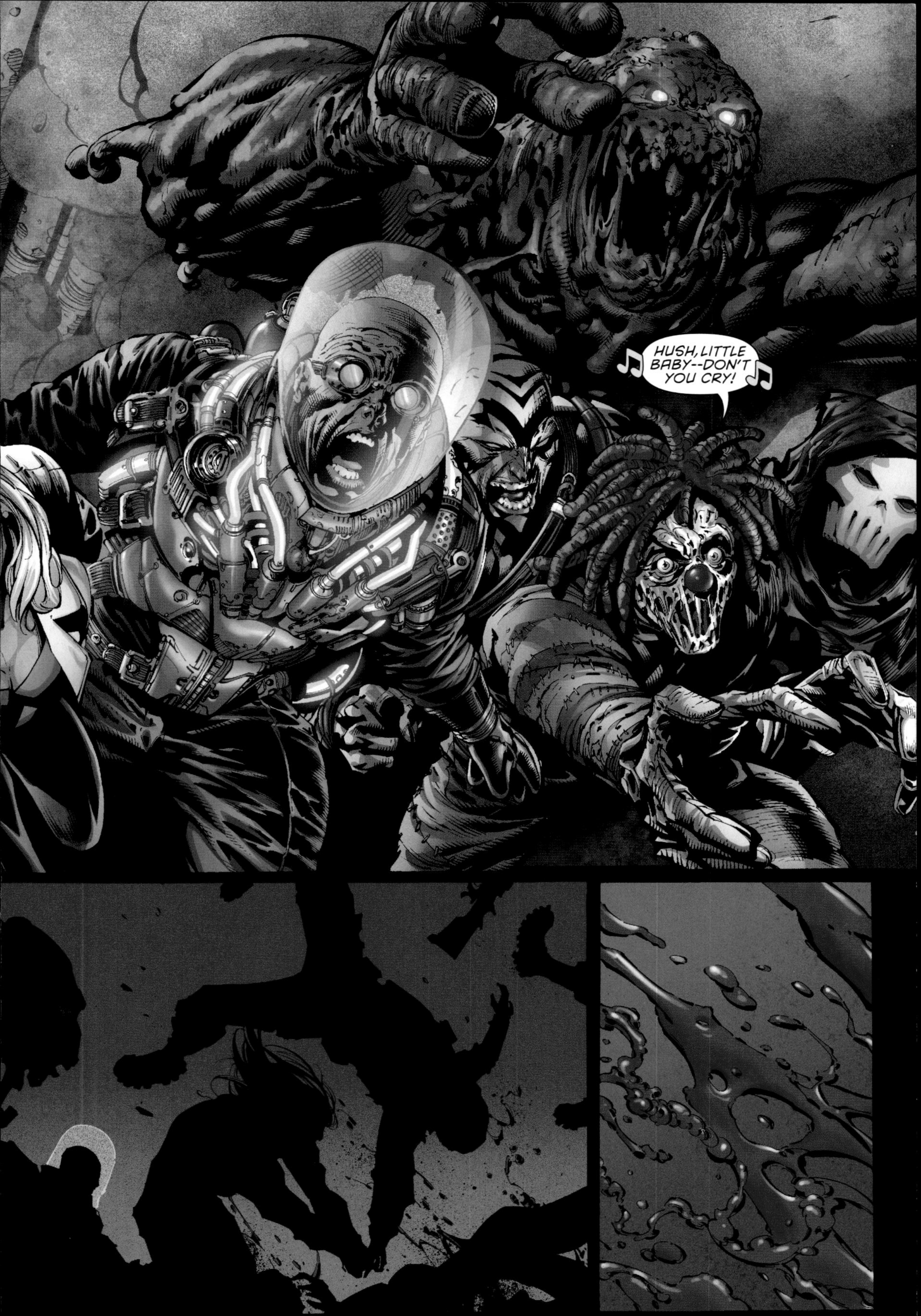
HUSH, LITTLE BABY--DON'T YOU CRY!

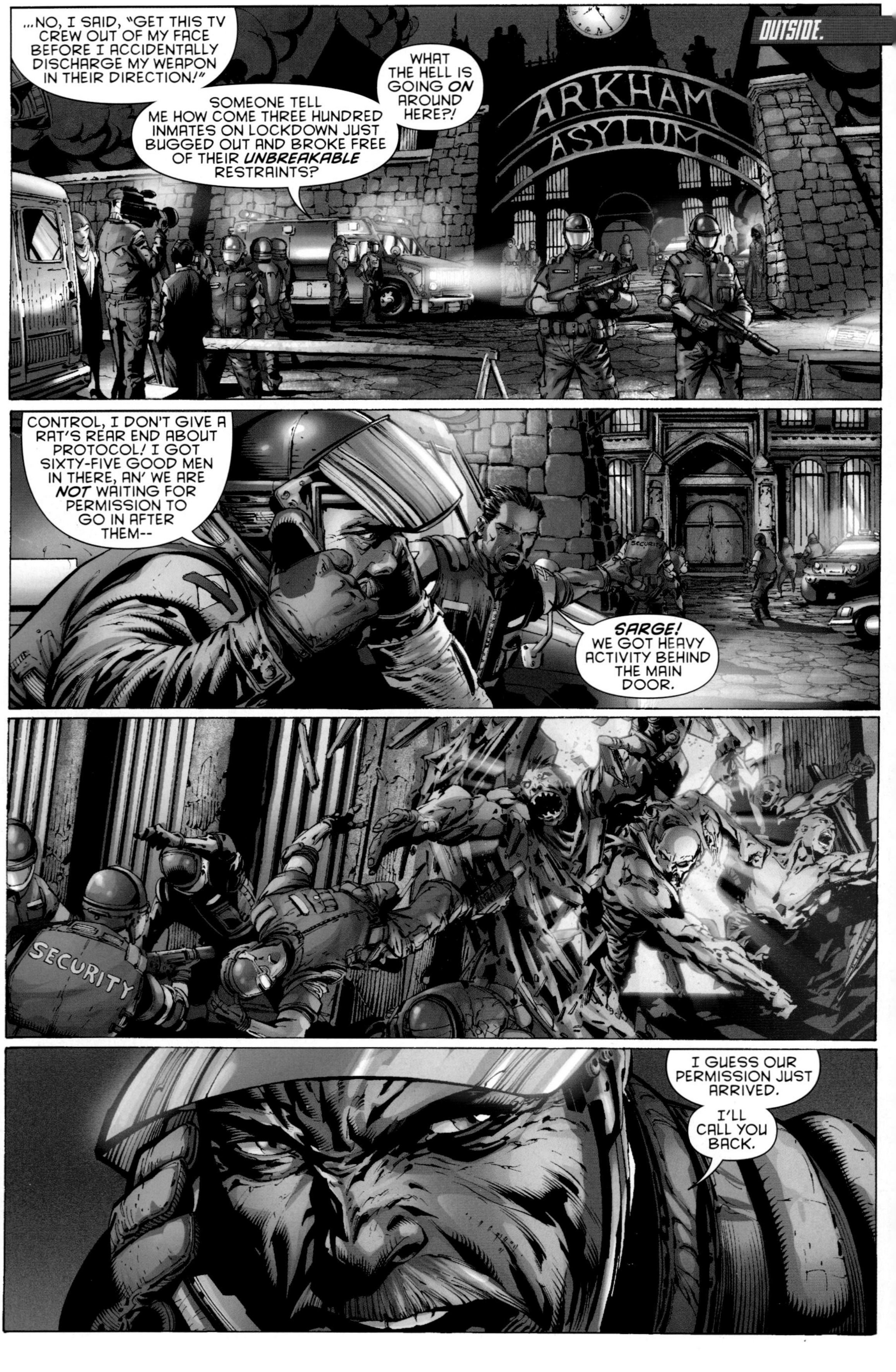
OUTSIDE.
...NO, I SAID, "GET THIS TV CREW OUT OF MY FACE BEFORE I ACCIDENTALLY DISCHARGE MY WEAPON IN THEIR DIRECTION!"
SOMEONE TELL ME HOW COME THREE HUNDRED INMATES ON LOCKDOWN JUST BUGGED OUT AND BROKE FREE OF THEIR UNBREAKABLE RESTRAINTS?
WHAT THE HELL IS GOING ON AROUND HERE?!
ARKHAM ASYLUM
CONTROL, I DON'T GIVE A RAT'S REAR END ABOUT PROTOCOL! I GOT SIXTY-FIVE GOOD MEN IN THERE, AN' WE ARE NOT WAITING FOR PERMISSION TO GO IN AFTER THEM--
SARGE! WE GOT HEAVY ACTIVITY BEHIND THE MAIN DOOR.
SECURITY
I GUESS OUR PERMISSION JUST ARRIVED.
I'LL CALL YOU BACK.

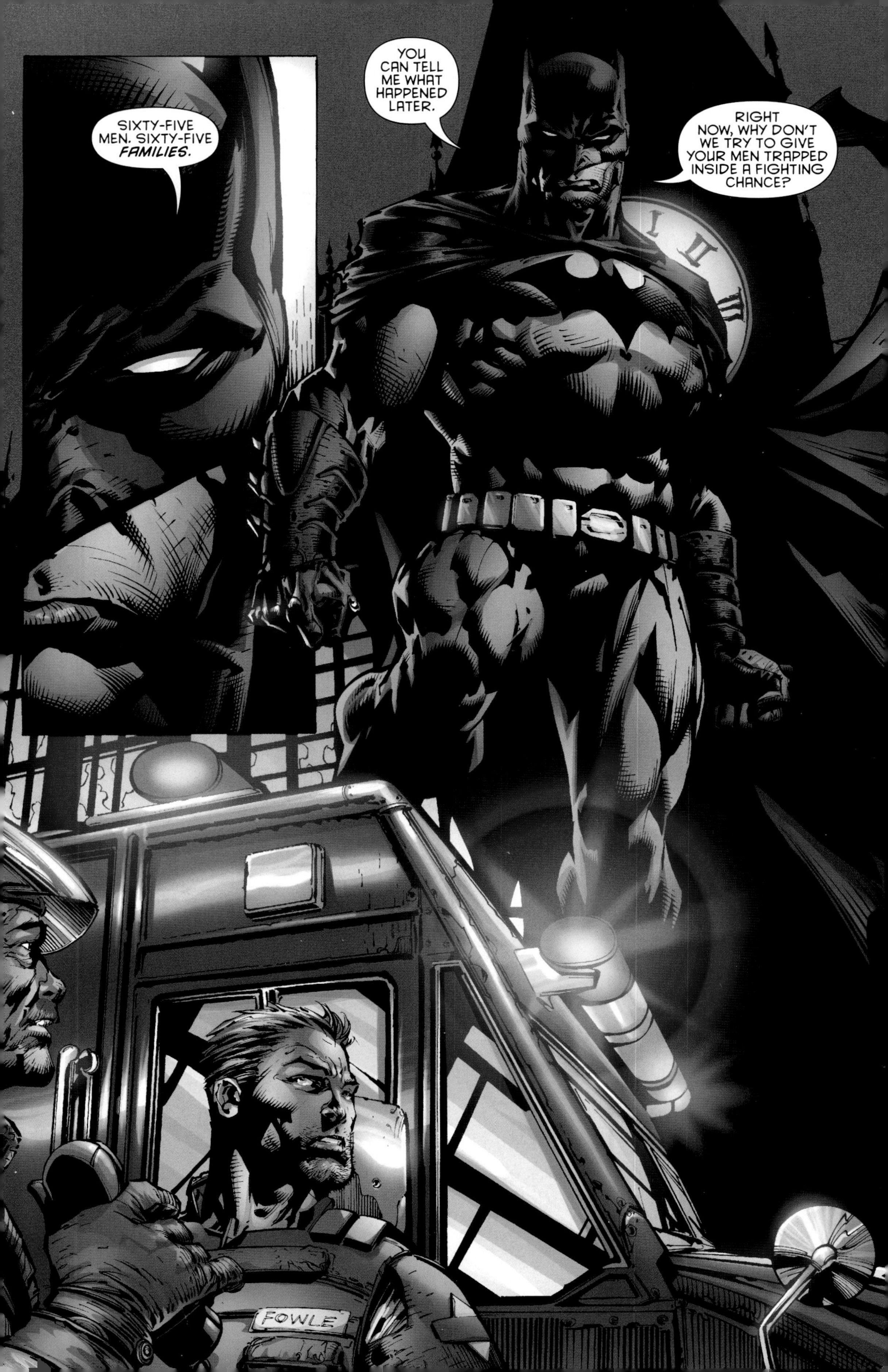
SIXTY-FIVE MEN. SIXTY-FIVE *FAMILIES*.
YOU CAN TELL ME WHAT HAPPENED LATER.
RIGHT NOW, WHY DON'T WE TRY TO GIVE YOUR MEN TRAPPED INSIDE A FIGHTING CHANCE?
FOWLE

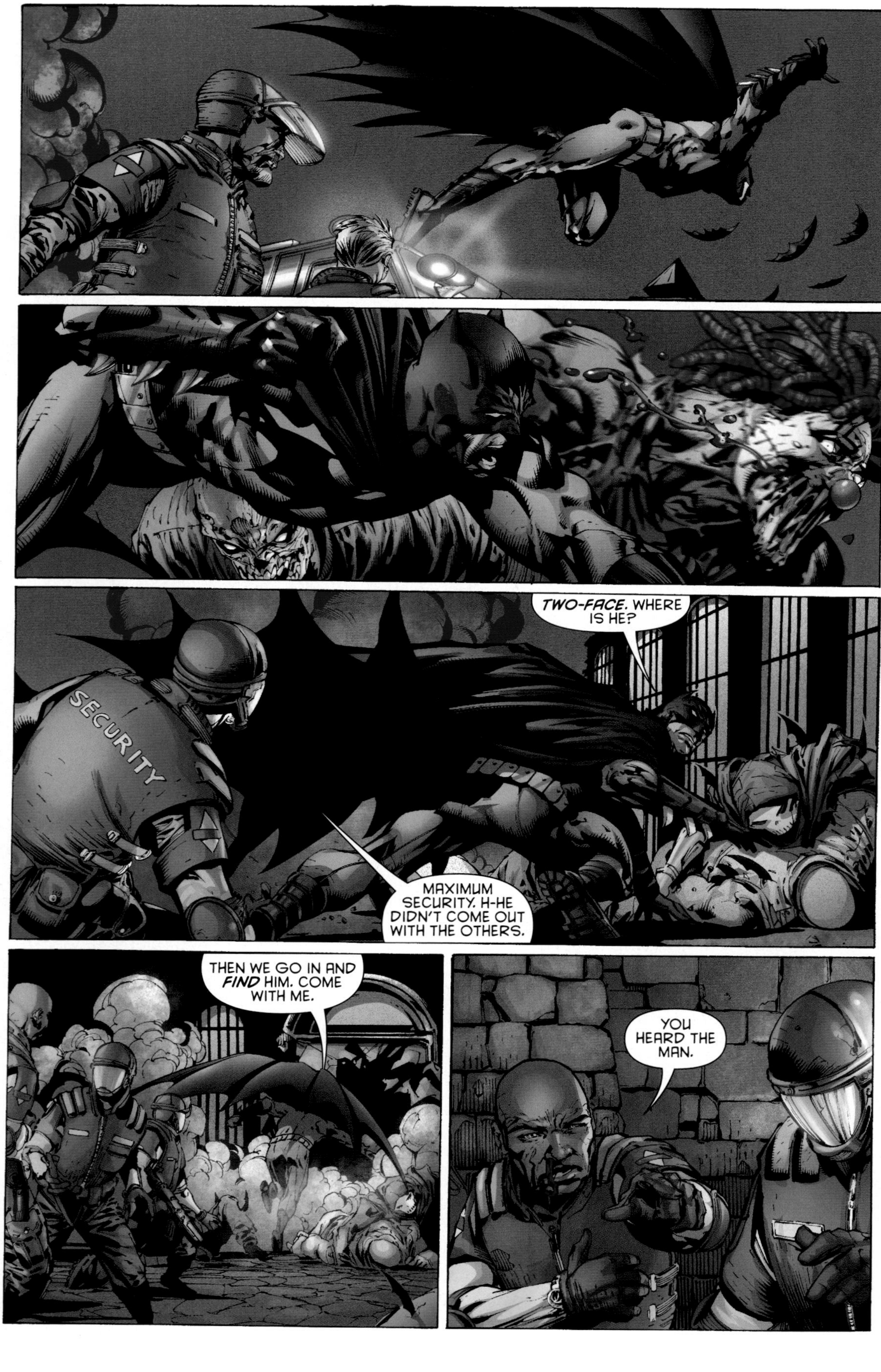
TWO-FACE. WHERE IS HE?
MAXIMUM SECURITY. H-HE DIDN'T COME OUT WITH THE OTHERS.
THEN WE GO IN AND FIND HIM. COME WITH ME.
YOU HEARD THE MAN.

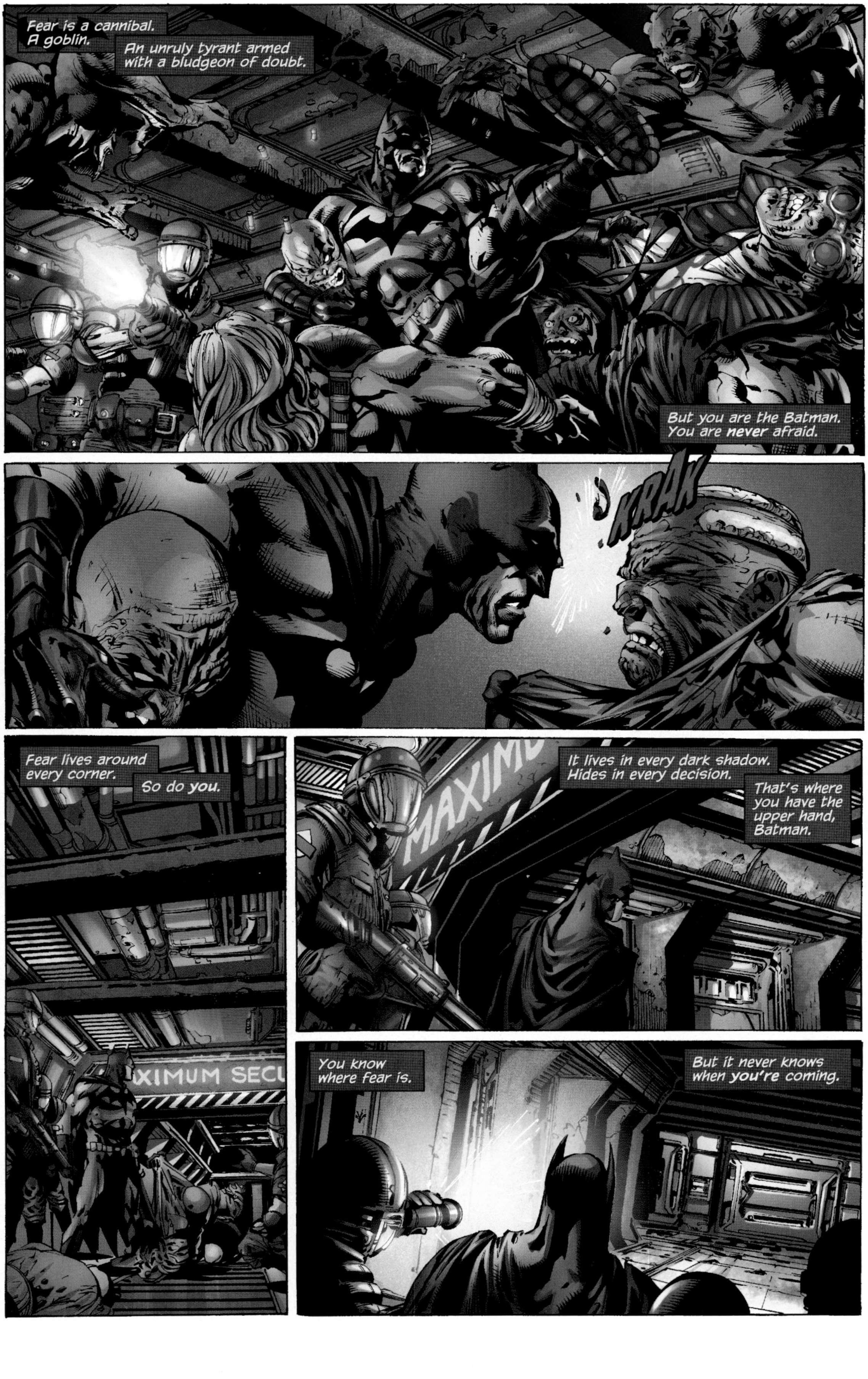
Fear is a cannibal. A goblin.
An unruly tyrant armed with a bludgeon of doubt.
But you are the Batman. You are **never** afraid.
KRAK
Fear lives around every corner.
So do **you**.
MAXIMUM SECU
MAXIMU
It lives in every dark shadow. Hides in every decision.
That's where you have the upper hand, Batman.
You know where fear is.
But it never knows when **you're** coming.

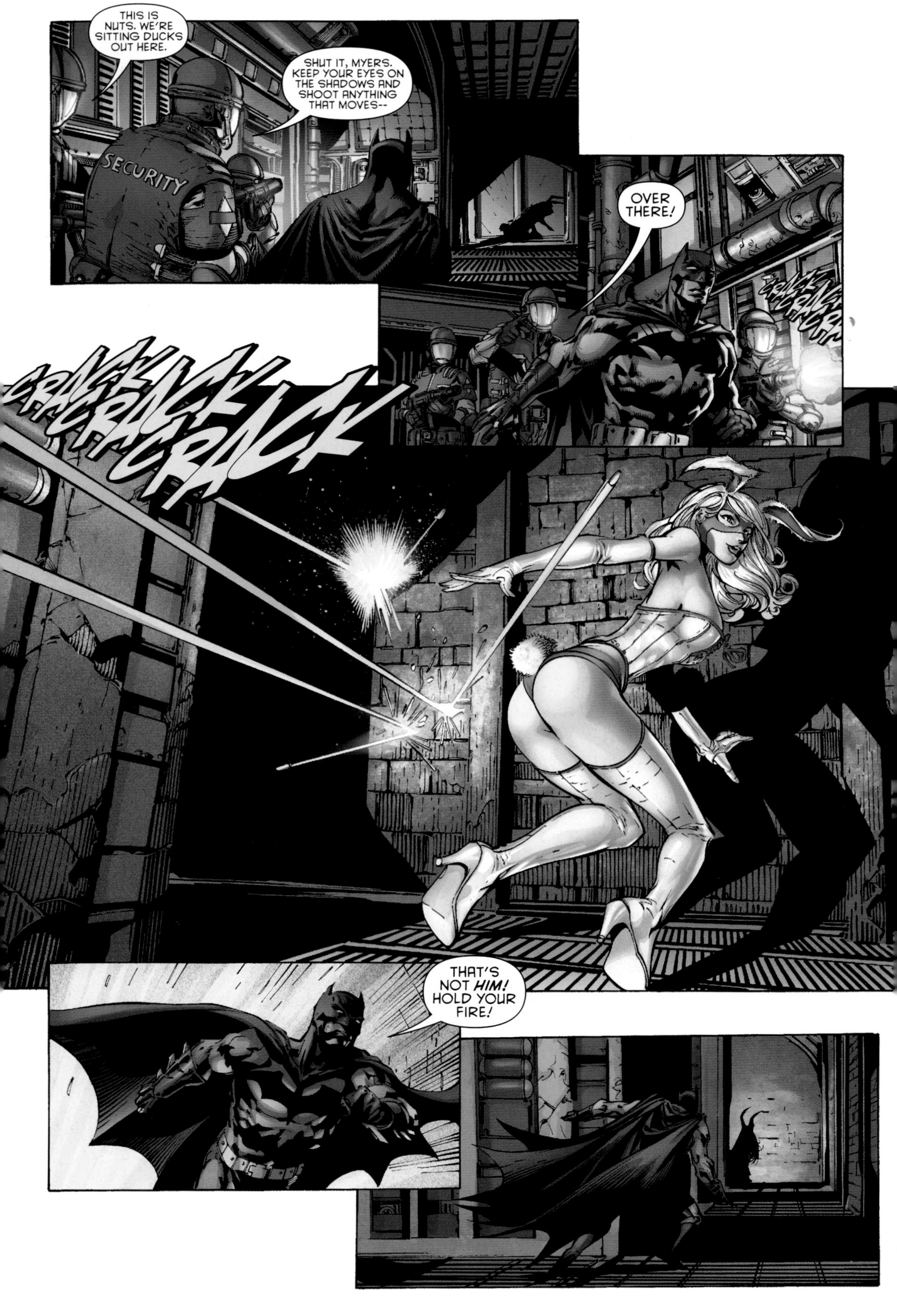

THIS IS NUTS. WE'RE SITTING DUCKS OUT HERE.
SHUT IT, MYERS. KEEP YOUR EYES ON THE SHADOWS AND SHOOT ANYTHING THAT MOVES--
SECURITY
OVER THERE!
CRACK CRACK CRACK
THAT'S NOT *HIM!* HOLD YOUR FIRE!

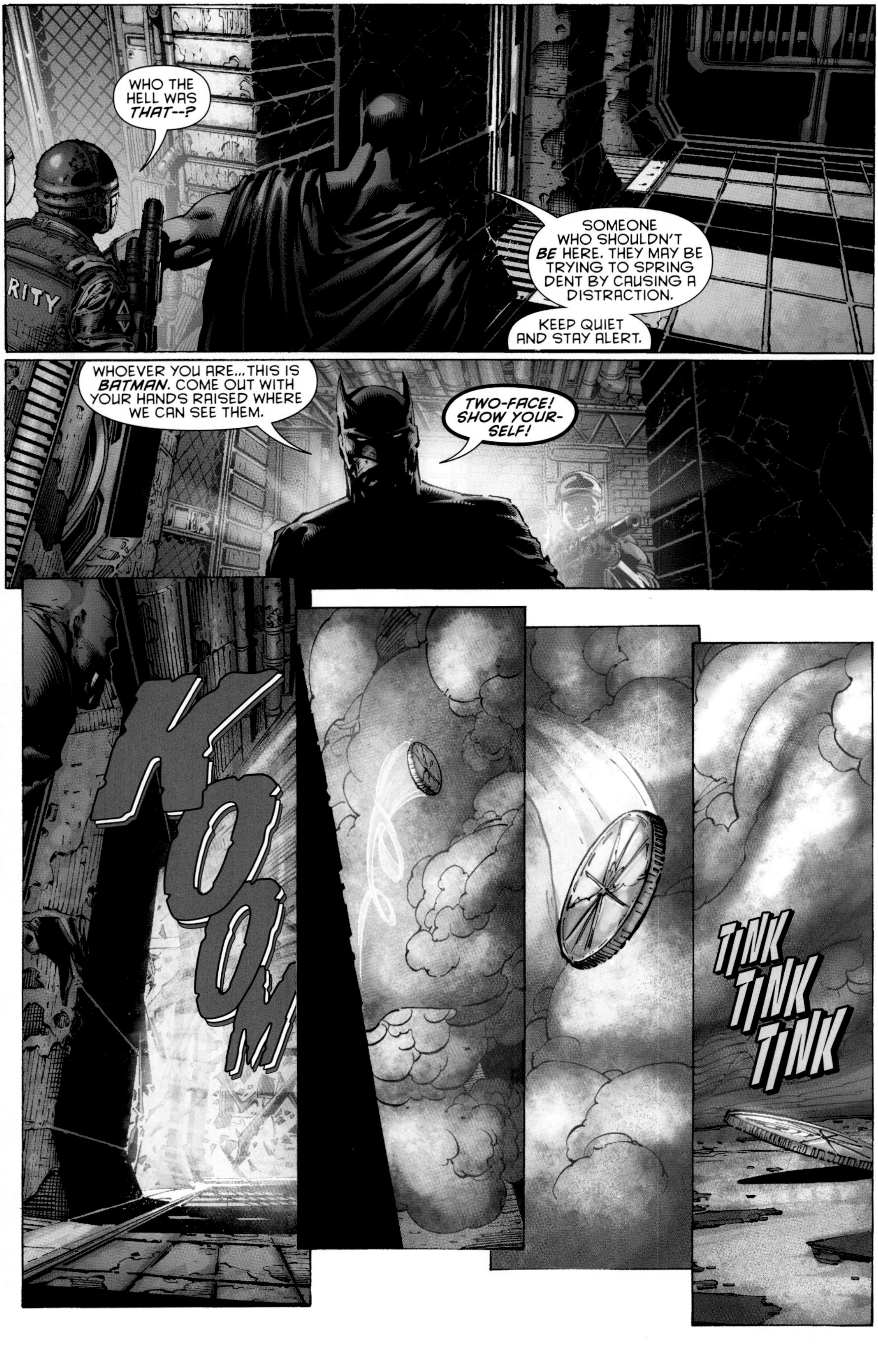
WHO THE HELL WAS *THAT*--?
SOMEONE WHO SHOULDN'T *BE* HERE. THEY MAY BE TRYING TO SPRING DENT BY CAUSING A DISTRACTION.
KEEP QUIET AND STAY ALERT.
RITY
WHOEVER YOU ARE...THIS IS *BATMAN.* COME OUT WITH YOUR HANDS RAISED WHERE WE CAN SEE THEM.
TWO-FACE! SHOW YOUR-SELF!
KOOM
TINK TINK TINK

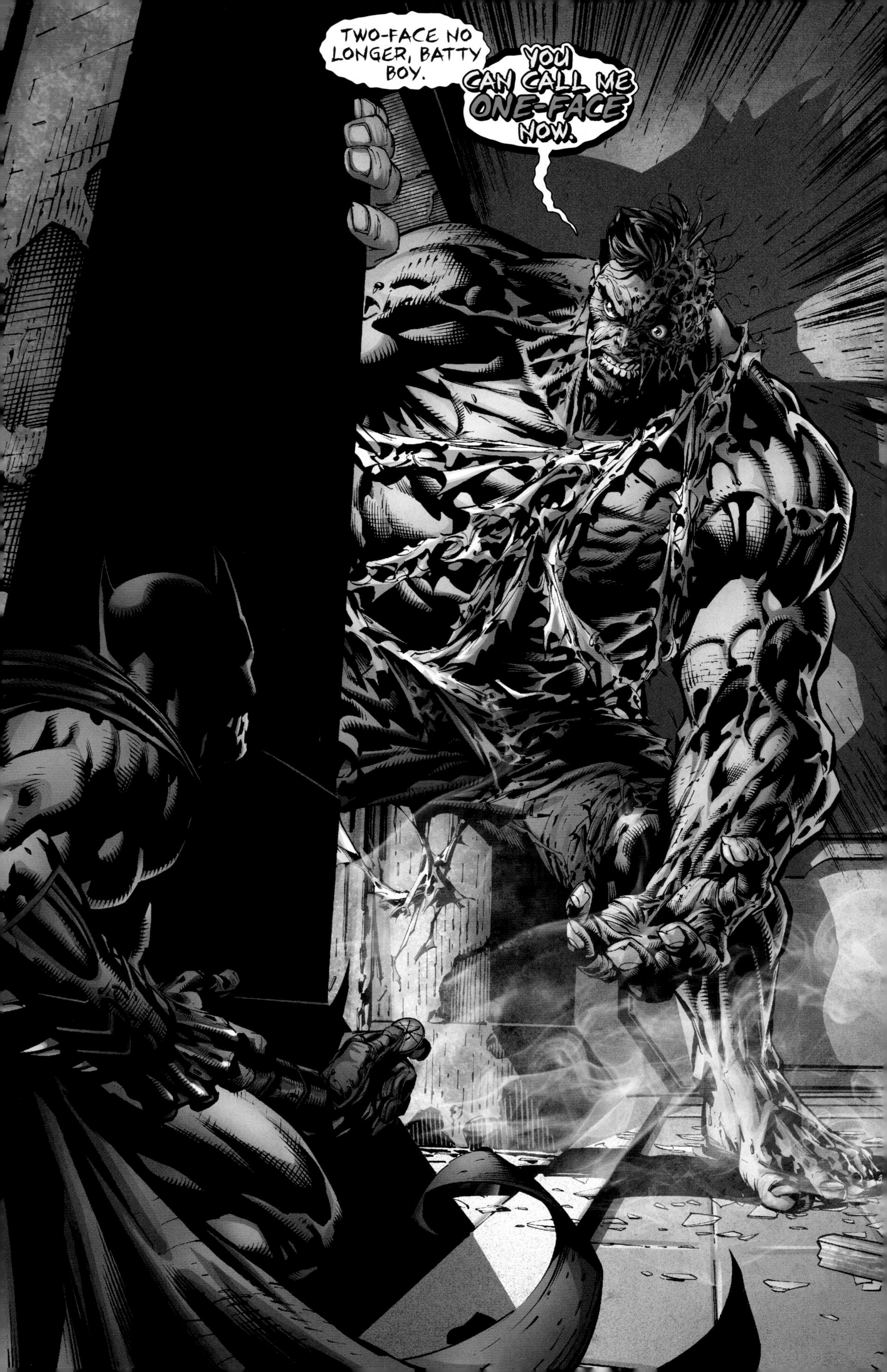
TWO-FACE NO LONGER, BATTY BOY.
YOU CAN CALL ME ONE-FACE NOW.

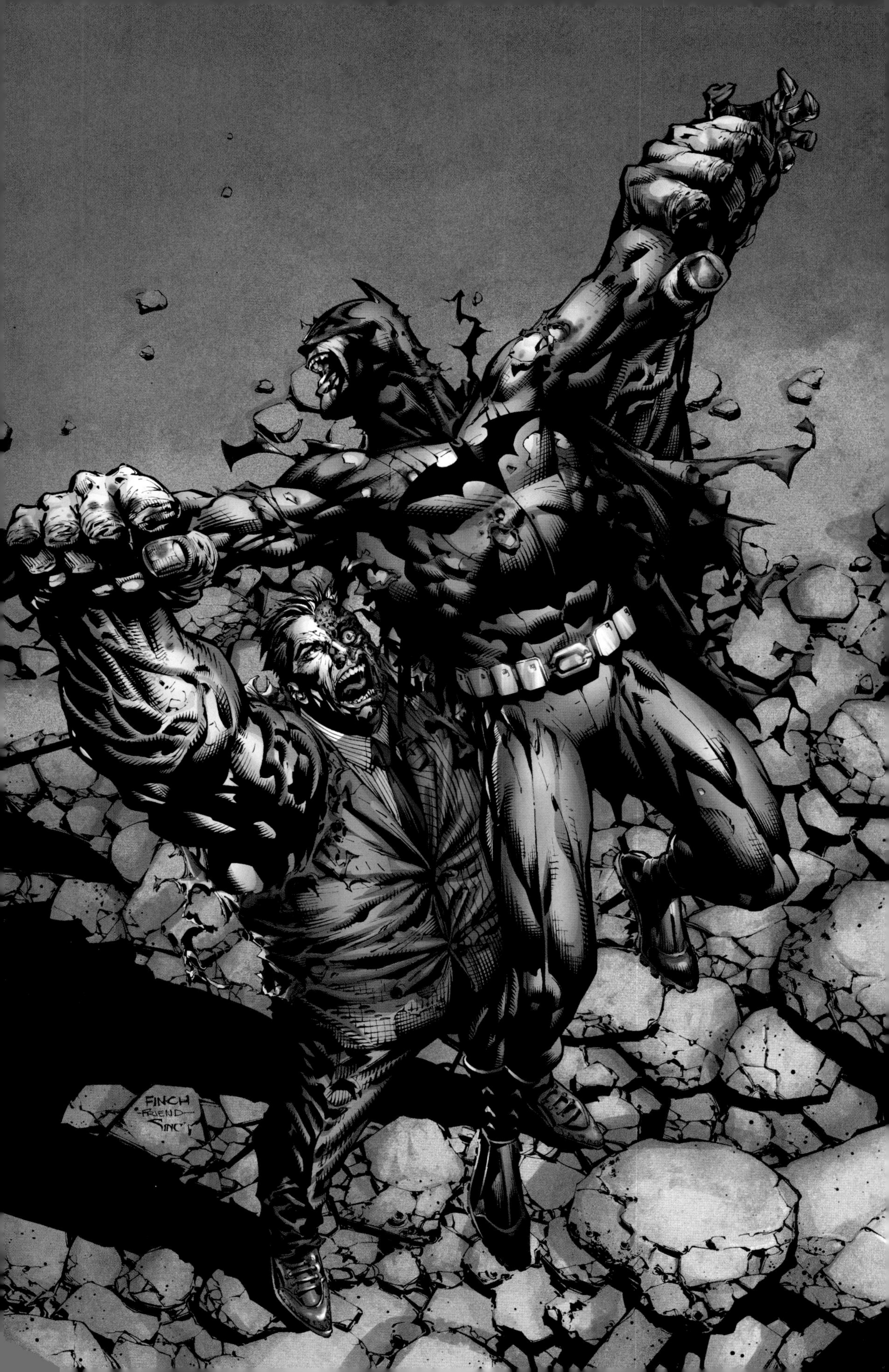
FINCH
FRIEND
SINC

A RUSH OF BLOOD

PAUL JENKINS writer/co-plotter **DAVID FINCH** penciller/co-plotter **RICHARD FRIEND** inker
cover art by **DAVID FINCH, RICHARD FRIEND & ALEX SINCLAIR**

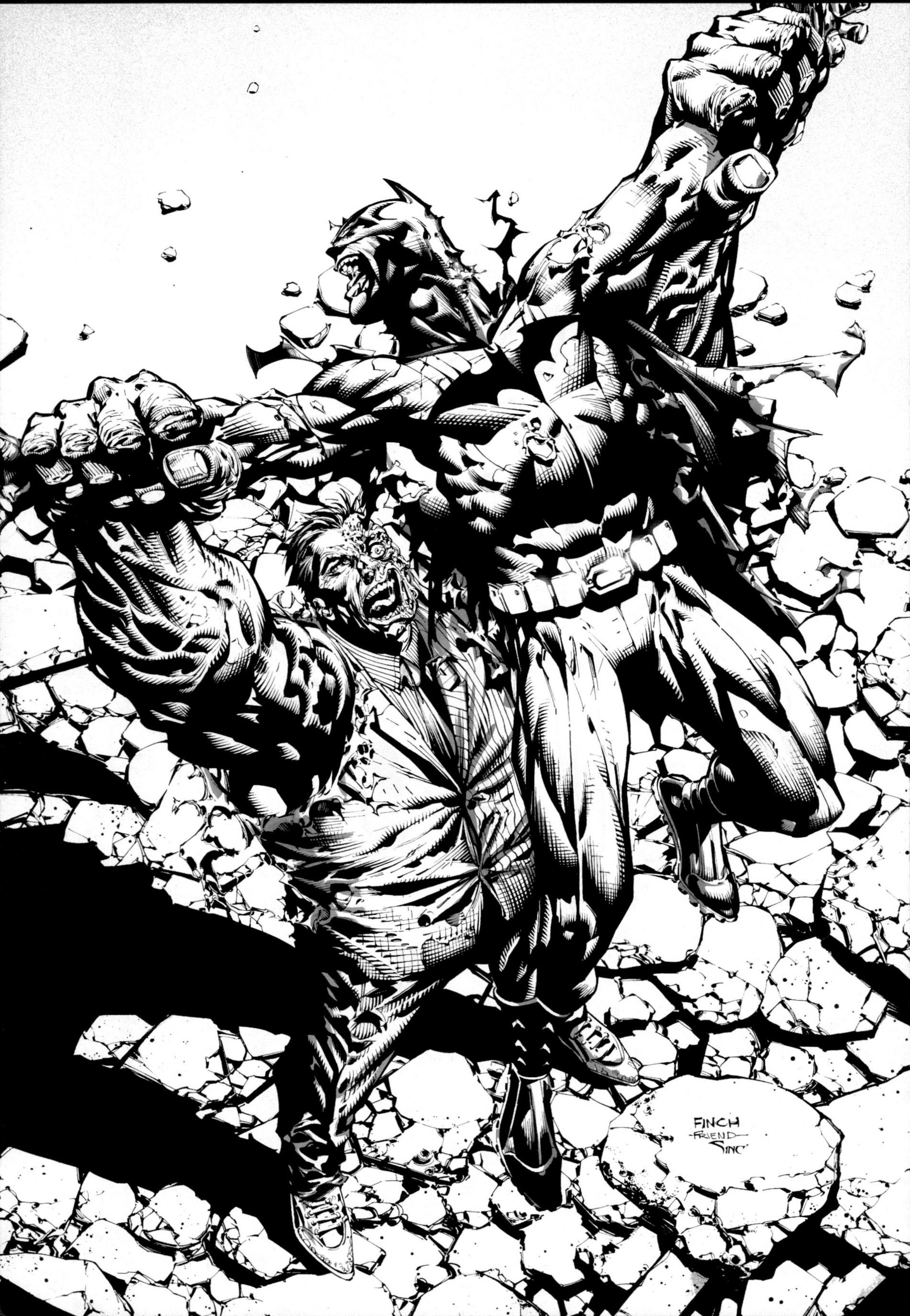
FINCH
FRIEND
SINC

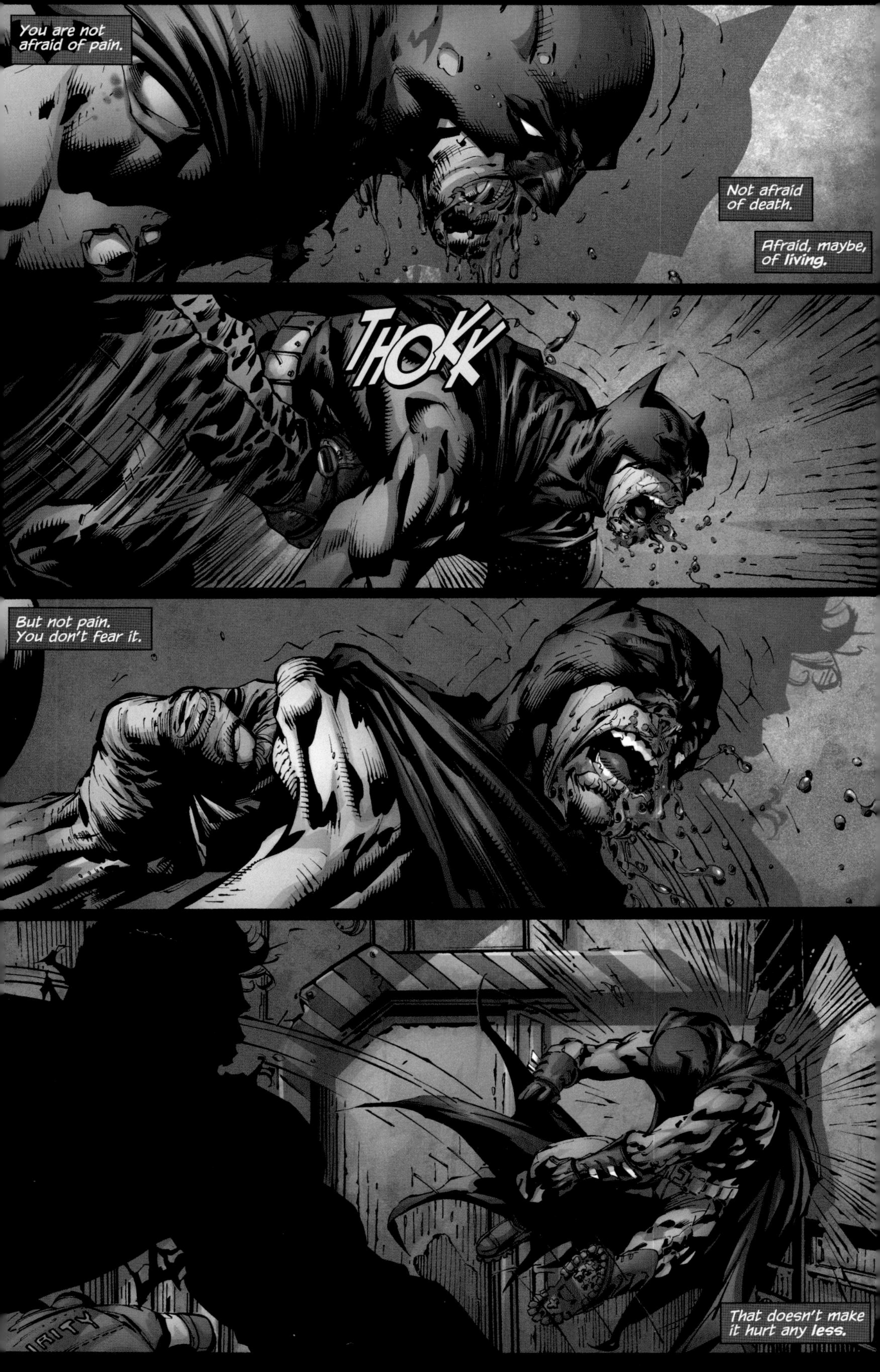
You are not afraid of pain.
Not afraid of death.
Afraid, maybe, of living.
THOKK
But not pain. You don't fear it.
That doesn't make it hurt any less.

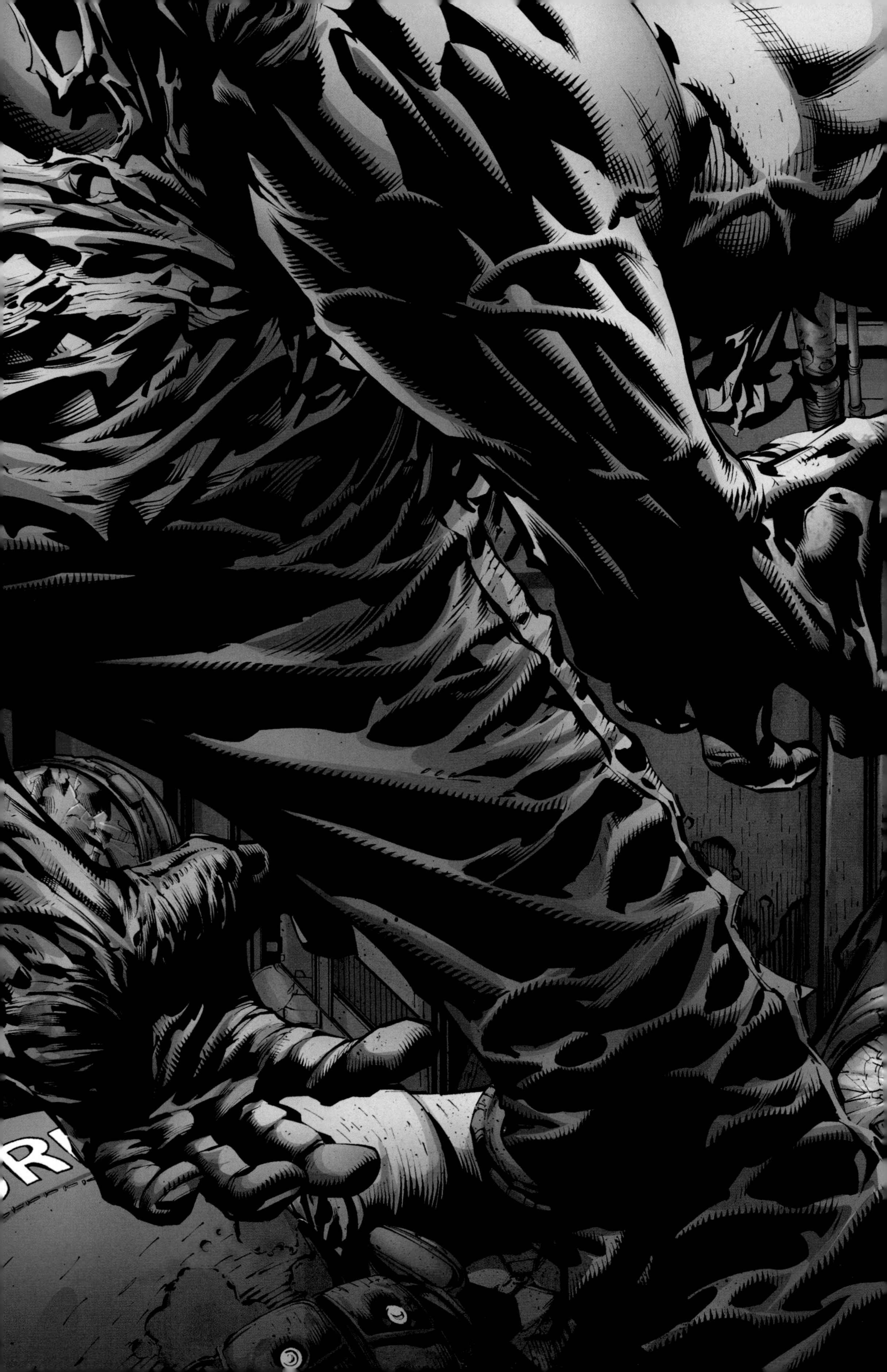

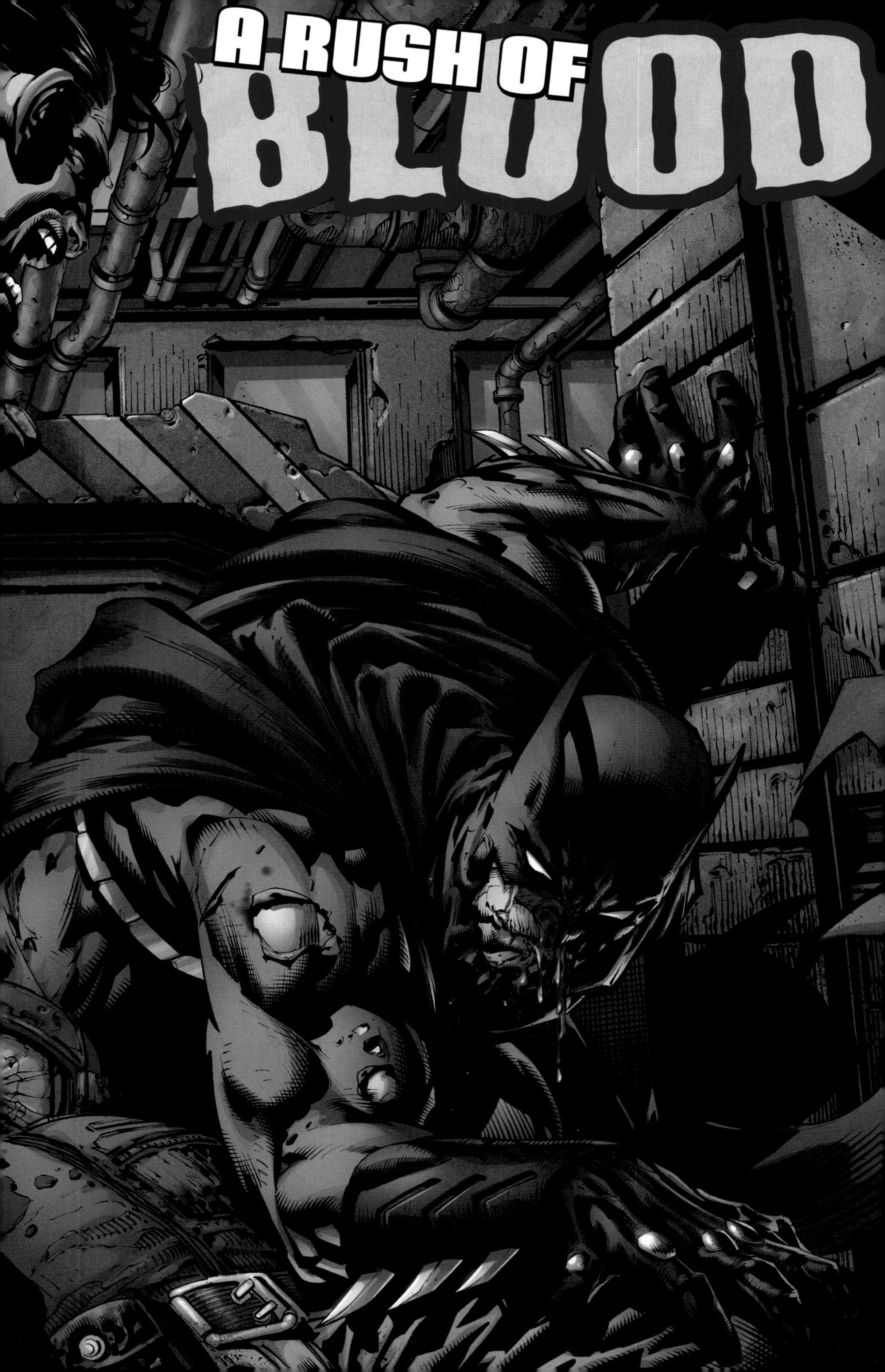
A RUSH OF
BLOOD

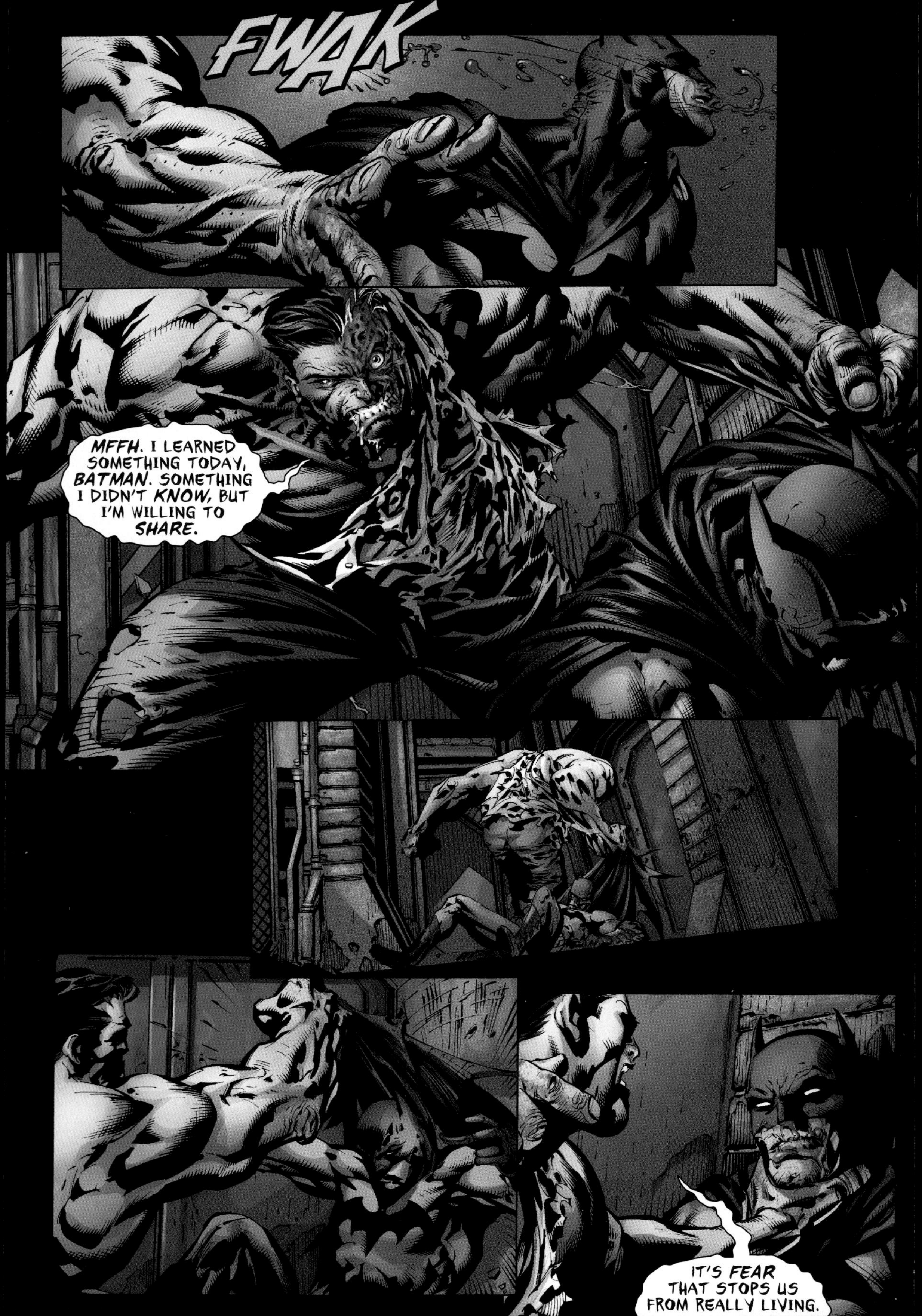
FWAK
MFFH. I LEARNED SOMETHING TODAY, BATMAN. SOMETHING I DIDN'T KNOW, BUT I'M WILLING TO SHARE.
IT'S FEAR THAT STOPS US FROM REALLY LIVING.

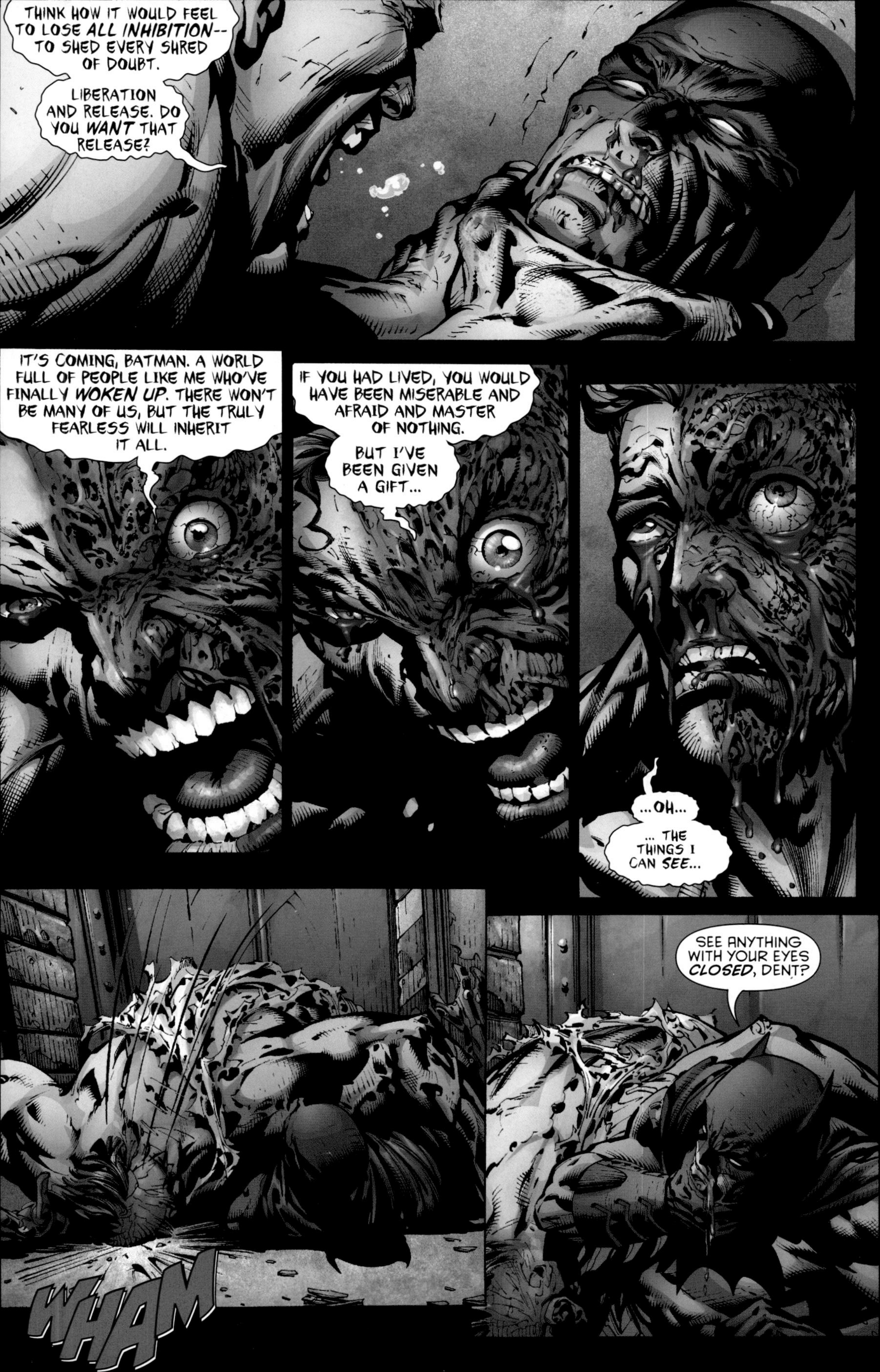
THINK HOW IT WOULD FEEL TO LOSE ALL INHIBITION-- TO SHED EVERY SHRED OF DOUBT.
LIBERATION AND RELEASE. DO YOU WANT THAT RELEASE?
IT'S COMING, BATMAN. A WORLD FULL OF PEOPLE LIKE ME WHO'VE FINALLY WOKEN UP. THERE WON'T BE MANY OF US, BUT THE TRULY FEARLESS WILL INHERIT IT ALL.
IF YOU HAD LIVED, YOU WOULD HAVE BEEN MISERABLE AND AFRAID AND MASTER OF NOTHING.
BUT I'VE BEEN GIVEN A GIFT...
...OH...
... THE THINGS I CAN SEE...
WHAM
SEE ANYTHING WITH YOUR EYES CLOSED, DENT?

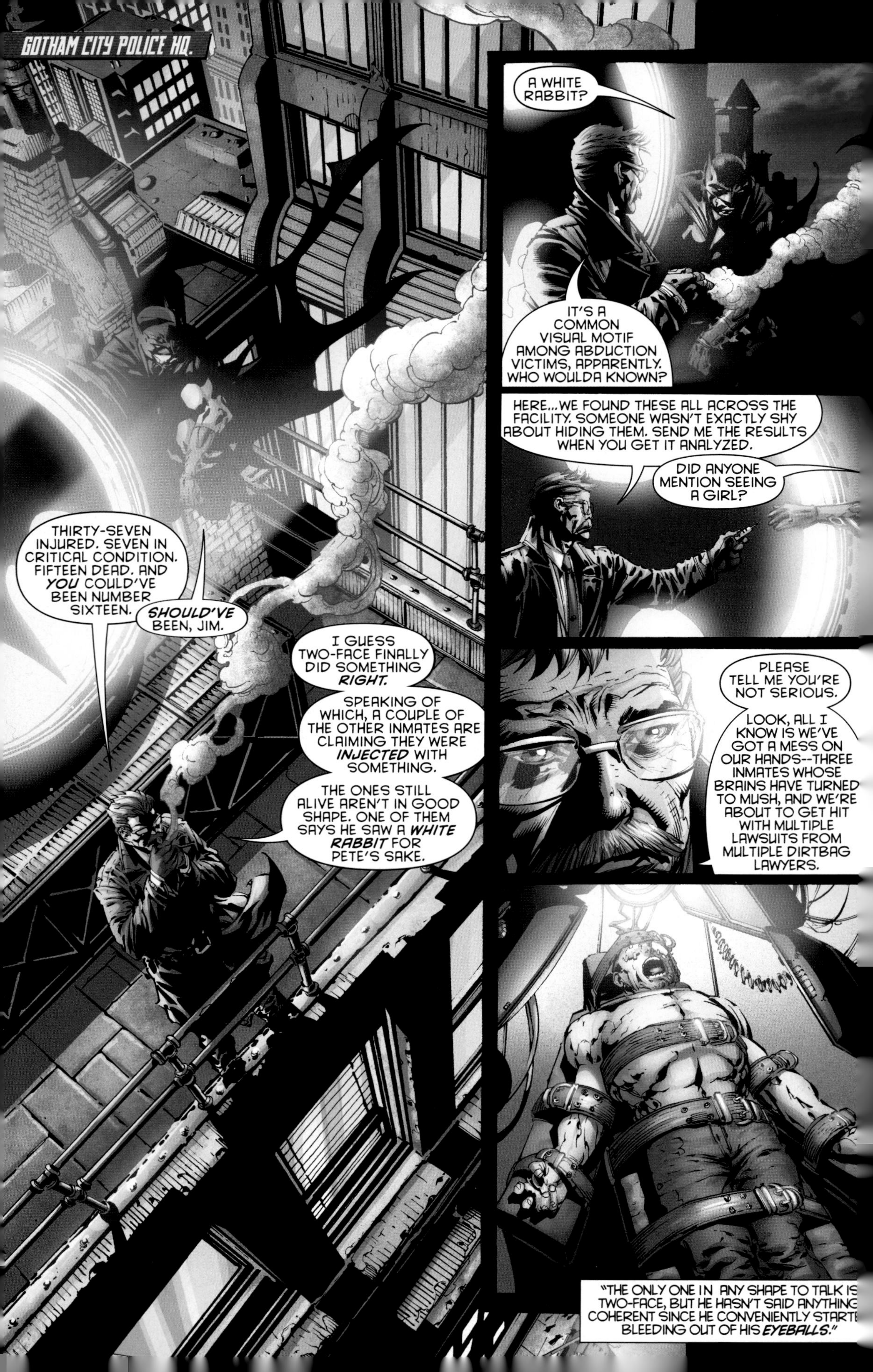
GOTHAM CITY POLICE HQ.
THIRTY-SEVEN INJURED. SEVEN IN CRITICAL CONDITION. FIFTEEN DEAD. AND YOU COULD'VE BEEN NUMBER SIXTEEN.
SHOULD'VE BEEN, JIM.
I GUESS TWO-FACE FINALLY DID SOMETHING RIGHT.
SPEAKING OF WHICH, A COUPLE OF THE OTHER INMATES ARE CLAIMING THEY WERE INJECTED WITH SOMETHING.
THE ONES STILL ALIVE AREN'T IN GOOD SHAPE. ONE OF THEM SAYS HE SAW A WHITE RABBIT FOR PETE'S SAKE.
A WHITE RABBIT?
IT'S A COMMON VISUAL MOTIF AMONG ABDUCTION VICTIMS, APPARENTLY. WHO WOULDA KNOWN?
HERE...WE FOUND THESE ALL ACROSS THE FACILITY. SOMEONE WASN'T EXACTLY SHY ABOUT HIDING THEM. SEND ME THE RESULTS WHEN YOU GET IT ANALYZED.
DID ANYONE MENTION SEEING A GIRL?
PLEASE TELL ME YOU'RE NOT SERIOUS.
LOOK, ALL I KNOW IS WE'VE GOT A MESS ON OUR HANDS--THREE INMATES WHOSE BRAINS HAVE TURNED TO MUSH, AND WE'RE ABOUT TO GET HIT WITH MULTIPLE LAWSUITS FROM MULTIPLE DIRTBAG LAWYERS.
"THE ONLY ONE IN ANY SHAPE TO TALK IS TWO-FACE, BUT HE HASN'T SAID ANYTHING COHERENT SINCE HE CONVENIENTLY STARTE BLEEDING OUT OF HIS EYEBALLS."

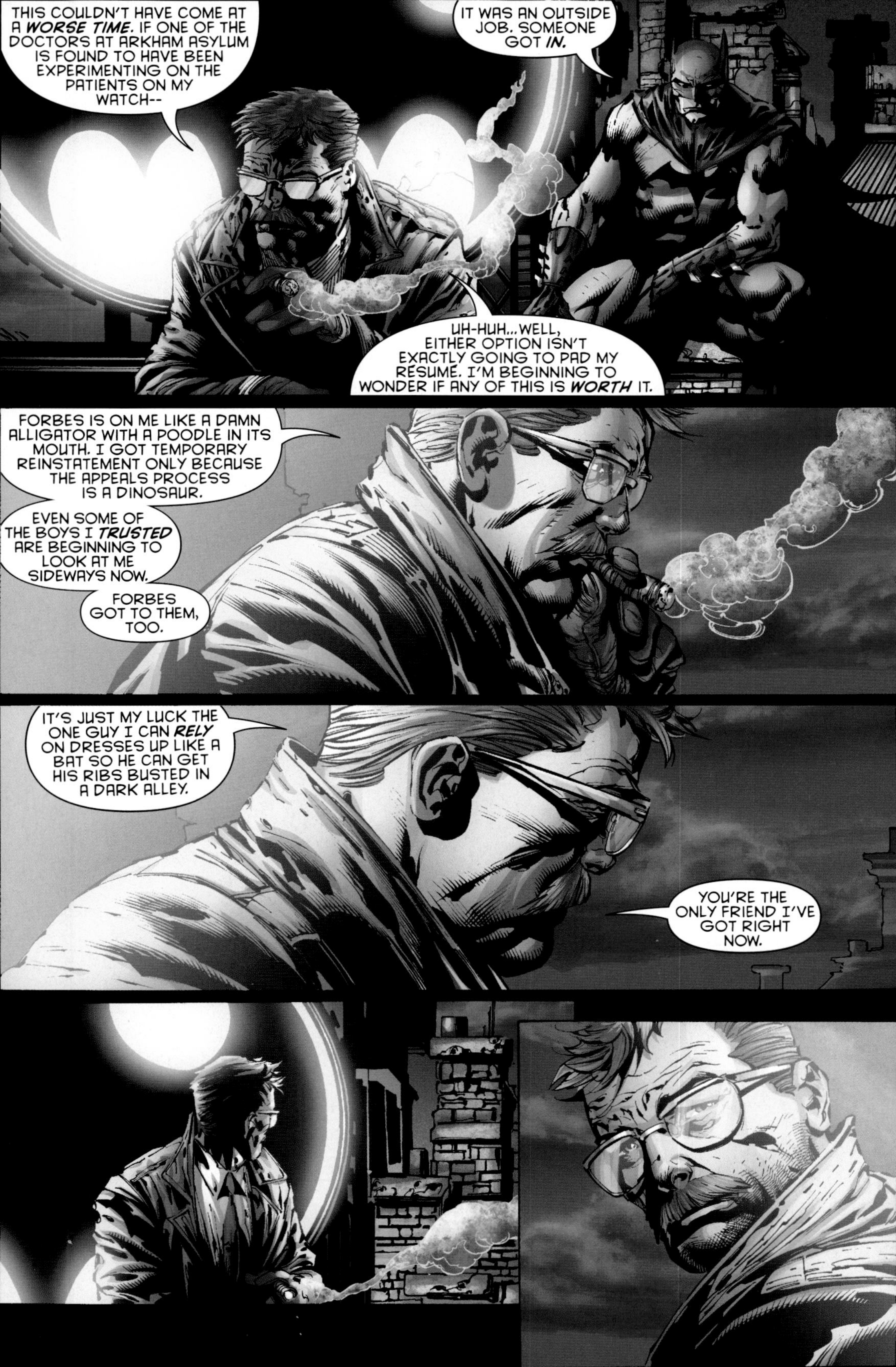

THIS COULDN'T HAVE COME AT A WORSE TIME. IF ONE OF THE DOCTORS AT ARKHAM ASYLUM IS FOUND TO HAVE BEEN EXPERIMENTING ON THE PATIENTS ON MY WATCH--
IT WAS AN OUTSIDE JOB. SOMEONE GOT IN.
UH-HUH...WELL, EITHER OPTION ISN'T EXACTLY GOING TO PAD MY RESUMÉ. I'M BEGINNING TO WONDER IF ANY OF THIS IS WORTH IT.
FORBES IS ON ME LIKE A DAMN ALLIGATOR WITH A POODLE IN ITS MOUTH. I GOT TEMPORARY REINSTATEMENT ONLY BECAUSE THE APPEALS PROCESS IS A DINOSAUR.
EVEN SOME OF THE BOYS I TRUSTED ARE BEGINNING TO LOOK AT ME SIDEWAYS NOW.
FORBES GOT TO THEM, TOO.
IT'S JUST MY LUCK THE ONE GUY I CAN RELY ON DRESSES UP LIKE A BAT SO HE CAN GET HIS RIBS BUSTED IN A DARK ALLEY.
YOU'RE THE ONLY FRIEND I'VE GOT RIGHT NOW.

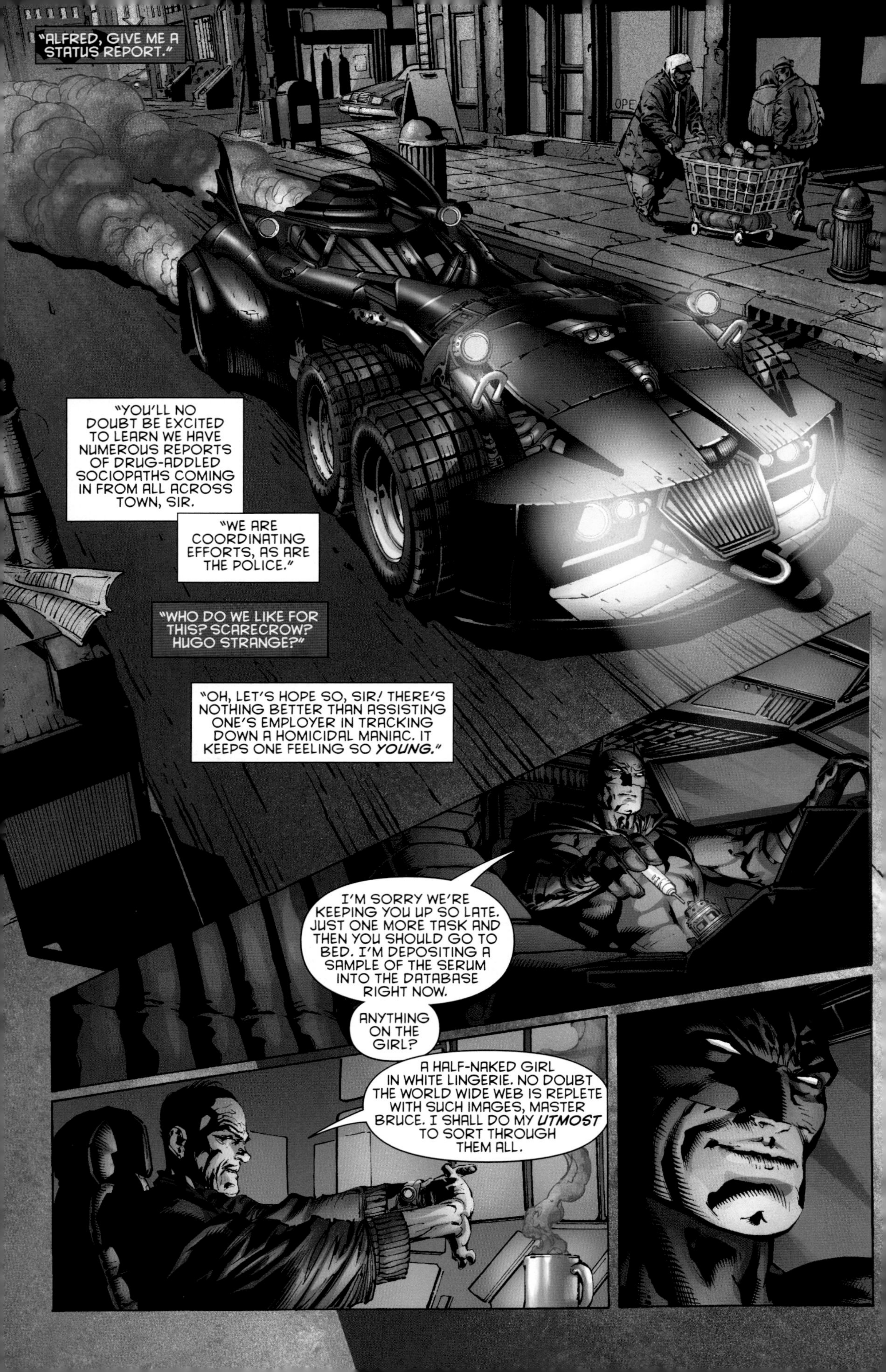
"ALFRED, GIVE ME A STATUS REPORT."
"YOU'LL NO DOUBT BE EXCITED TO LEARN WE HAVE NUMEROUS REPORTS OF DRUG-ADDLED SOCIOPATHS COMING IN FROM ALL ACROSS TOWN, SIR.
"WE ARE COORDINATING EFFORTS, AS ARE THE POLICE."
"WHO DO WE LIKE FOR THIS? SCARECROW? HUGO STRANGE?"
"OH, LET'S HOPE SO, SIR! THERE'S NOTHING BETTER THAN ASSISTING ONE'S EMPLOYER IN TRACKING DOWN A HOMICIDAL MANIAC. IT KEEPS ONE FEELING SO *YOUNG.*"
I'M SORRY WE'RE KEEPING YOU UP SO LATE. JUST ONE MORE TASK AND THEN YOU SHOULD GO TO BED. I'M DEPOSITING A SAMPLE OF THE SERUM INTO THE DATABASE RIGHT NOW.
ANYTHING ON THE GIRL?
A HALF-NAKED GIRL IN WHITE LINGERIE. NO DOUBT THE WORLD WIDE WEB IS REPLETE WITH SUCH IMAGES, MASTER BRUCE. I SHALL DO MY *UTMOST* TO SORT THROUGH THEM ALL.

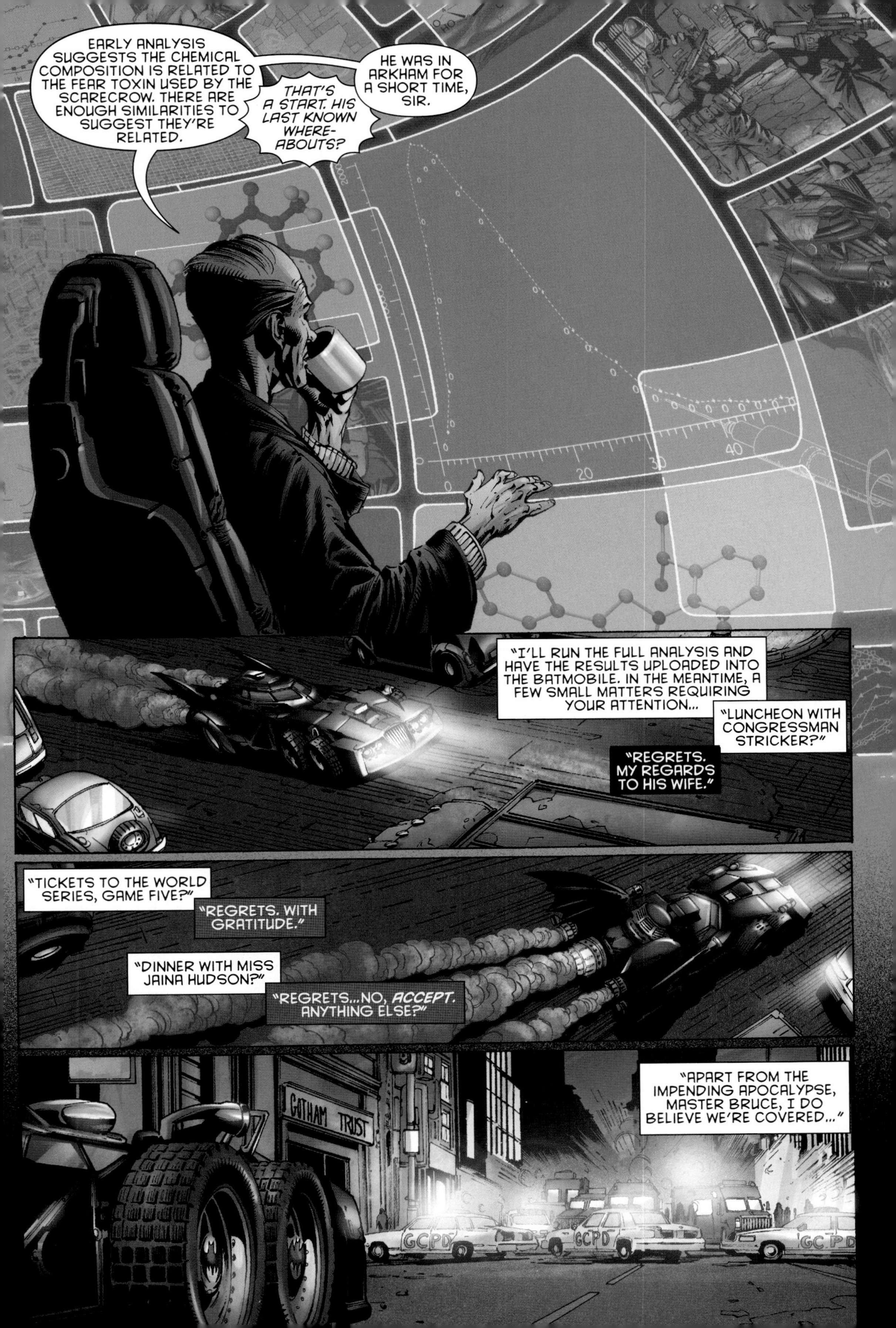
EARLY ANALYSIS SUGGESTS THE CHEMICAL COMPOSITION IS RELATED TO THE FEAR TOXIN USED BY THE SCARECROW. THERE ARE ENOUGH SIMILARITIES TO SUGGEST THEY'RE RELATED.
THAT'S A START. HIS LAST KNOWN WHERE-ABOUTS?
HE WAS IN ARKHAM FOR A SHORT TIME, SIR.
"I'LL RUN THE FULL ANALYSIS AND HAVE THE RESULTS UPLOADED INTO THE BATMOBILE. IN THE MEANTIME, A FEW SMALL MATTERS REQUIRING YOUR ATTENTION...
"LUNCHEON WITH CONGRESSMAN STRICKER?"
"REGRETS. MY REGARDS TO HIS WIFE."
"TICKETS TO THE WORLD SERIES, GAME FIVE?"
"REGRETS. WITH GRATITUDE."
"DINNER WITH MISS JAINA HUDSON?"
"REGRETS...NO, *ACCEPT.* ANYTHING ELSE?"
"APART FROM THE IMPENDING APOCALYPSE, MASTER BRUCE, I DO BELIEVE WE'RE COVERED..."
GOTHAM TRUST
GCPD
GCPD
GCPD

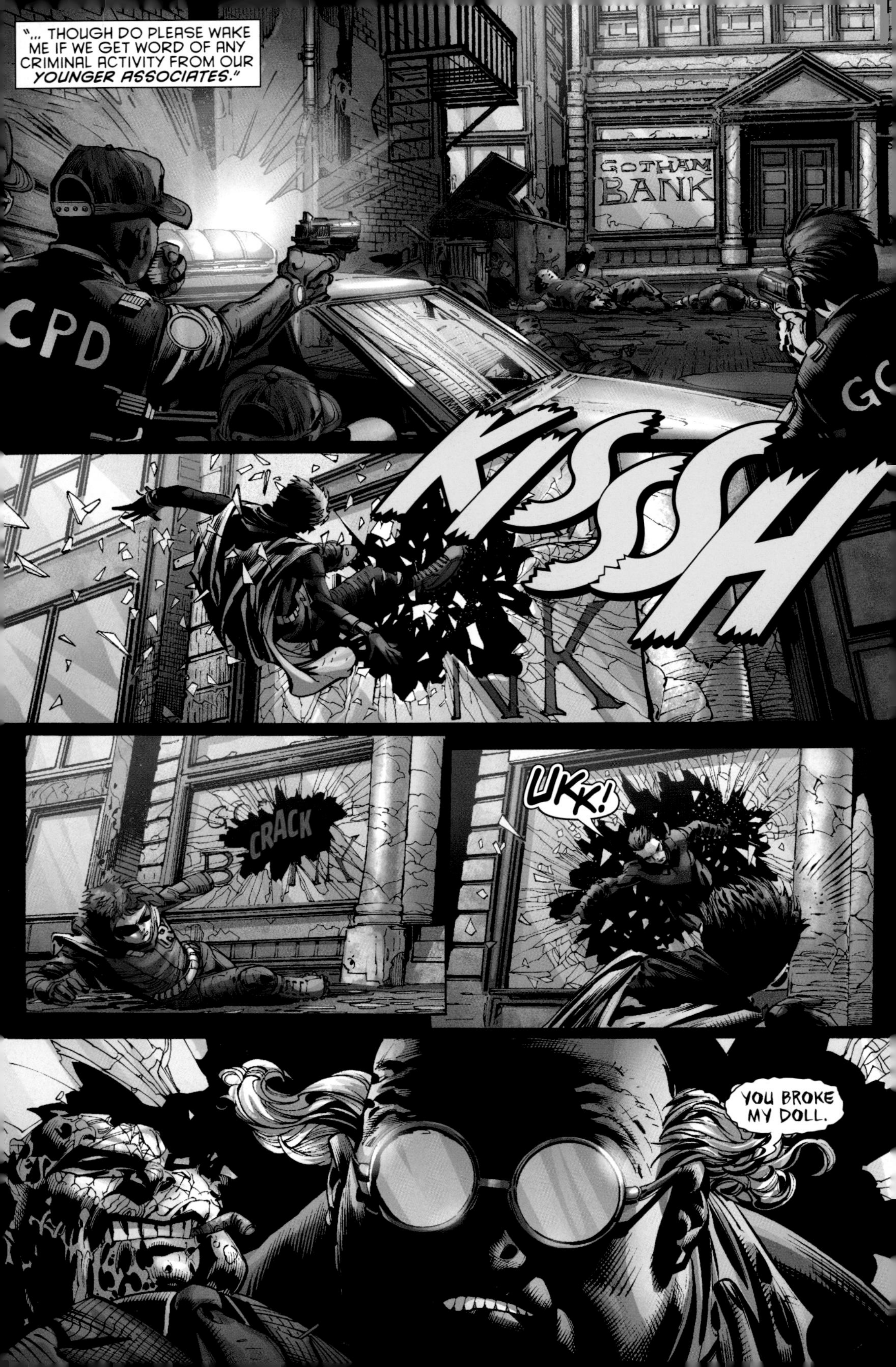
"... THOUGH DO PLEASE WAKE ME IF WE GET WORD OF ANY CRIMINAL ACTIVITY FROM OUR *YOUNGER ASSOCIATES*."
GOTHAM BANK
CPD
KSSSH
CRACK
UKK!
YOU BROKE MY DOLL.

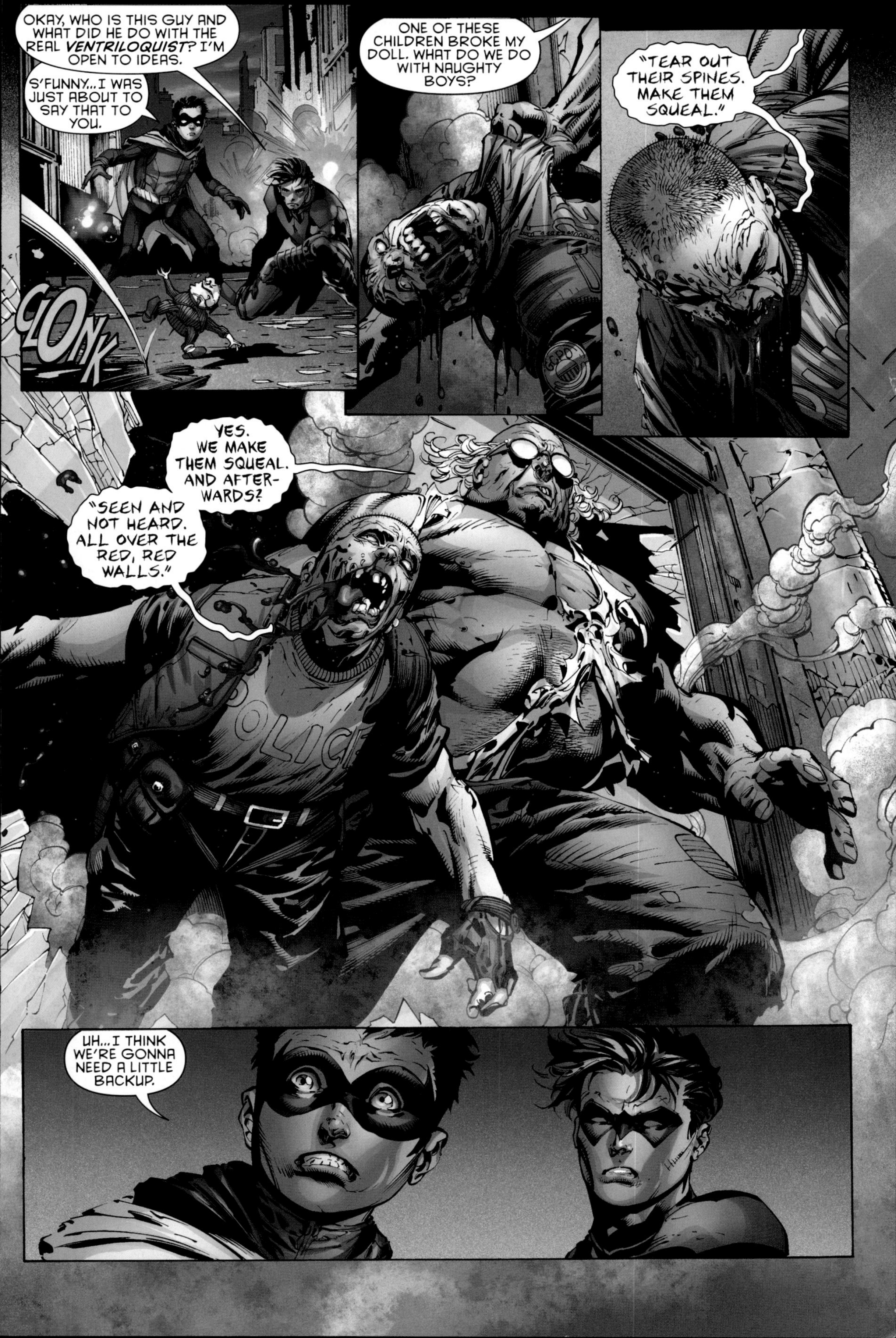
OKAY, WHO IS THIS GUY AND WHAT DID HE DO WITH THE REAL VENTRILOQUIST? I'M OPEN TO IDEAS.
S'FUNNY...I WAS JUST ABOUT TO SAY THAT TO YOU.
CLONK
ONE OF THESE CHILDREN BROKE MY DOLL. WHAT DO WE DO WITH NAUGHTY BOYS?
"TEAR OUT THEIR SPINES. MAKE THEM SQUEAL."
YES. WE MAKE THEM SQUEAL. AND AFTER-WARDS?
"SEEN AND NOT HEARD. ALL OVER THE RED, RED WALLS."
POLICE
UH...I THINK WE'RE GONNA NEED A LITTLE BACKUP.

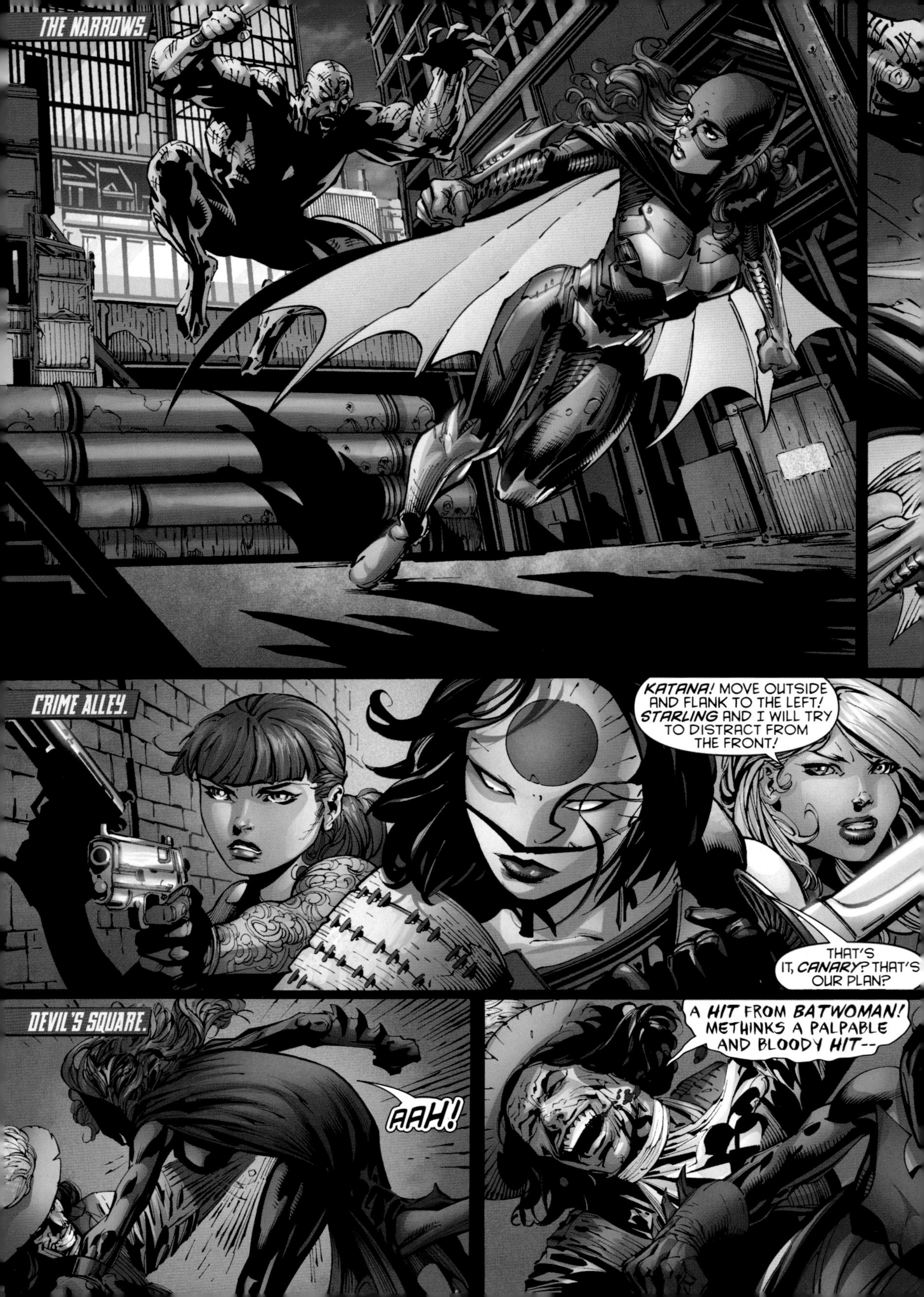
THE NARROWS.
CRIME ALLEY.
KATANA! MOVE OUTSIDE AND FLANK TO THE LEFT! STARLING AND I WILL TRY TO DISTRACT FROM THE FRONT!
THAT'S IT, CANARY? THAT'S OUR PLAN?
DEVIL'S SQUARE.
AAH!
A HIT FROM BATWOMAN! METHINKS A PALPABLE AND BLOODY HIT--

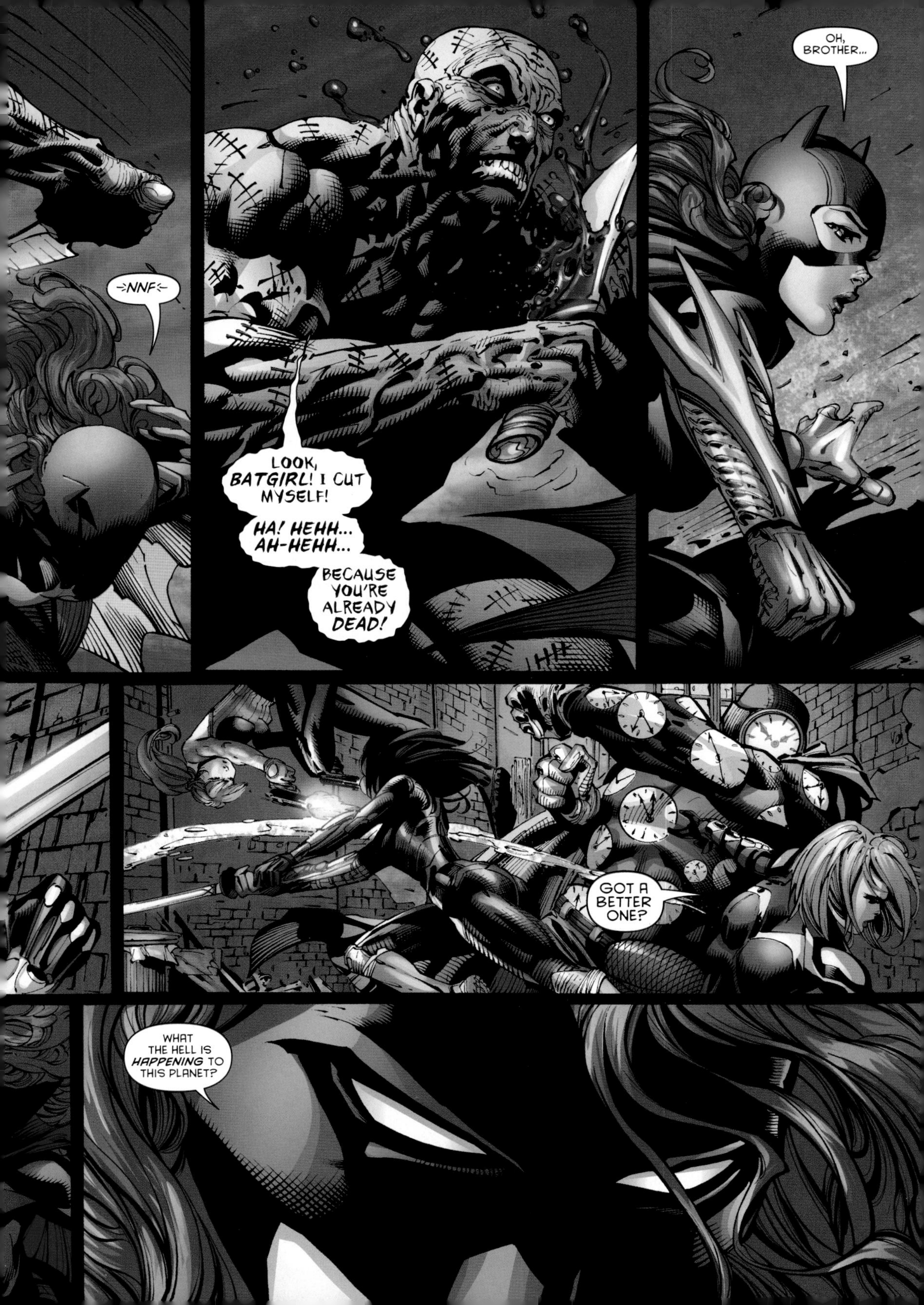

NNF
LOOK, BATGIRL! I CUT MYSELF!
HA! HEHH... AH-HEHH...
BECAUSE YOU'RE ALREADY DEAD!
OH, BROTHER...
GOT A BETTER ONE?
WHAT THE HELL IS HAPPENING TO THIS PLANET?

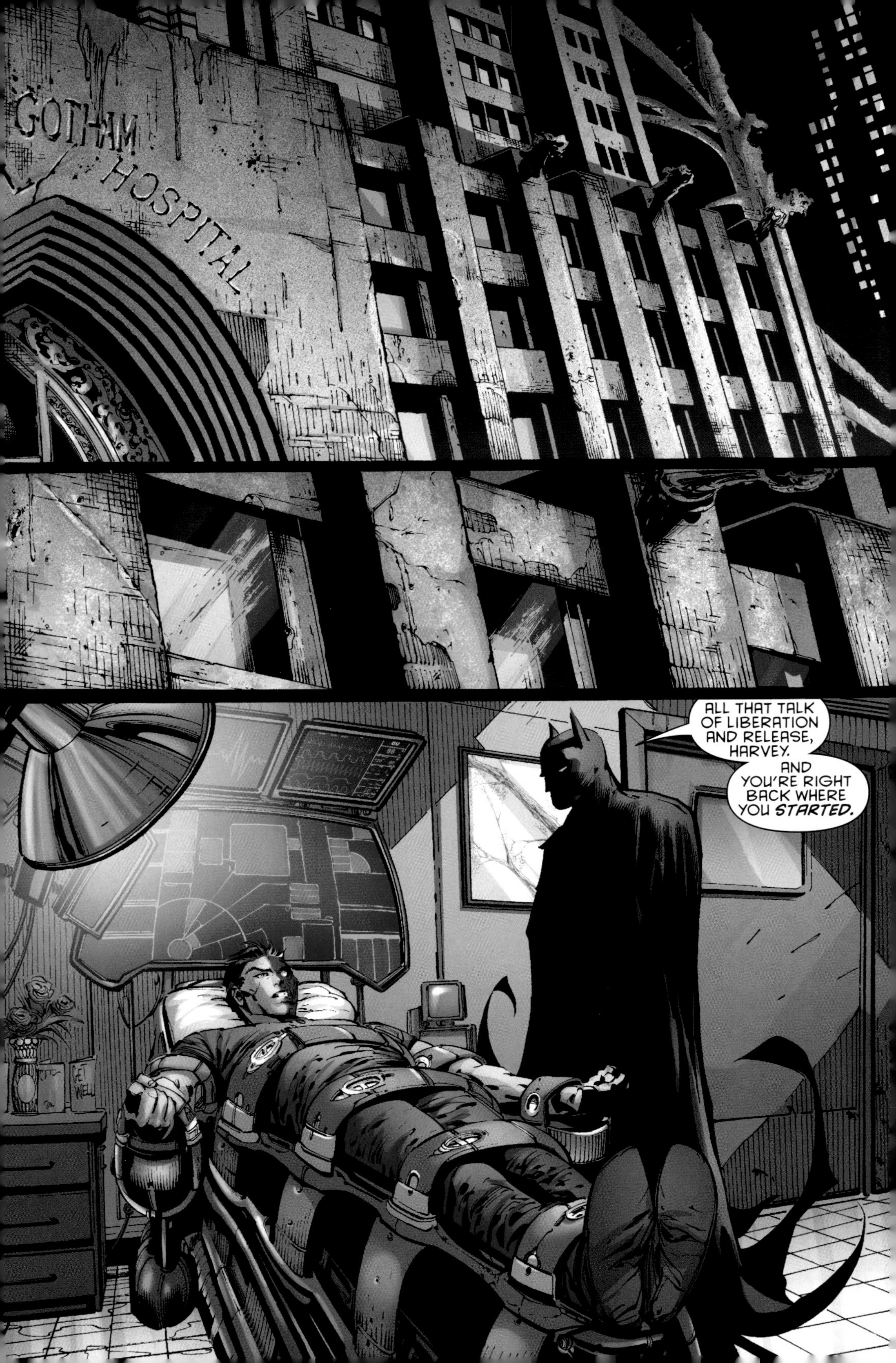
GOTHAM HOSPITAL
ALL THAT TALK OF LIBERATION AND RELEASE, HARVEY.
AND YOU'RE RIGHT BACK WHERE YOU STARTED.
GET WELL

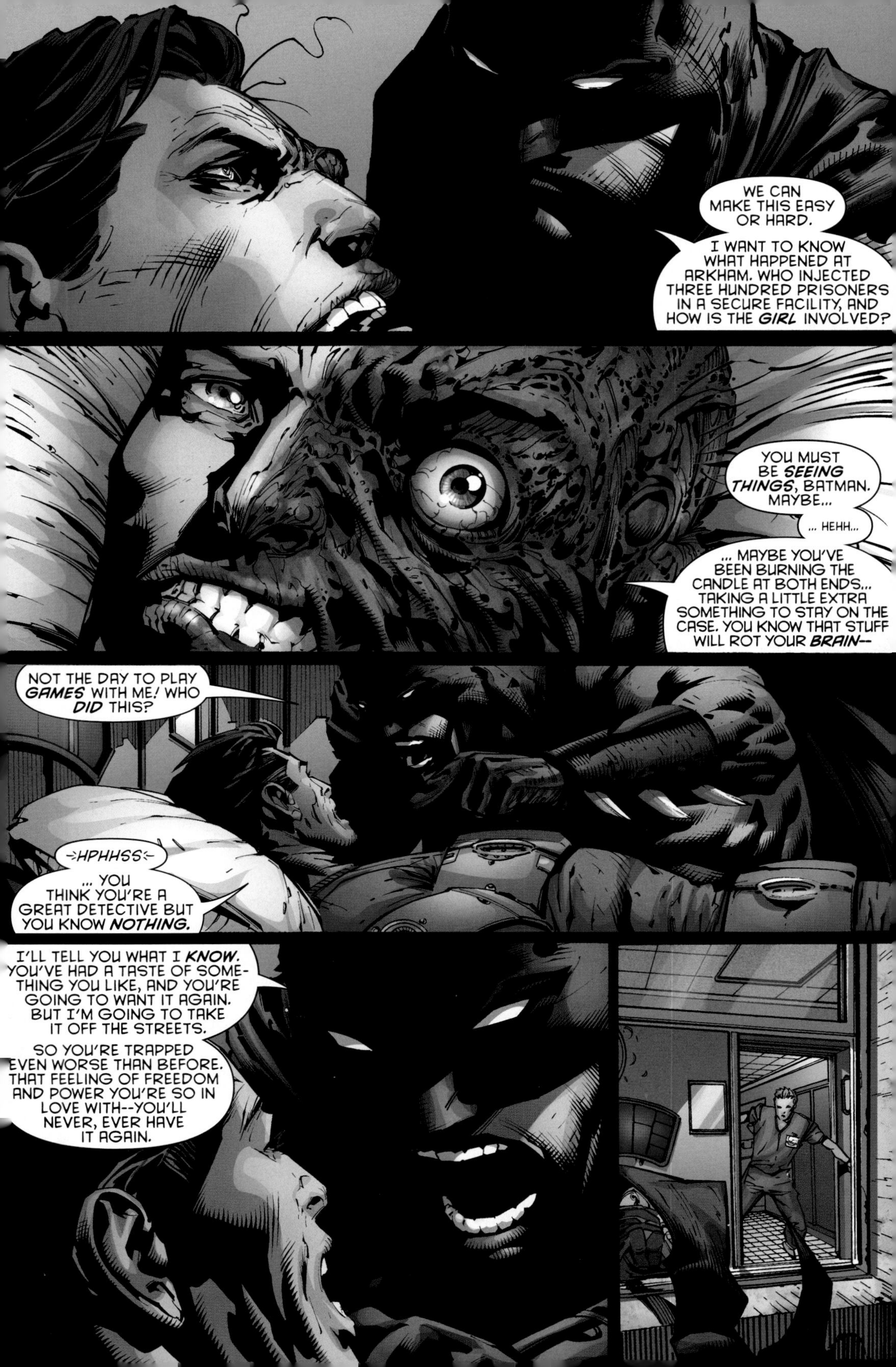
WE CAN MAKE THIS EASY OR HARD.
I WANT TO KNOW WHAT HAPPENED AT ARKHAM. WHO INJECTED THREE HUNDRED PRISONERS IN A SECURE FACILITY, AND HOW IS THE GIRL INVOLVED?
YOU MUST BE SEEING THINGS, BATMAN. MAYBE...
... HEHH...
... MAYBE YOU'VE BEEN BURNING THE CANDLE AT BOTH ENDS... TAKING A LITTLE EXTRA SOMETHING TO STAY ON THE CASE. YOU KNOW THAT STUFF WILL ROT YOUR BRAIN--
NOT THE DAY TO PLAY GAMES WITH ME! WHO DID THIS?
HPHHSS
... YOU THINK YOU'RE A GREAT DETECTIVE BUT YOU KNOW NOTHING.
I'LL TELL YOU WHAT I KNOW. YOU'VE HAD A TASTE OF SOMETHING YOU LIKE, AND YOU'RE GOING TO WANT IT AGAIN. BUT I'M GOING TO TAKE IT OFF THE STREETS.
SO YOU'RE TRAPPED EVEN WORSE THAN BEFORE. THAT FEELING OF FREEDOM AND POWER YOU'RE SO IN LOVE WITH--YOU'LL NEVER, EVER HAVE IT AGAIN.

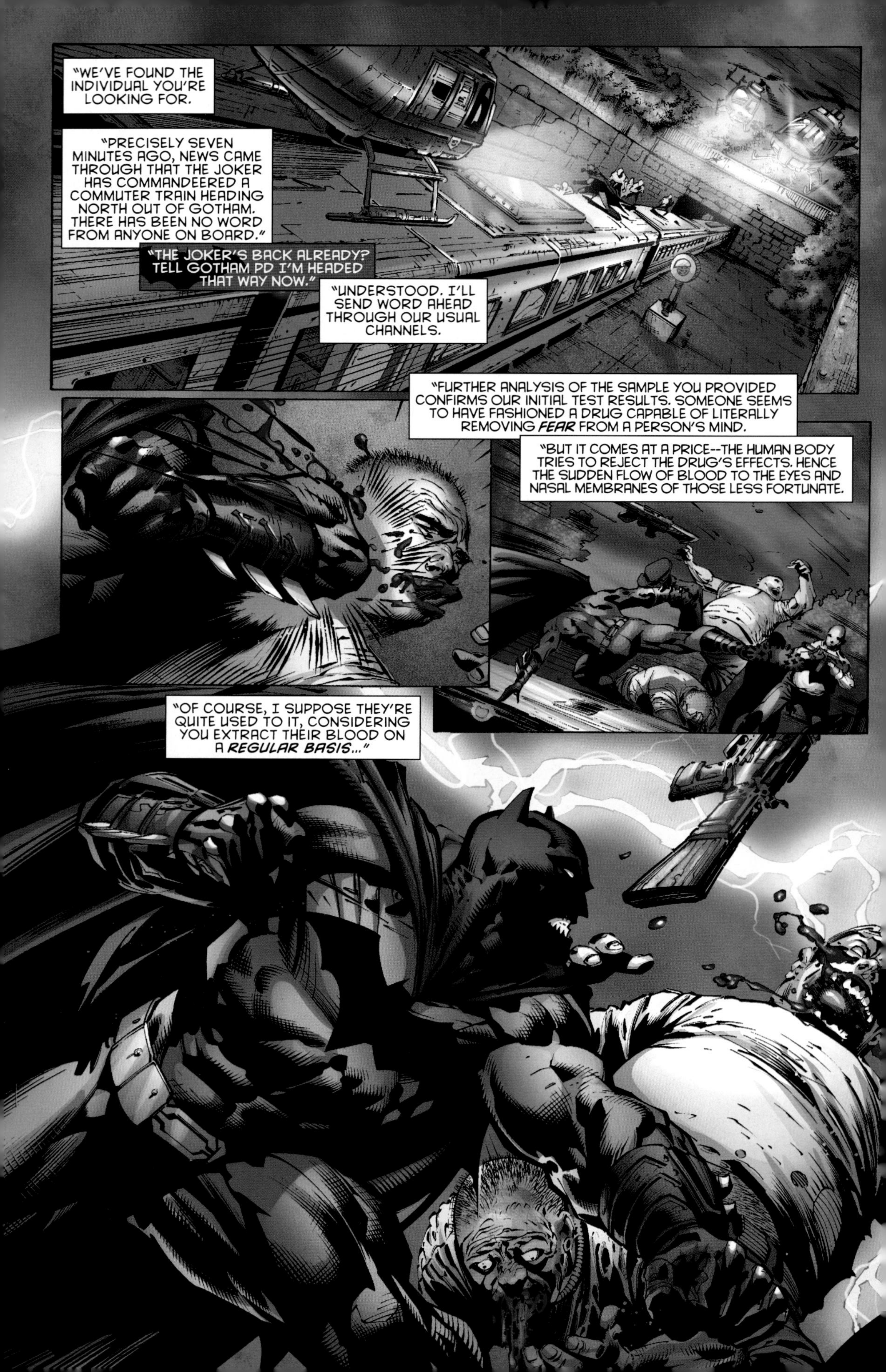
"WE'VE FOUND THE INDIVIDUAL YOU'RE LOOKING FOR.
"PRECISELY SEVEN MINUTES AGO, NEWS CAME THROUGH THAT THE JOKER HAS COMMANDEERED A COMMUTER TRAIN HEADING NORTH OUT OF GOTHAM. THERE HAS BEEN NO WORD FROM ANYONE ON BOARD."
"THE JOKER'S BACK ALREADY? TELL GOTHAM PD I'M HEADED THAT WAY NOW."
"UNDERSTOOD. I'LL SEND WORD AHEAD THROUGH OUR USUAL CHANNELS.
"FURTHER ANALYSIS OF THE SAMPLE YOU PROVIDED CONFIRMS OUR INITIAL TEST RESULTS. SOMEONE SEEMS TO HAVE FASHIONED A DRUG CAPABLE OF LITERALLY REMOVING FEAR FROM A PERSON'S MIND.
"BUT IT COMES AT A PRICE--THE HUMAN BODY TRIES TO REJECT THE DRUG'S EFFECTS. HENCE THE SUDDEN FLOW OF BLOOD TO THE EYES AND NASAL MEMBRANES OF THOSE LESS FORTUNATE.
"OF COURSE, I SUPPOSE THEY'RE QUITE USED TO IT, CONSIDERING YOU EXTRACT THEIR BLOOD ON A REGULAR BASIS..."

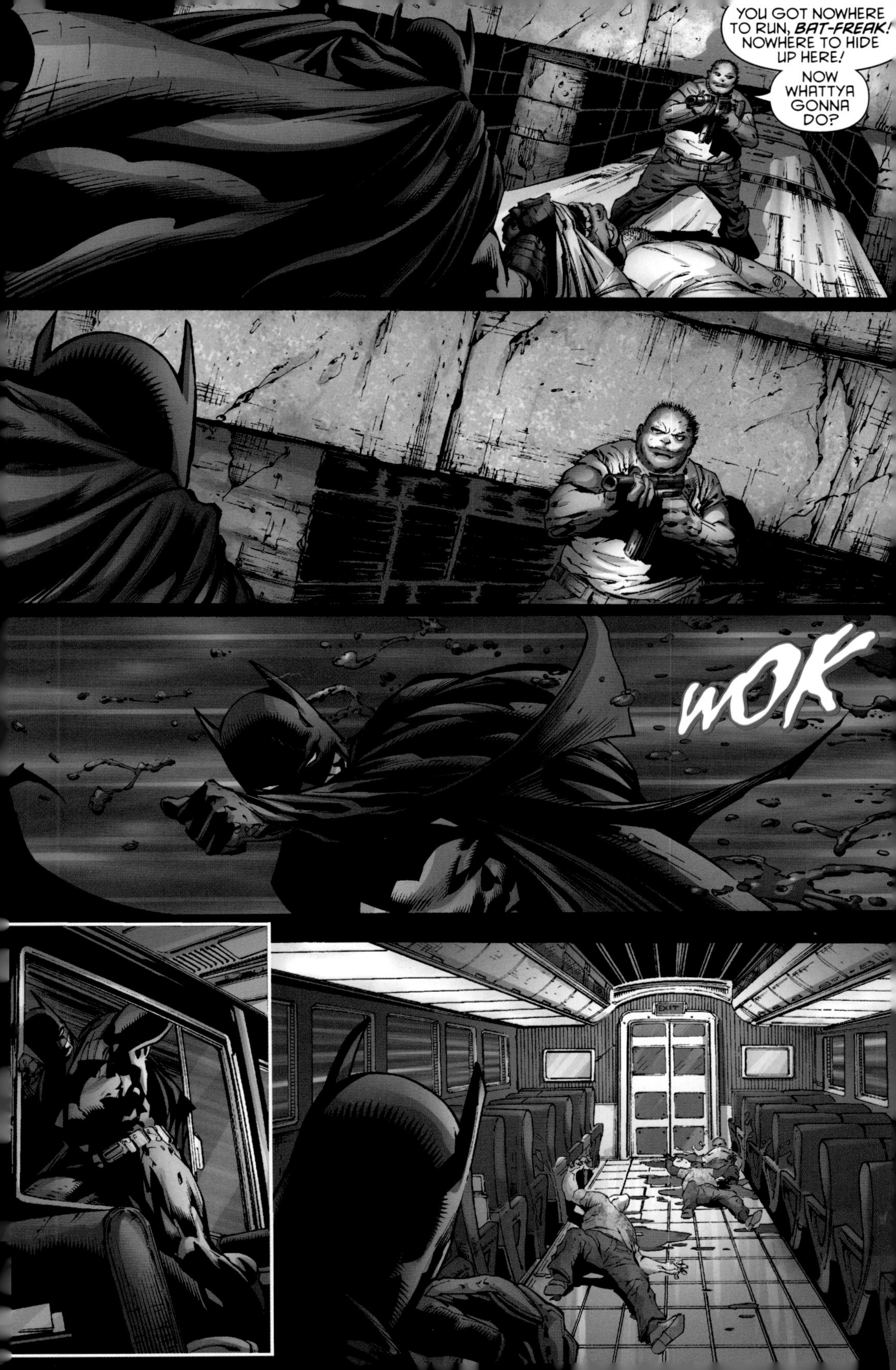
YOU GOT NOWHERE TO RUN, BAT-FREAK! NOWHERE TO HIDE UP HERE!
NOW WHATTYA GONNA DO?
WOK
EXIT

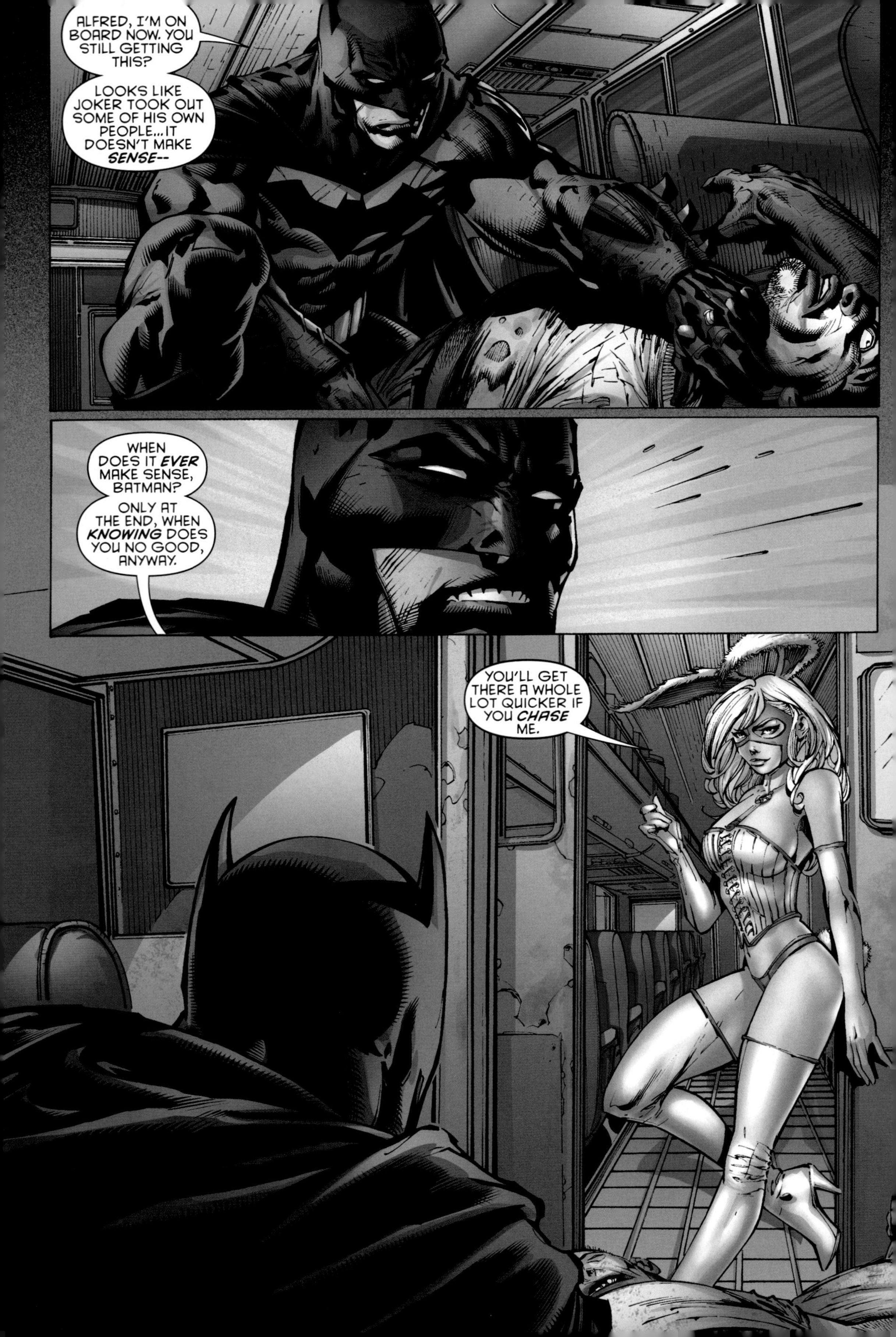
ALFRED, I'M ON BOARD NOW. YOU STILL GETTING THIS?
LOOKS LIKE JOKER TOOK OUT SOME OF HIS OWN PEOPLE...IT DOESN'T MAKE *SENSE*--
WHEN DOES IT *EVER* MAKE SENSE, BATMAN?
ONLY AT THE END, WHEN *KNOWING* DOES YOU NO GOOD, ANYWAY.
YOU'LL GET THERE A WHOLE LOT QUICKER IF YOU *CHASE* ME.

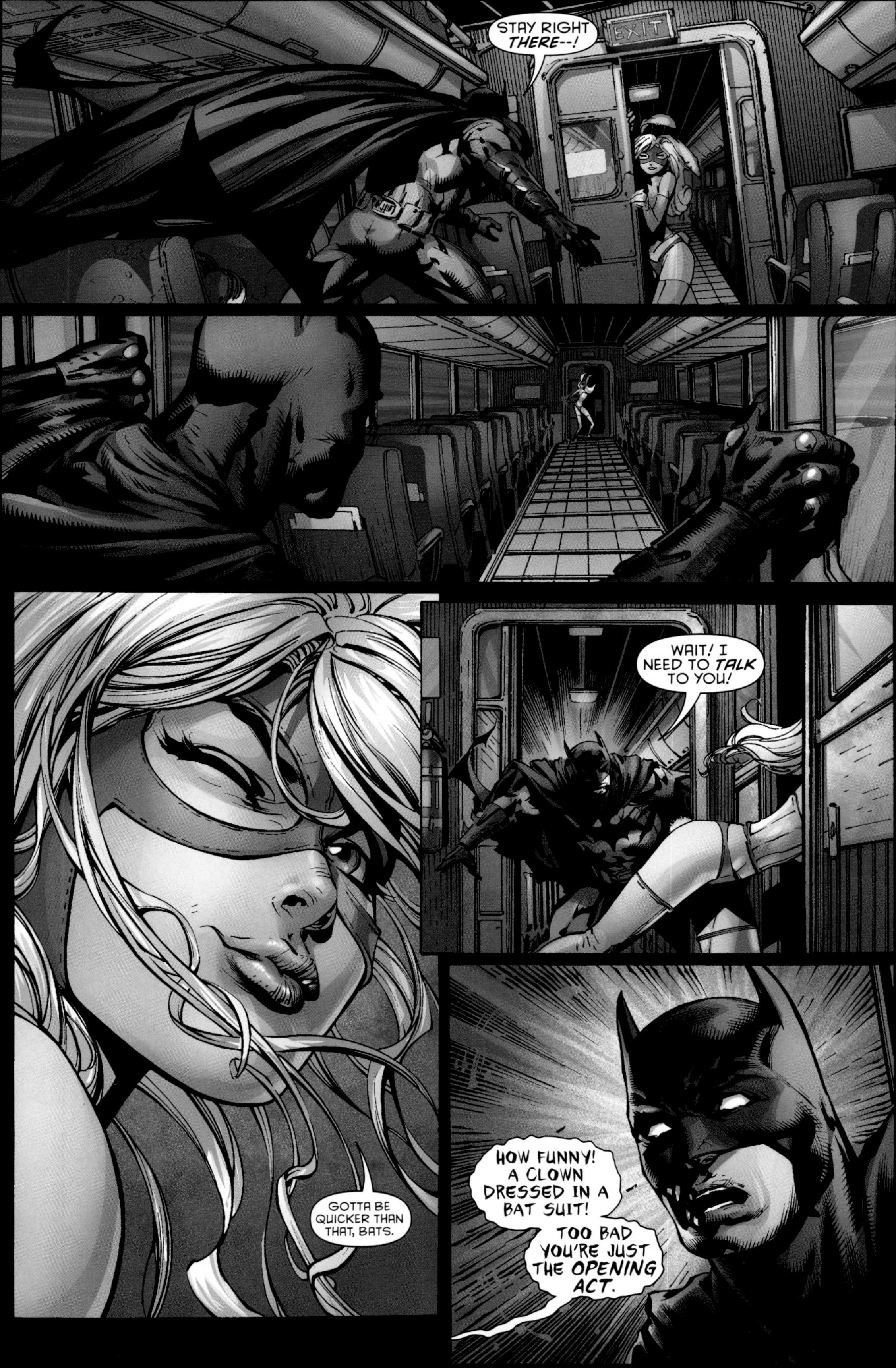
EXIT
STAY RIGHT THERE--!
WAIT! I NEED TO TALK TO YOU!
GOTTA BE QUICKER THAN THAT, BATS.
HOW FUNNY! A CLOWN DRESSED IN A BAT SUIT!
TOO BAD YOU'RE JUST THE OPENING ACT.

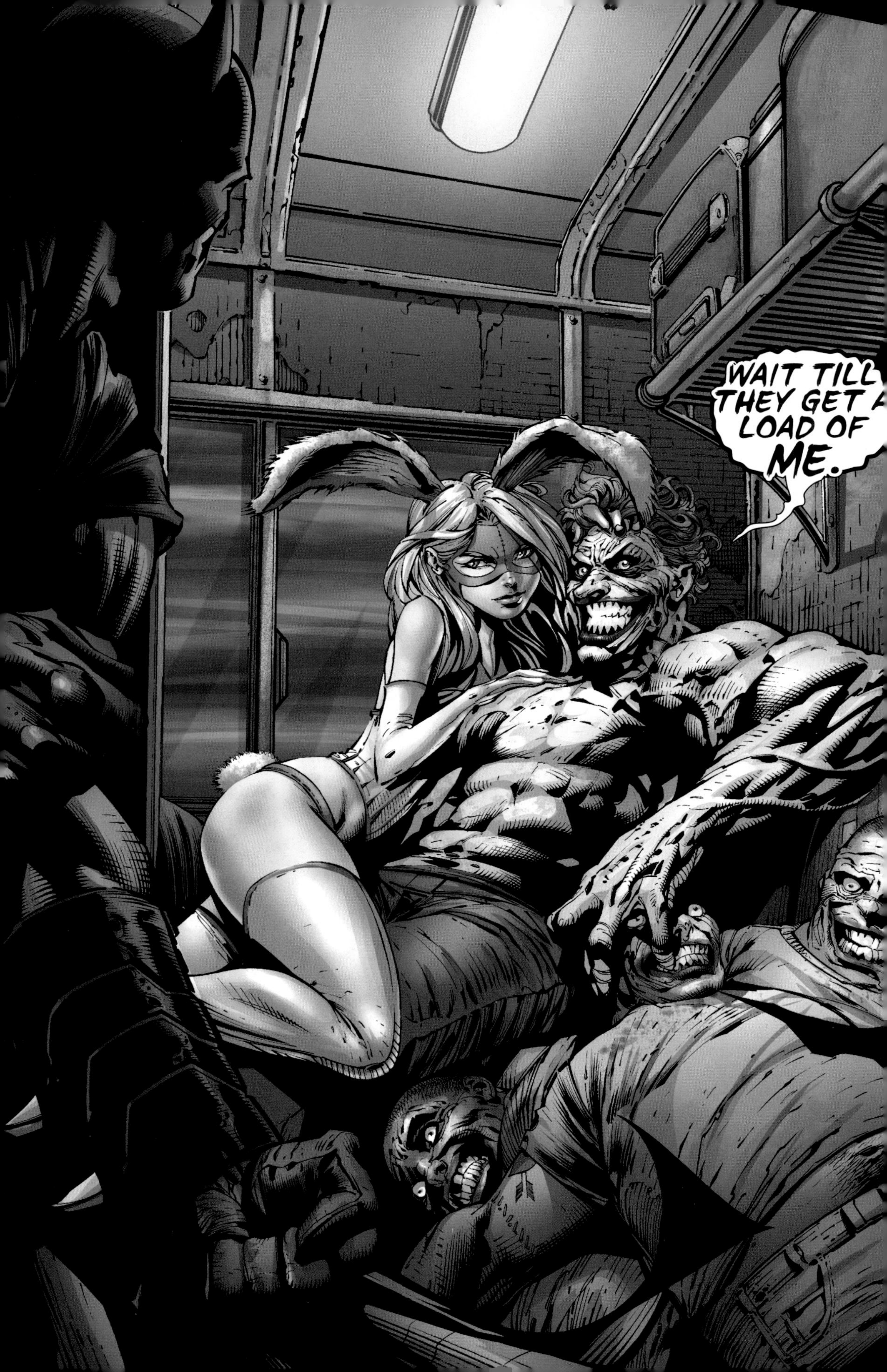
WAIT TILL THEY GET A LOAD OF ME.

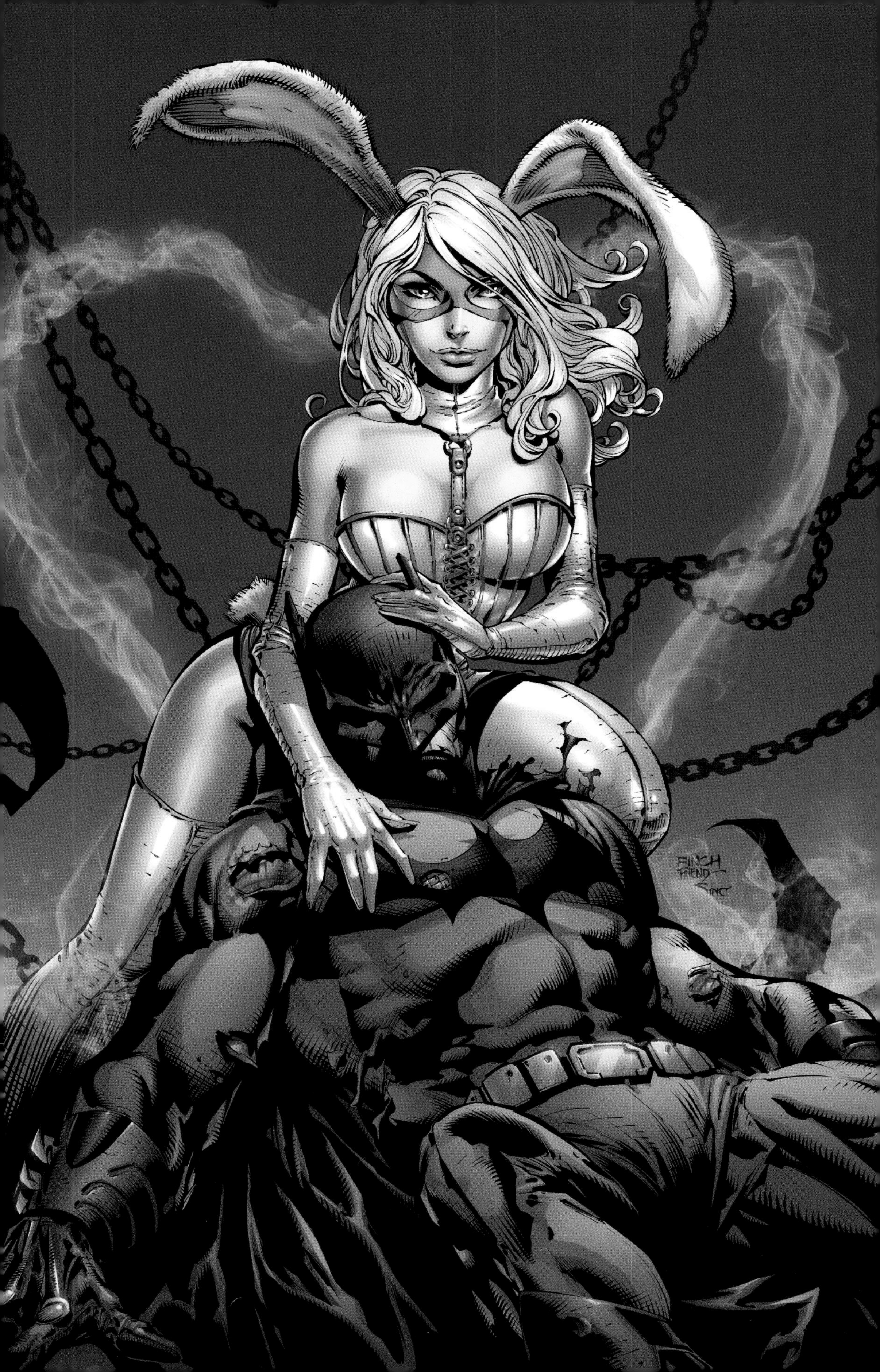
FINCH
FRIEND
SINC

CATCH ME IF YOU CAN

PAUL JENKINS writer/co-plotter **DAVID FINCH** penciller/co-plotter **RICHARD FRIEND** inker

cover art by **DAVID FINCH, RICHARD FRIEND & ALEX SINCLAIR**

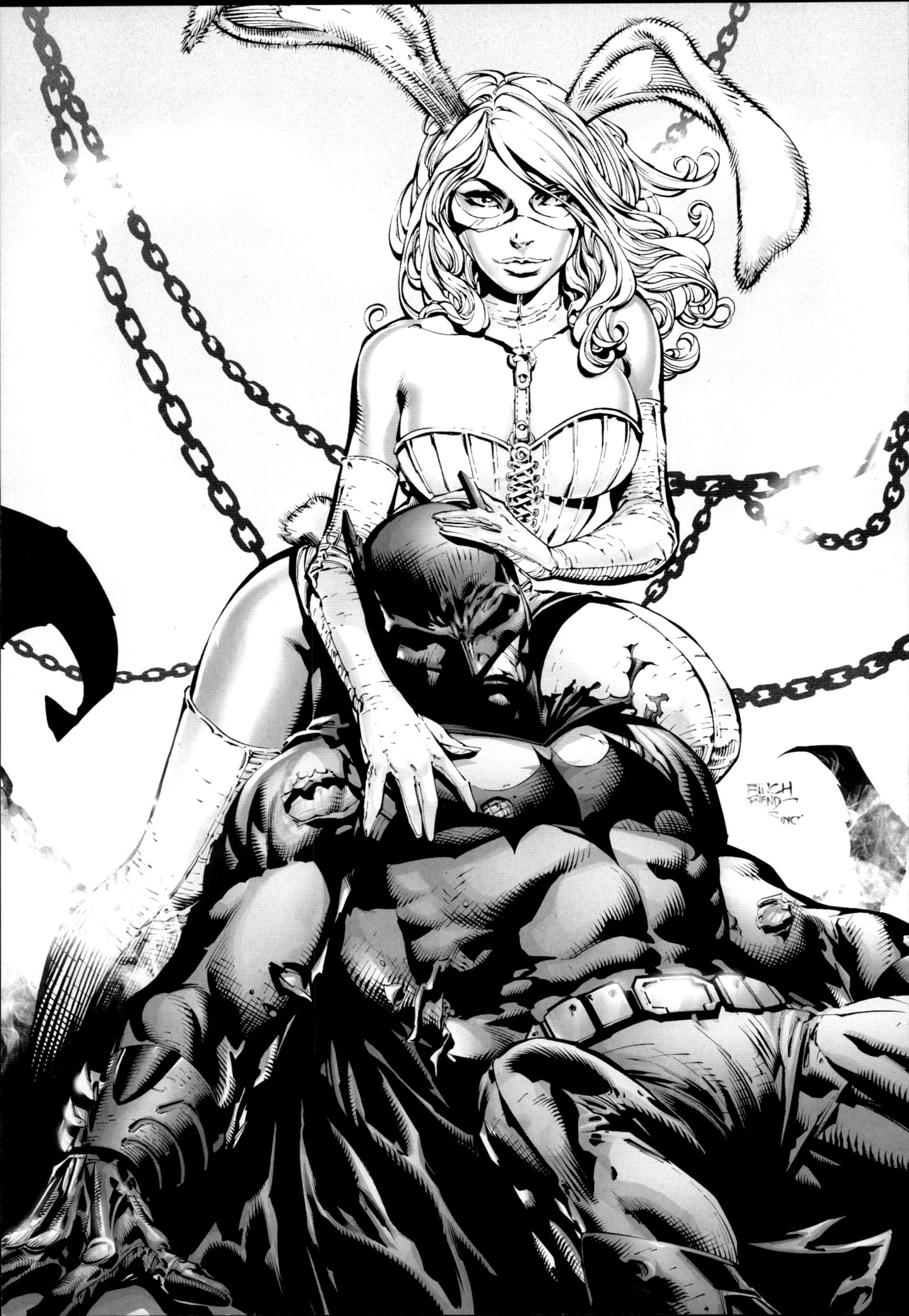
FINCH
FRIEND

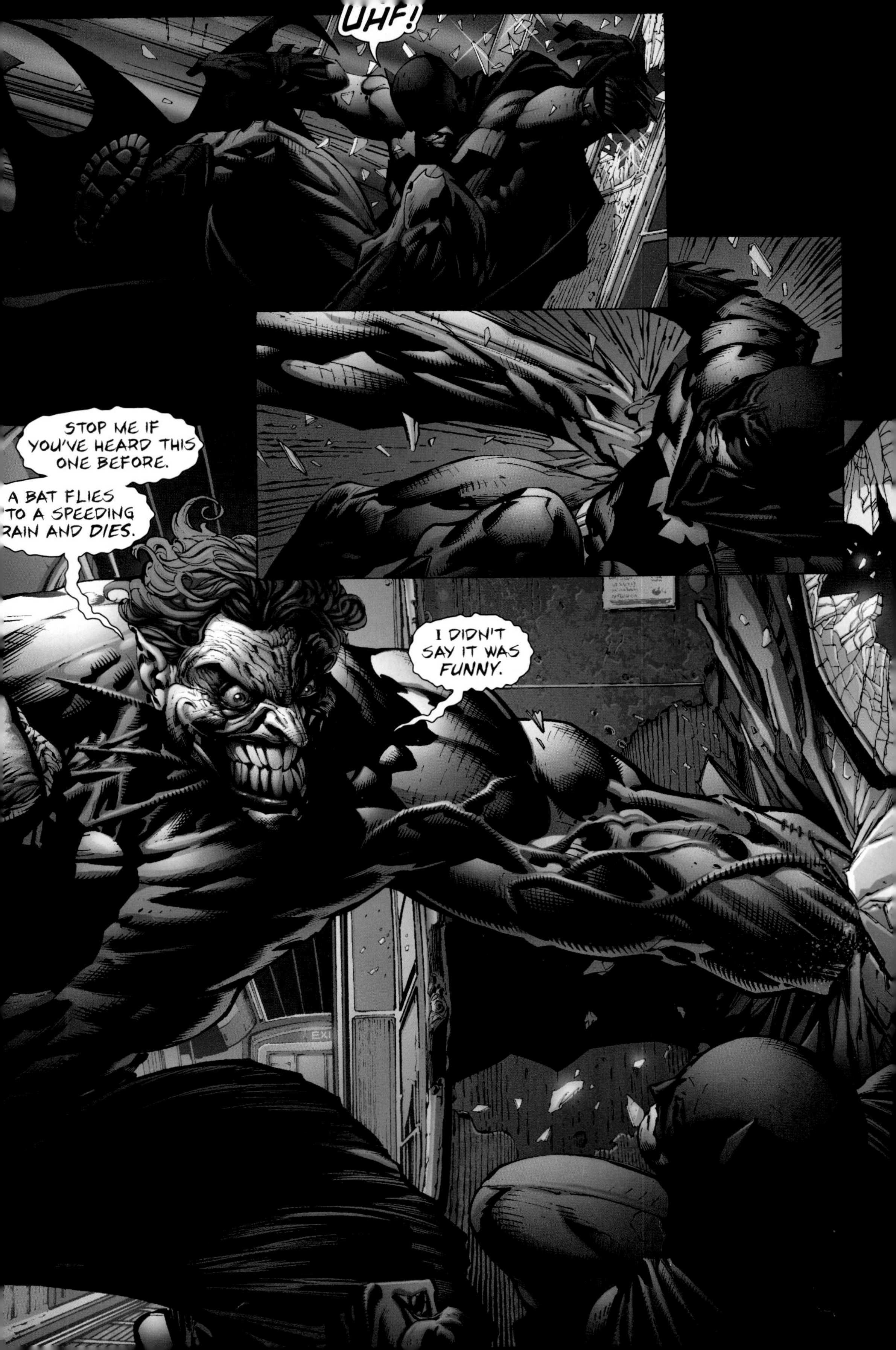
UHF!
STOP ME IF YOU'VE HEARD THIS ONE BEFORE.
A BAT FLIES TO A SPEEDING RAIN AND DIES.
I DIDN'T SAY IT WAS FUNNY.
EXI

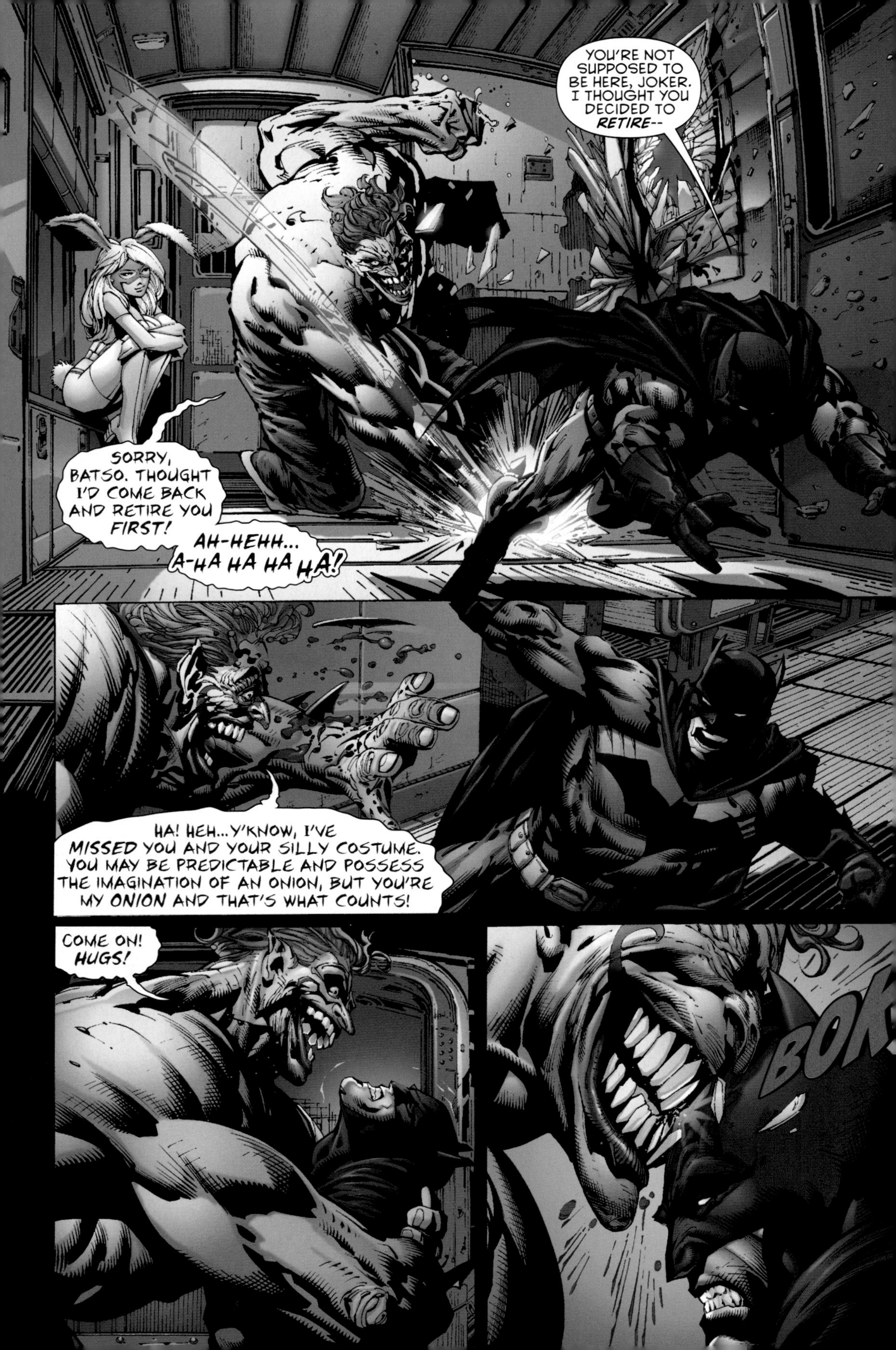
YOU'RE NOT SUPPOSED TO BE HERE, JOKER. I THOUGHT YOU DECIDED TO RETIRE--
SORRY, BATSO. THOUGHT I'D COME BACK AND RETIRE YOU FIRST!
AH-HEHH... A-HA HA HA HA HA!
HA! HEH...Y'KNOW, I'VE MISSED YOU AND YOUR SILLY COSTUME. YOU MAY BE PREDICTABLE AND POSSESS THE IMAGINATION OF AN ONION, BUT YOU'RE MY ONION AND THAT'S WHAT COUNTS!
COME ON! HUGS!
BOK

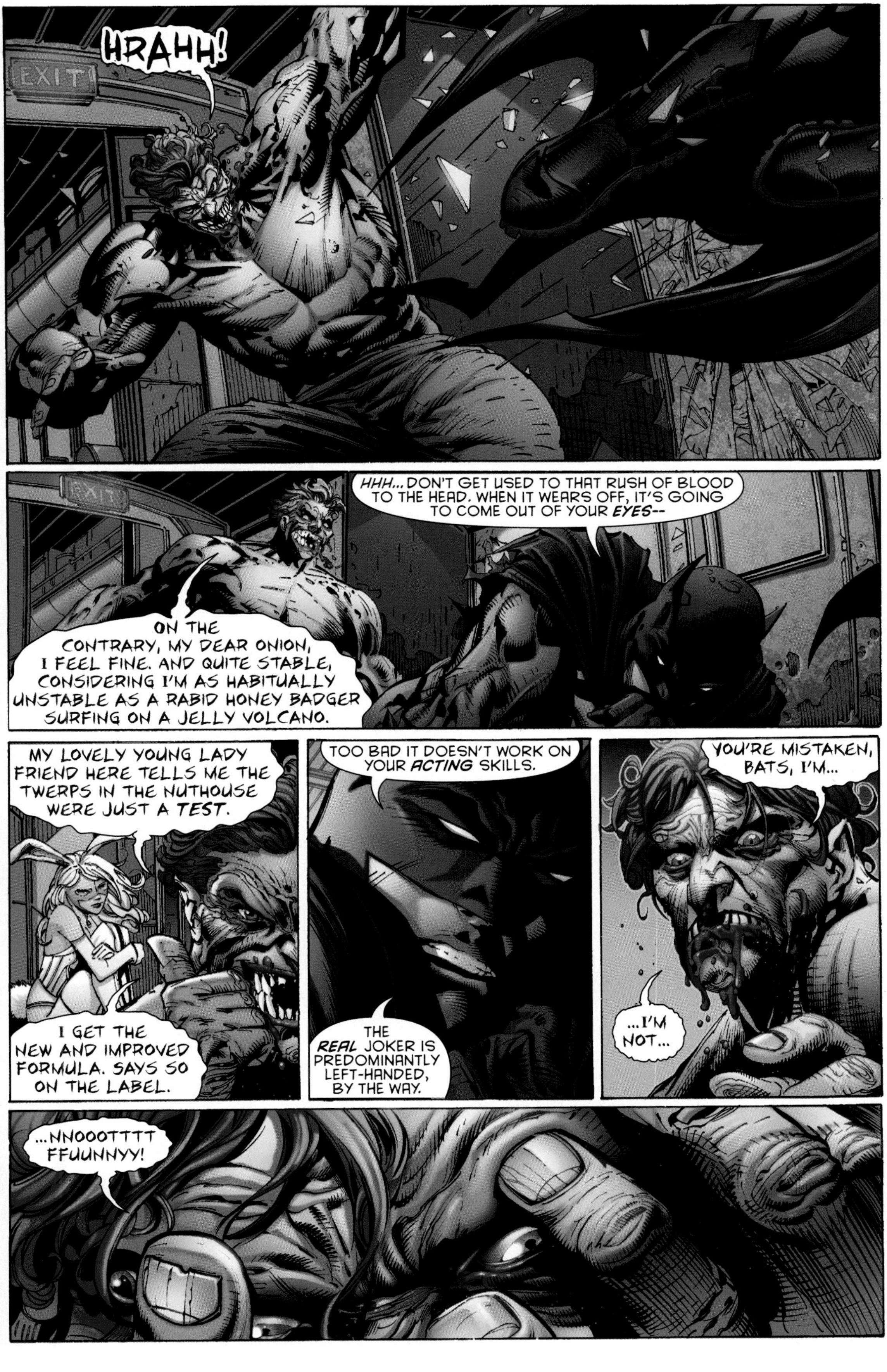
HRAHH!
EXIT
EXIT
HHH... DON'T GET USED TO THAT RUSH OF BLOOD TO THE HEAD. WHEN IT WEARS OFF, IT'S GOING TO COME OUT OF YOUR EYES--
ON THE CONTRARY, MY DEAR ONION, I FEEL FINE. AND QUITE STABLE, CONSIDERING I'M AS HABITUALLY UNSTABLE AS A RABID HONEY BADGER SURFING ON A JELLY VOLCANO.
MY LOVELY YOUNG LADY FRIEND HERE TELLS ME THE TWERPS IN THE NUTHOUSE WERE JUST A TEST.
I GET THE NEW AND IMPROVED FORMULA. SAYS SO ON THE LABEL.
TOO BAD IT DOESN'T WORK ON YOUR ACTING SKILLS.
THE REAL JOKER IS PREDOMINANTLY LEFT-HANDED, BY THE WAY.
YOU'RE MISTAKEN, BATS, I'M...
...I'M NOT...
...NNOOOTTTT FFUUNNYY!

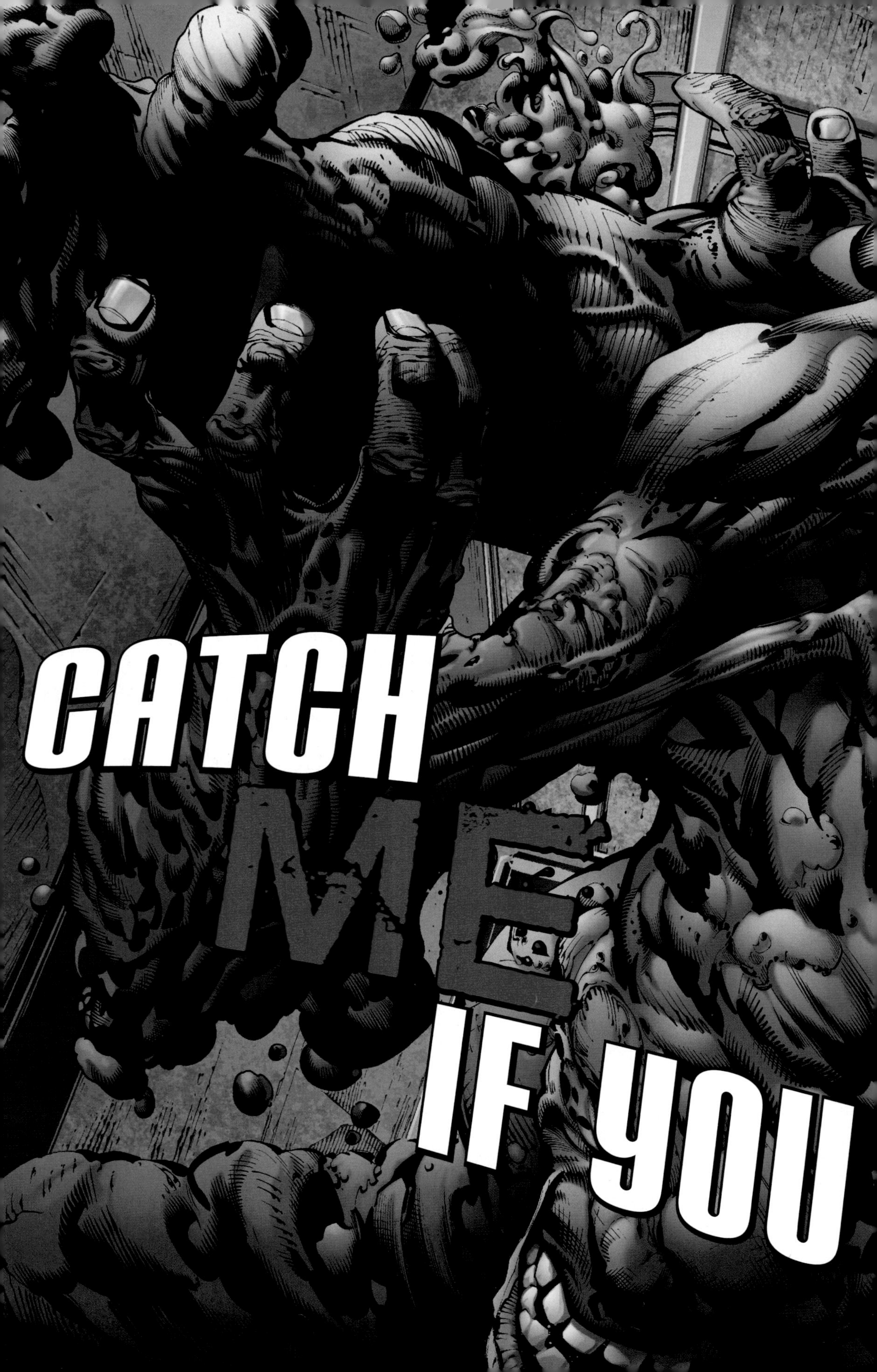
CATCH
ME
IF YOU

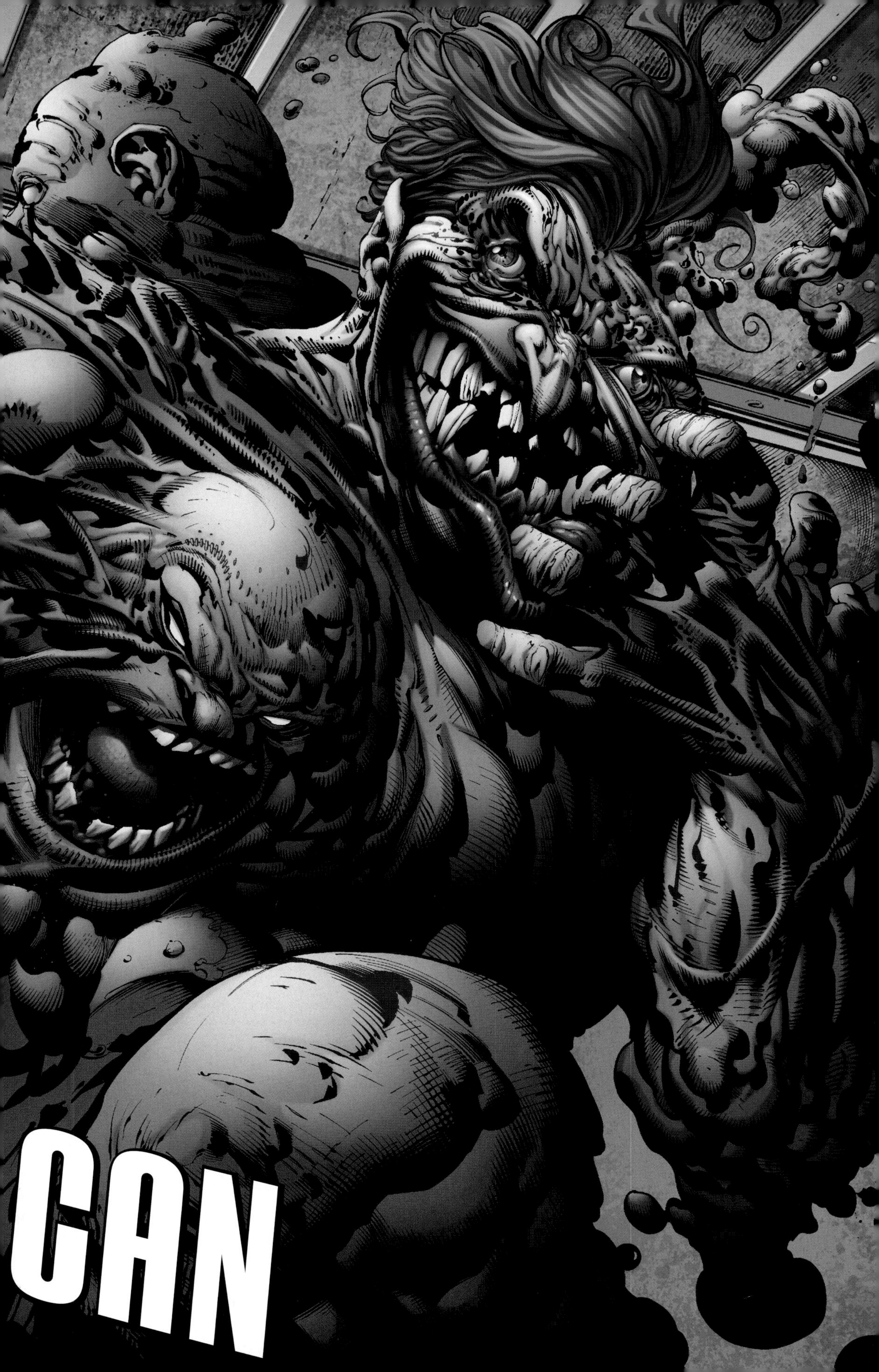
CAN

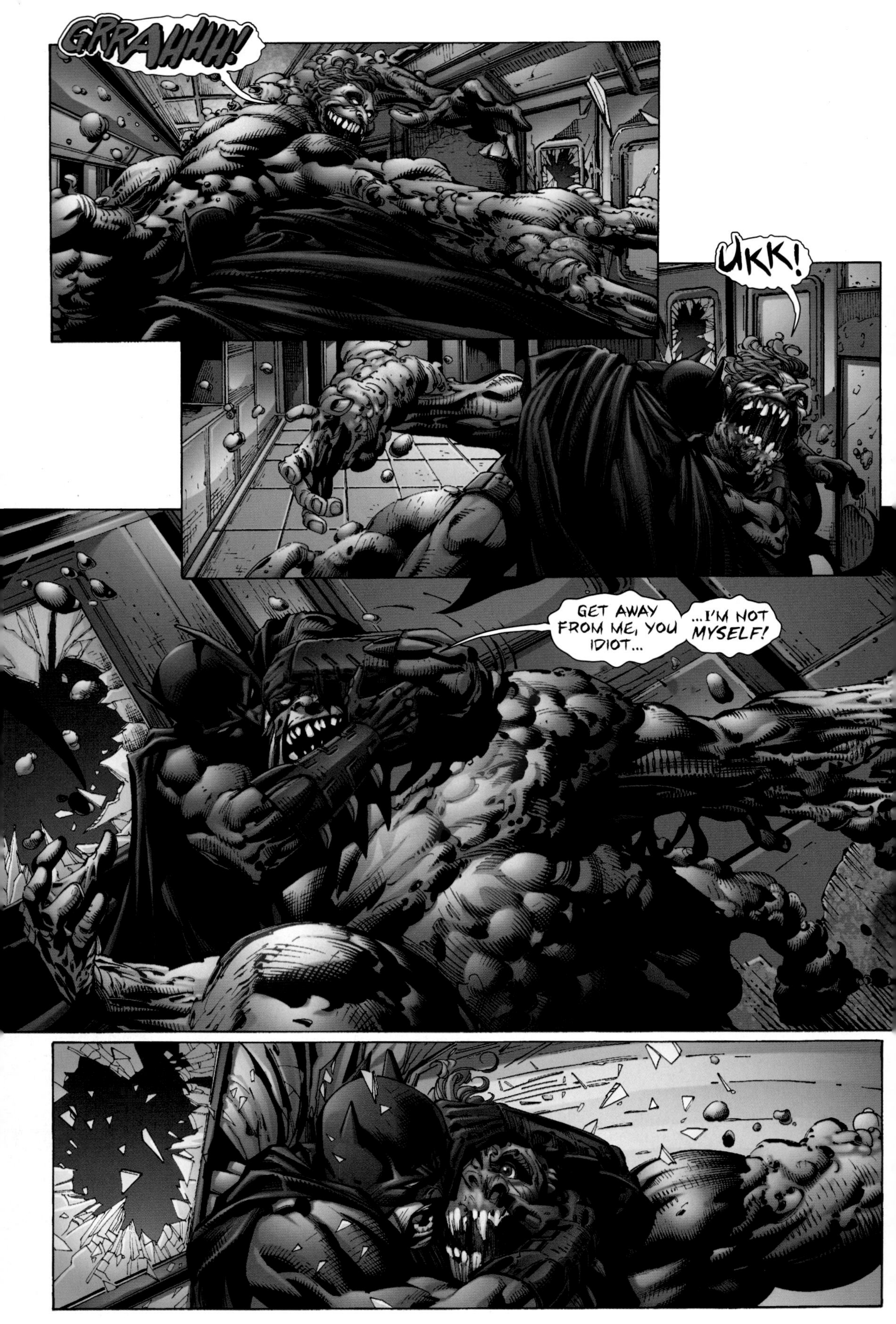
GRRAHHH!
UKK!
GET AWAY FROM ME, YOU IDIOT...
...I'M NOT MYSELF!

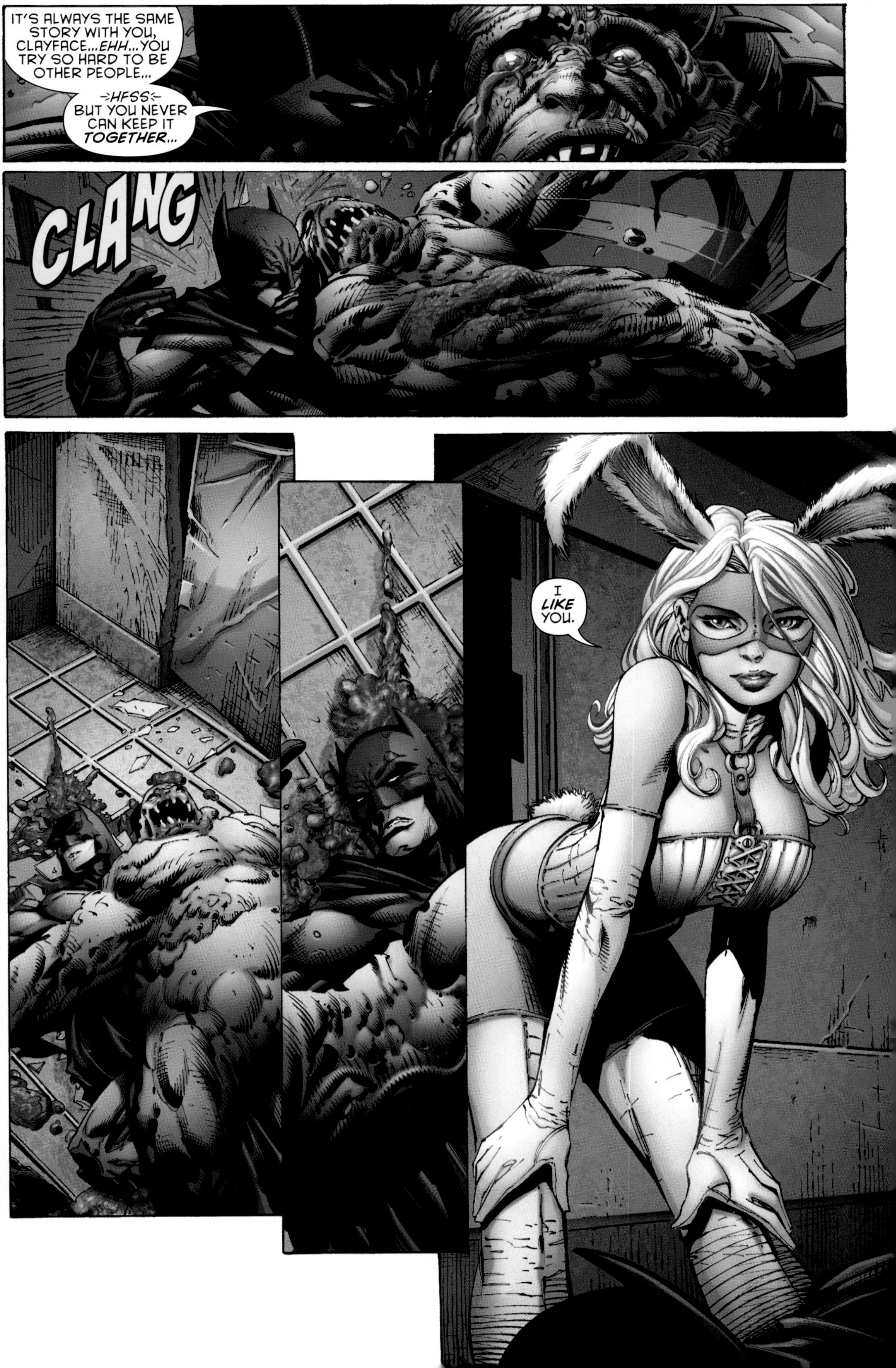
IT'S ALWAYS THE SAME STORY WITH YOU, CLAYFACE...EHH...YOU TRY SO HARD TO BE OTHER PEOPLE...
-HFSS- BUT YOU NEVER CAN KEEP IT TOGETHER...
CLANG
I LIKE YOU.

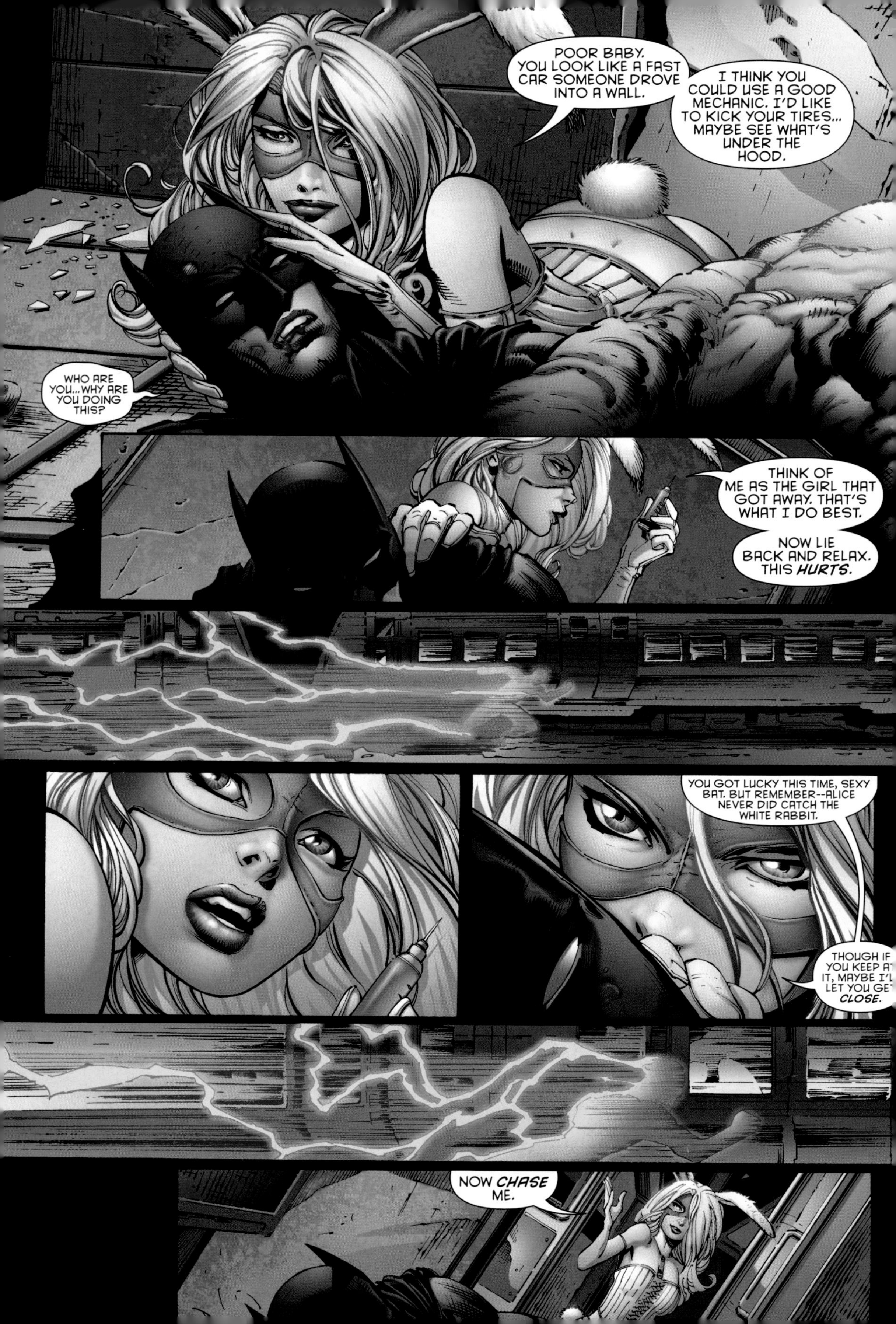
POOR BABY. YOU LOOK LIKE A FAST CAR SOMEONE DROVE INTO A WALL.
I THINK YOU COULD USE A GOOD MECHANIC. I'D LIKE TO KICK YOUR TIRES... MAYBE SEE WHAT'S UNDER THE HOOD.
WHO ARE YOU... WHY ARE YOU DOING THIS?
THINK OF ME AS THE GIRL THAT GOT AWAY. THAT'S WHAT I DO BEST.
NOW LIE BACK AND RELAX. THIS *HURTS*.
YOU GOT LUCKY THIS TIME, SEXY BAT. BUT REMEMBER--ALICE NEVER DID CATCH THE WHITE RABBIT.
THOUGH IF YOU KEEP AT IT, MAYBE I'LL LET YOU GET *CLOSE*.
NOW *CHASE* ME.

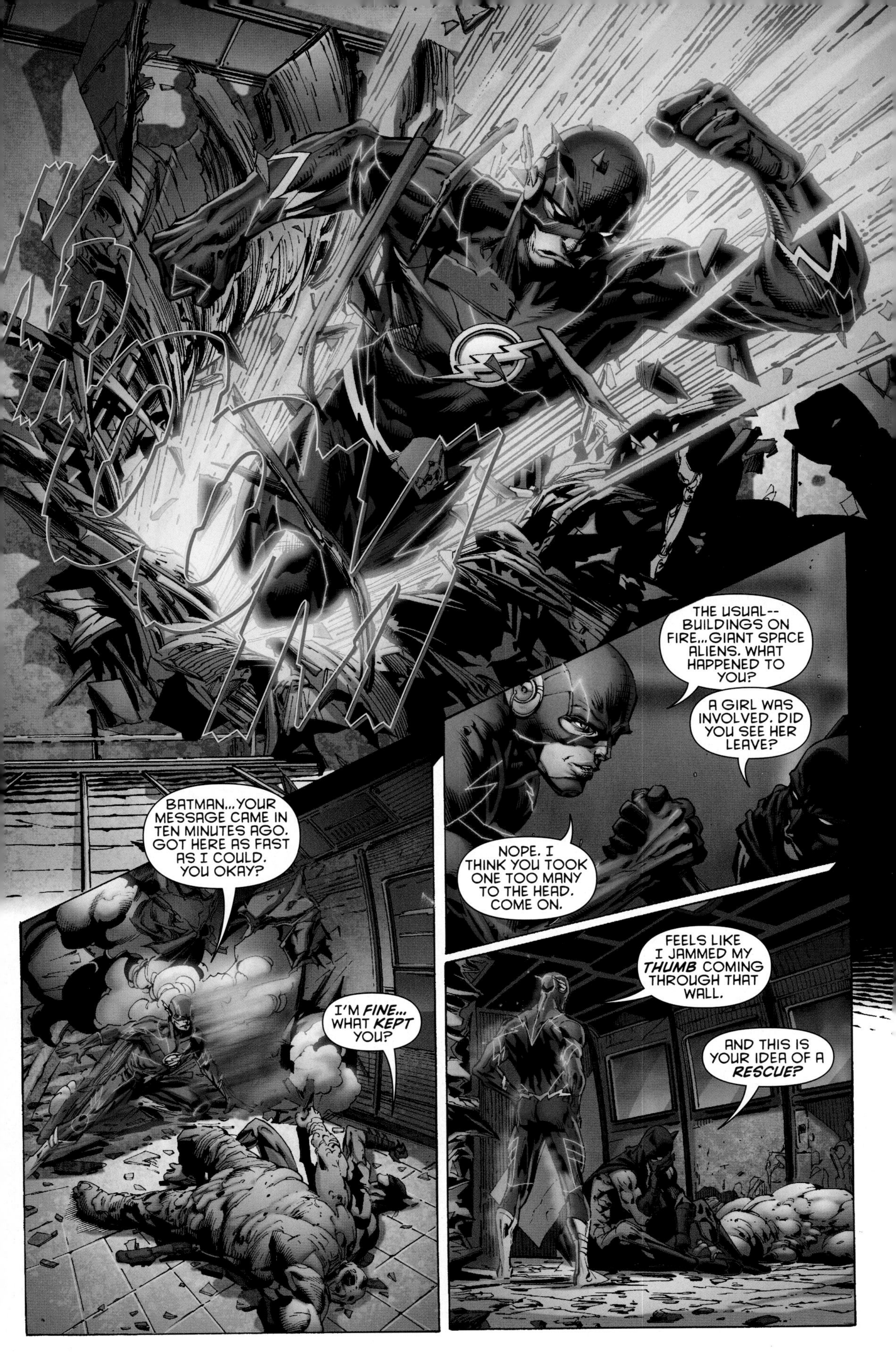

KRAKOOM
BATMAN...YOUR MESSAGE CAME IN TEN MINUTES AGO. GOT HERE AS FAST AS I COULD. YOU OKAY?
I'M FINE... WHAT KEPT YOU?
THE USUAL-- BUILDINGS ON FIRE...GIANT SPACE ALIENS. WHAT HAPPENED TO YOU?
A GIRL WAS INVOLVED. DID YOU SEE HER LEAVE?
NOPE. I THINK YOU TOOK ONE TOO MANY TO THE HEAD. COME ON.
FEELS LIKE I JAMMED MY THUMB COMING THROUGH THAT WALL.
AND THIS IS YOUR IDEA OF A RESCUE?

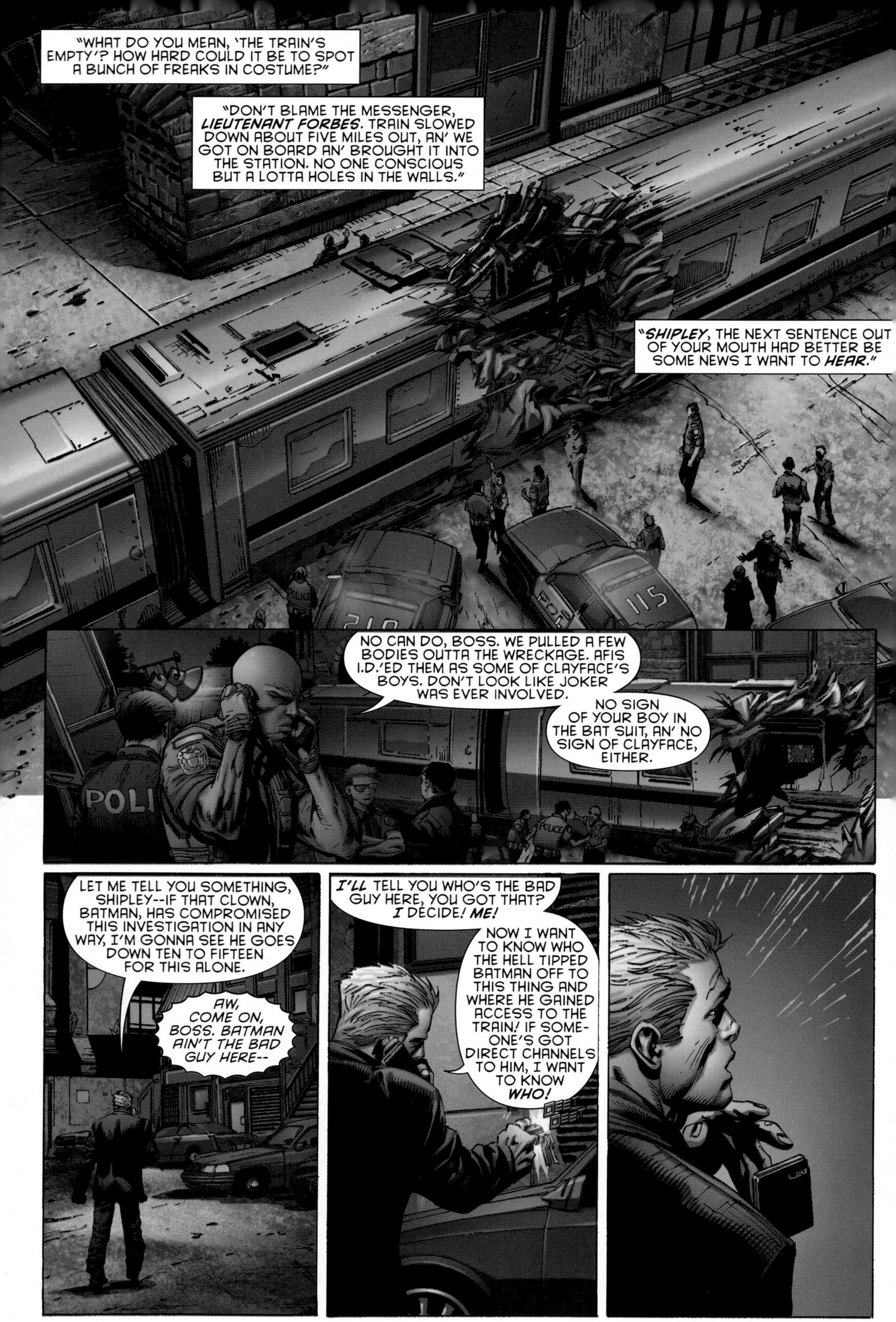
"WHAT DO YOU MEAN, 'THE TRAIN'S EMPTY'? HOW HARD COULD IT BE TO SPOT A BUNCH OF FREAKS IN COSTUME?"
"DON'T BLAME THE MESSENGER, LIEUTENANT FORBES. TRAIN SLOWED DOWN ABOUT FIVE MILES OUT, AN' WE GOT ON BOARD AN' BROUGHT IT INTO THE STATION. NO ONE CONSCIOUS BUT A LOTTA HOLES IN THE WALLS."
"SHIPLEY, THE NEXT SENTENCE OUT OF YOUR MOUTH HAD BETTER BE SOME NEWS I WANT TO HEAR."
POLICE
115
210
NO CAN DO, BOSS. WE PULLED A FEW BODIES OUTTA THE WRECKAGE. AFIS I.D.'ED THEM AS SOME OF CLAYFACE'S BOYS. DON'T LOOK LIKE JOKER WAS EVER INVOLVED.
NO SIGN OF YOUR BOY IN THE BAT SUIT, AN' NO SIGN OF CLAYFACE, EITHER.
POLI
POLICE
LET ME TELL YOU SOMETHING, SHIPLEY--IF THAT CLOWN, BATMAN, HAS COMPROMISED THIS INVESTIGATION IN ANY WAY, I'M GONNA SEE HE GOES DOWN TEN TO FIFTEEN FOR THIS ALONE.
AW, COME ON, BOSS. BATMAN AIN'T THE BAD GUY HERE--
I'LL TELL YOU WHO'S THE BAD GUY HERE, YOU GOT THAT? I DECIDE! ME!
NOW I WANT TO KNOW WHO THE HELL TIPPED BATMAN OFF TO THIS THING AND WHERE HE GAINED ACCESS TO THE TRAIN! IF SOME-ONE'S GOT DIRECT CHANNELS TO HIM, I WANT TO KNOW WHO!
DEET DEET

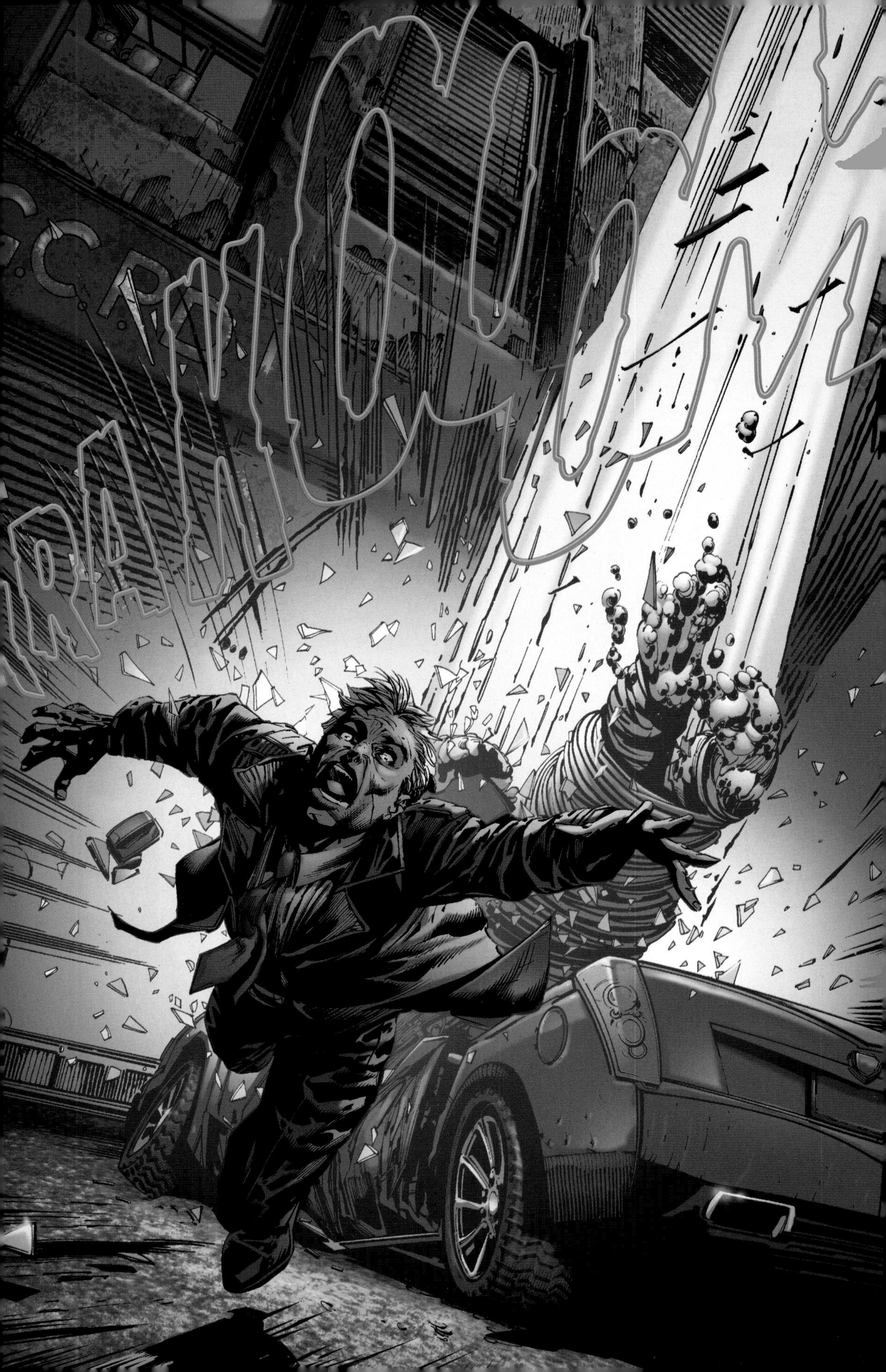

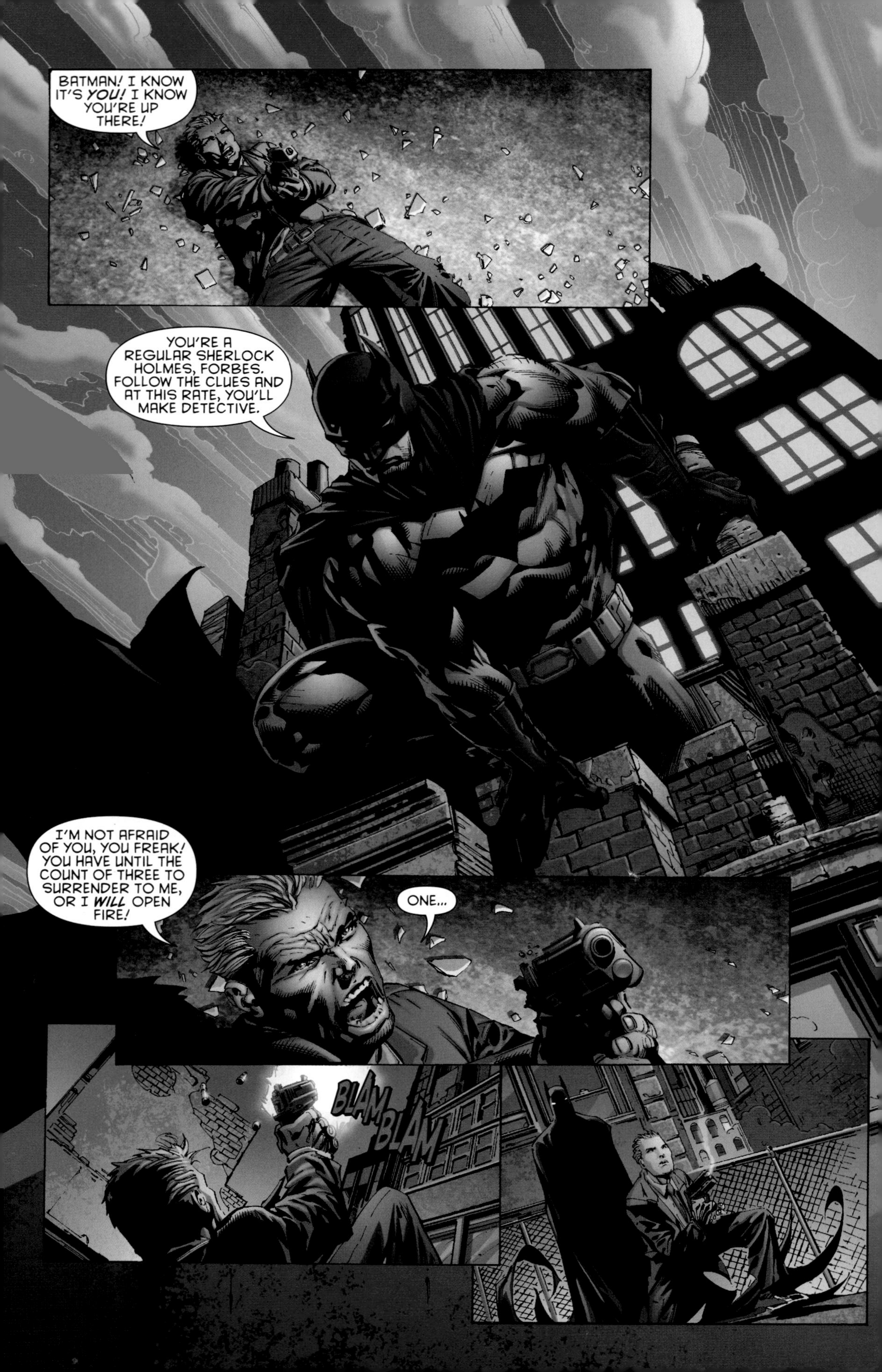
BATMAN! I KNOW IT'S YOU! I KNOW YOU'RE UP THERE!
YOU'RE A REGULAR SHERLOCK HOLMES, FORBES. FOLLOW THE CLUES AND AT THIS RATE, YOU'LL MAKE DETECTIVE.
I'M NOT AFRAID OF YOU, YOU FREAK! YOU HAVE UNTIL THE COUNT OF THREE TO SURRENDER TO ME, OR I WILL OPEN FIRE!
ONE...
BLAM BLAM

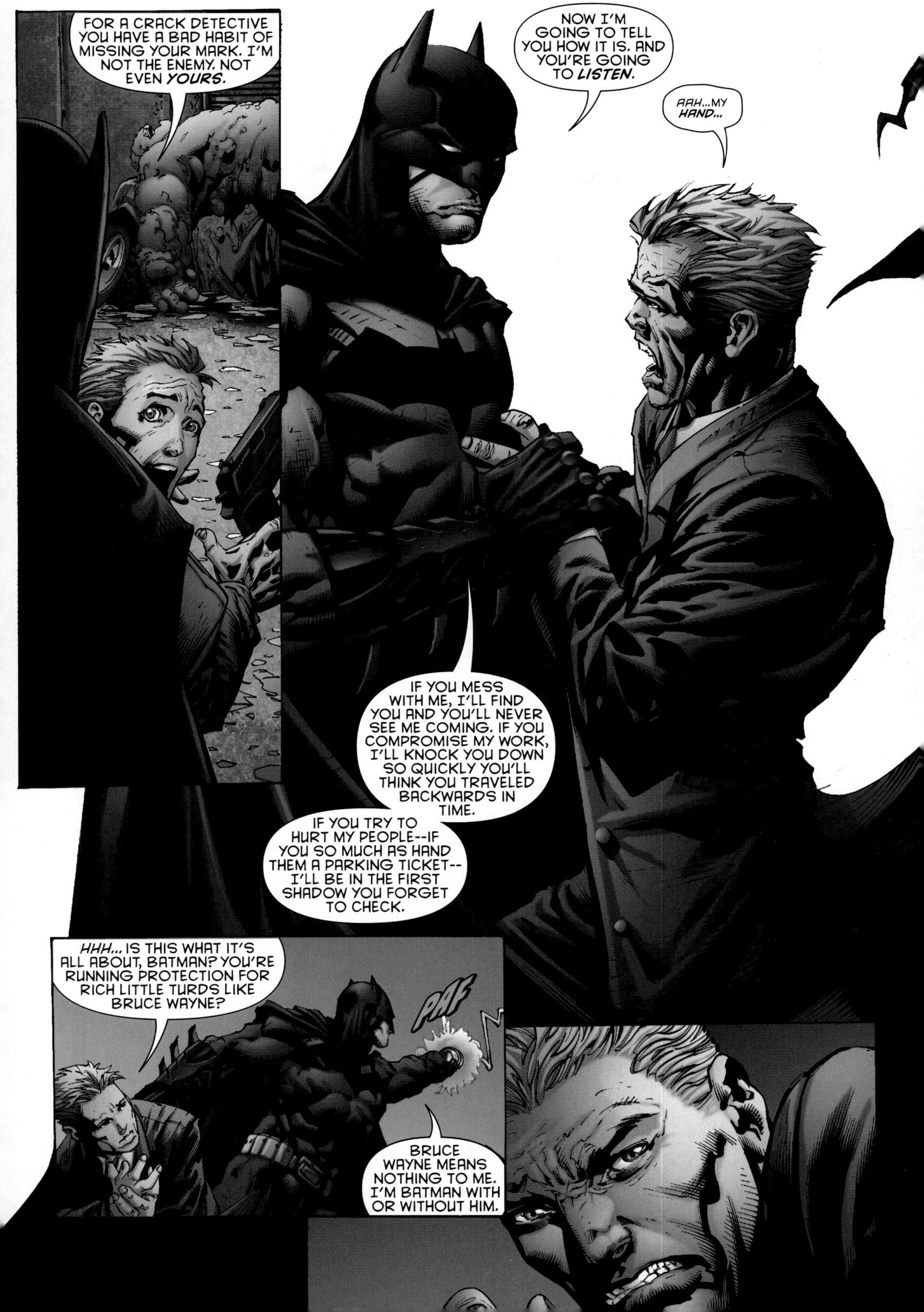
FOR A CRACK DETECTIVE YOU HAVE A BAD HABIT OF MISSING YOUR MARK. I'M NOT THE ENEMY. NOT EVEN *YOURS*.
NOW I'M GOING TO TELL YOU HOW IT IS. AND YOU'RE GOING TO *LISTEN*.
AAH...MY HAND...
IF YOU MESS WITH ME, I'LL FIND YOU AND YOU'LL NEVER SEE ME COMING. IF YOU COMPROMISE MY WORK, I'LL KNOCK YOU DOWN SO QUICKLY YOU'LL THINK YOU TRAVELED BACKWARDS IN TIME.
IF YOU TRY TO HURT MY PEOPLE--IF YOU SO MUCH AS HAND THEM A PARKING TICKET--I'LL BE IN THE FIRST SHADOW YOU FORGET TO CHECK.
HHH... IS THIS WHAT IT'S ALL ABOUT, BATMAN? YOU'RE RUNNING PROTECTION FOR RICH LITTLE TURDS LIKE BRUCE WAYNE?
PAF
BRUCE WAYNE MEANS NOTHING TO ME. I'M BATMAN WITH OR WITHOUT HIM.

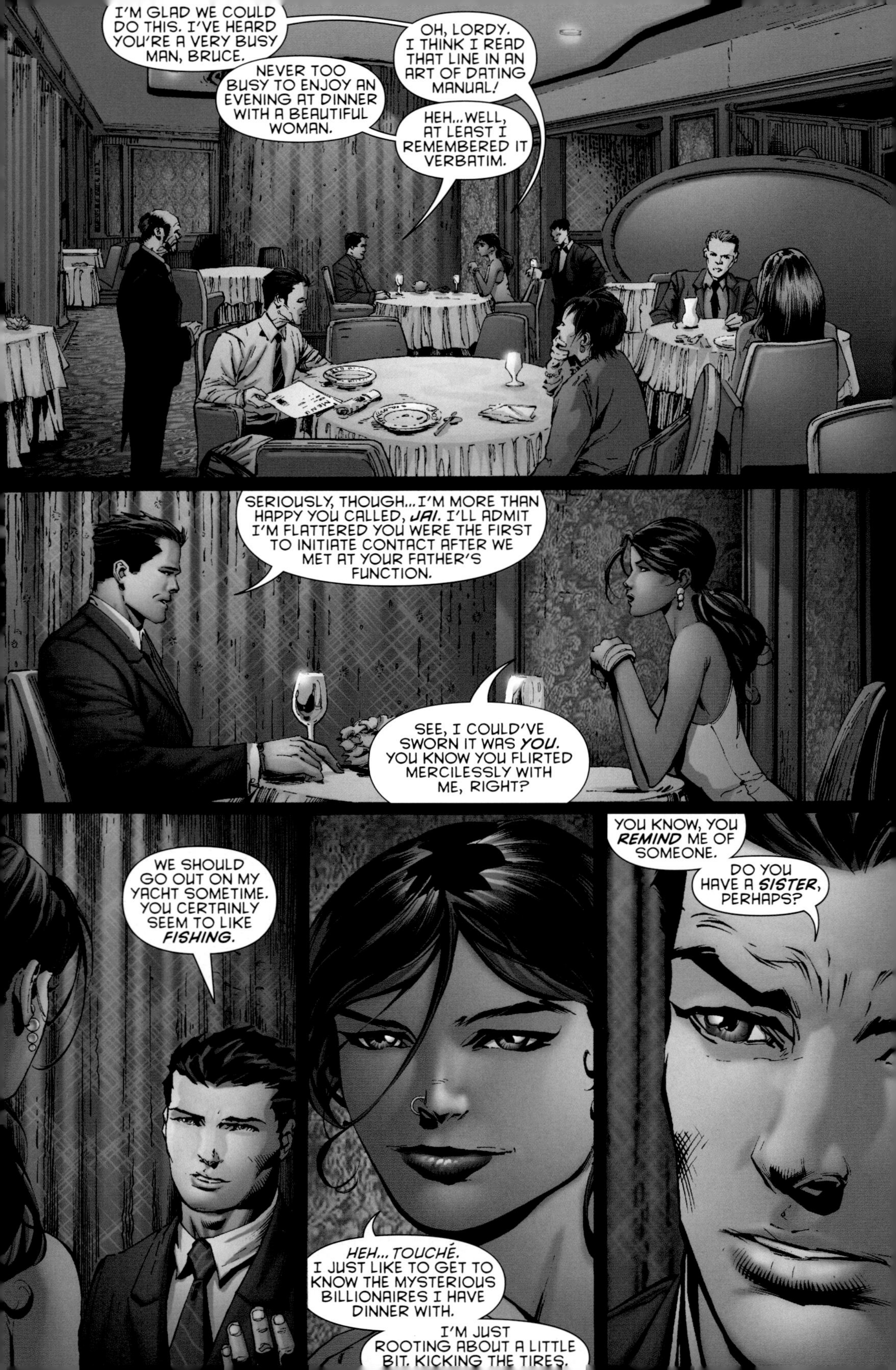
I'M GLAD WE COULD DO THIS. I'VE HEARD YOU'RE A VERY BUSY MAN, BRUCE.
NEVER TOO BUSY TO ENJOY AN EVENING AT DINNER WITH A BEAUTIFUL WOMAN.
OH, LORDY. I THINK I READ THAT LINE IN AN ART OF DATING MANUAL!
HEH... WELL, AT LEAST I REMEMBERED IT VERBATIM.
MENU
SERIOUSLY, THOUGH... I'M MORE THAN HAPPY YOU CALLED, *JAI*. I'LL ADMIT I'M FLATTERED YOU WERE THE FIRST TO INITIATE CONTACT AFTER WE MET AT YOUR FATHER'S FUNCTION.
SEE, I COULD'VE SWORN IT WAS *YOU*. YOU KNOW YOU FLIRTED MERCILESSLY WITH ME, RIGHT?
WE SHOULD GO OUT ON MY YACHT SOMETIME. YOU CERTAINLY SEEM TO LIKE *FISHING*.
HEH... TOUCHÉ. I JUST LIKE TO GET TO KNOW THE MYSTERIOUS BILLIONAIRES I HAVE DINNER WITH.
I'M JUST ROOTING ABOUT A LITTLE BIT. KICKING THE TIRES.
YOU KNOW, YOU *REMIND* ME OF SOMEONE.
DO YOU HAVE A *SISTER*, PERHAPS?

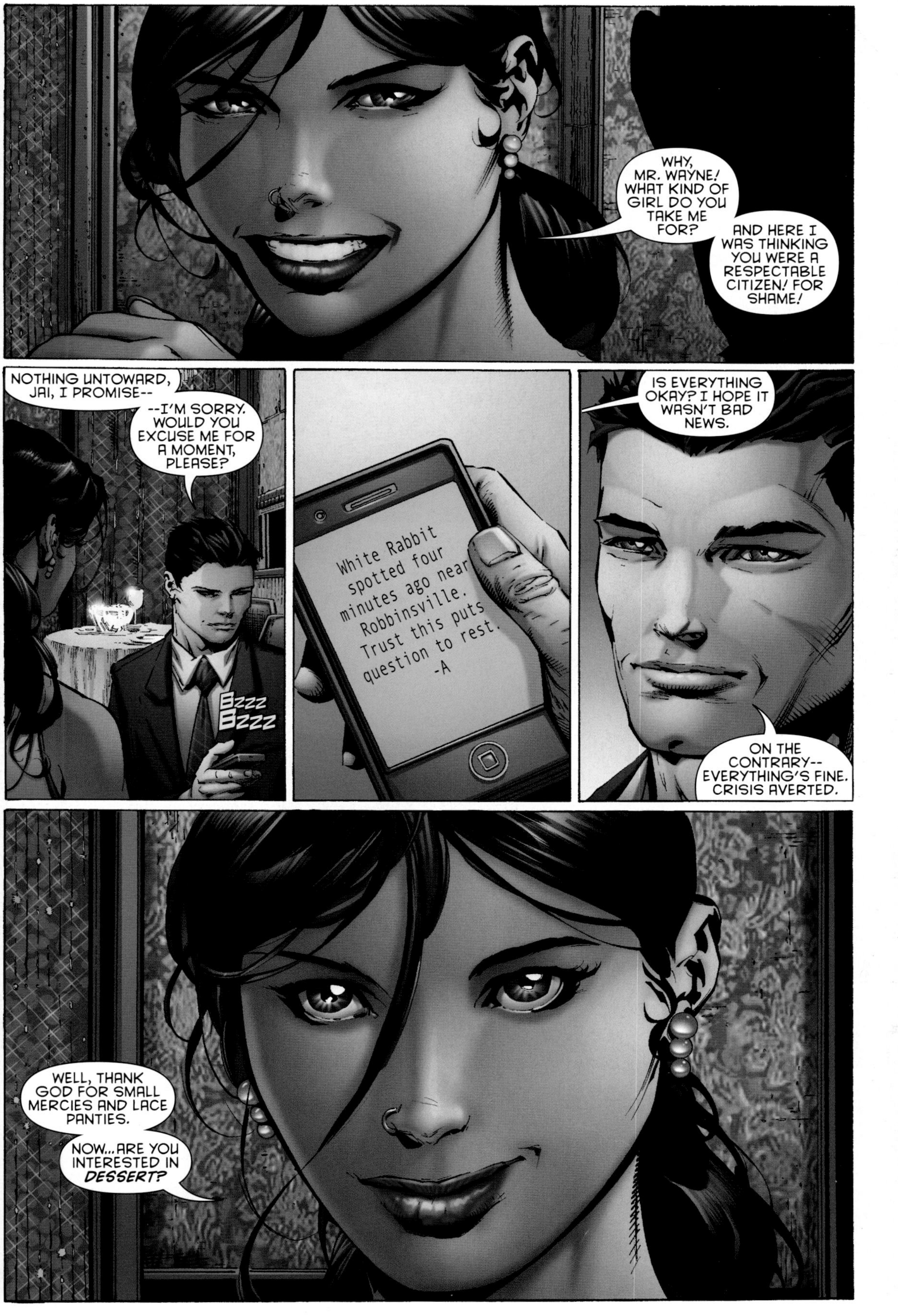
WHY, MR. WAYNE! WHAT KIND OF GIRL DO YOU TAKE ME FOR?
AND HERE I WAS THINKING YOU WERE A RESPECTABLE CITIZEN! FOR SHAME!
NOTHING UNTOWARD, JAI, I PROMISE--
--I'M SORRY. WOULD YOU EXCUSE ME FOR A MOMENT, PLEASE?
BZZZ BZZZ
White Rabbit spotted four minutes ago near Robbinsville. Trust this puts question to rest. -A
IS EVERYTHING OKAY? I HOPE IT WASN'T BAD NEWS.
ON THE CONTRARY-- EVERYTHING'S FINE. CRISIS AVERTED.
WELL, THANK GOD FOR SMALL MERCIES AND LACE PANTIES.
NOW...ARE YOU INTERESTED IN DESSERT?

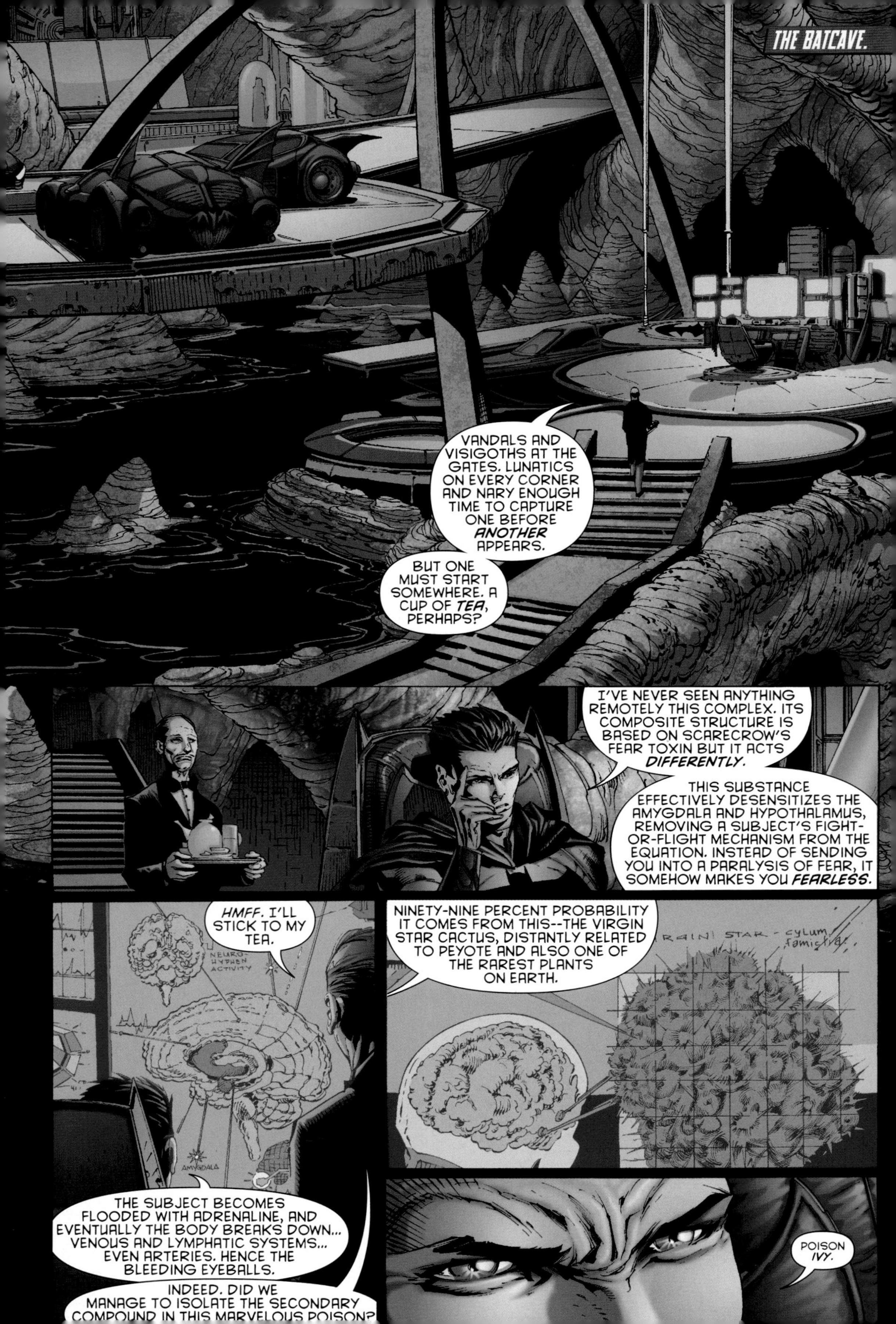
THE BATCAVE.
VANDALS AND VISIGOTHS AT THE GATES. LUNATICS ON EVERY CORNER AND NARY ENOUGH TIME TO CAPTURE ONE BEFORE *ANOTHER* APPEARS.
BUT ONE MUST START SOMEWHERE. A CUP OF *TEA*, PERHAPS?
I'VE NEVER SEEN ANYTHING REMOTELY THIS COMPLEX. ITS COMPOSITE STRUCTURE IS BASED ON SCARECROW'S FEAR TOXIN BUT IT ACTS *DIFFERENTLY*.
THIS SUBSTANCE EFFECTIVELY DESENSITIZES THE AMYGDALA AND HYPOTHALAMUS, REMOVING A SUBJECT'S FIGHT-OR-FLIGHT MECHANISM FROM THE EQUATION. INSTEAD OF SENDING YOU INTO A PARALYSIS OF FEAR, IT SOMEHOW MAKES YOU *FEARLESS*.
HMFF. I'LL STICK TO MY TEA.
AMYGDALA
NINETY-NINE PERCENT PROBABILITY IT COMES FROM THIS--THE VIRGIN STAR CACTUS, DISTANTLY RELATED TO PEYOTE AND ALSO ONE OF THE RAREST PLANTS ON EARTH.
THE SUBJECT BECOMES FLOODED WITH ADRENALINE, AND EVENTUALLY THE BODY BREAKS DOWN... VENOUS AND LYMPHATIC SYSTEMS... EVEN ARTERIES. HENCE THE BLEEDING EYEBALLS.
INDEED. DID WE MANAGE TO ISOLATE THE SECONDARY COMPOUND IN THIS MARVELOUS POISON?
POISON *IVY*.

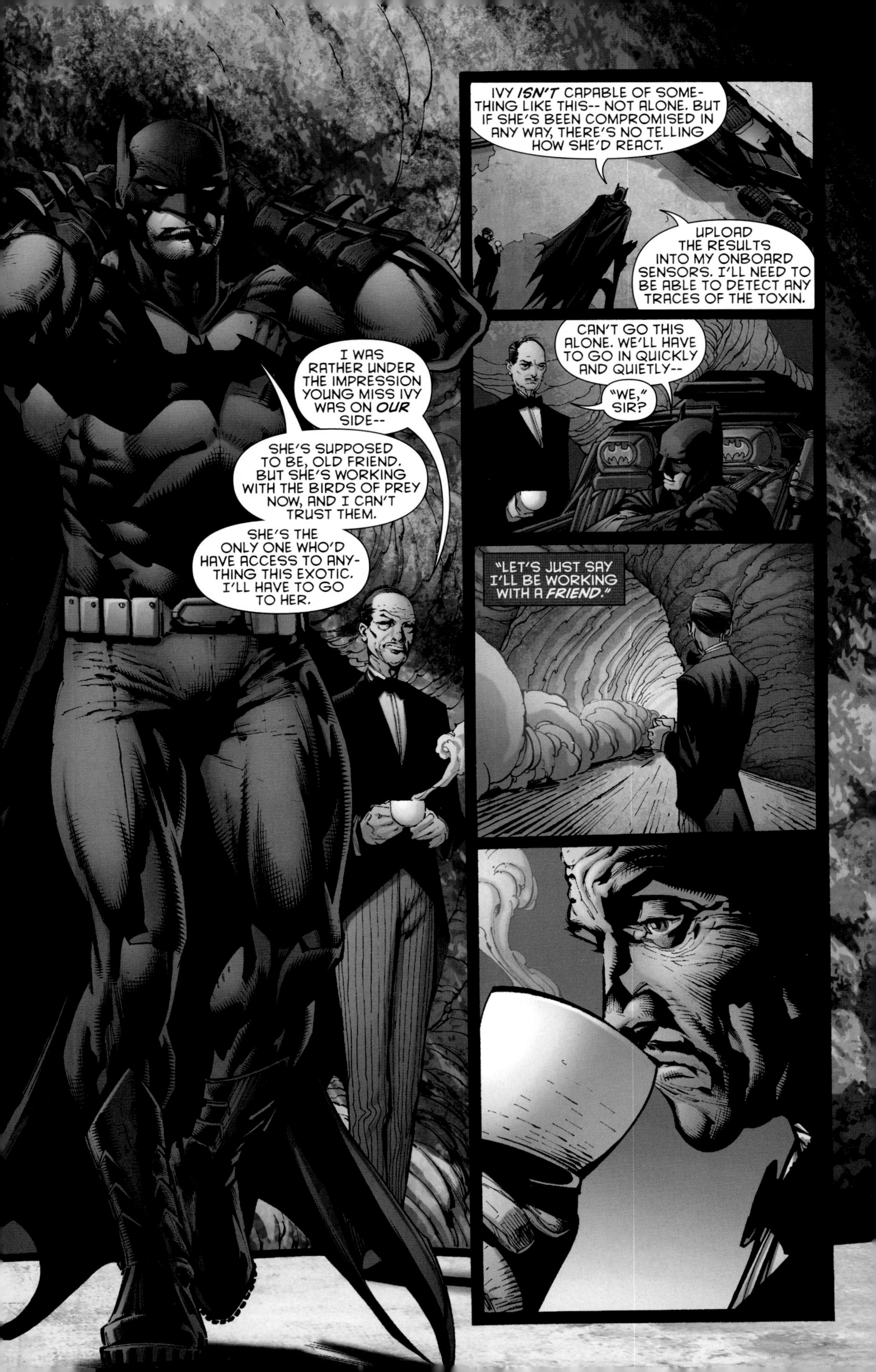

I WAS RATHER UNDER THE IMPRESSION YOUNG MISS IVY WAS ON OUR SIDE--
SHE'S SUPPOSED TO BE, OLD FRIEND. BUT SHE'S WORKING WITH THE BIRDS OF PREY NOW, AND I CAN'T TRUST THEM.
SHE'S THE ONLY ONE WHO'D HAVE ACCESS TO ANYTHING THIS EXOTIC. I'LL HAVE TO GO TO HER.
IVY ISN'T CAPABLE OF SOMETHING LIKE THIS-- NOT ALONE. BUT IF SHE'S BEEN COMPROMISED IN ANY WAY, THERE'S NO TELLING HOW SHE'D REACT.
UPLOAD THE RESULTS INTO MY ONBOARD SENSORS. I'LL NEED TO BE ABLE TO DETECT ANY TRACES OF THE TOXIN.
CAN'T GO THIS ALONE. WE'LL HAVE TO GO IN QUICKLY AND QUIETLY--
"WE," SIR?
"LET'S JUST SAY I'LL BE WORKING WITH A FRIEND."

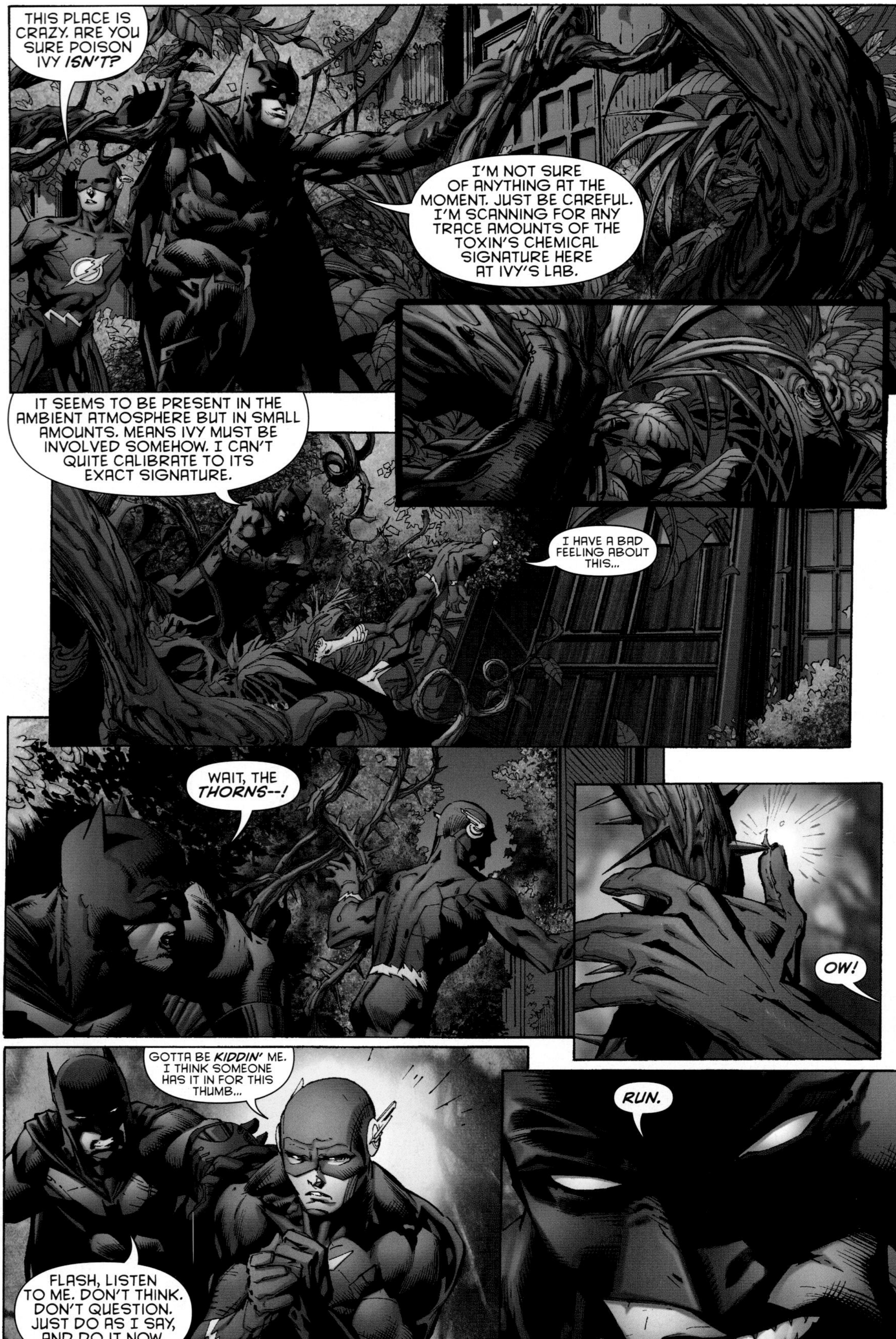
THIS PLACE IS CRAZY. ARE YOU SURE POISON IVY *ISN'T?*
I'M NOT SURE OF ANYTHING AT THE MOMENT. JUST BE CAREFUL. I'M SCANNING FOR ANY TRACE AMOUNTS OF THE TOXIN'S CHEMICAL SIGNATURE HERE AT IVY'S LAB.
IT SEEMS TO BE PRESENT IN THE AMBIENT ATMOSPHERE BUT IN SMALL AMOUNTS. MEANS IVY MUST BE INVOLVED SOMEHOW. I CAN'T QUITE CALIBRATE TO ITS EXACT SIGNATURE.
I HAVE A BAD FEELING ABOUT THIS...
WAIT, THE *THORNS--!*
OW!
GOTTA BE *KIDDIN'* ME. I THINK SOMEONE HAS IT IN FOR THIS THUMB...
FLASH, LISTEN TO ME. DON'T THINK. DON'T QUESTION. JUST DO AS I SAY, AND DO IT NOW.
RUN.

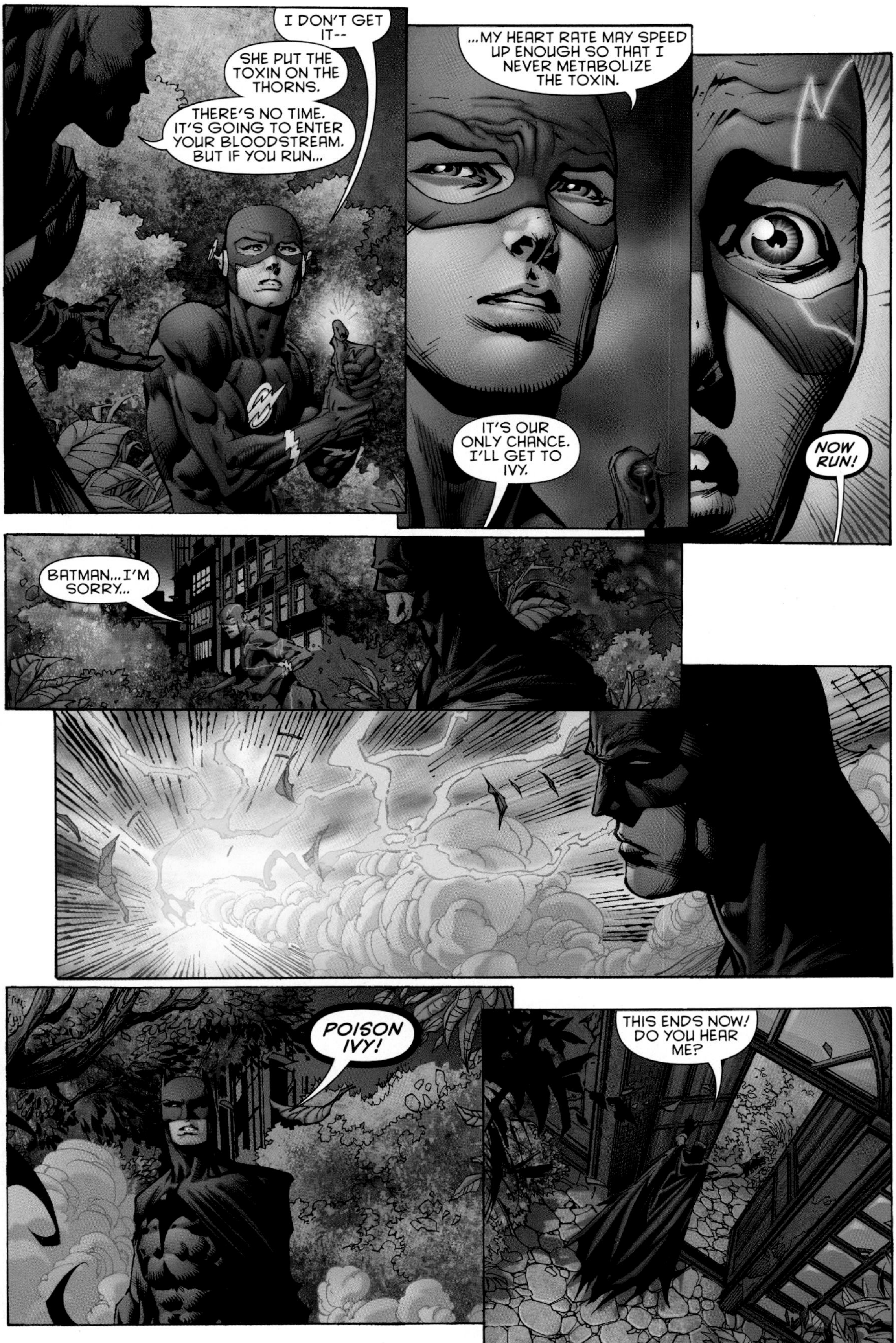
I DON'T GET IT--
SHE PUT THE TOXIN ON THE THORNS.
THERE'S NO TIME. IT'S GOING TO ENTER YOUR BLOODSTREAM. BUT IF YOU RUN...
...MY HEART RATE MAY SPEED UP ENOUGH SO THAT I NEVER METABOLIZE THE TOXIN.
IT'S OUR ONLY CHANCE. I'LL GET TO IVY.
NOW RUN!
BATMAN...I'M SORRY...
POISON IVY!
THIS ENDS NOW! DO YOU HEAR ME?

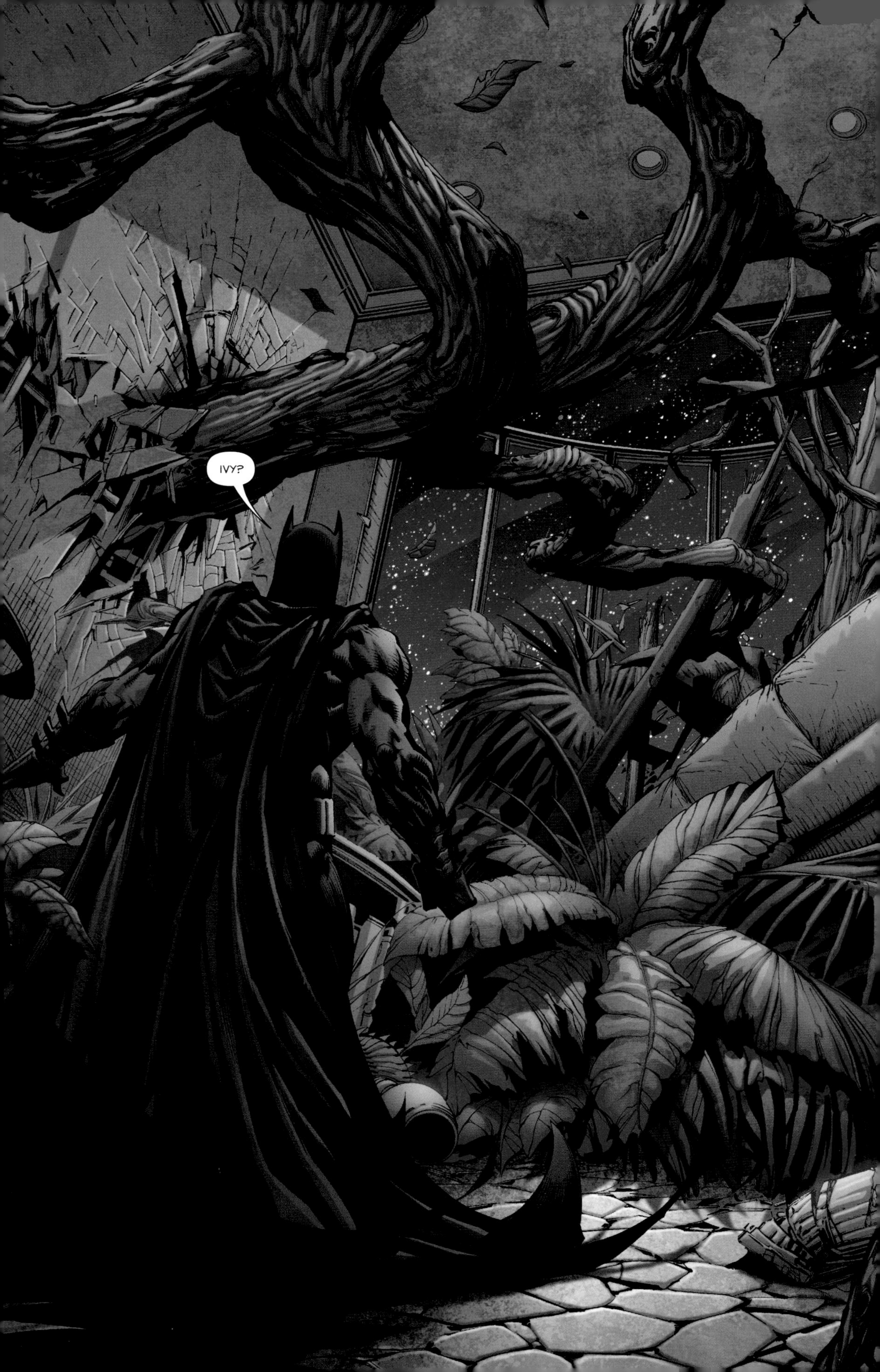
IVY?

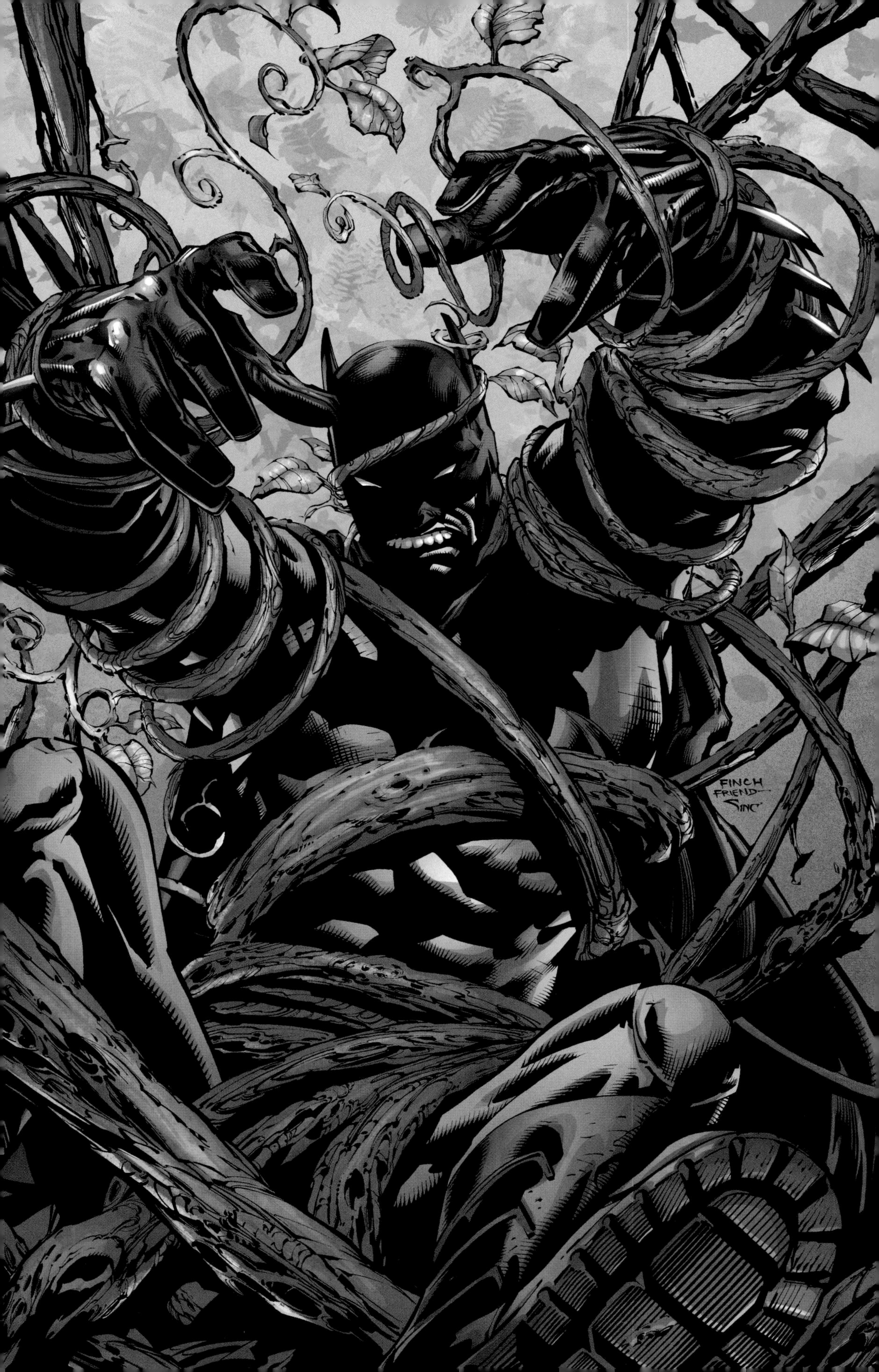
FINCH
FRIEND
SINC

PAUL JENKINS writer/co-plotter DAVID FINCH penciller/co-plotter RICHARD FRIEND inker
cover art by DAVID FINCH, RICHARD FRIEND & ALEX SINCLAIR

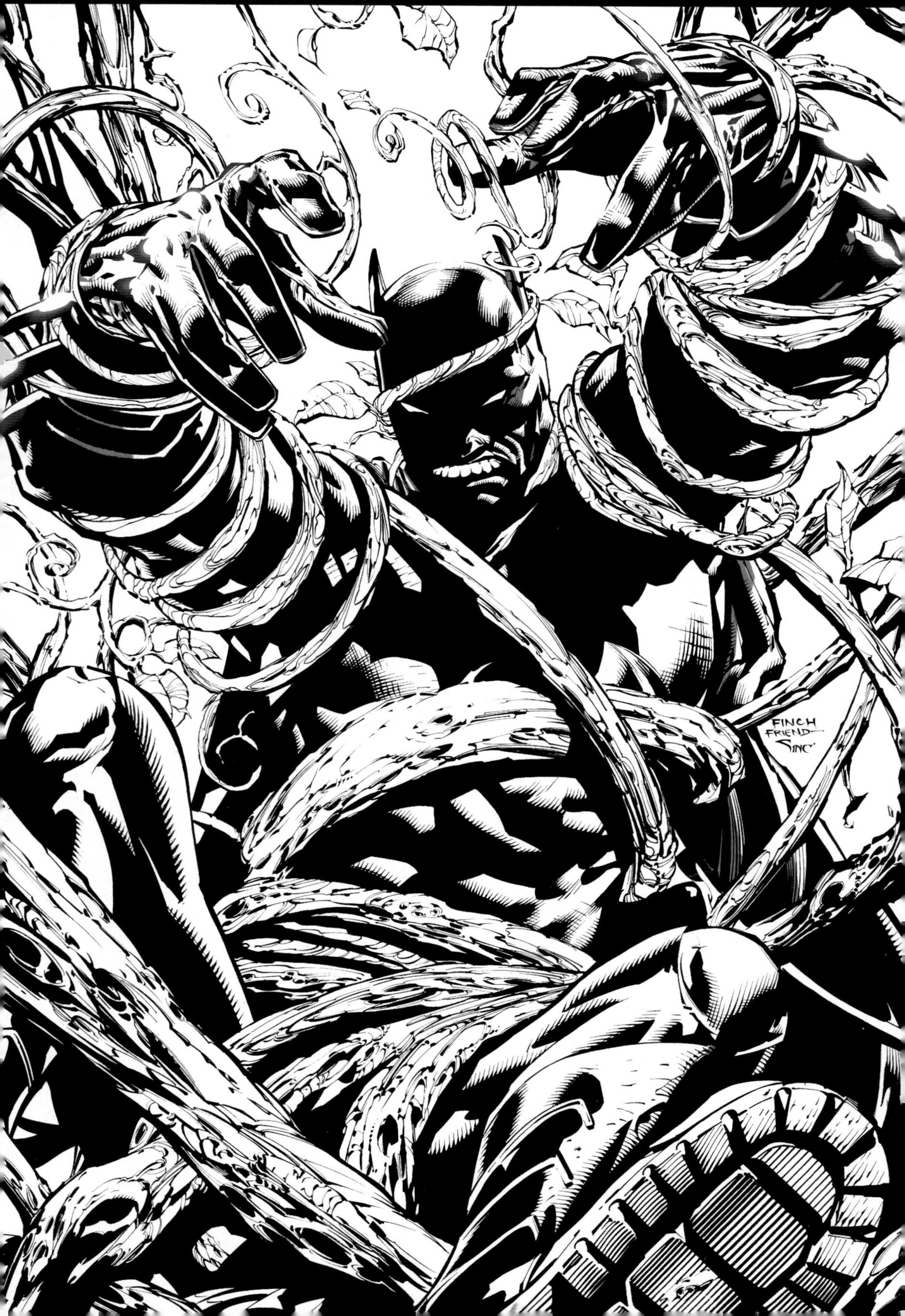
FINCH
FRIEND
SINC

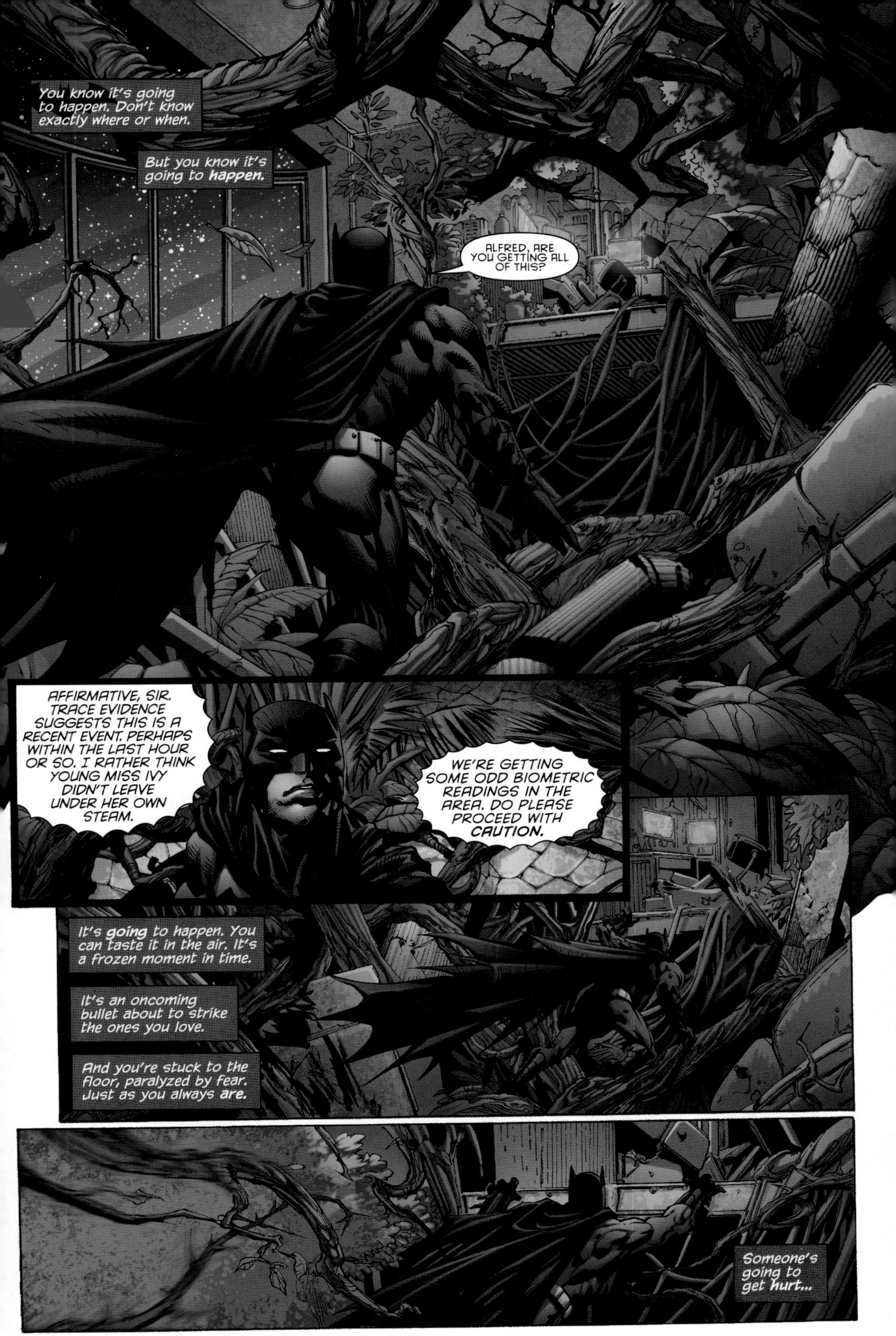
You know it's going to happen. Don't know exactly where or when.
But you know it's going to **happen**.
ALFRED, ARE YOU GETTING ALL OF THIS?
AFFIRMATIVE, SIR. TRACE EVIDENCE SUGGESTS THIS IS A RECENT EVENT. PERHAPS WITHIN THE LAST HOUR OR SO. I RATHER THINK YOUNG MISS IVY DIDN'T LEAVE UNDER HER OWN STEAM.
WE'RE GETTING SOME ODD BIOMETRIC READINGS IN THE AREA. DO PLEASE PROCEED WITH **CAUTION.**
It's **going** to happen. You can taste it in the air. It's a frozen moment in time.
It's an oncoming bullet about to strike the ones you love.
And you're stuck to the floor, paralyzed by fear. Just as you always **are**.
Someone's going to get **hurt...**

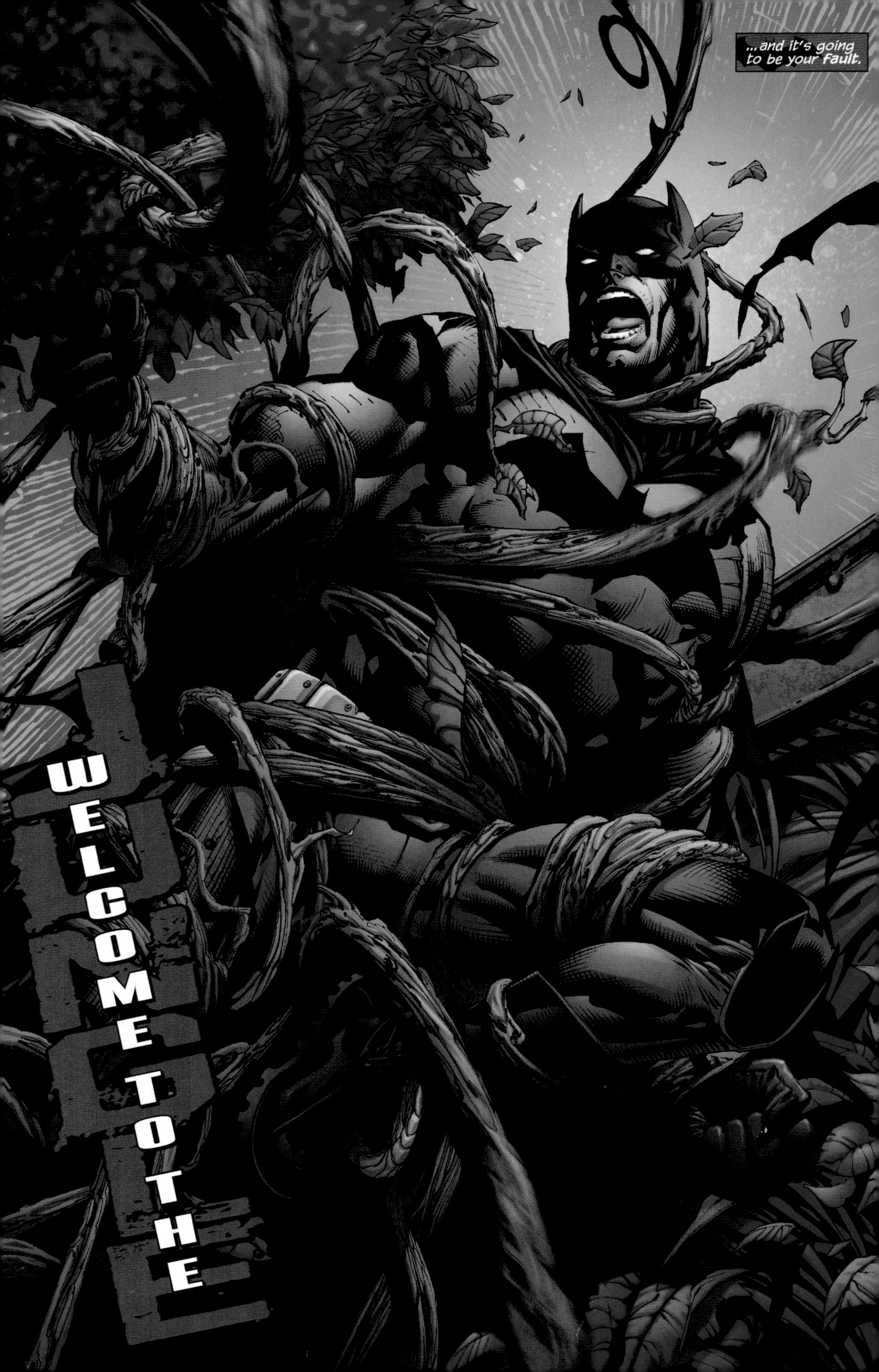
...and it's going to be your fault.
WELCOME TO THE
JUNGLE

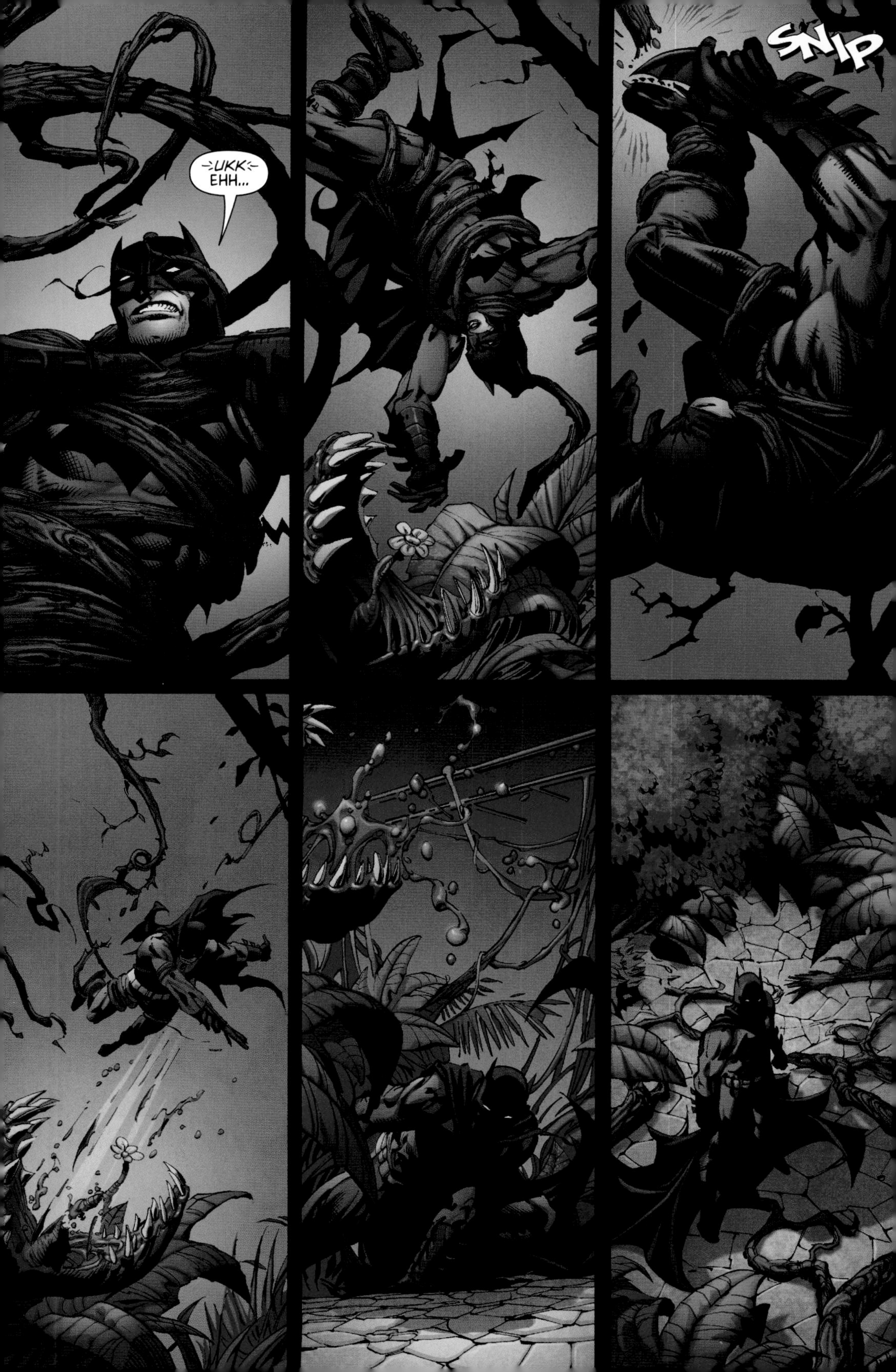

=UKK=
EHH...
SNIP

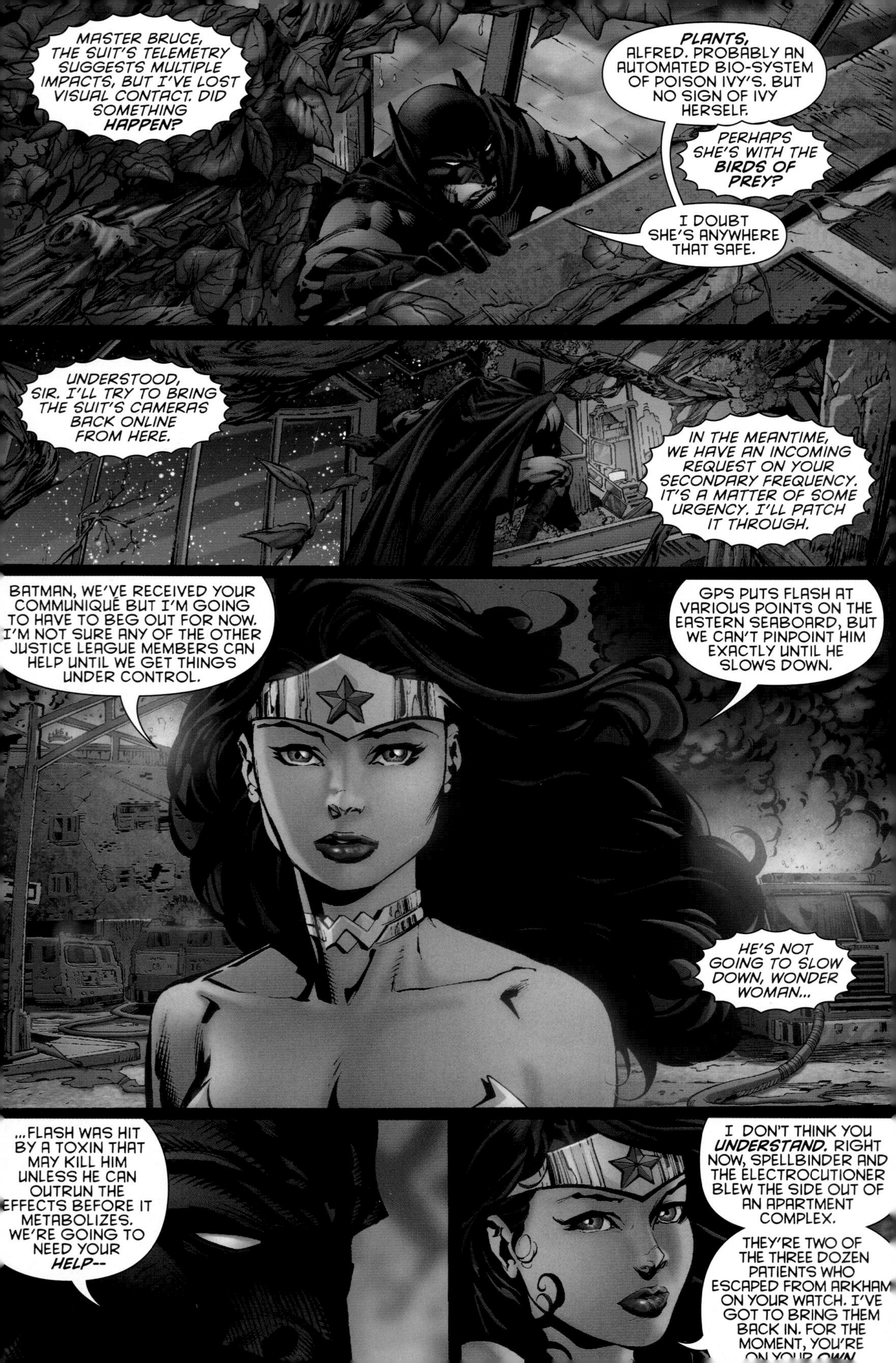
MASTER BRUCE, THE SUIT'S TELEMETRY SUGGESTS MULTIPLE IMPACTS, BUT I'VE LOST VISUAL CONTACT. DID SOMETHING HAPPEN?
PLANTS, ALFRED. PROBABLY AN AUTOMATED BIO-SYSTEM OF POISON IVY'S. BUT NO SIGN OF IVY HERSELF.
PERHAPS SHE'S WITH THE BIRDS OF PREY?
I DOUBT SHE'S ANYWHERE THAT SAFE.
UNDERSTOOD, SIR. I'LL TRY TO BRING THE SUIT'S CAMERAS BACK ONLINE FROM HERE.
IN THE MEANTIME, WE HAVE AN INCOMING REQUEST ON YOUR SECONDARY FREQUENCY. IT'S A MATTER OF SOME URGENCY. I'LL PATCH IT THROUGH.
BATMAN, WE'VE RECEIVED YOUR COMMUNIQUÉ BUT I'M GOING TO HAVE TO BEG OUT FOR NOW. I'M NOT SURE ANY OF THE OTHER JUSTICE LEAGUE MEMBERS CAN HELP UNTIL WE GET THINGS UNDER CONTROL.
GPS PUTS FLASH AT VARIOUS POINTS ON THE EASTERN SEABOARD, BUT WE CAN'T PINPOINT HIM EXACTLY UNTIL HE SLOWS DOWN.
HE'S NOT GOING TO SLOW DOWN, WONDER WOMAN...
...FLASH WAS HIT BY A TOXIN THAT MAY KILL HIM UNLESS HE CAN OUTRUN THE EFFECTS BEFORE IT METABOLIZES. WE'RE GOING TO NEED YOUR HELP--
I DON'T THINK YOU UNDERSTAND. RIGHT NOW, SPELLBINDER AND THE ELECTROCUTIONER BLEW THE SIDE OUT OF AN APARTMENT COMPLEX.
THEY'RE TWO OF THE THREE DOZEN PATIENTS WHO ESCAPED FROM ARKHAM ON YOUR WATCH. I'VE GOT TO BRING THEM BACK IN. FOR THE MOMENT, YOU'RE ON YOUR OWN.

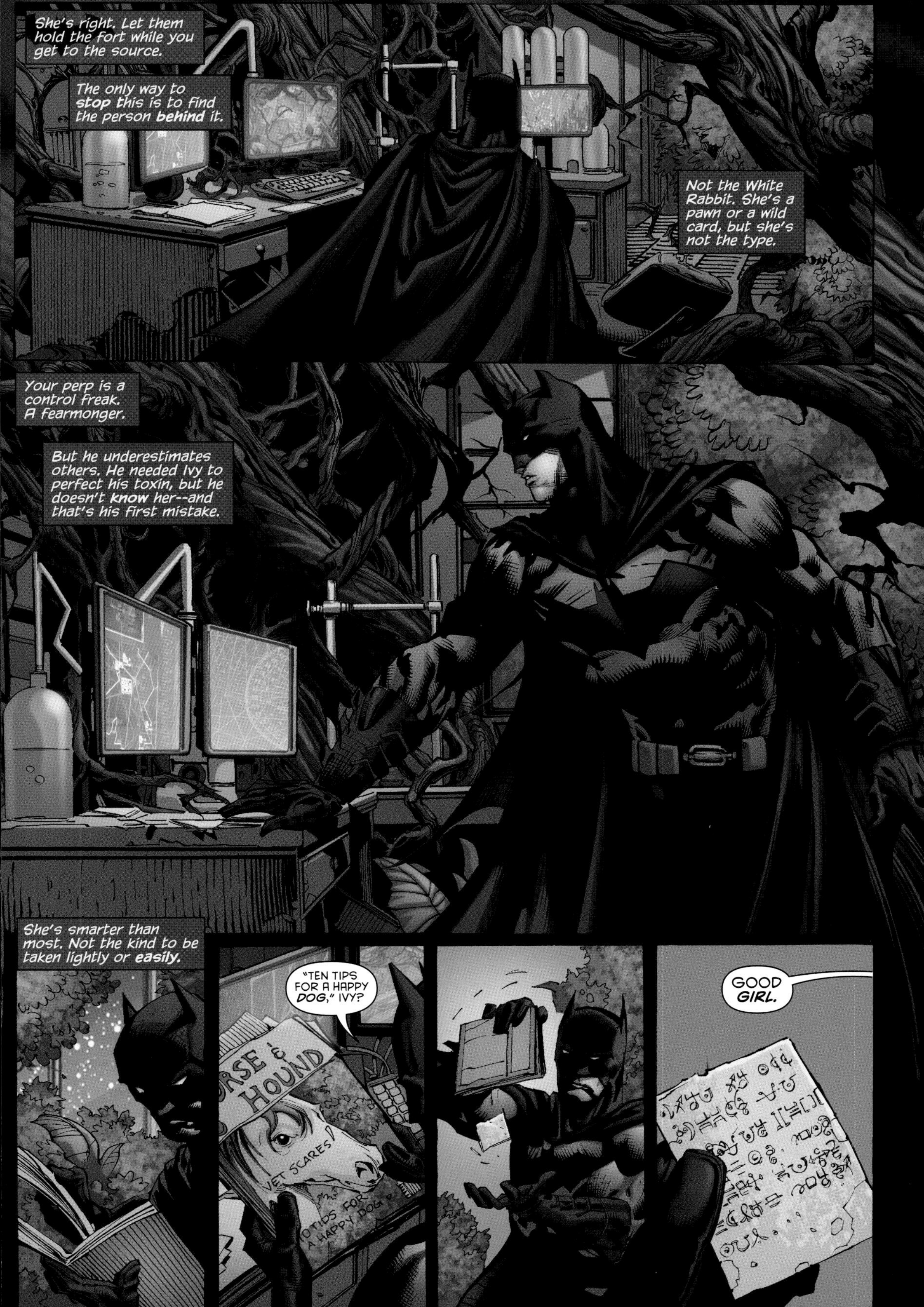

She's right. Let them hold the fort while you get to the source.
The only way to **stop this** is to find the person **behind** it.
Not the White Rabbit. She's a pawn or a wild card, but she's not the type.
Your perp is a control freak. A fearmonger.
But he underestimates others. He needed Ivy to perfect his toxin, but he doesn't **know** her--and that's his first mistake.
She's smarter than most. Not the kind to be taken lightly or **easily**.
"TEN TIPS FOR A HAPPY *DOG*," IVY?
HORSE & HOUND
VET SCARES!
10 TIPS FOR A HAPPY DOG
GOOD **GIRL.**

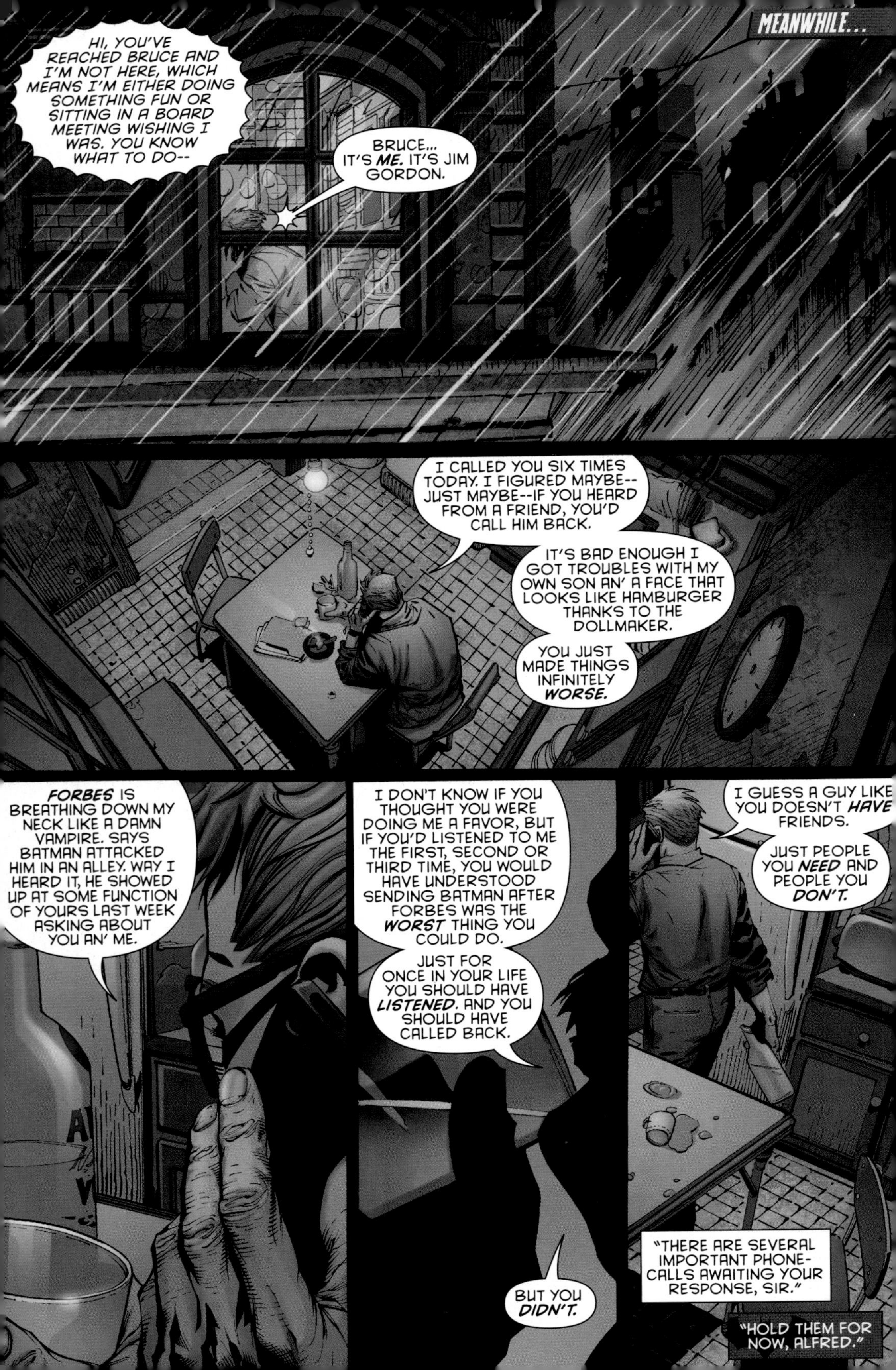
MEANWHILE...
HI, YOU'VE REACHED BRUCE AND I'M NOT HERE, WHICH MEANS I'M EITHER DOING SOMETHING FUN OR SITTING IN A BOARD MEETING WISHING I WAS. YOU KNOW WHAT TO DO--
BRUCE... IT'S ME. IT'S JIM GORDON.
I CALLED YOU SIX TIMES TODAY. I FIGURED MAYBE-- JUST MAYBE--IF YOU HEARD FROM A FRIEND, YOU'D CALL HIM BACK.
IT'S BAD ENOUGH I GOT TROUBLES WITH MY OWN SON AN' A FACE THAT LOOKS LIKE HAMBURGER THANKS TO THE DOLLMAKER.
YOU JUST MADE THINGS INFINITELY WORSE.
FORBES IS BREATHING DOWN MY NECK LIKE A DAMN VAMPIRE. SAYS BATMAN ATTACKED HIM IN AN ALLEY. WAY I HEARD IT, HE SHOWED UP AT SOME FUNCTION OF YOURS LAST WEEK ASKING ABOUT YOU AN' ME.
I DON'T KNOW IF YOU THOUGHT YOU WERE DOING ME A FAVOR, BUT IF YOU'D LISTENED TO ME THE FIRST, SECOND OR THIRD TIME, YOU WOULD HAVE UNDERSTOOD SENDING BATMAN AFTER FORBES WAS THE WORST THING YOU COULD DO.
JUST FOR ONCE IN YOUR LIFE YOU SHOULD HAVE LISTENED. AND YOU SHOULD HAVE CALLED BACK.
BUT YOU DIDN'T.
I GUESS A GUY LIKE YOU DOESN'T HAVE FRIENDS.
JUST PEOPLE YOU NEED AND PEOPLE YOU DON'T.
"THERE ARE SEVERAL IMPORTANT PHONE-CALLS AWAITING YOUR RESPONSE, SIR."
"HOLD THEM FOR NOW, ALFRED."

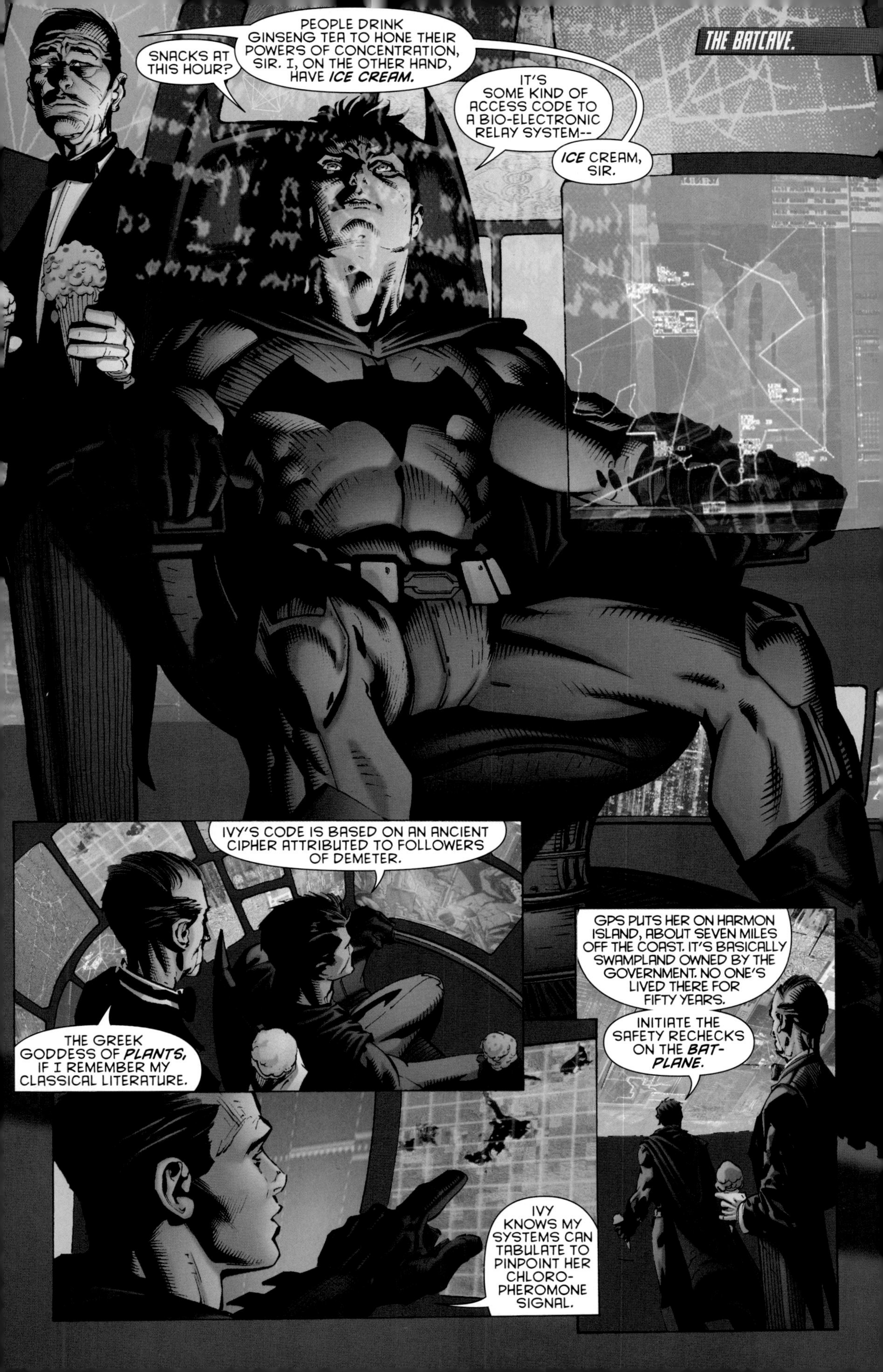
THE BATCAVE.
SNACKS AT THIS HOUR?
PEOPLE DRINK GINSENG TEA TO HONE THEIR POWERS OF CONCENTRATION, SIR. I, ON THE OTHER HAND, HAVE ICE CREAM.
IT'S SOME KIND OF ACCESS CODE TO A BIO-ELECTRONIC RELAY SYSTEM--
ICE CREAM, SIR.
IVY'S CODE IS BASED ON AN ANCIENT CIPHER ATTRIBUTED TO FOLLOWERS OF DEMETER.
THE GREEK GODDESS OF PLANTS, IF I REMEMBER MY CLASSICAL LITERATURE.
IVY KNOWS MY SYSTEMS CAN TABULATE TO PINPOINT HER CHLORO-PHEROMONE SIGNAL.
GPS PUTS HER ON HARMON ISLAND, ABOUT SEVEN MILES OFF THE COAST. IT'S BASICALLY SWAMPLAND OWNED BY THE GOVERNMENT. NO ONE'S LIVED THERE FOR FIFTY YEARS.
INITIATE THE SAFETY RECHECKS ON THE BAT-PLANE.

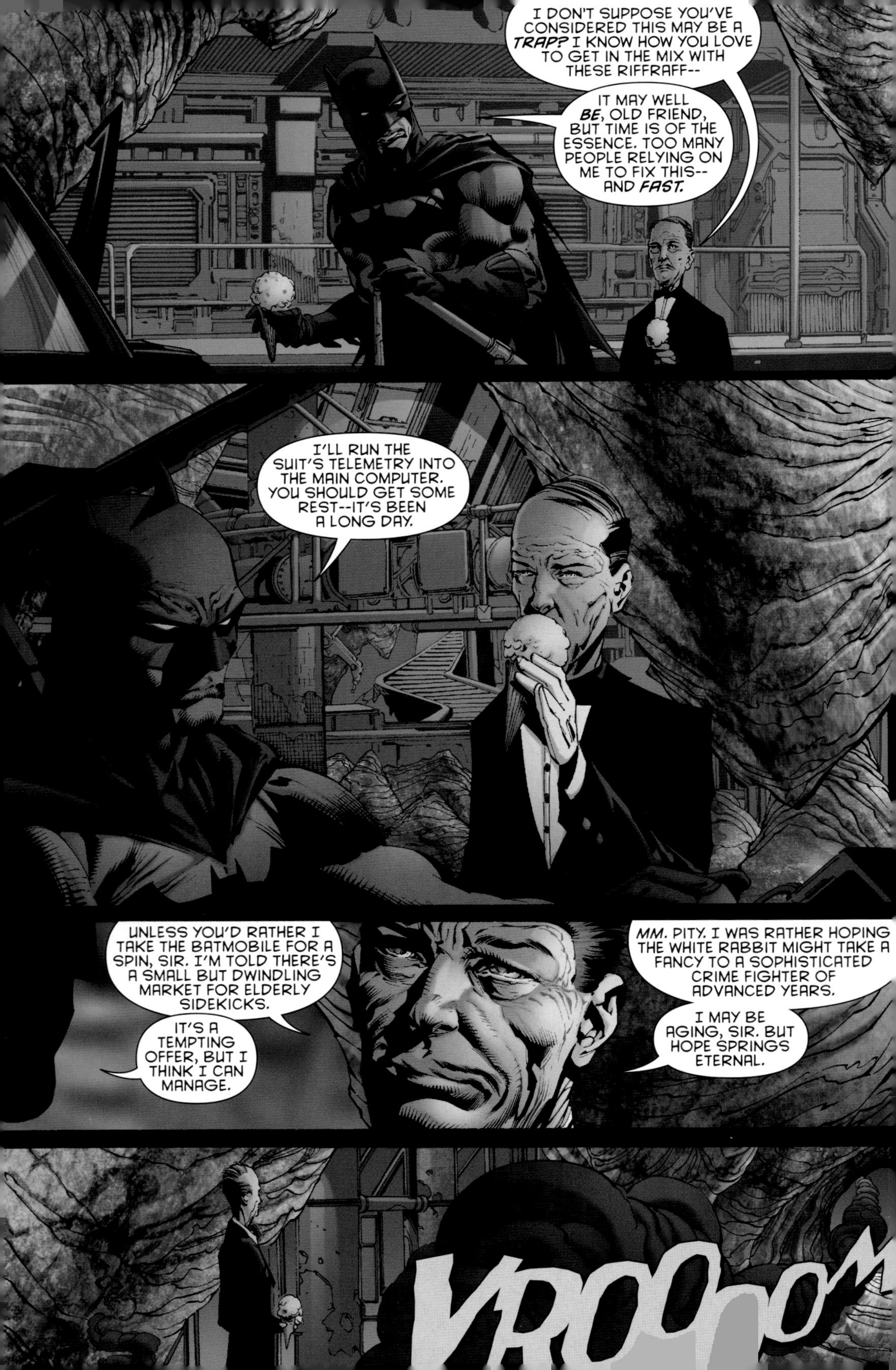
I DON'T SUPPOSE YOU'VE CONSIDERED THIS MAY BE A *TRAP?* I KNOW HOW YOU LOVE TO GET IN THE MIX WITH THESE RIFFRAFF--
IT MAY WELL *BE*, OLD FRIEND, BUT TIME IS OF THE ESSENCE. TOO MANY PEOPLE RELYING ON ME TO FIX THIS-- AND *FAST.*
I'LL RUN THE SUIT'S TELEMETRY INTO THE MAIN COMPUTER. YOU SHOULD GET SOME REST--IT'S BEEN A LONG DAY.
UNLESS YOU'D RATHER I TAKE THE BATMOBILE FOR A SPIN, SIR. I'M TOLD THERE'S A SMALL BUT DWINDLING MARKET FOR ELDERLY SIDEKICKS.
IT'S A TEMPTING OFFER, BUT I THINK I CAN MANAGE.
MM. PITY. I WAS RATHER HOPING THE WHITE RABBIT MIGHT TAKE A FANCY TO A SOPHISTICATED CRIME FIGHTER OF ADVANCED YEARS.
I MAY BE AGING, SIR. BUT HOPE SPRINGS ETERNAL.
VROOOOOM

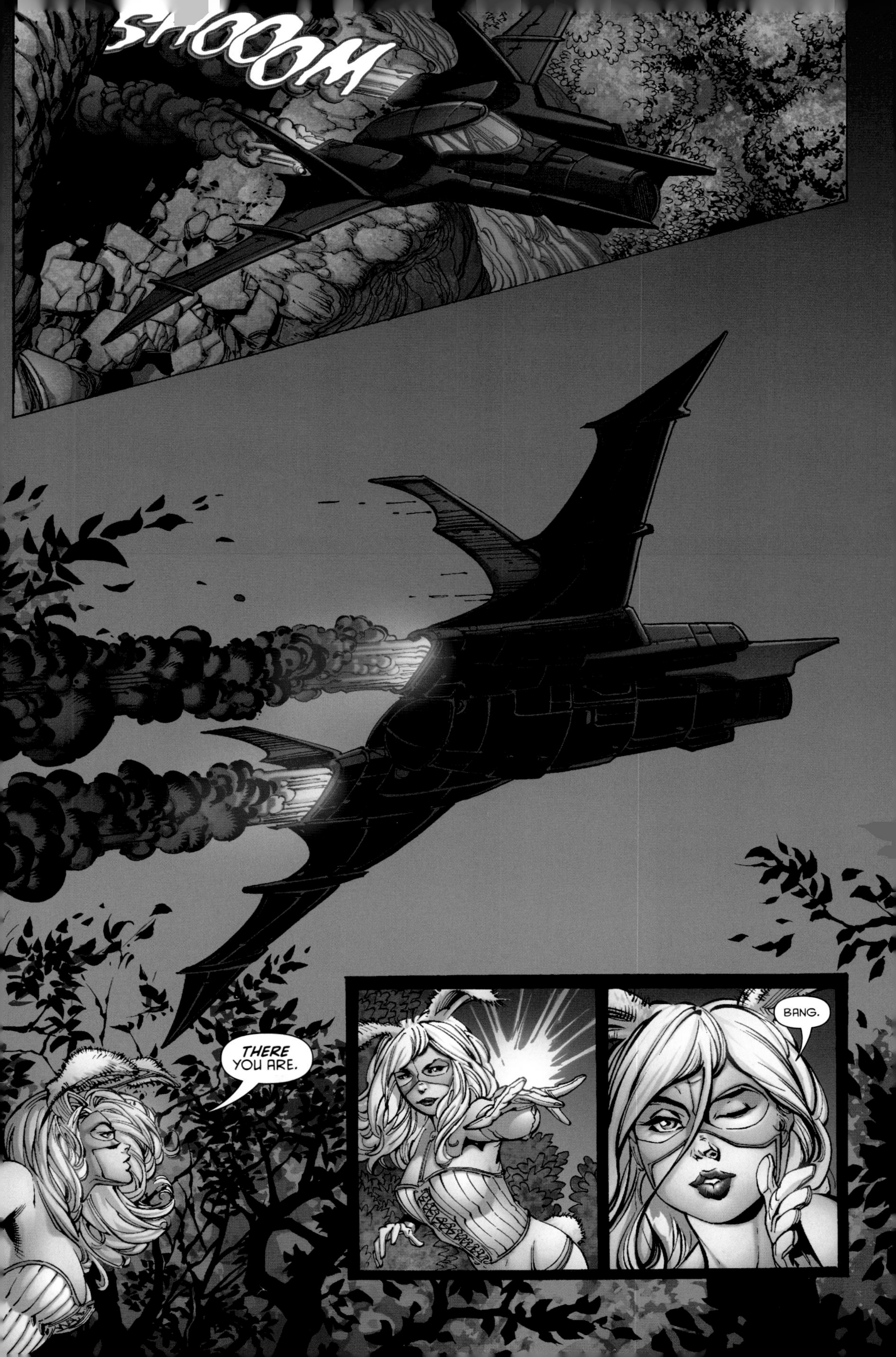
SHOOOM
THERE YOU ARE.
BANG.

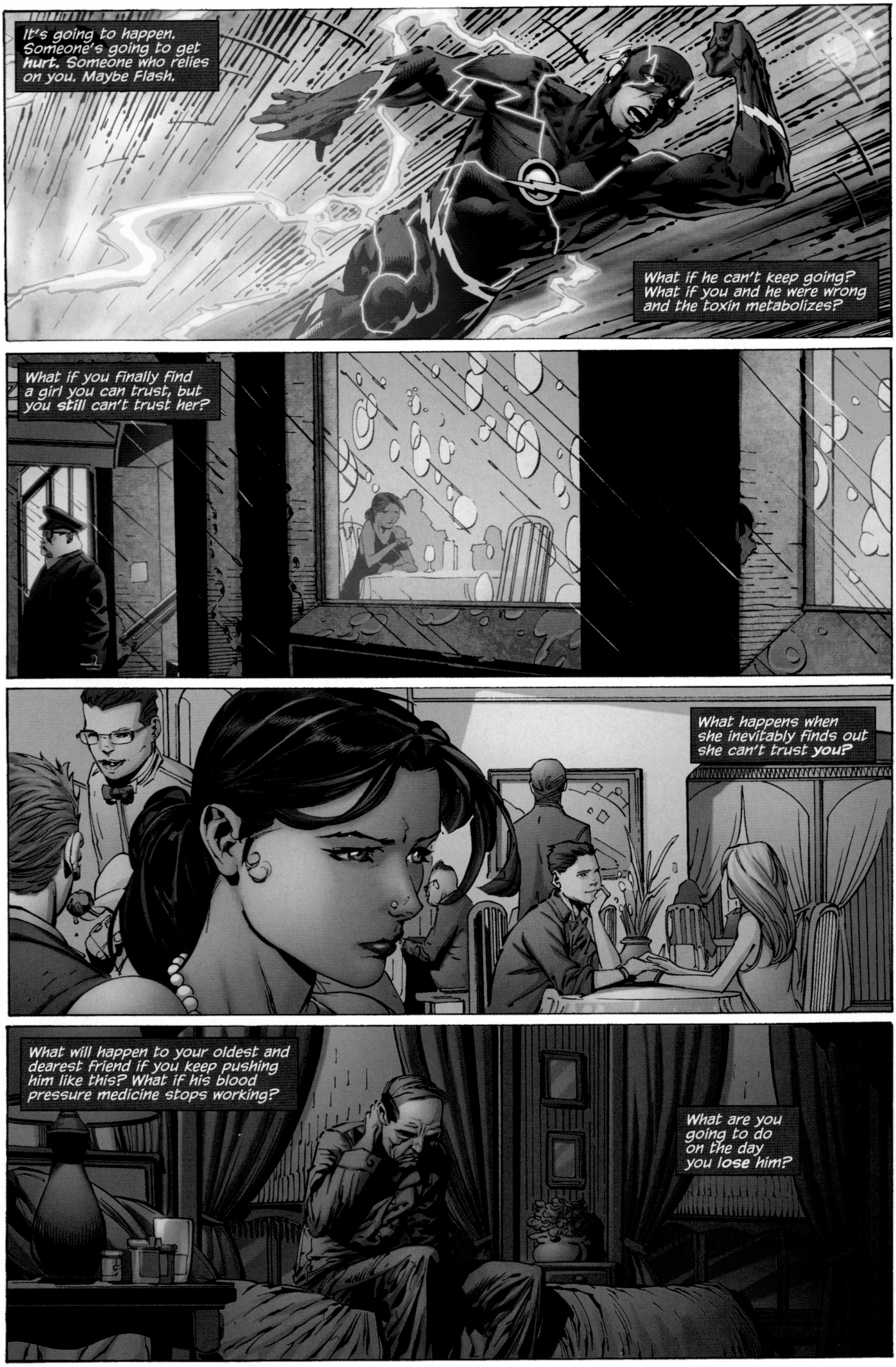
It's going to happen. Someone's going to get **hurt.** Someone who relies on you. Maybe Flash.
What if he can't keep going? What if you and he were wrong and the toxin metabolizes?
What if you finally find a girl you can trust, but you **still** can't trust her?
What happens when she inevitably finds out she can't trust **you?**
What will happen to your oldest and dearest friend if you keep pushing him like this? What if his blood pressure medicine stops working?
What are you going to do on the day you **lose** him?

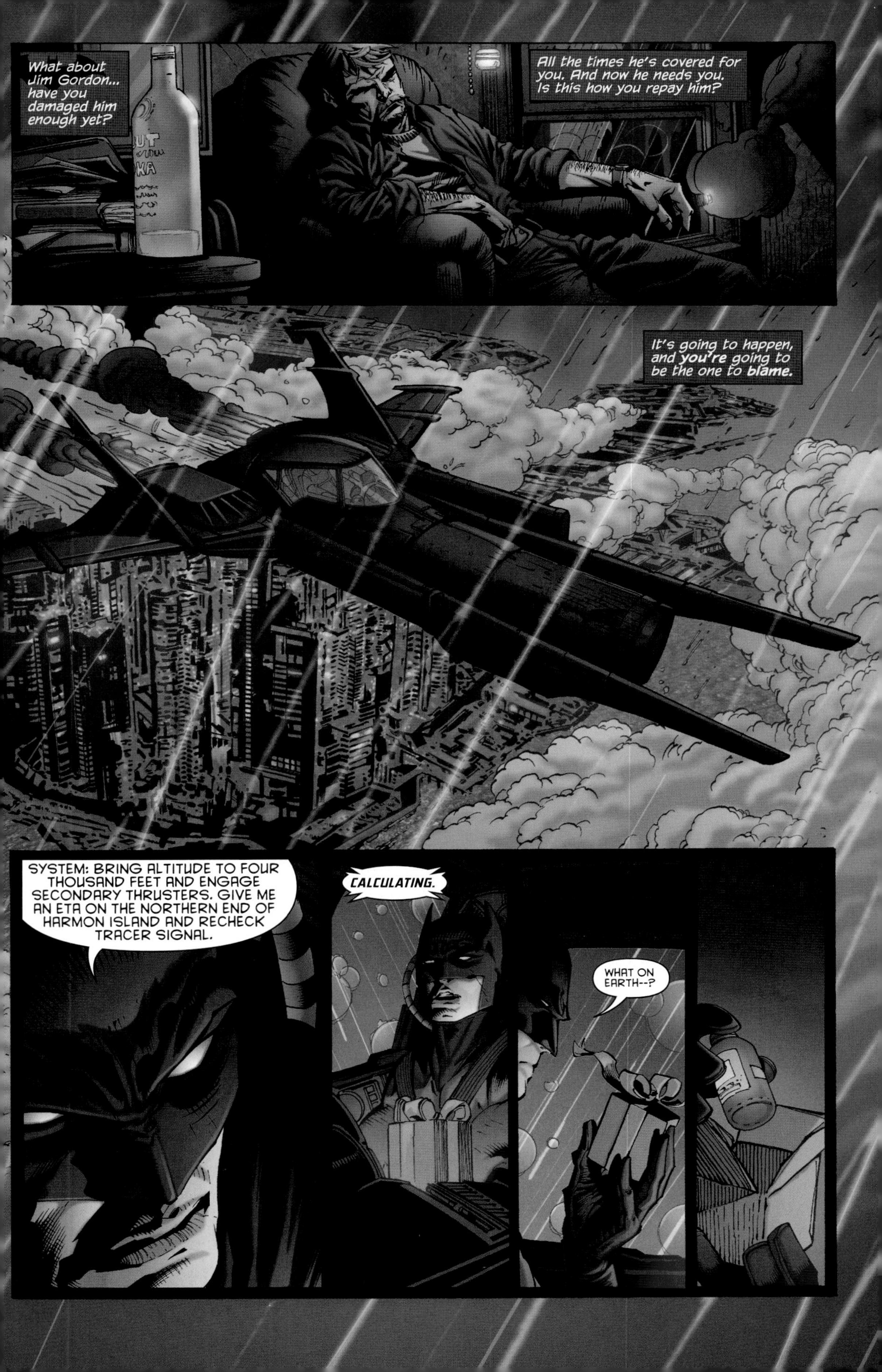
What about Jim Gordon... have you damaged him enough yet?
All the times he's covered for you. And now he needs you. Is this how you repay him?
It's going to happen, and you're going to be the one to blame.
SYSTEM: BRING ALTITUDE TO FOUR THOUSAND FEET AND ENGAGE SECONDARY THRUSTERS. GIVE ME AN ETA ON THE NORTHERN END OF HARMON ISLAND AND RECHECK TRACER SIGNAL.
CALCULATING.
WHAT ON EARTH--?

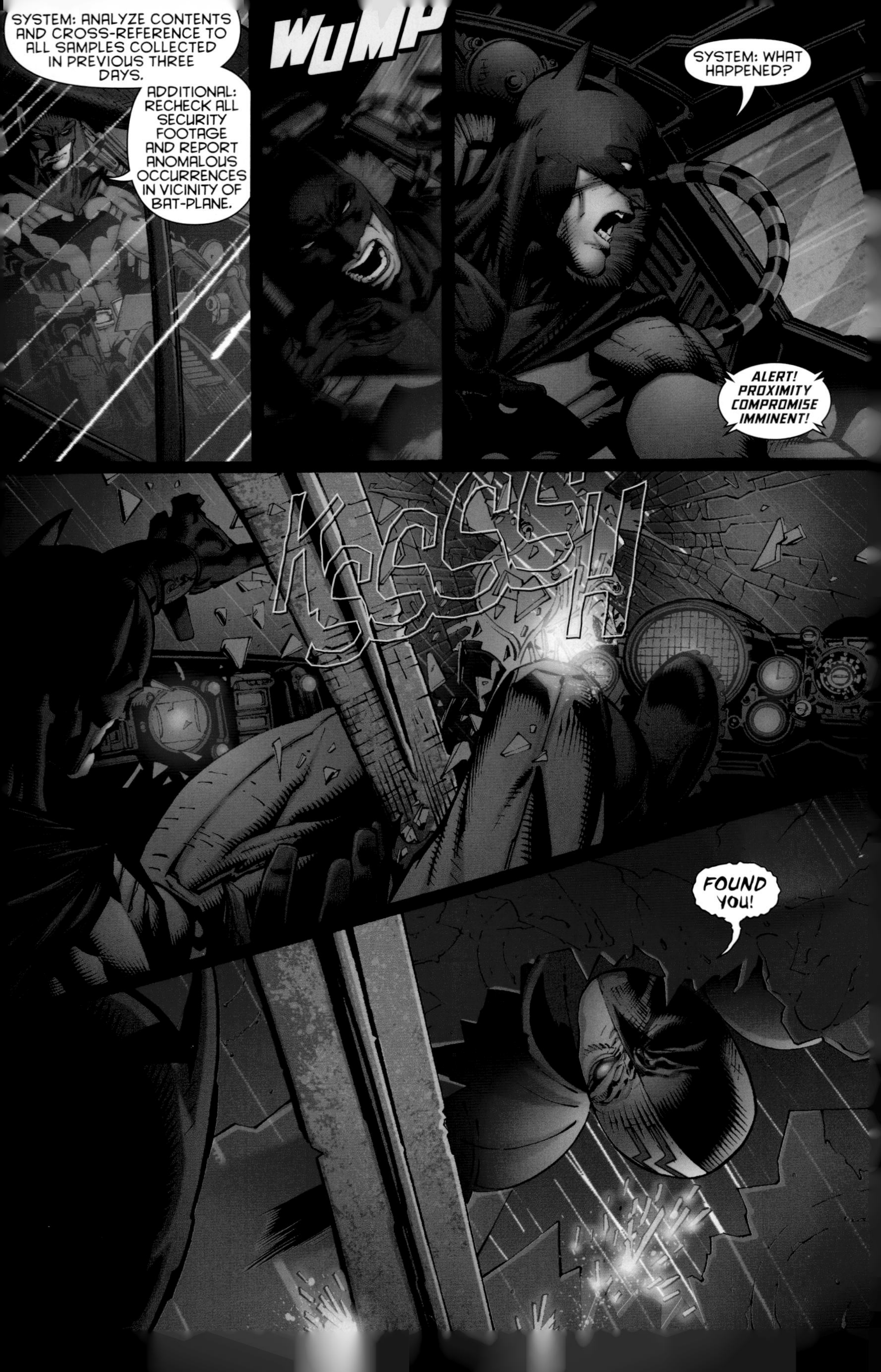
SYSTEM: ANALYZE CONTENTS AND CROSS-REFERENCE TO ALL SAMPLES COLLECTED IN PREVIOUS THREE DAYS.
ADDITIONAL: RECHECK ALL SECURITY FOOTAGE AND REPORT ANOMALOUS OCCURRENCES IN VICINITY OF BAT-PLANE.
WUMP
SYSTEM: WHAT HAPPENED?
ALERT! PROXIMITY COMPROMISE IMMINENT!
KRSSSH
FOUND YOU!

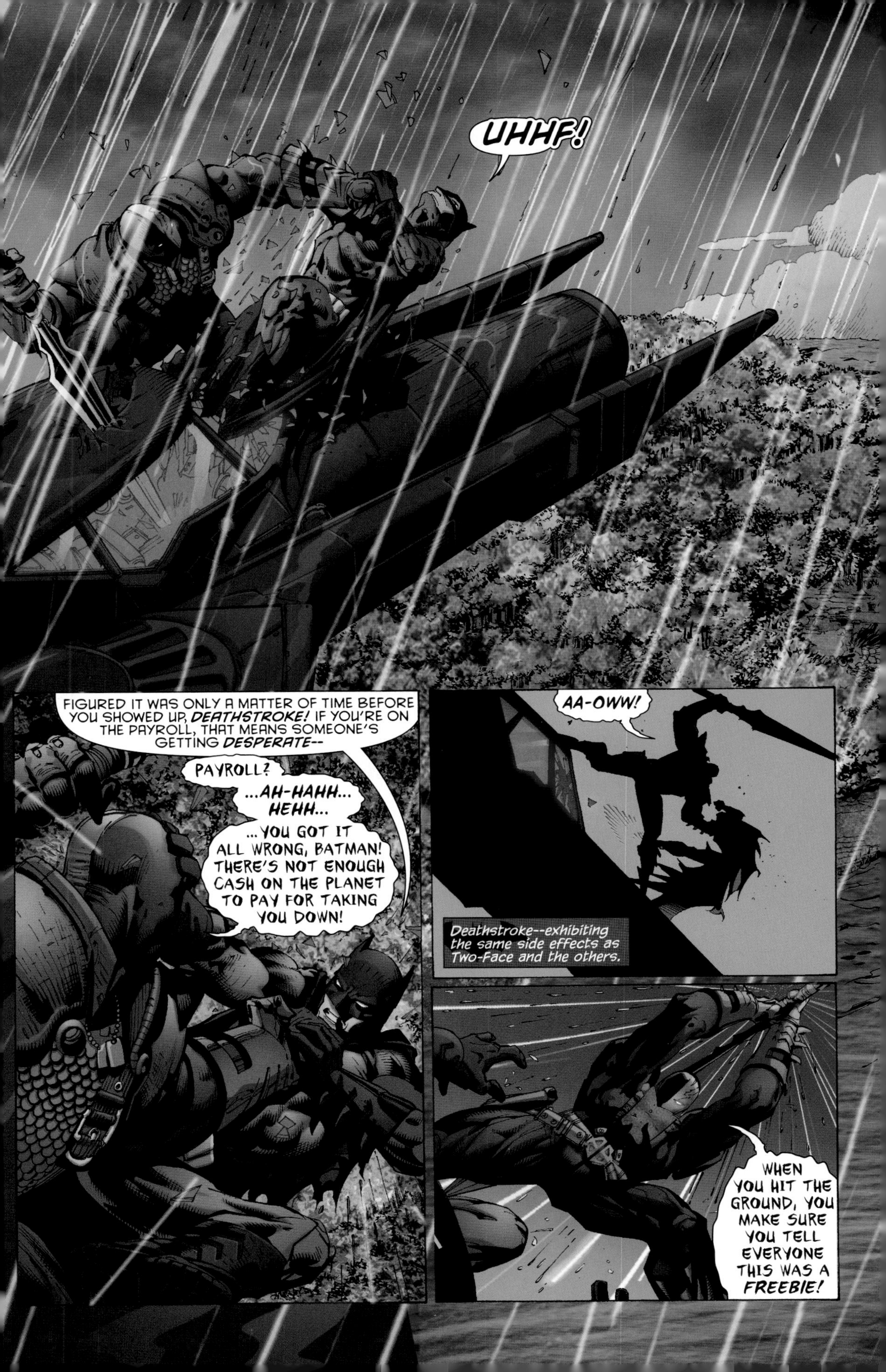
UHHF!
FIGURED IT WAS ONLY A MATTER OF TIME BEFORE YOU SHOWED UP, DEATHSTROKE! IF YOU'RE ON THE PAYROLL, THAT MEANS SOMEONE'S GETTING DESPERATE--
PAYROLL?
...AH-HAHH... HEHH...
...YOU GOT IT ALL WRONG, BATMAN! THERE'S NOT ENOUGH CASH ON THE PLANET TO PAY FOR TAKING YOU DOWN!
AA-OWW!
Deathstroke--exhibiting the same side effects as Two-Face and the others.
WHEN YOU HIT THE GROUND, YOU MAKE SURE YOU TELL EVERYONE THIS WAS A FREEBIE!

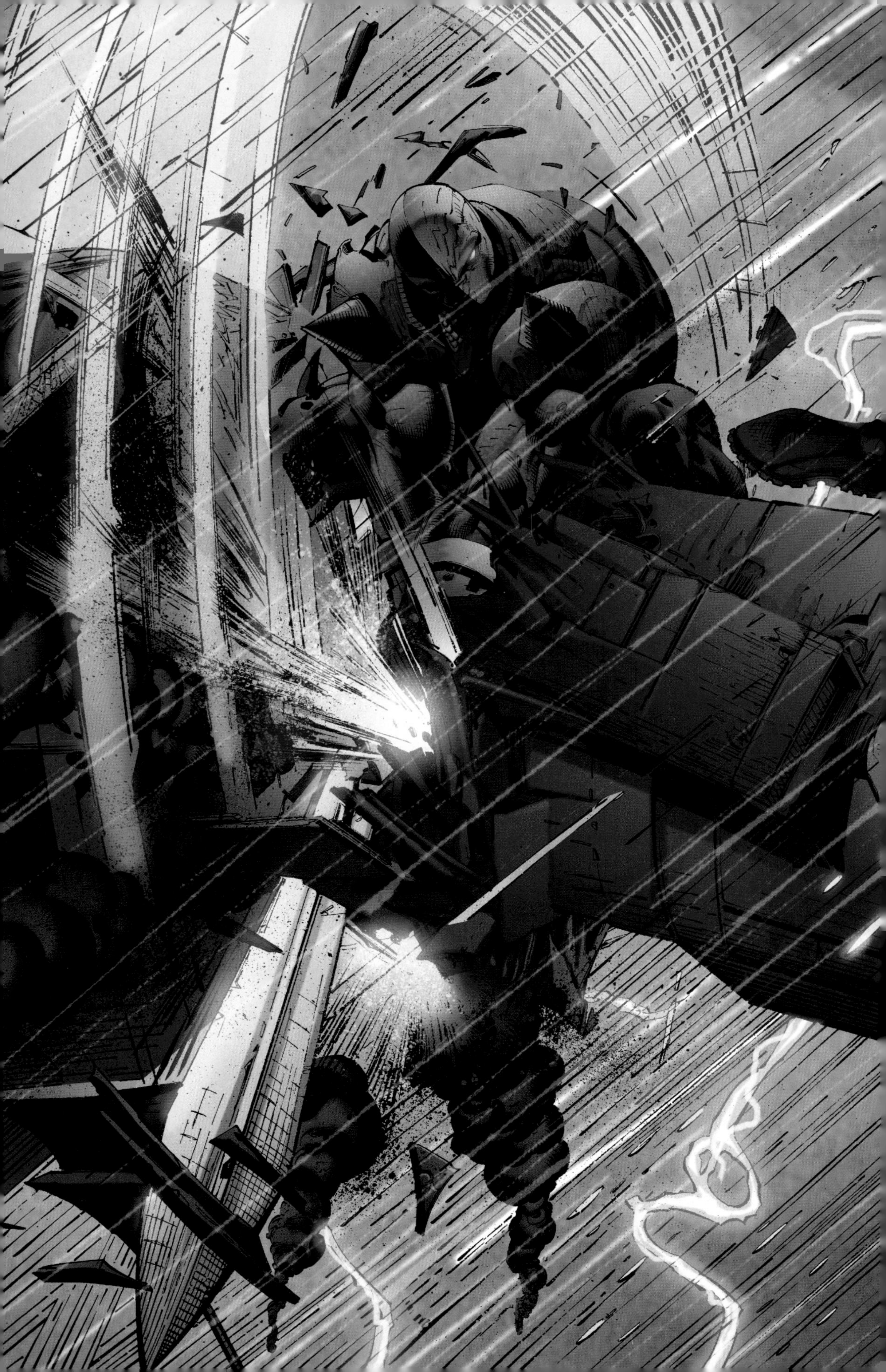

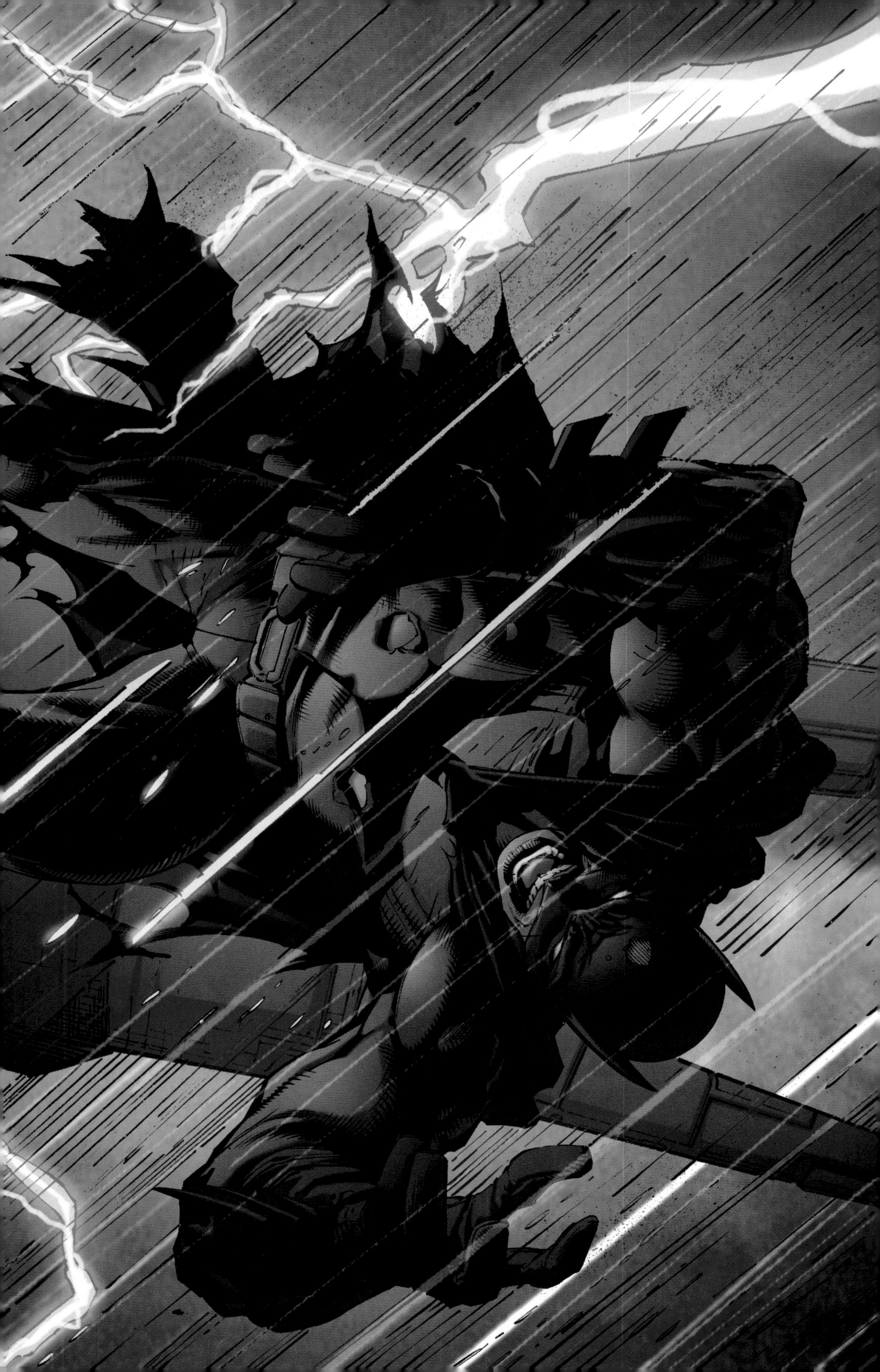

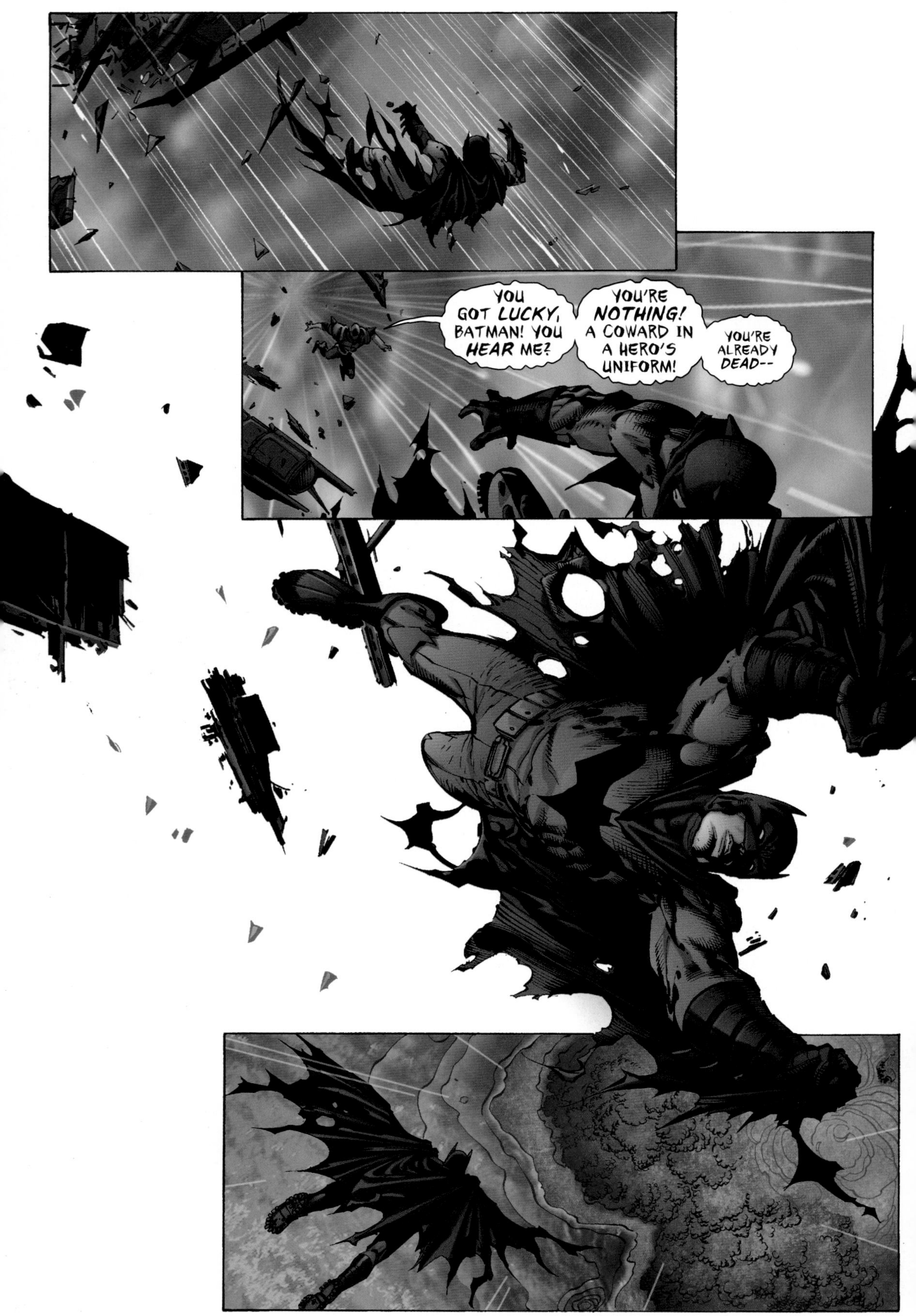
YOU GOT LUCKY, BATMAN! YOU HEAR ME?
YOU'RE NOTHING! A COWARD IN A HERO'S UNIFORM!
YOU'RE ALREADY DEAD--

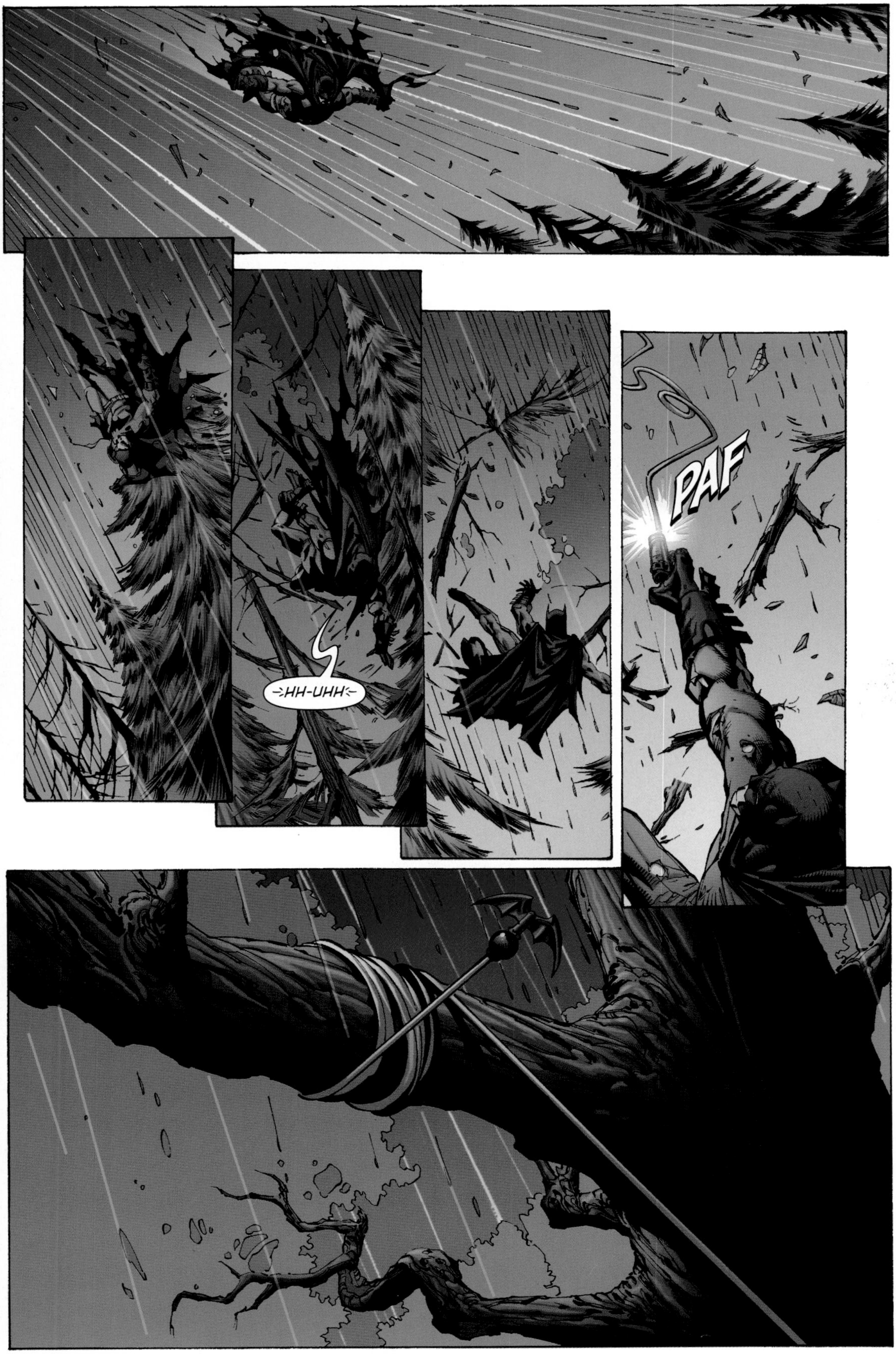
HH-UHH
PAF

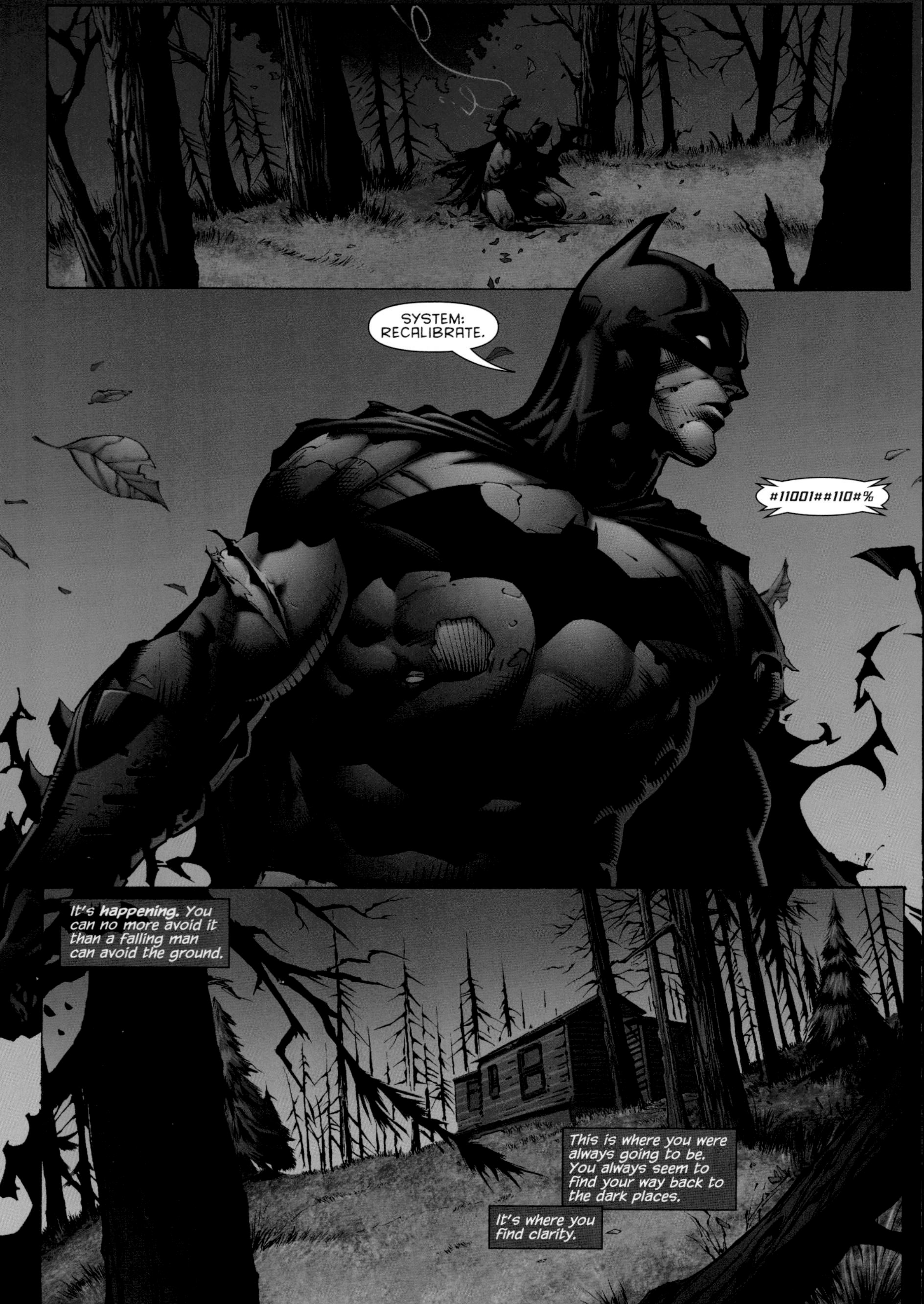
SYSTEM: RECALIBRATE.
#11001##110#%
It's **happening.** You can no more avoid it than a falling man can avoid the ground.
This is where you were always going to be. You always seem to find your way back to the dark places.
It's where you find clarity.

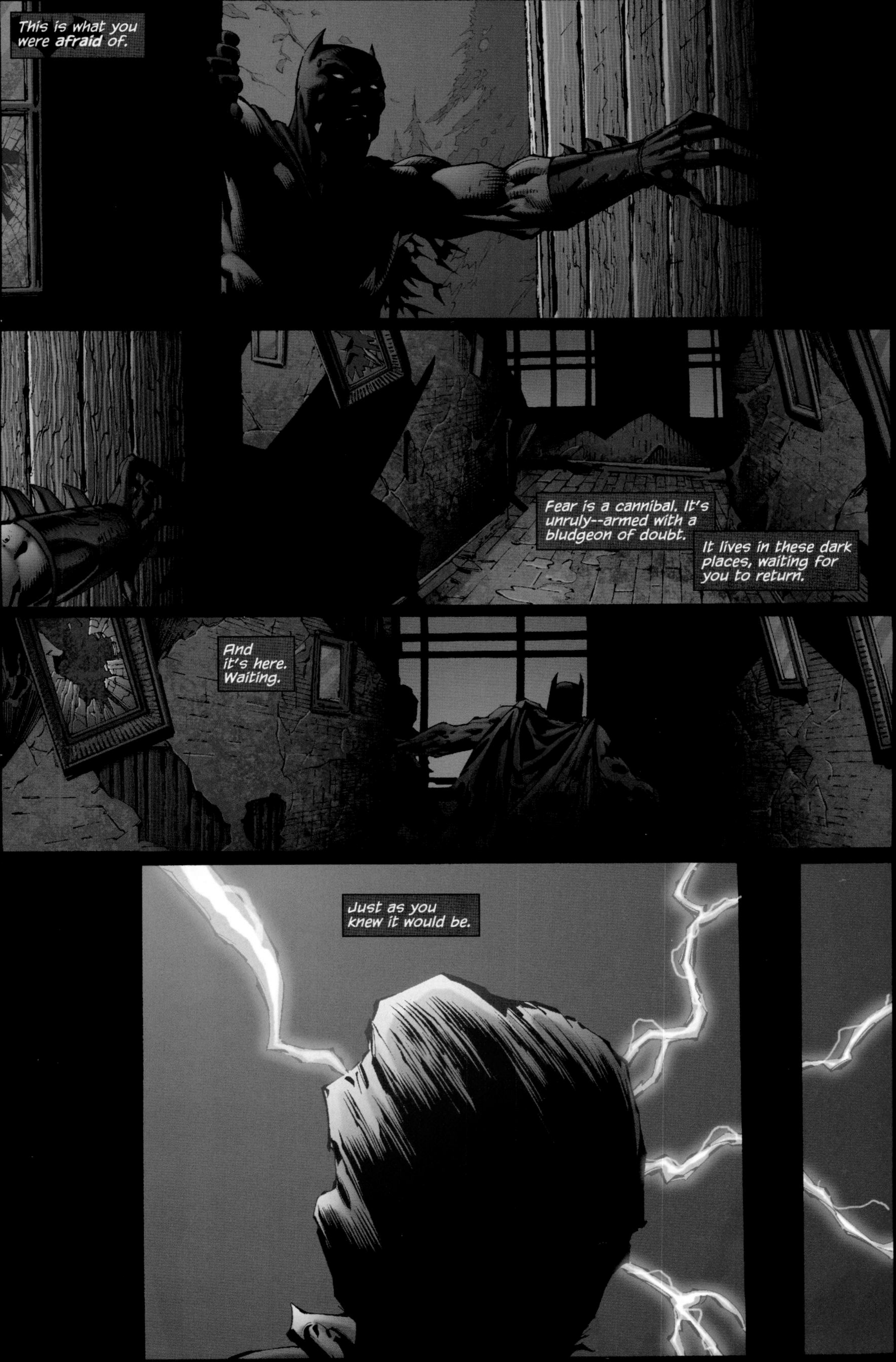
This is what you were afraid of.
Fear is a cannibal. It's unruly--armed with a bludgeon of doubt.
It lives in these dark places, waiting for you to return.
And it's here. Waiting.
Just as you knew it would be.

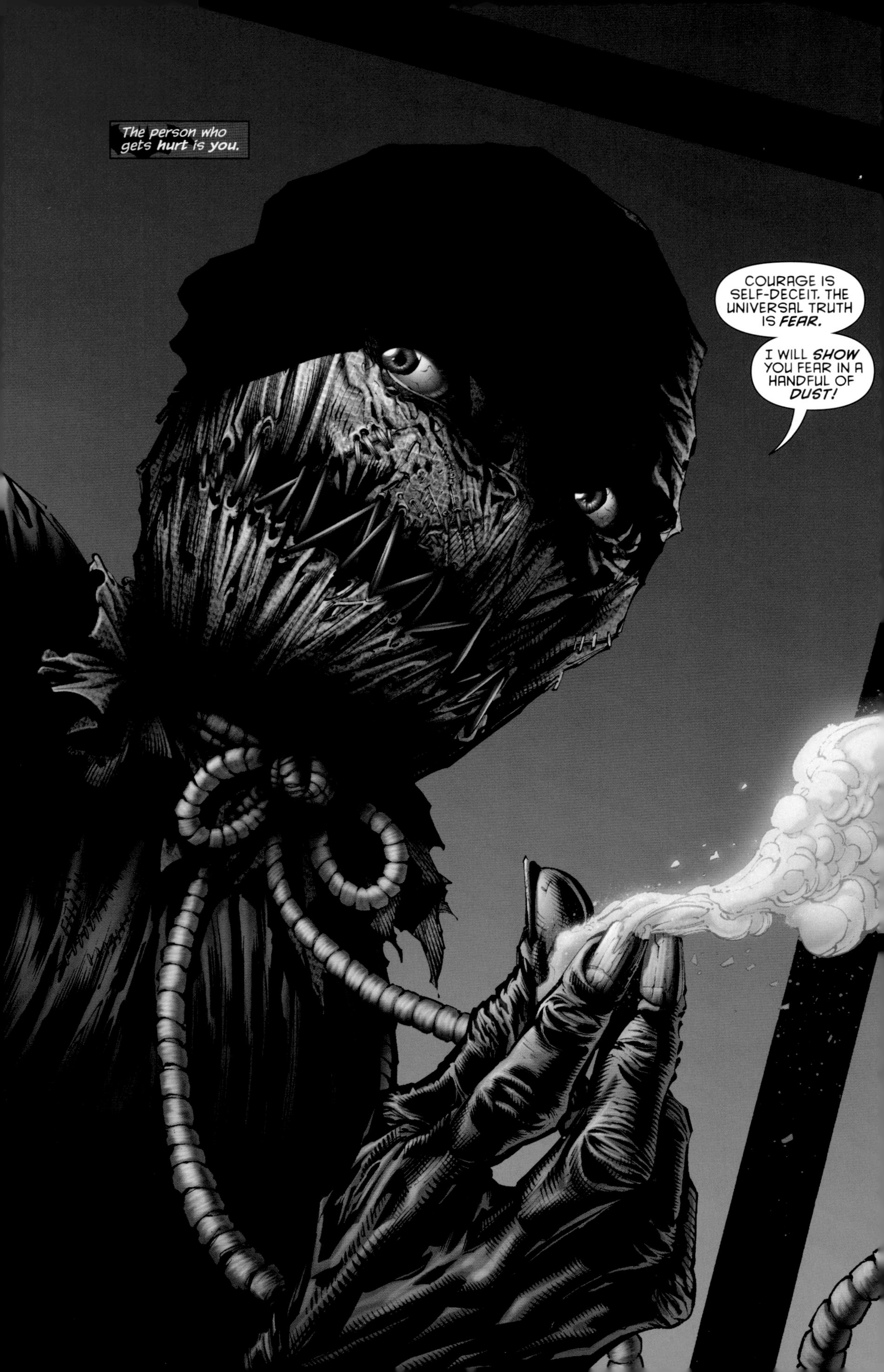
The person who gets hurt is you.
COURAGE IS SELF-DECEIT. THE UNIVERSAL TRUTH IS FEAR.
I WILL SHOW YOU FEAR IN A HANDFUL OF DUST!

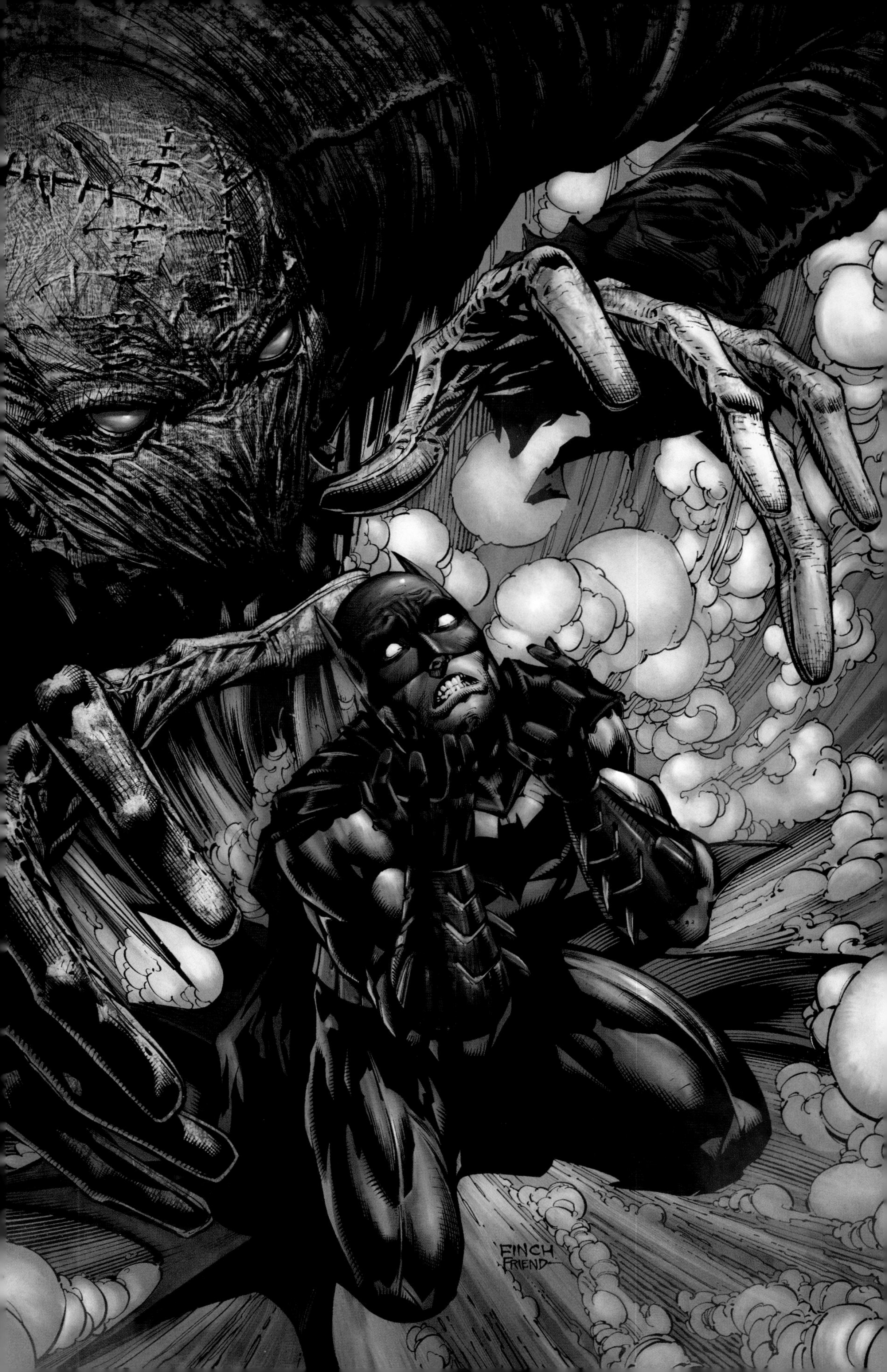
FINCH
FRIEND

HANDFUL OF DUST

PAUL JENKINS writer/co-plotter **DAVID FINCH** penciller/co-plotter **RICHARD FRIEND** inker
cover art by **DAVID FINCH, RICHARD FRIEND & ALEX SINCLAIR**

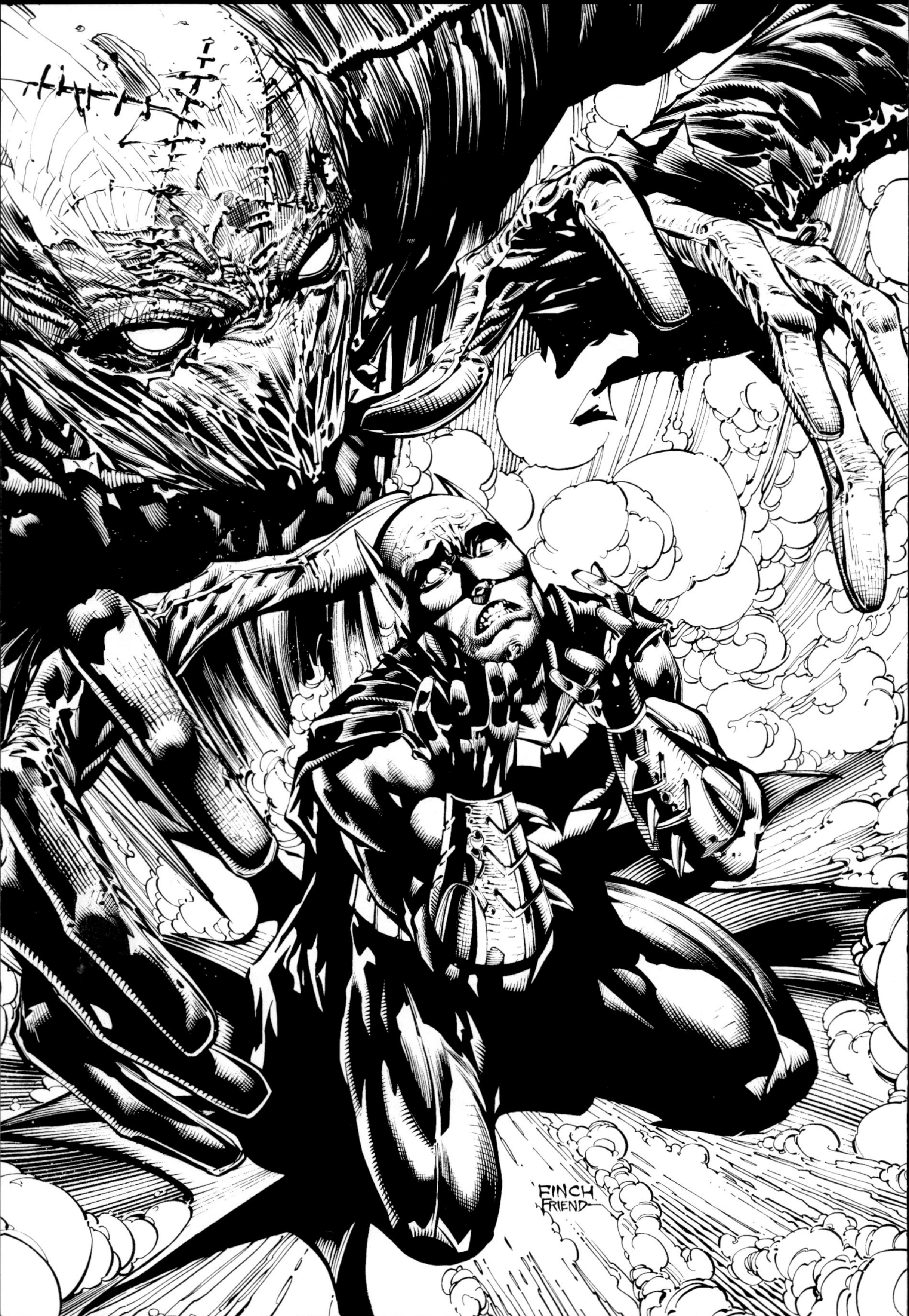
FINCH
FRIEND

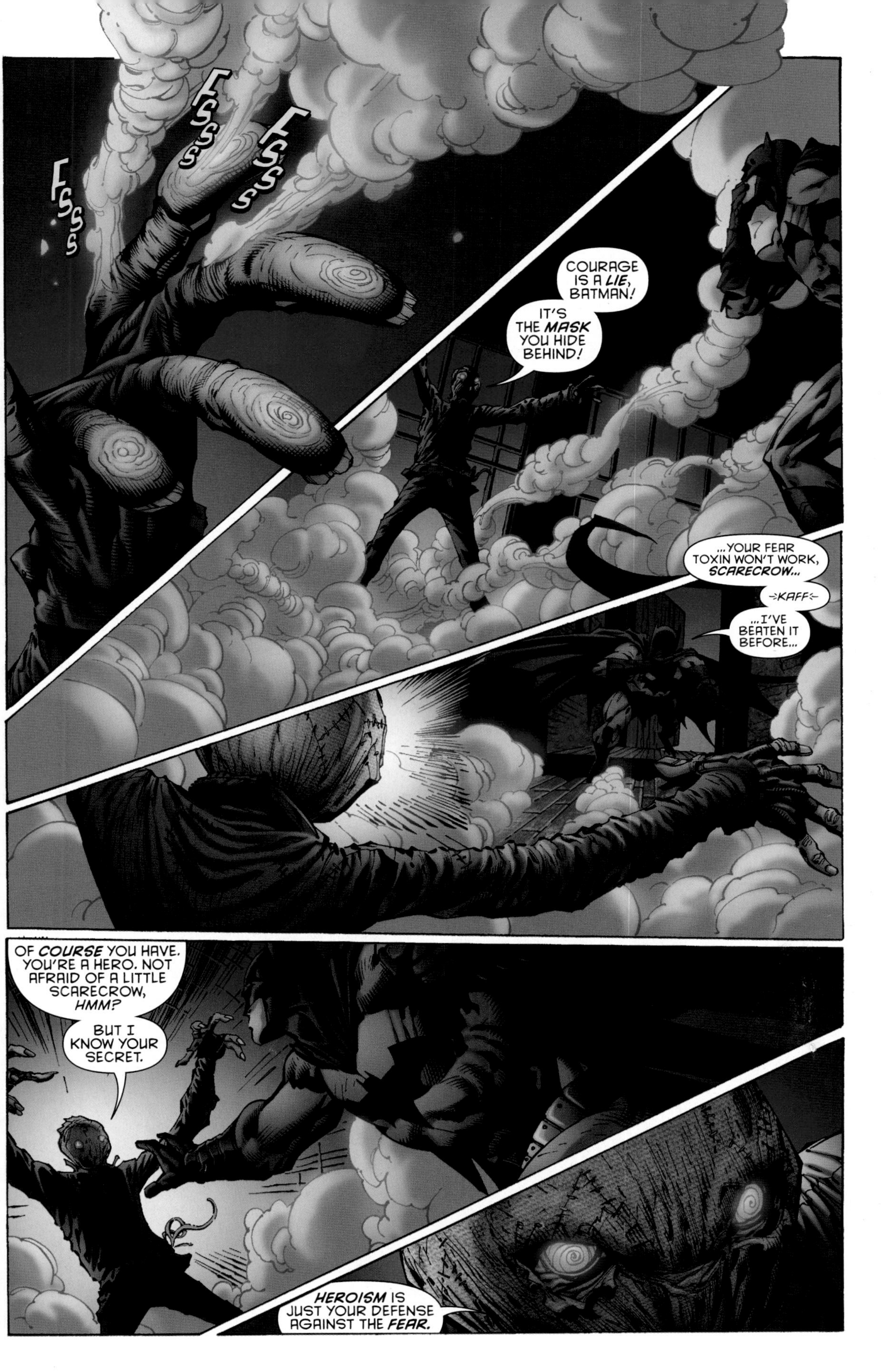
FSSS
FSSS
FSSS
COURAGE IS A LIE, BATMAN!
IT'S THE MASK YOU HIDE BEHIND!
...YOUR FEAR TOXIN WON'T WORK, SCARECROW...
KAFF
...I'VE BEATEN IT BEFORE...
OF COURSE YOU HAVE. YOU'RE A HERO. NOT AFRAID OF A LITTLE SCARECROW, HMM?
BUT I KNOW YOUR SECRET.
HEROISM IS JUST YOUR DEFENSE AGAINST THE FEAR.

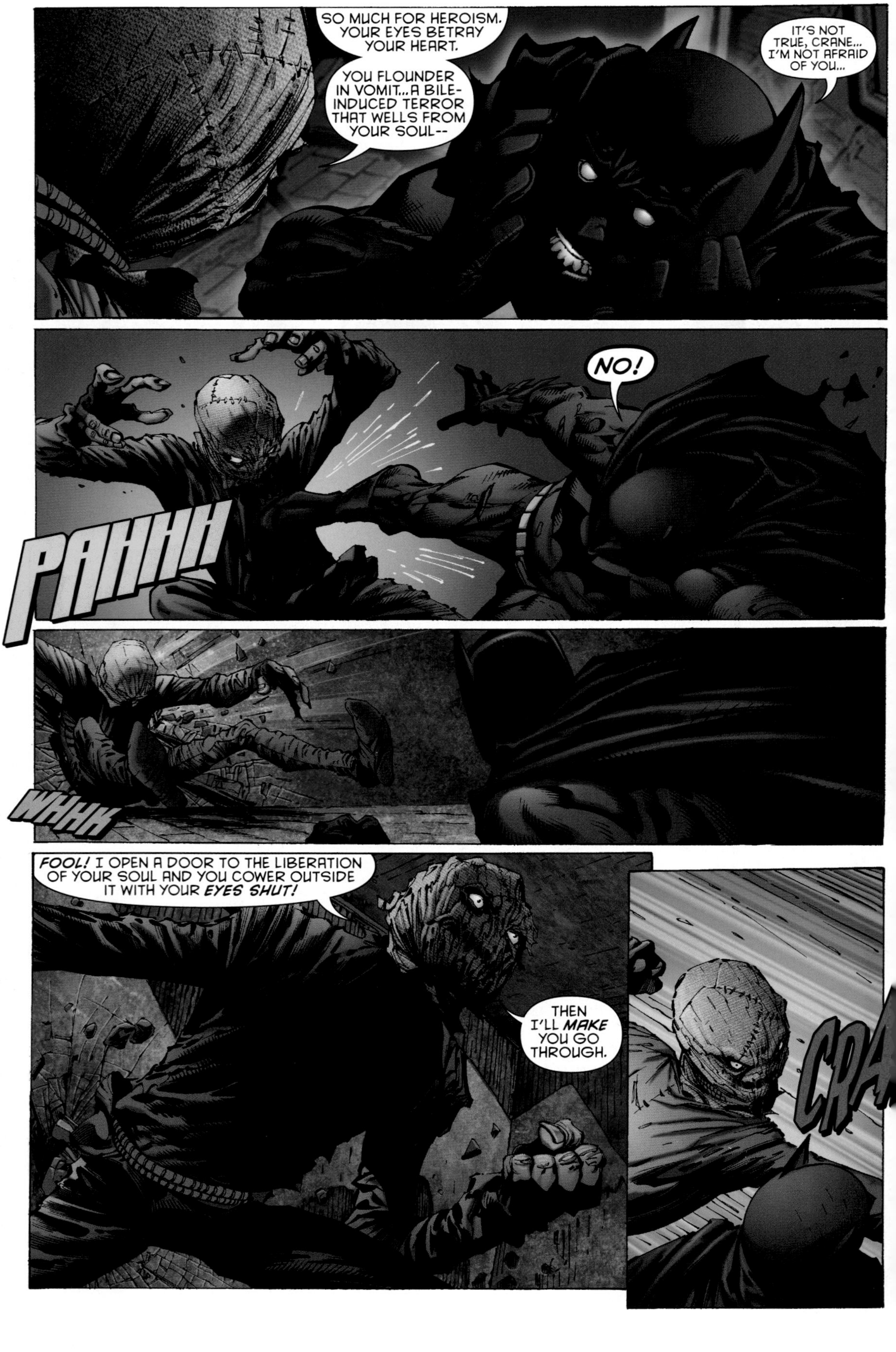
SO MUCH FOR HEROISM. YOUR EYES BETRAY YOUR HEART.
YOU FLOUNDER IN VOMIT...A BILE-INDUCED TERROR THAT WELLS FROM YOUR SOUL--
IT'S NOT TRUE, CRANE... I'M NOT AFRAID OF YOU...
NO!
PAHHH
WHHK
FOOL! I OPEN A DOOR TO THE LIBERATION OF YOUR SOUL AND YOU COWER OUTSIDE IT WITH YOUR EYES SHUT!
THEN I'LL MAKE YOU GO THROUGH.

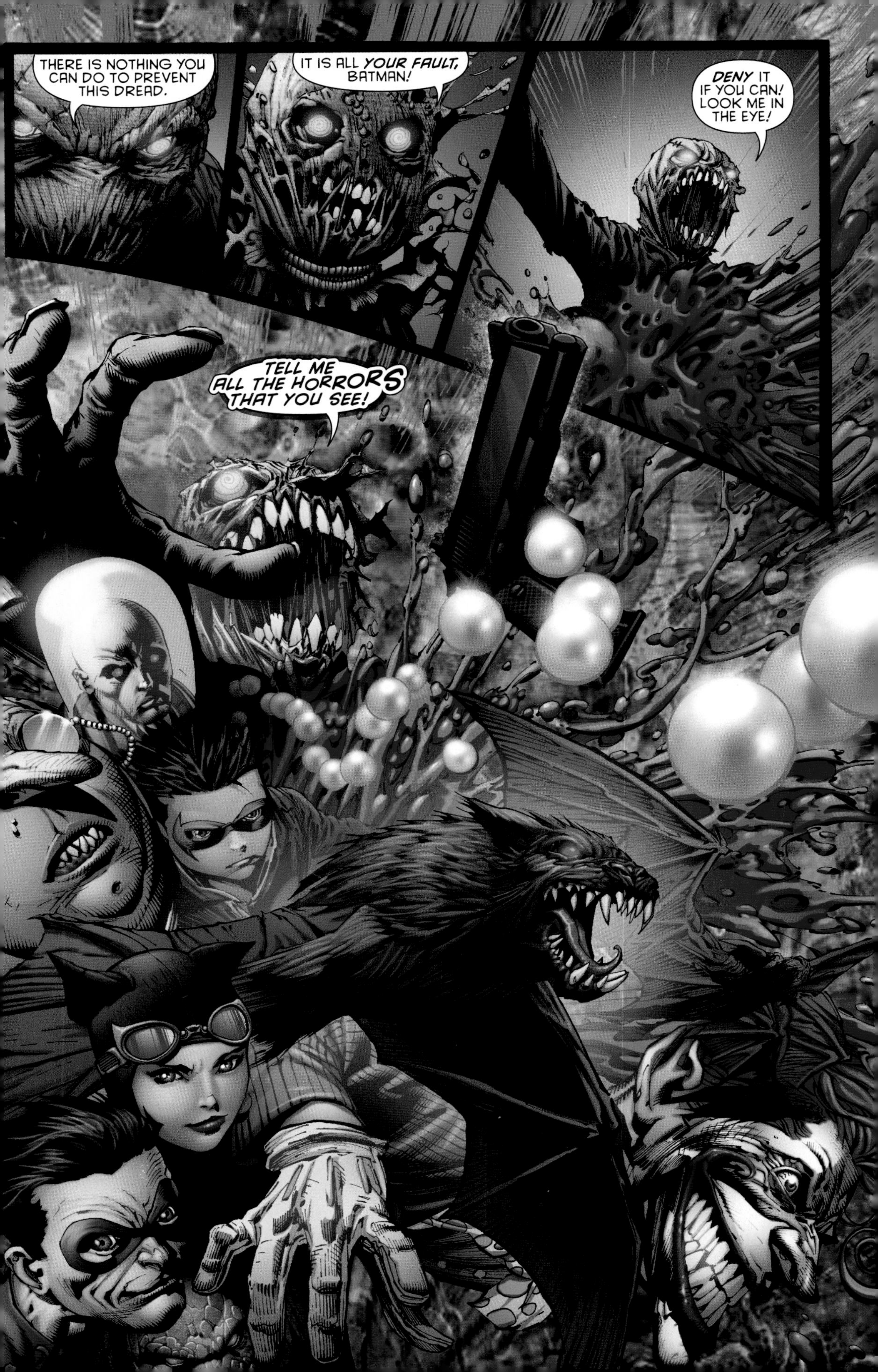
THERE IS NOTHING YOU CAN DO TO PREVENT THIS DREAD.
IT IS ALL YOUR FAULT, BATMAN!
DENY IT IF YOU CAN! LOOK ME IN THE EYE!
TELL ME ALL THE HORRORS THAT YOU SEE!

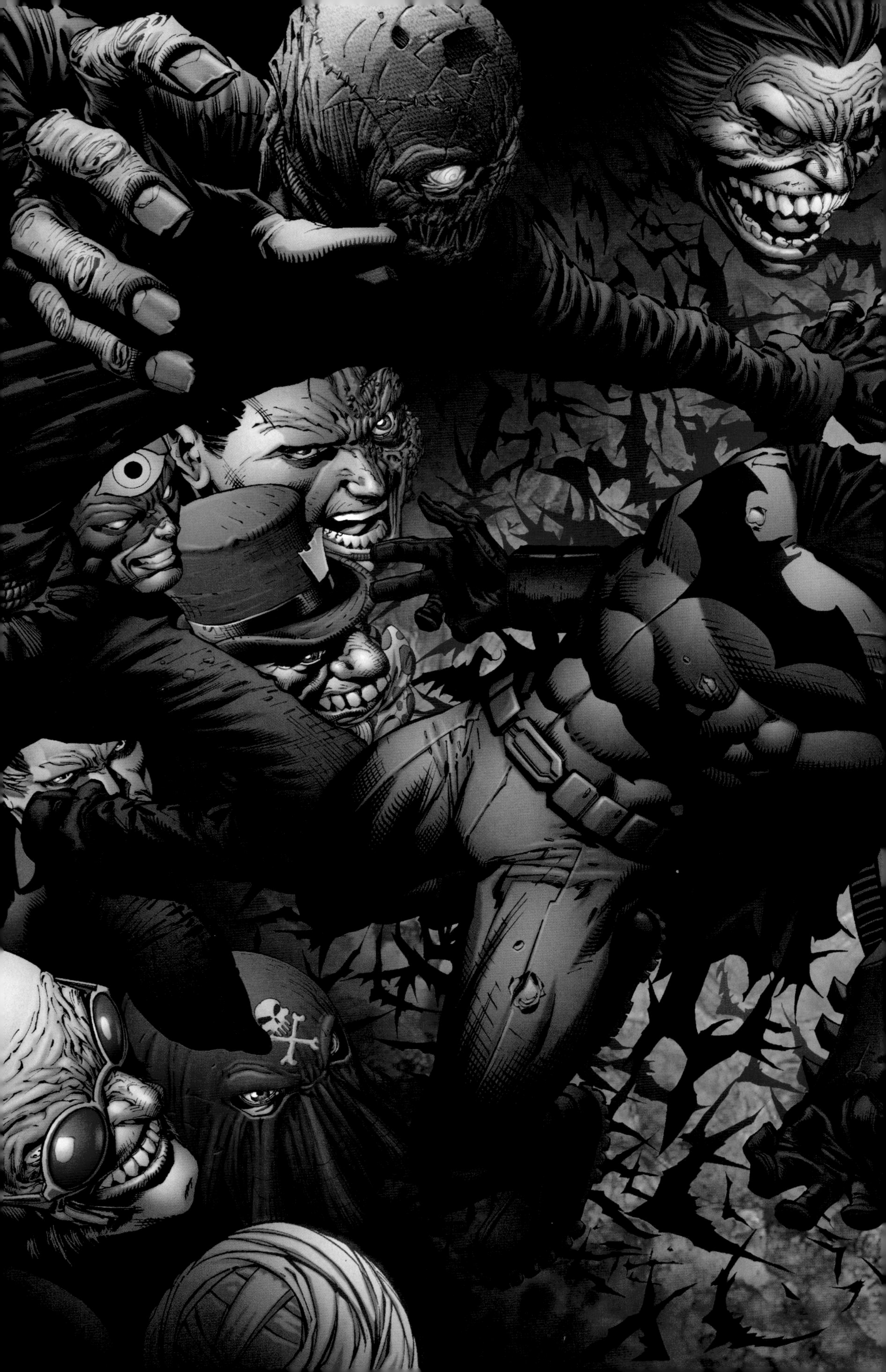

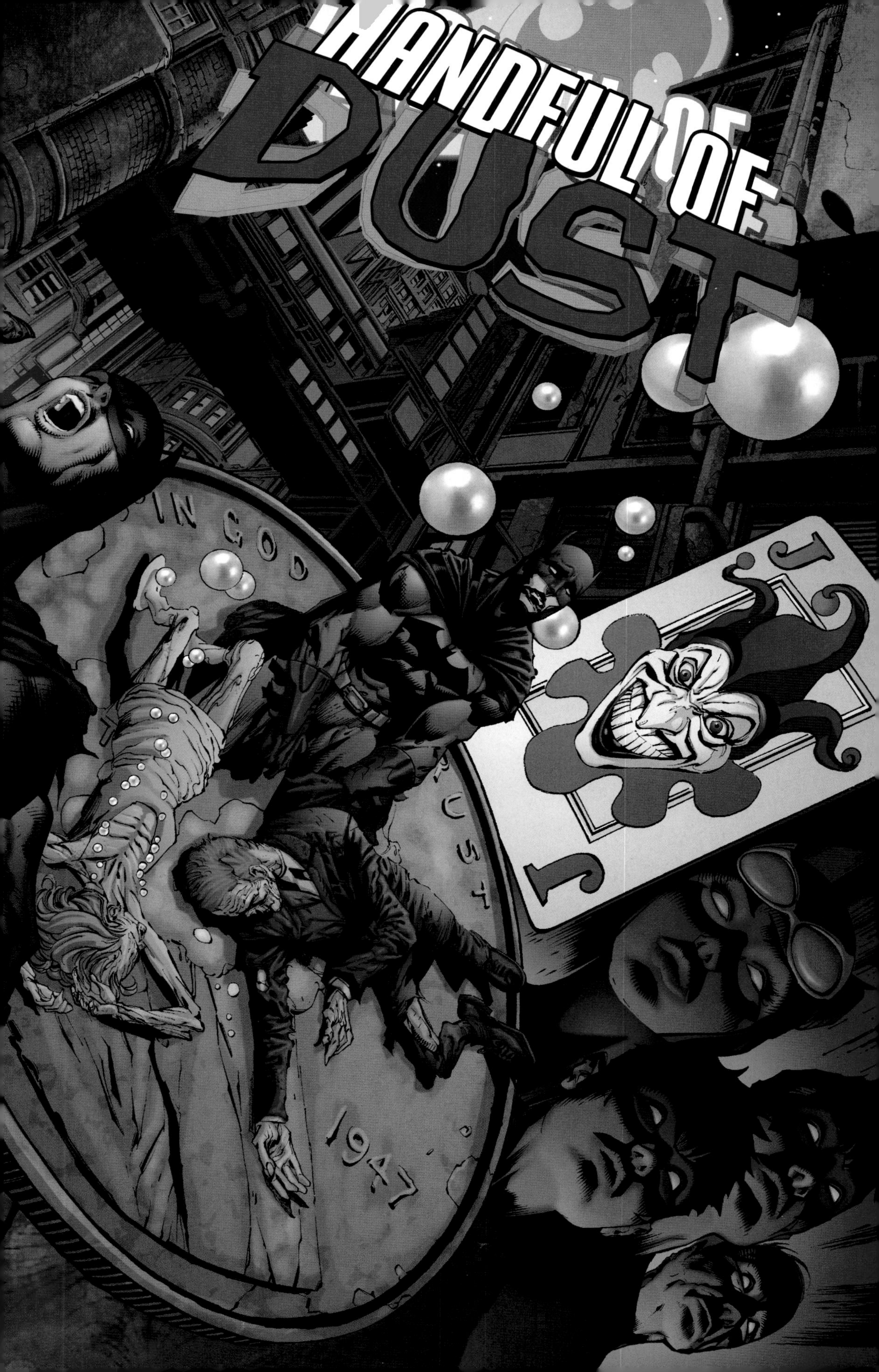
HANDFUL OF
DUST
IN GOD
RUST
1947
J
J

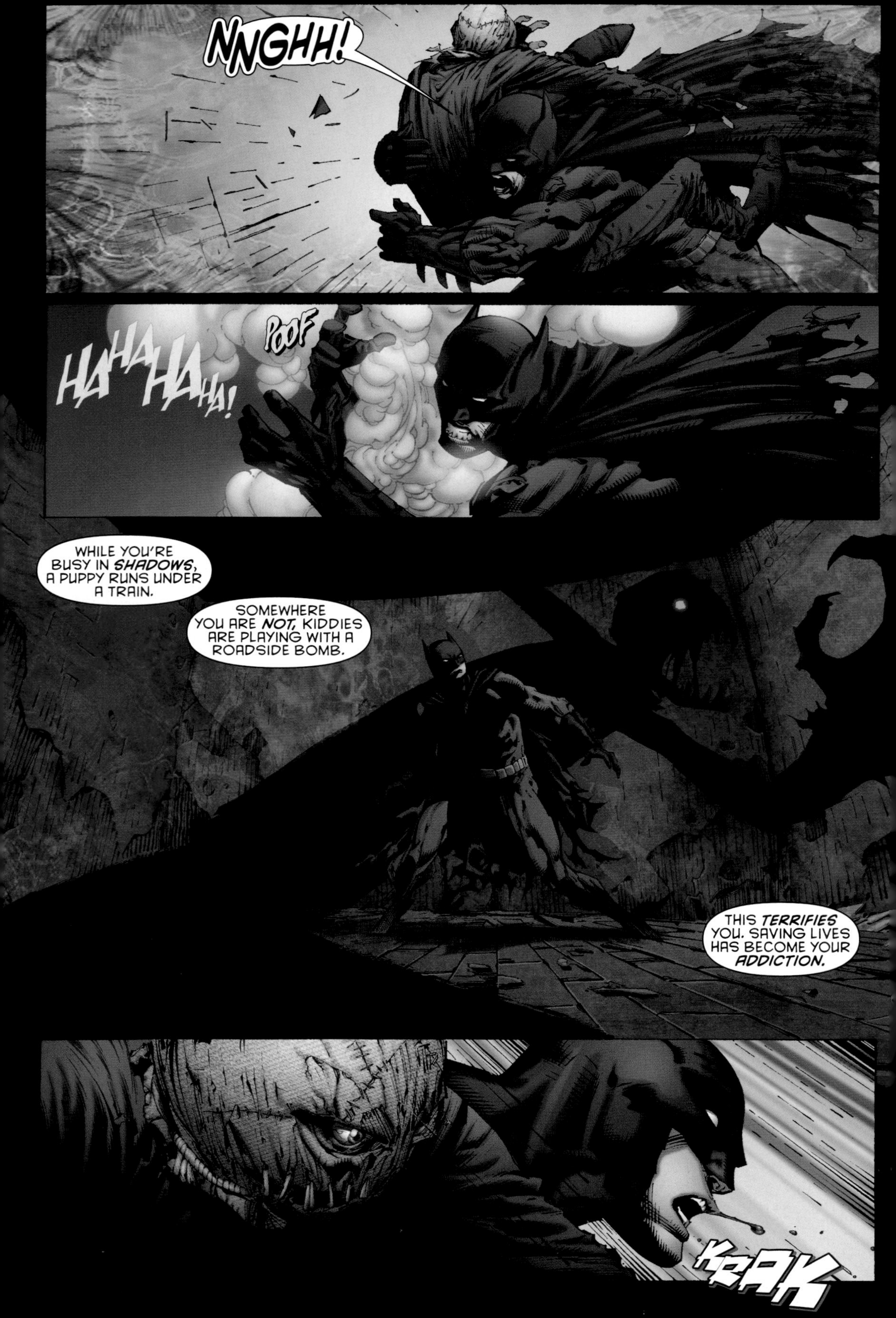
NNGHH!
POOF
HAHAHAHAHA!
WHILE YOU'RE BUSY IN SHADOWS, A PUPPY RUNS UNDER A TRAIN.
SOMEWHERE YOU ARE NOT, KIDDIES ARE PLAYING WITH A ROADSIDE BOMB.
THIS TERRIFIES YOU. SAVING LIVES HAS BECOME YOUR ADDICTION.
KRAK

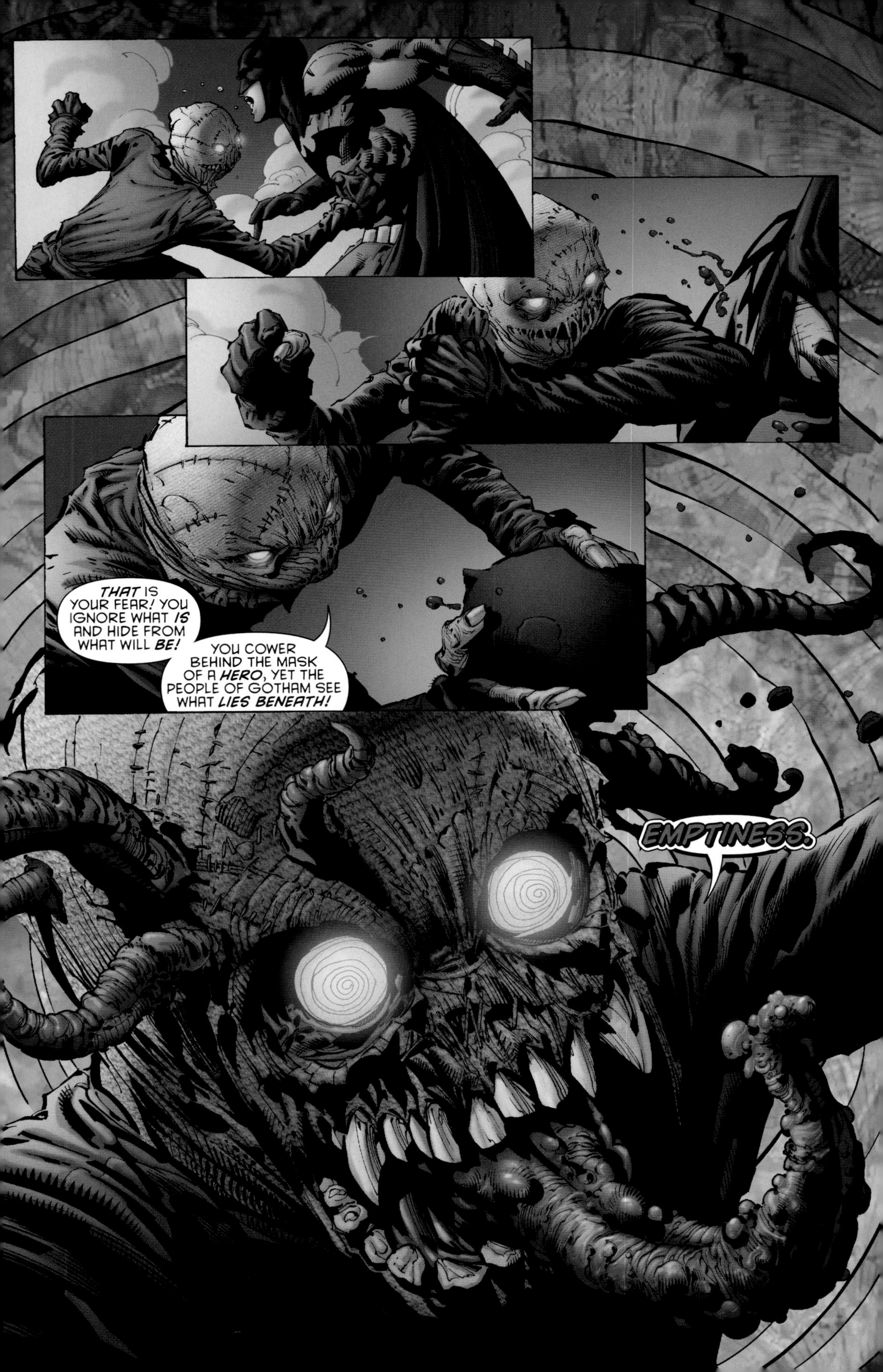
THAT IS YOUR FEAR! YOU IGNORE WHAT IS AND HIDE FROM WHAT WILL BE!
YOU COWER BEHIND THE MASK OF A HERO, YET THE PEOPLE OF GOTHAM SEE WHAT LIES BENEATH!
EMPTINESS.

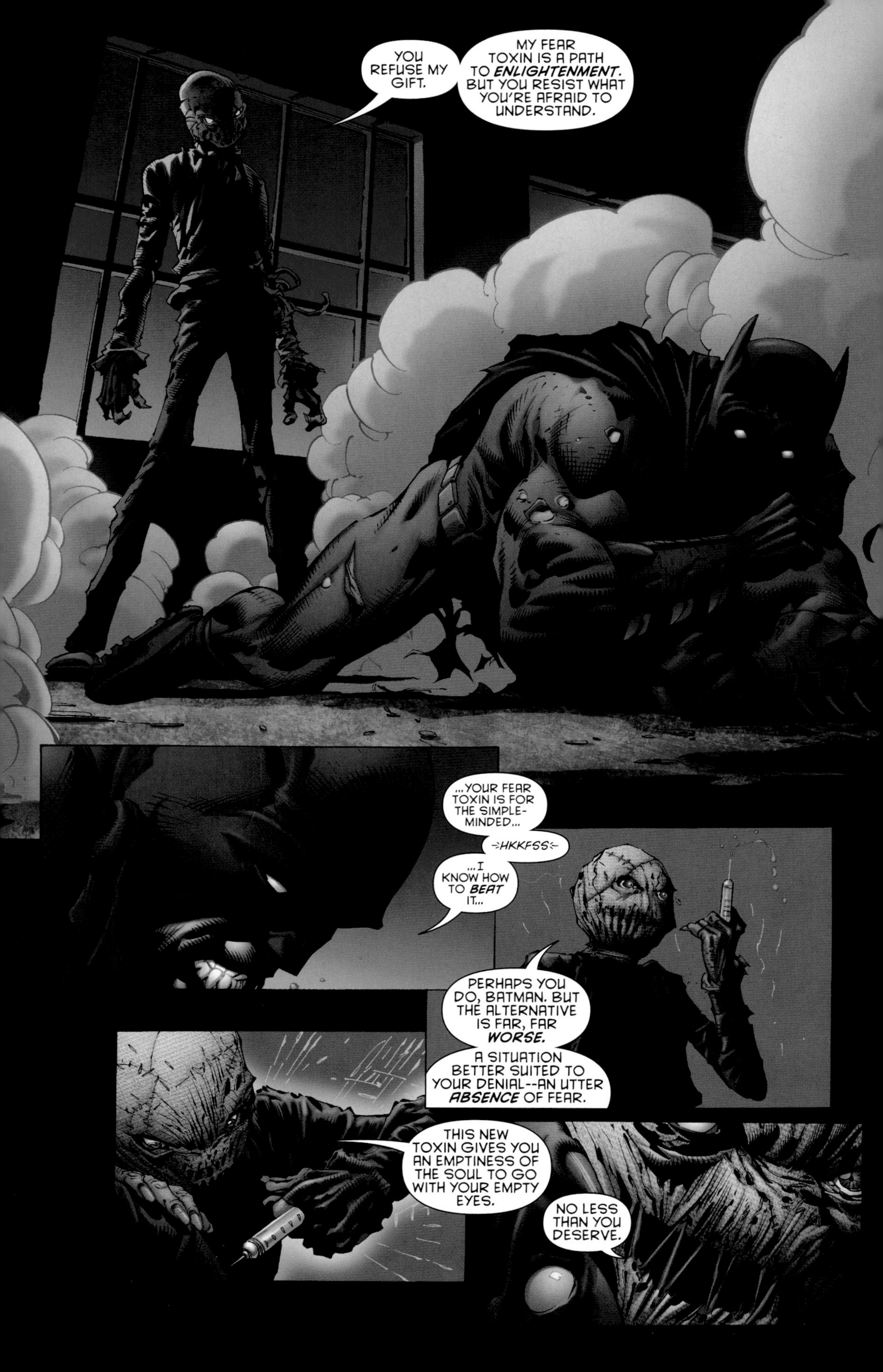

YOU REFUSE MY GIFT.
MY FEAR TOXIN IS A PATH TO ENLIGHTENMENT. BUT YOU RESIST WHAT YOU'RE AFRAID TO UNDERSTAND.
...YOUR FEAR TOXIN IS FOR THE SIMPLE-MINDED...
HKKFSS
...I KNOW HOW TO BEAT IT...
PERHAPS YOU DO, BATMAN. BUT THE ALTERNATIVE IS FAR, FAR WORSE.
A SITUATION BETTER SUITED TO YOUR DENIAL--AN UTTER ABSENCE OF FEAR.
THIS NEW TOXIN GIVES YOU AN EMPTINESS OF THE SOUL TO GO WITH YOUR EMPTY EYES.
NO LESS THAN YOU DESERVE.

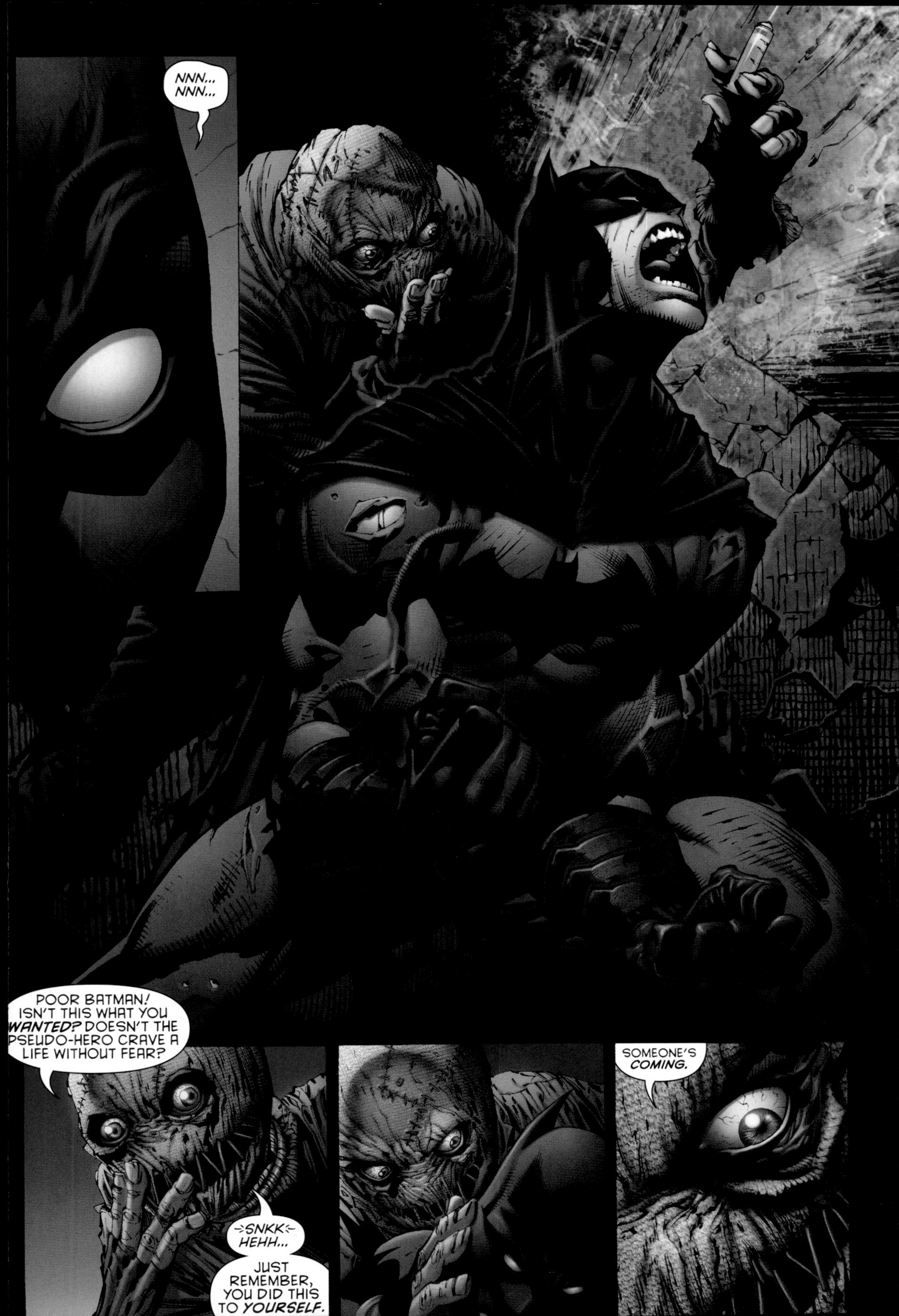
NNN... NNN...
POOR BATMAN! ISN'T THIS WHAT YOU WANTED? DOESN'T THE PSEUDO-HERO CRAVE A LIFE WITHOUT FEAR?
SNKK HEHH...
JUST REMEMBER, YOU DID THIS TO YOURSELF.
SOMEONE'S COMING.

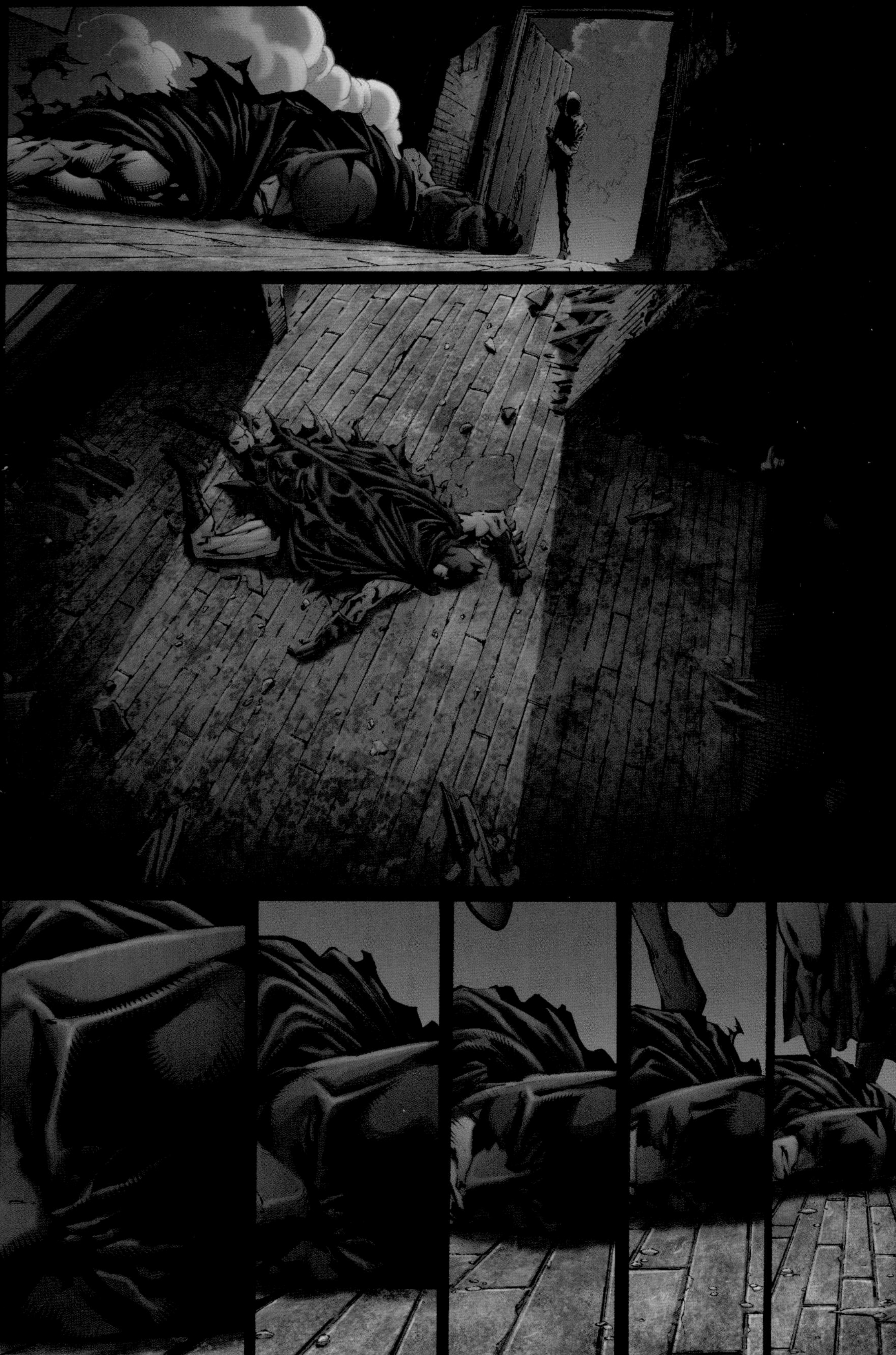

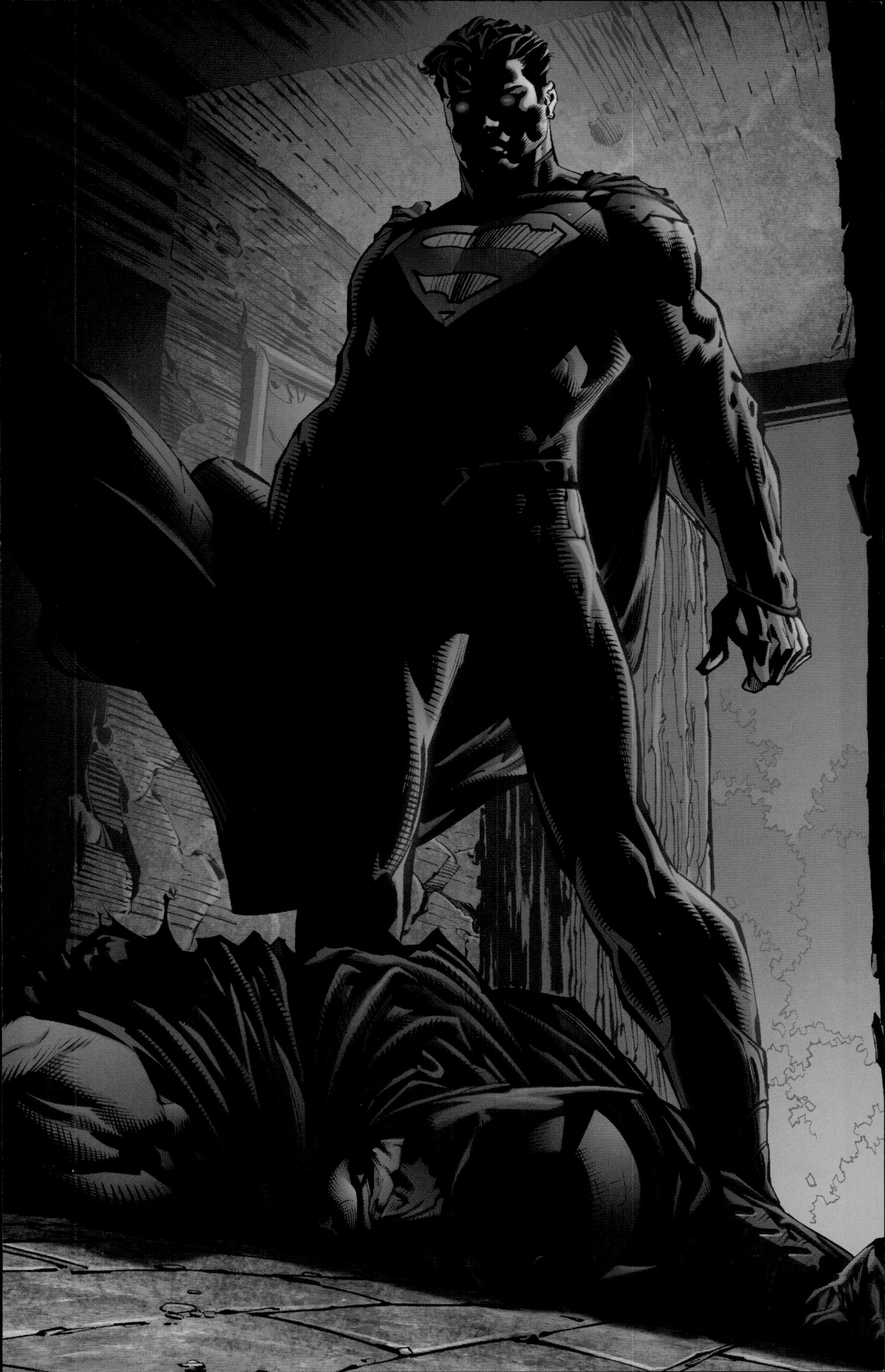

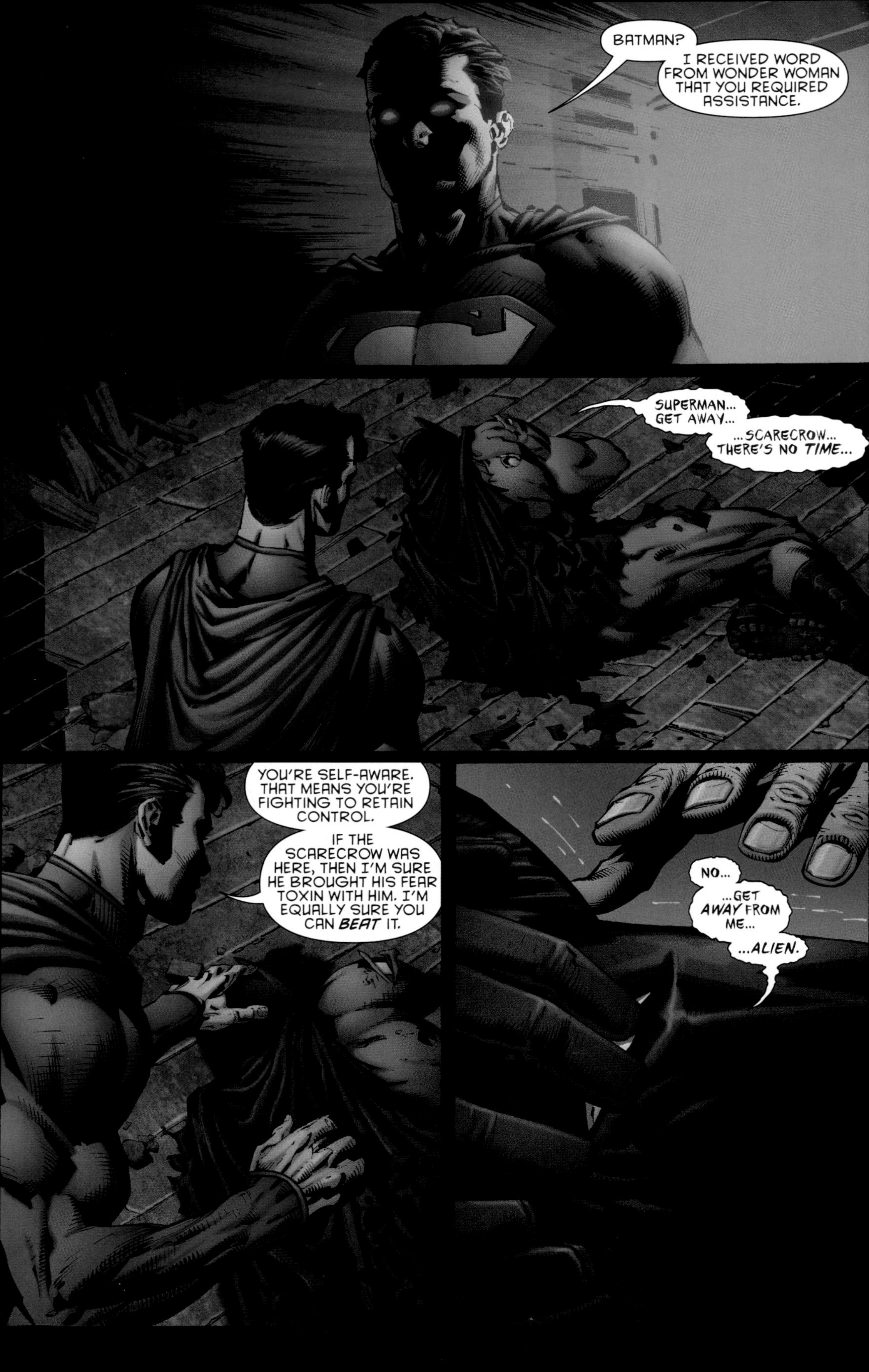
BATMAN?
I RECEIVED WORD FROM WONDER WOMAN THAT YOU REQUIRED ASSISTANCE.
SUPERMAN... GET AWAY...
...SCARECROW... THERE'S NO TIME...
YOU'RE SELF-AWARE. THAT MEANS YOU'RE FIGHTING TO RETAIN CONTROL.
IF THE SCARECROW WAS HERE, THEN I'M SURE HE BROUGHT HIS FEAR TOXIN WITH HIM. I'M EQUALLY SURE YOU CAN BEAT IT.
NO...
...GET AWAY FROM ME...
...ALIEN.

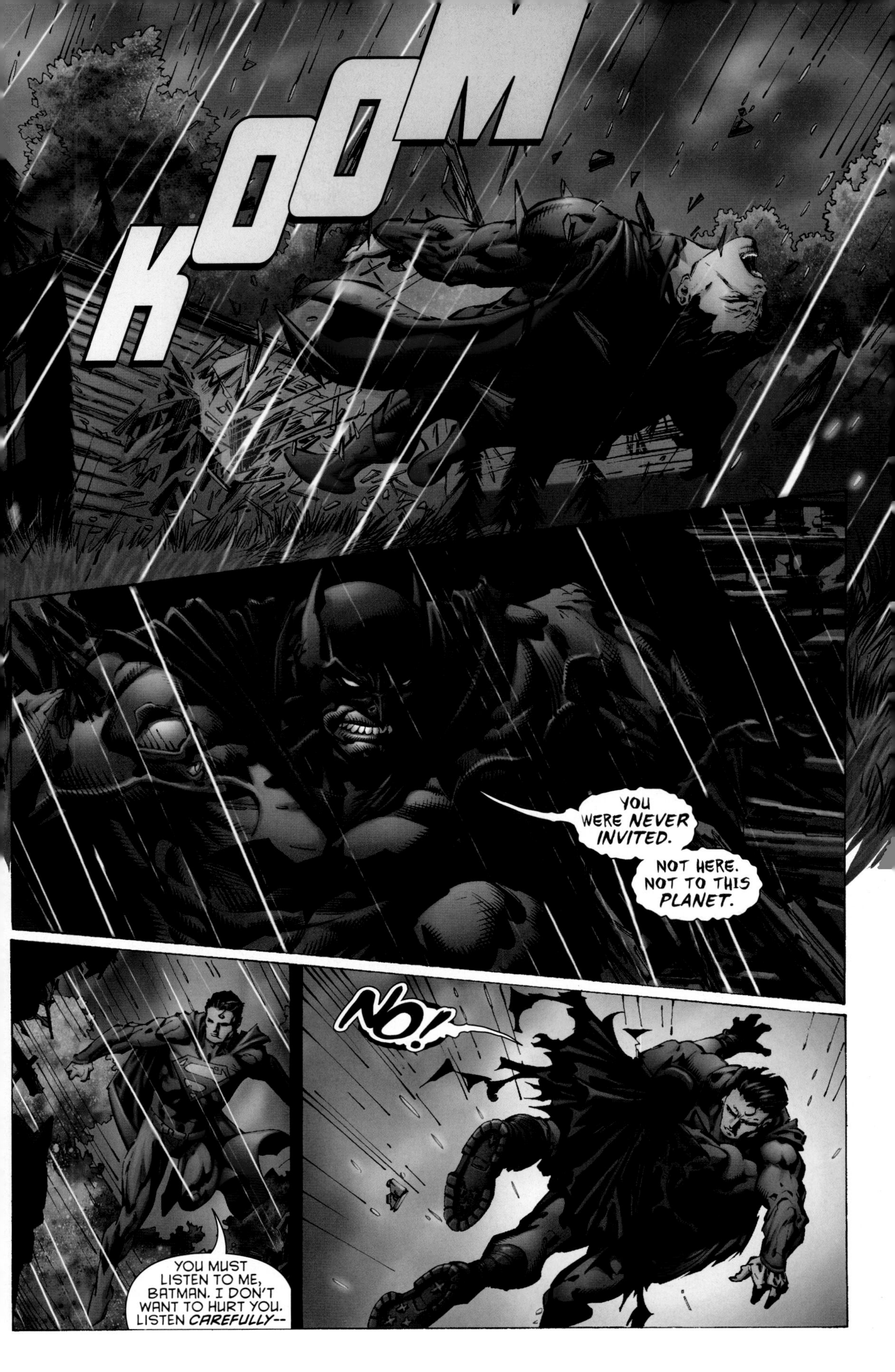
KOOOM
YOU WERE NEVER INVITED.
NOT HERE. NOT TO THIS PLANET.
YOU MUST LISTEN TO ME, BATMAN. I DON'T WANT TO HURT YOU. LISTEN CAREFULLY--
NO!

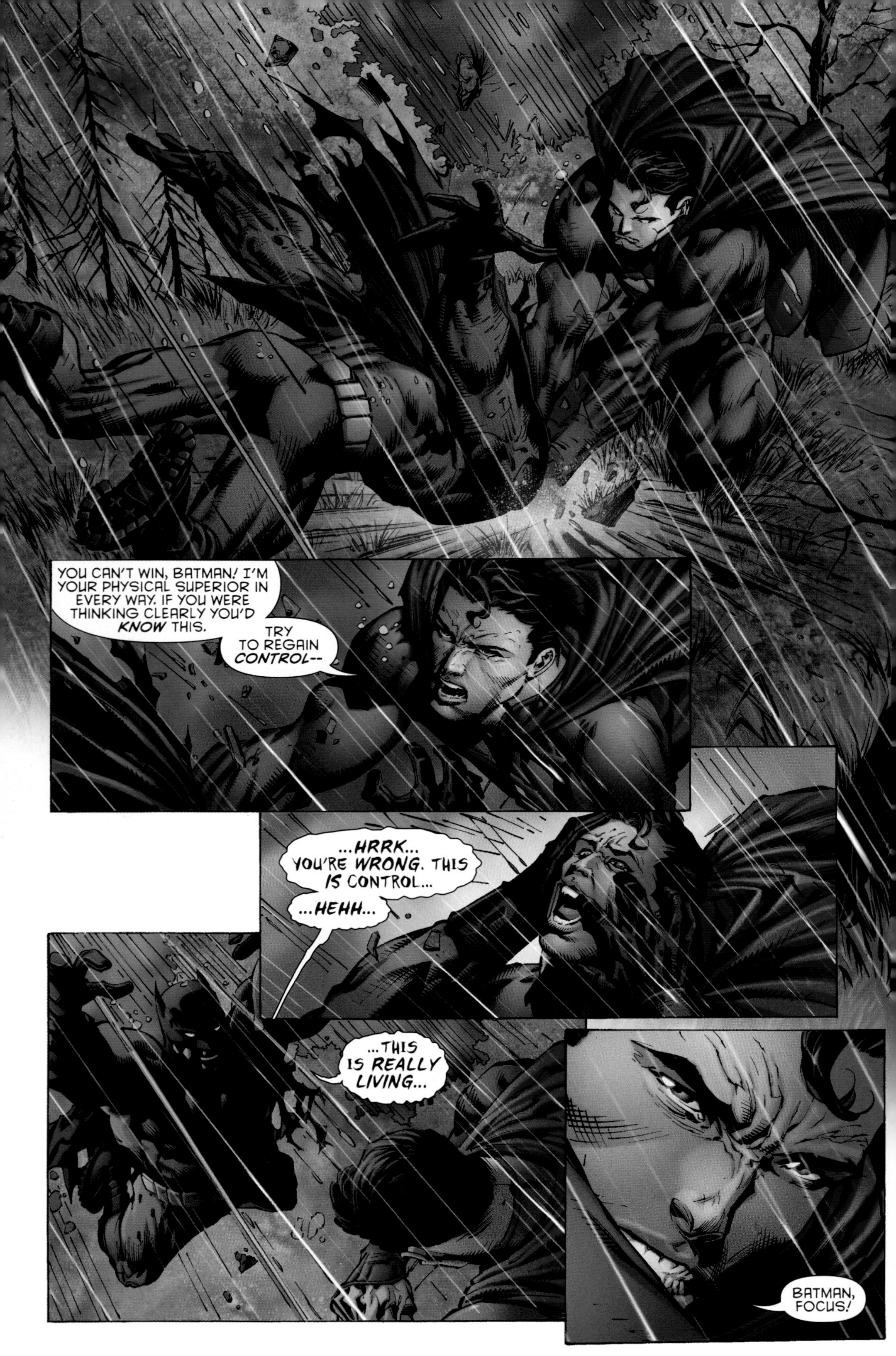
YOU CAN'T WIN, BATMAN! I'M YOUR PHYSICAL SUPERIOR IN EVERY WAY. IF YOU WERE THINKING CLEARLY YOU'D KNOW THIS.
TRY TO REGAIN CONTROL--
...HRRK... YOU'RE WRONG. THIS IS CONTROL...
...HEHH...
...THIS IS REALLY LIVING...
BATMAN, FOCUS!

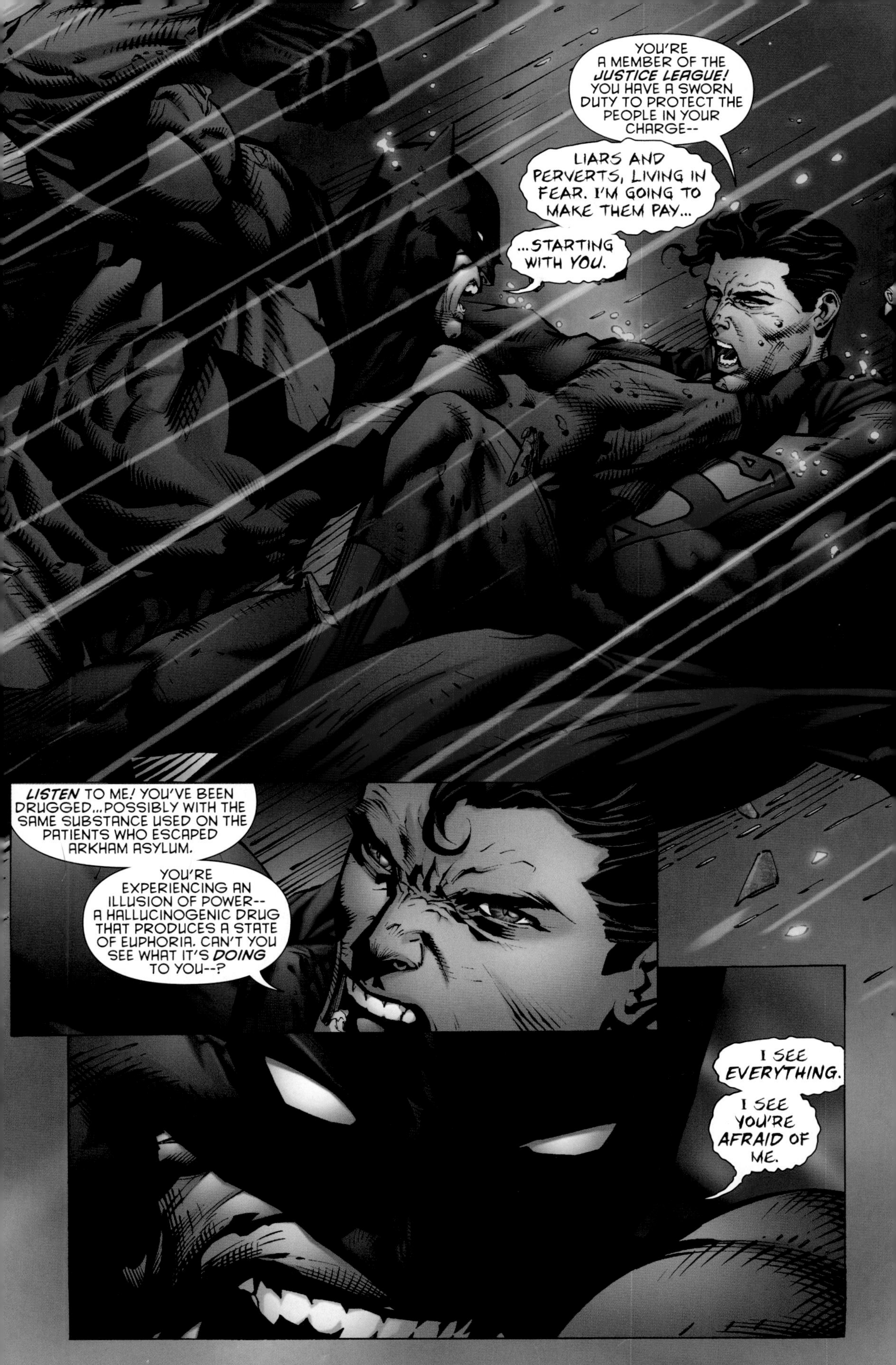
YOU'RE A MEMBER OF THE JUSTICE LEAGUE! YOU HAVE A SWORN DUTY TO PROTECT THE PEOPLE IN YOUR CHARGE--
LIARS AND PERVERTS, LIVING IN FEAR. I'M GOING TO MAKE THEM PAY...
...STARTING WITH YOU.
LISTEN TO ME! YOU'VE BEEN DRUGGED...POSSIBLY WITH THE SAME SUBSTANCE USED ON THE PATIENTS WHO ESCAPED ARKHAM ASYLUM.
YOU'RE EXPERIENCING AN ILLUSION OF POWER-- A HALLUCINOGENIC DRUG THAT PRODUCES A STATE OF EUPHORIA. CAN'T YOU SEE WHAT IT'S DOING TO YOU--?
I SEE EVERYTHING.
I SEE YOU'RE AFRAID OF ME.

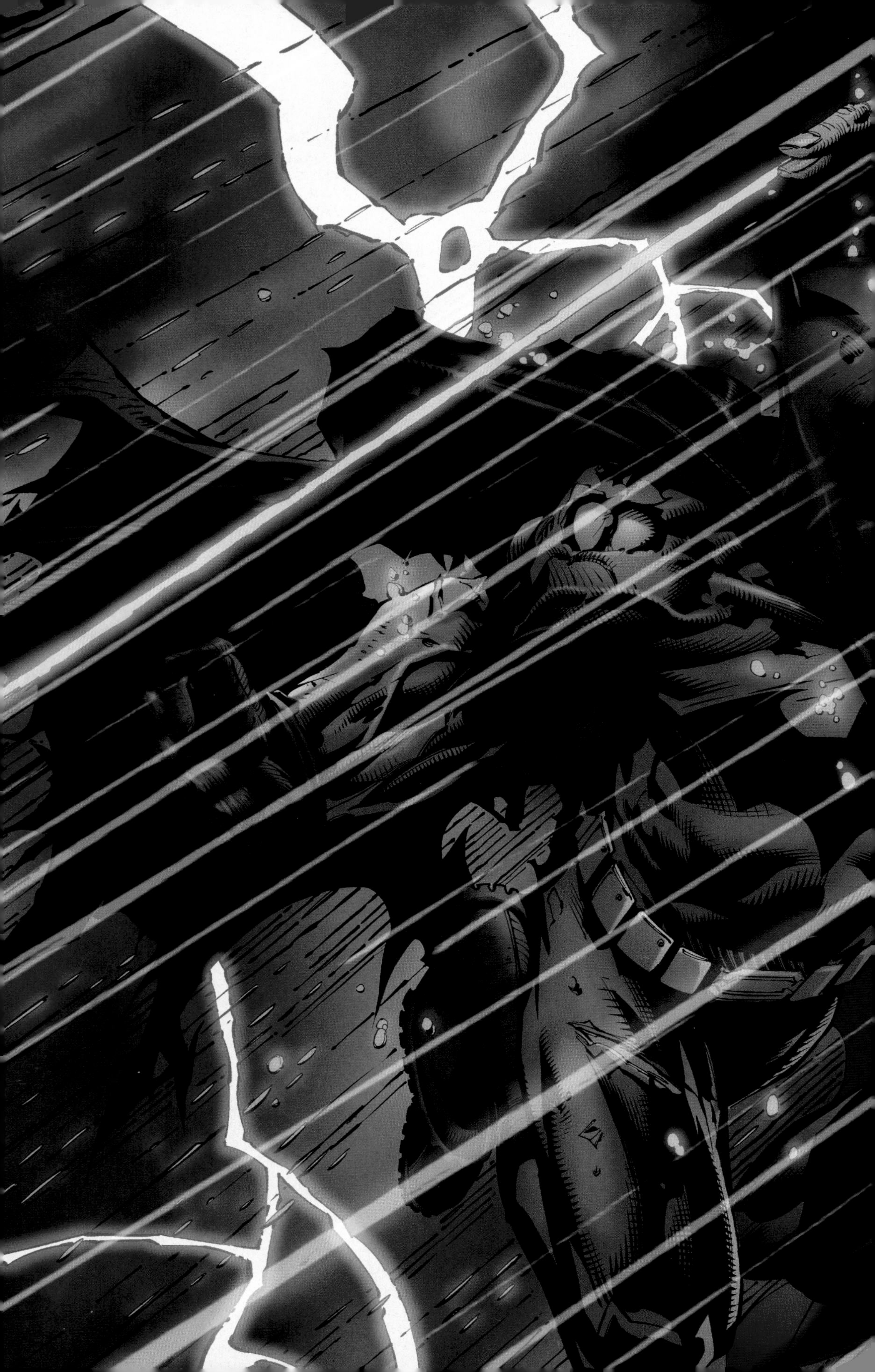

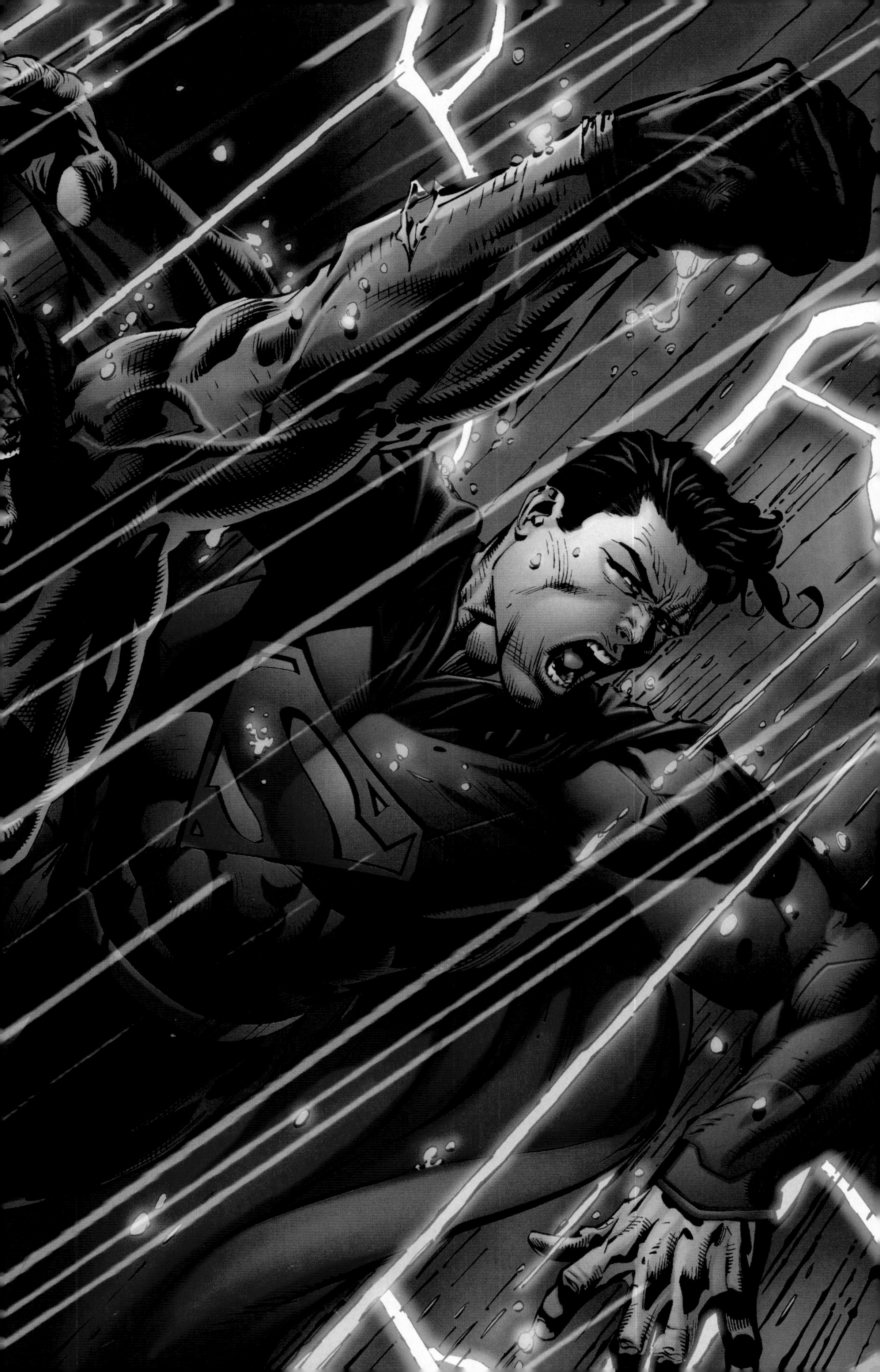

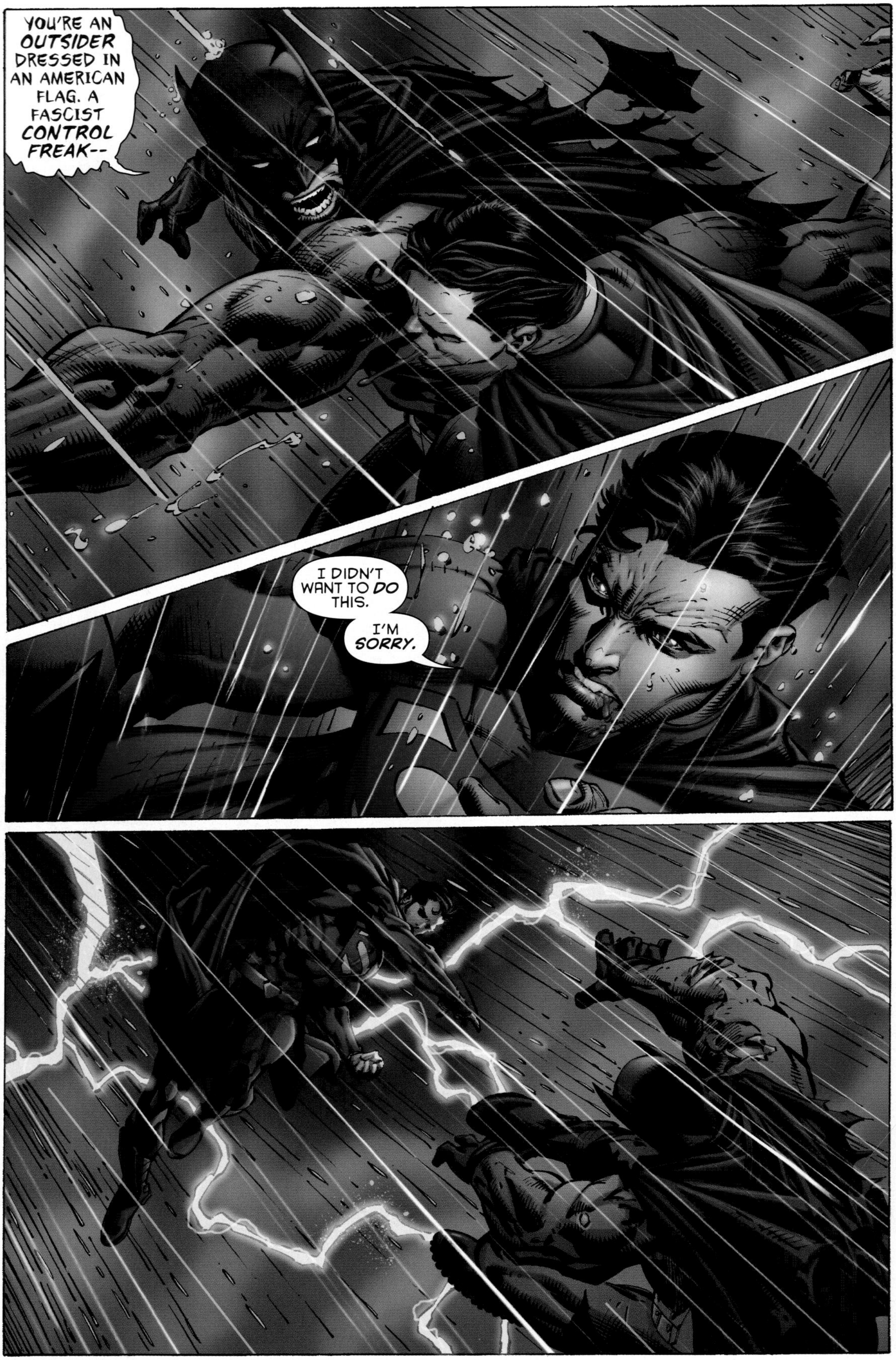
YOU'RE AN OUTSIDER DRESSED IN AN AMERICAN FLAG. A FASCIST CONTROL FREAK--
I DIDN'T WANT TO DO THIS.
I'M SORRY.

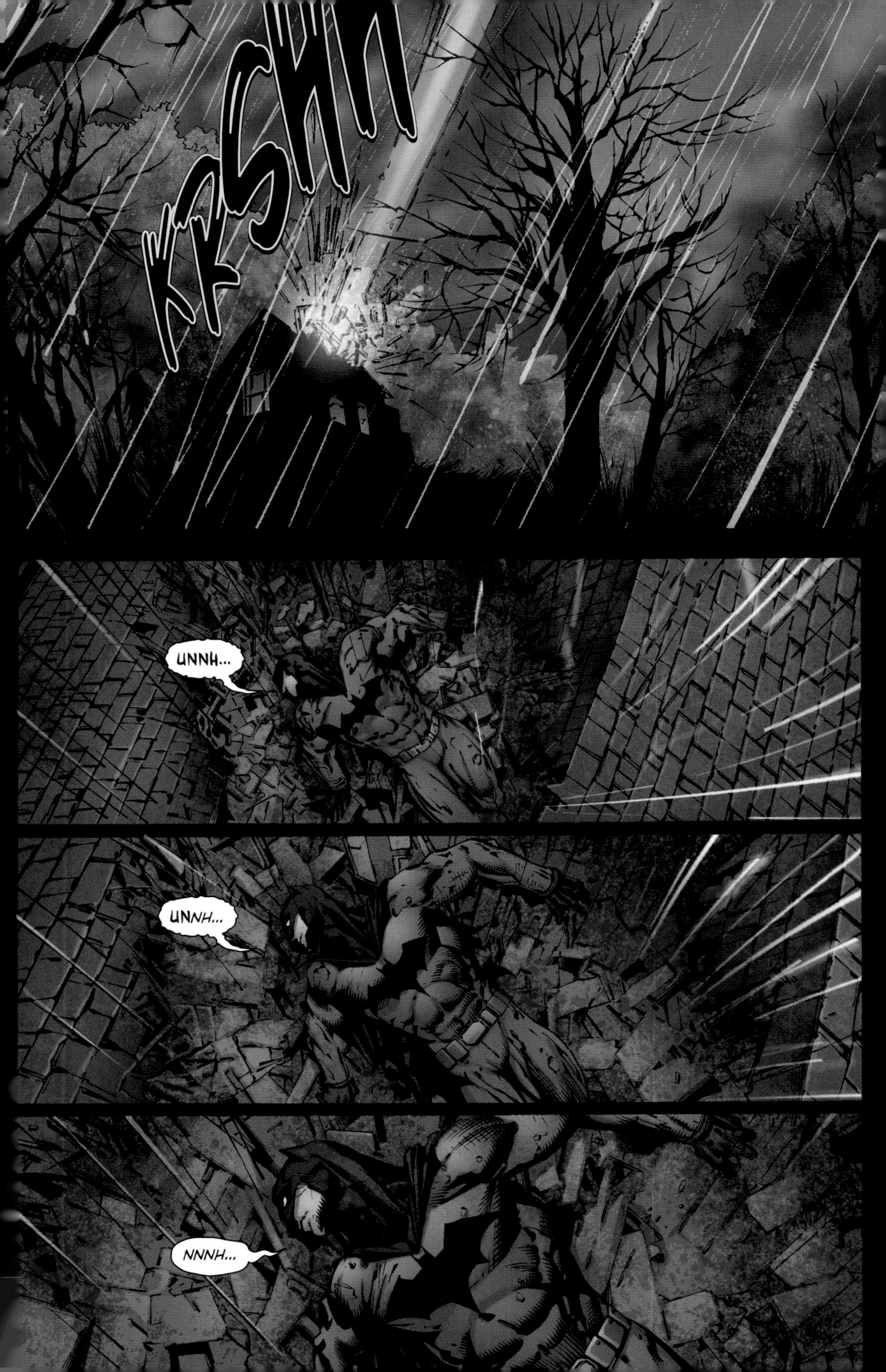
KRSHH
UNNH...
UNNH...
NNNH...

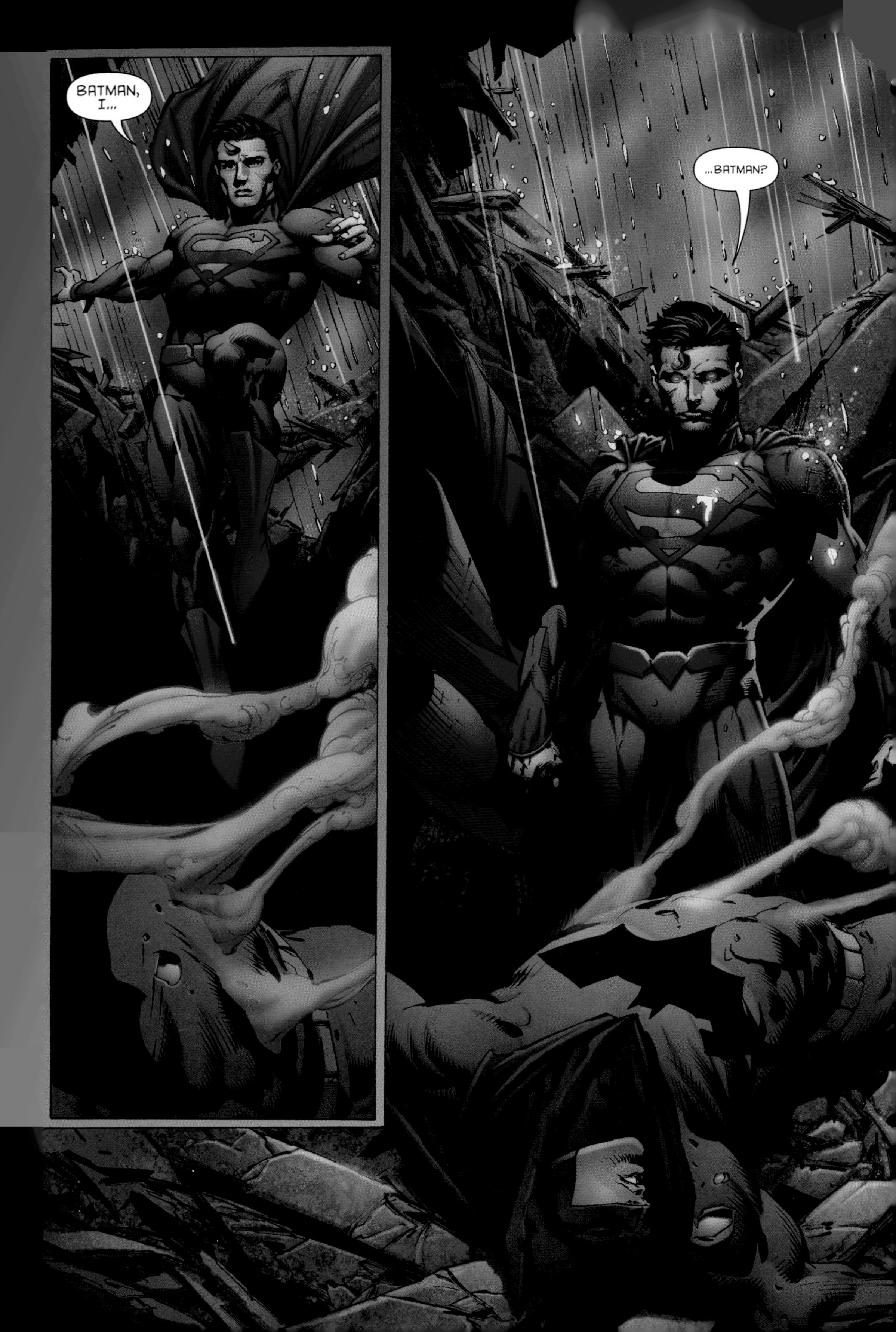
BATMAN, I...
...BATMAN?

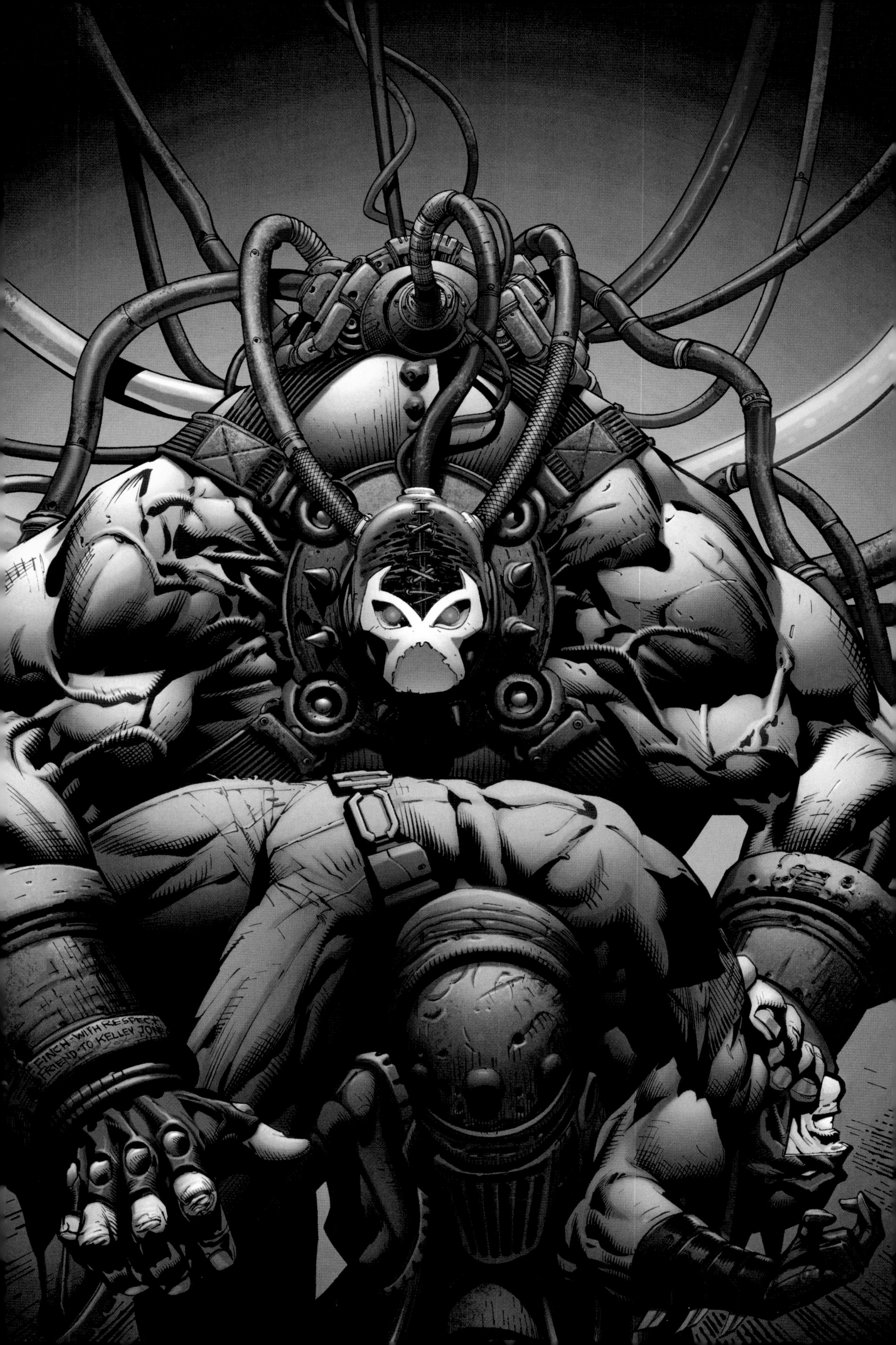
FINCH · WITH
FRIEND · TO KELLEY

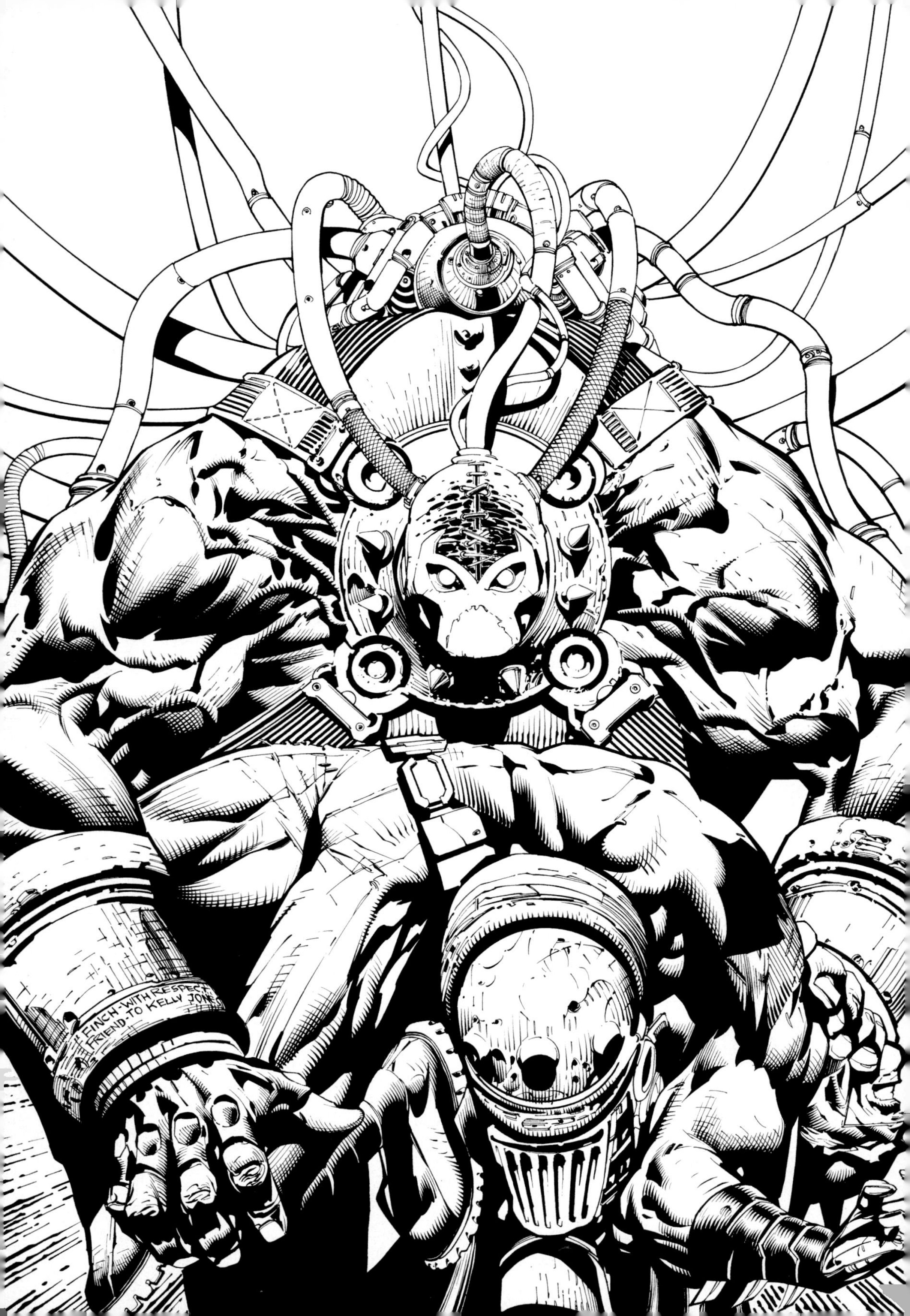
FINCH - WITH RESPECT
FRIEND - TO KELLY JONES

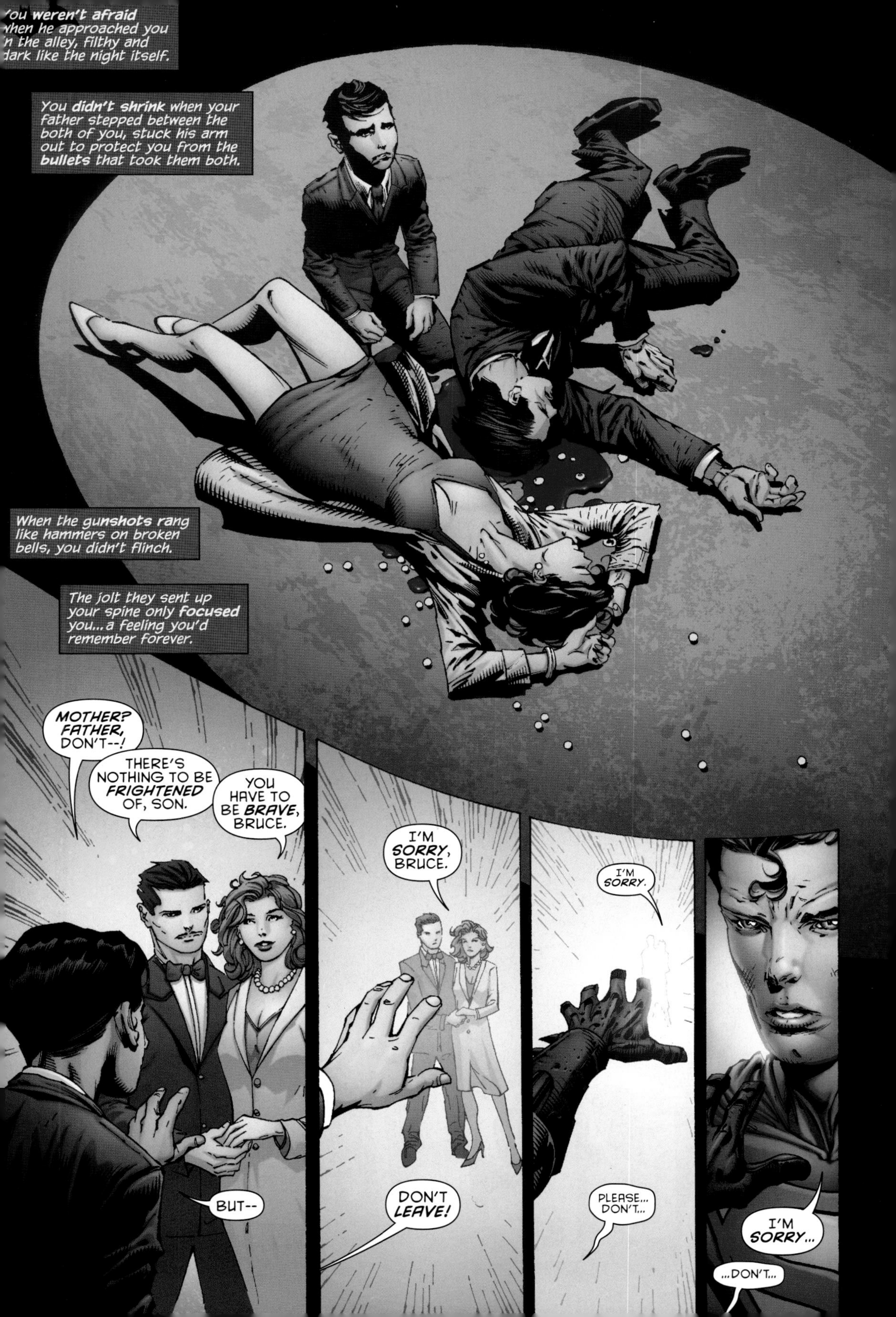
You weren't afraid when he approached you in the alley, filthy and dark like the night itself.
You didn't shrink when your father stepped between the both of you, stuck his arm out to protect you from the bullets that took them both.
When the gunshots rang like hammers on broken bells, you didn't flinch.
The jolt they sent up your spine only focused you...a feeling you'd remember forever.
MOTHER? FATHER, DON'T--!
THERE'S NOTHING TO BE FRIGHTENED OF, SON.
YOU HAVE TO BE BRAVE, BRUCE.
BUT--
I'M SORRY, BRUCE.
DON'T LEAVE!
I'M SORRY.
PLEASE... DON'T...
I'M SORRY...
...DON'T...

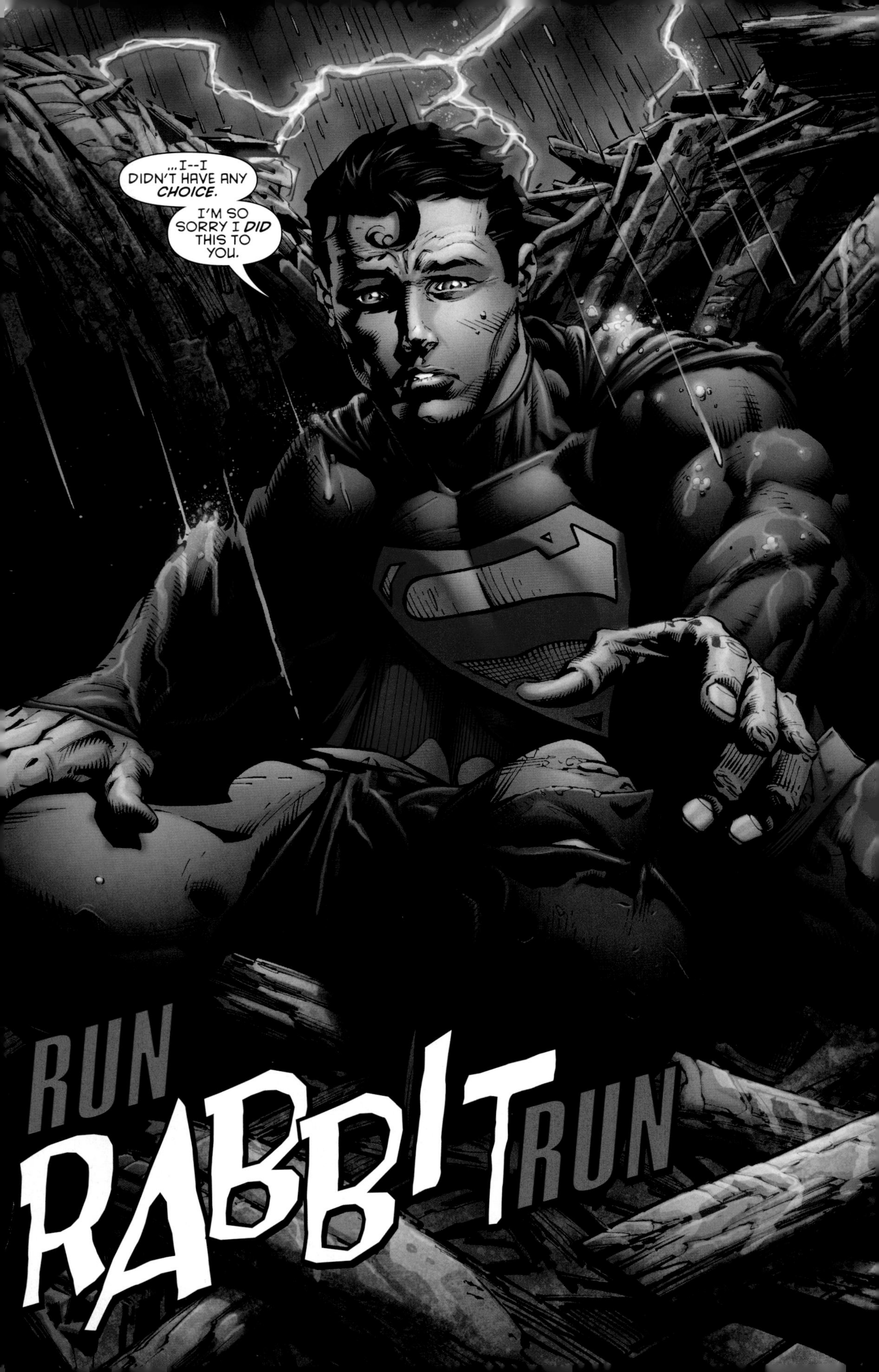
...I--I DIDN'T HAVE ANY CHOICE.
I'M SO SORRY I DID THIS TO YOU.
RUN RABBIT RUN

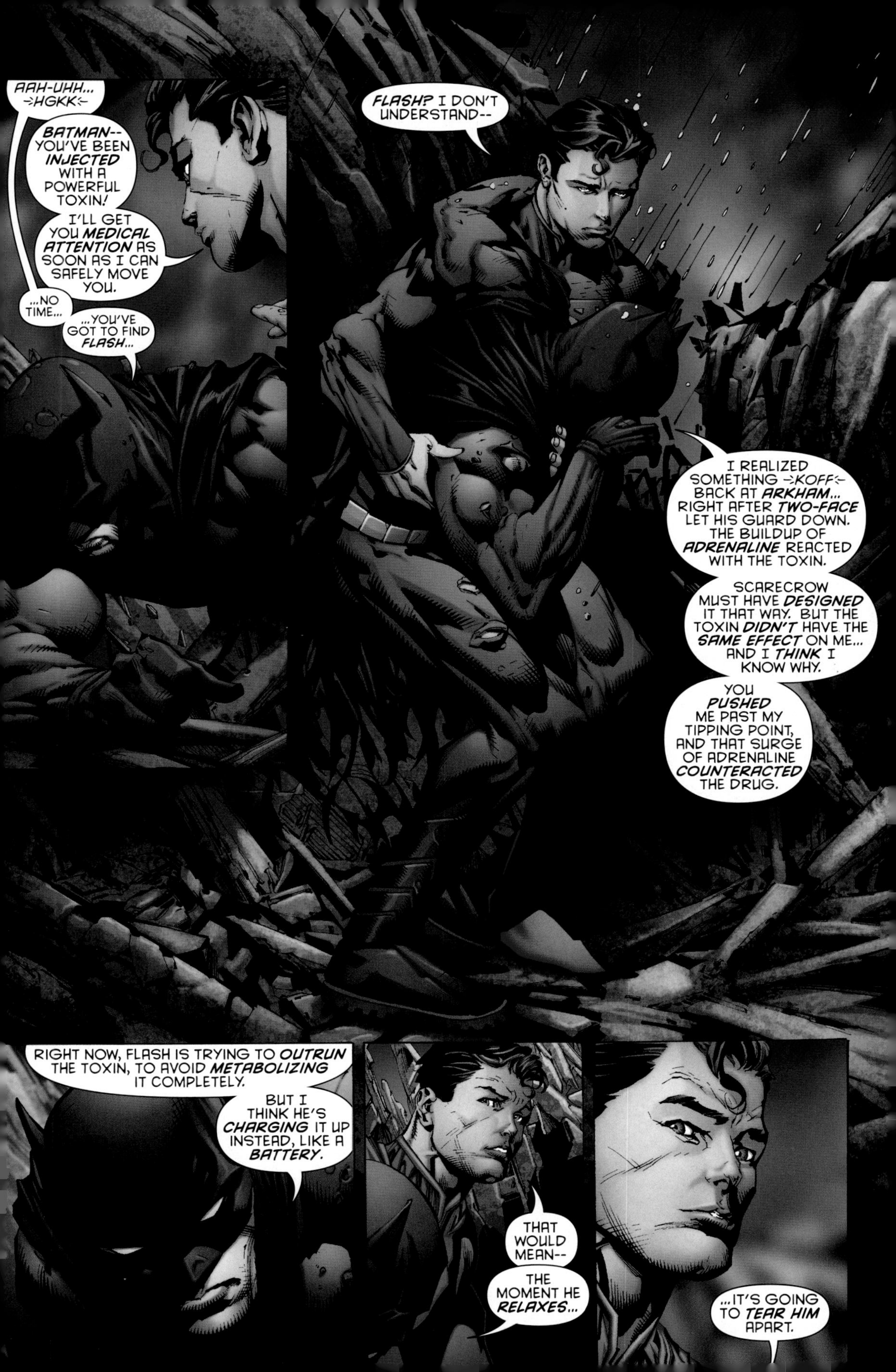
AAH-UHH... -HGKK-
BATMAN-- YOU'VE BEEN INJECTED WITH A POWERFUL TOXIN!
I'LL GET YOU MEDICAL ATTENTION AS SOON AS I CAN SAFELY MOVE YOU.
...NO TIME...
...YOU'VE GOT TO FIND FLASH...
FLASH? I DON'T UNDERSTAND--
I REALIZED SOMETHING -KOFF- BACK AT ARKHAM... RIGHT AFTER TWO-FACE LET HIS GUARD DOWN. THE BUILDUP OF ADRENALINE REACTED WITH THE TOXIN.
SCARECROW MUST HAVE DESIGNED IT THAT WAY. BUT THE TOXIN DIDN'T HAVE THE SAME EFFECT ON ME... AND I THINK I KNOW WHY.
YOU PUSHED ME PAST MY TIPPING POINT, AND THAT SURGE OF ADRENALINE COUNTERACTED THE DRUG.
RIGHT NOW, FLASH IS TRYING TO OUTRUN THE TOXIN, TO AVOID METABOLIZING IT COMPLETELY.
BUT I THINK HE'S CHARGING IT UP INSTEAD, LIKE A BATTERY.
THAT WOULD MEAN--
THE MOMENT HE RELAXES...
...IT'S GOING TO TEAR HIM APART.

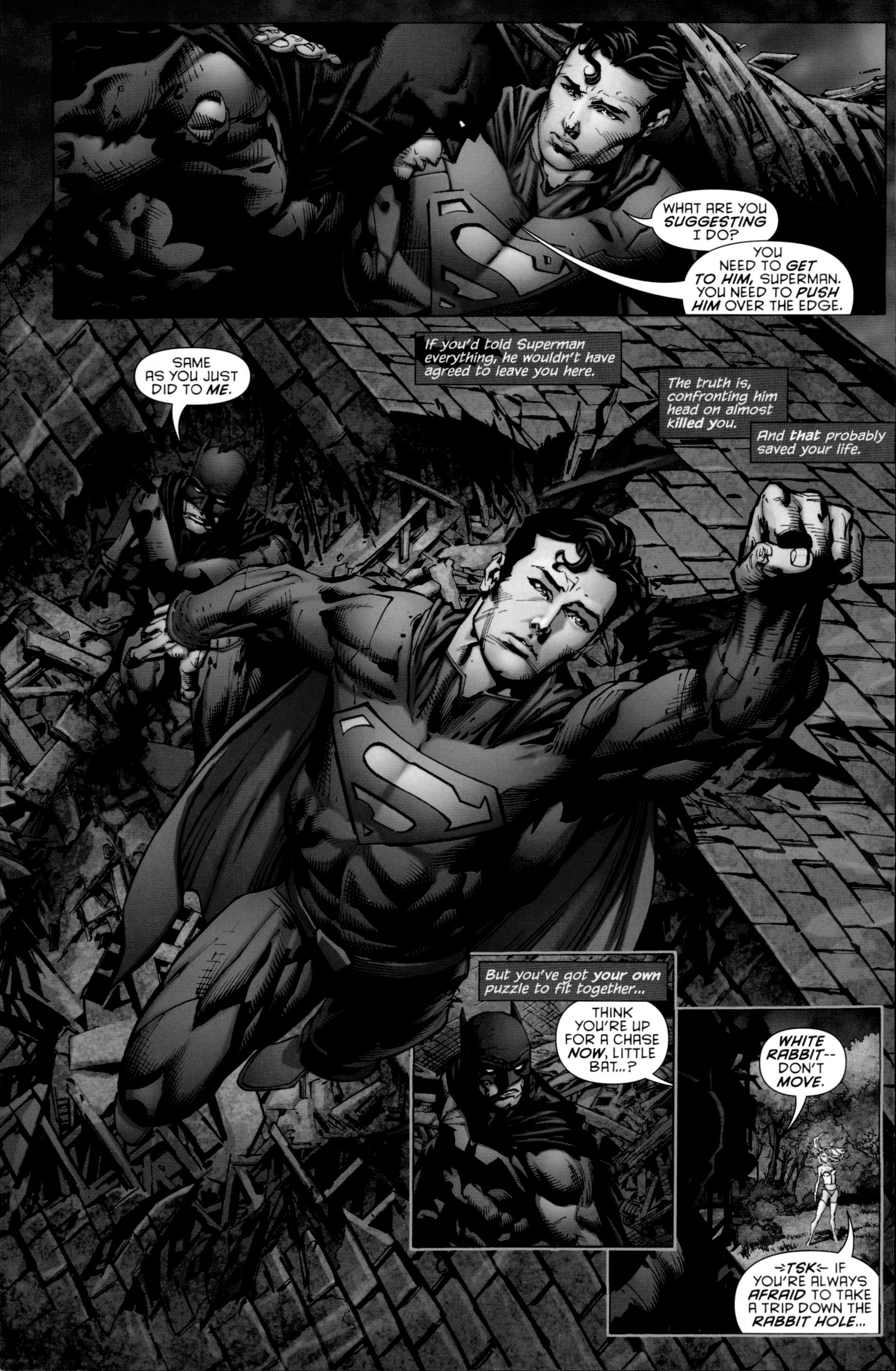
WHAT ARE YOU SUGGESTING I DO?
YOU NEED TO GET TO HIM, SUPERMAN. YOU NEED TO PUSH HIM OVER THE EDGE.
SAME AS YOU JUST DID TO ME.
If you'd told Superman everything, he wouldn't have agreed to leave you here.
The truth is, confronting him head on almost killed you.
And that probably saved your life.
But you've got your own puzzle to fit together...
THINK YOU'RE UP FOR A CHASE NOW, LITTLE BAT...?
WHITE RABBIT-- DON'T MOVE.
TSK IF YOU'RE ALWAYS AFRAID TO TAKE A TRIP DOWN THE RABBIT HOLE...

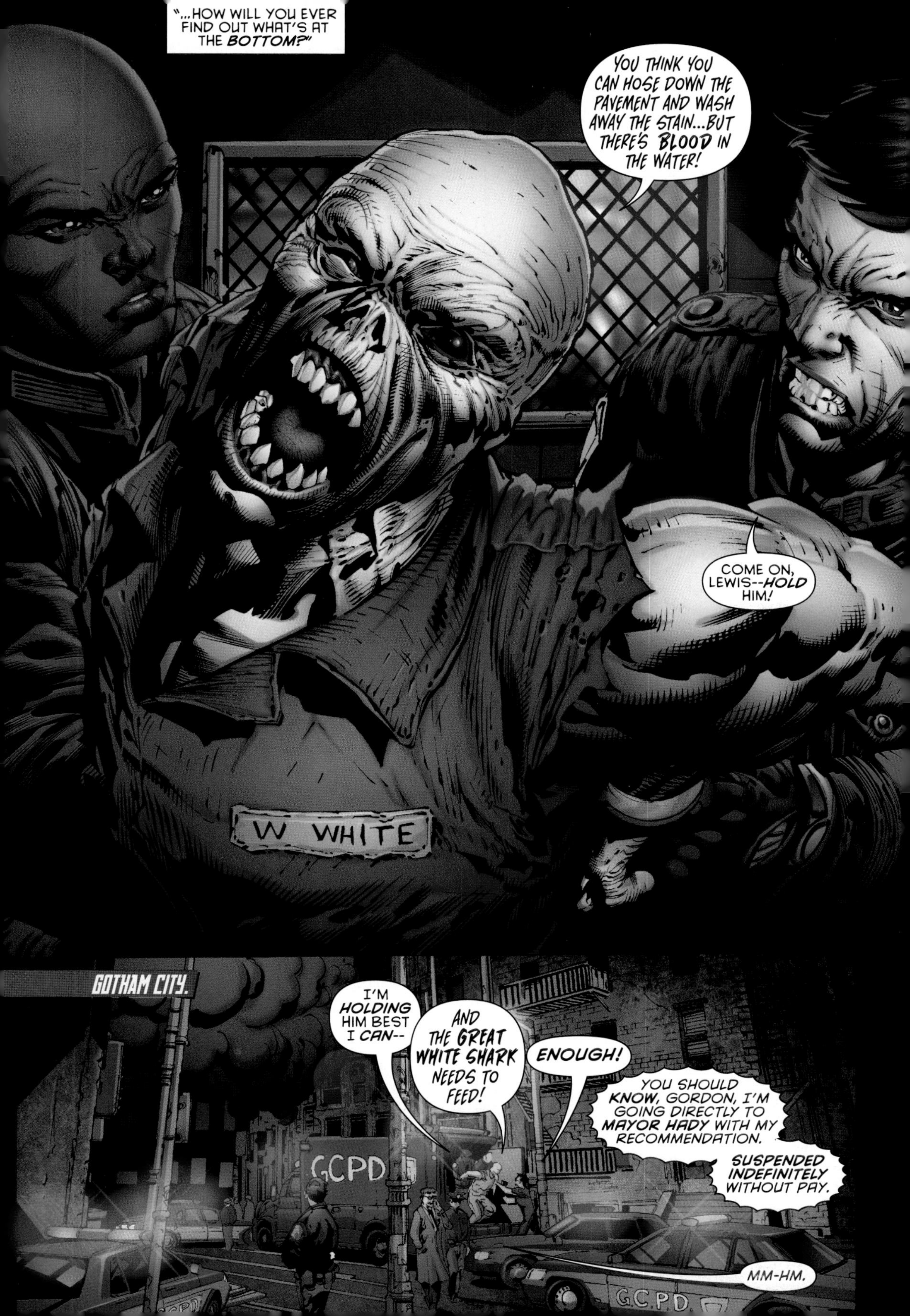
"...HOW WILL YOU EVER FIND OUT WHAT'S AT THE BOTTOM?"
YOU THINK YOU CAN HOSE DOWN THE PAVEMENT AND WASH AWAY THE STAIN...BUT THERE'S BLOOD IN THE WATER!
COME ON, LEWIS--HOLD HIM!
W WHITE
GOTHAM CITY.
I'M HOLDING HIM BEST I CAN--
AND THE GREAT WHITE SHARK NEEDS TO FEED!
ENOUGH!
YOU SHOULD KNOW, GORDON, I'M GOING DIRECTLY TO MAYOR HADY WITH MY RECOMMENDATION.
SUSPENDED INDEFINITELY WITHOUT PAY.
MM-HM.
GCPD
G.C.P.D.

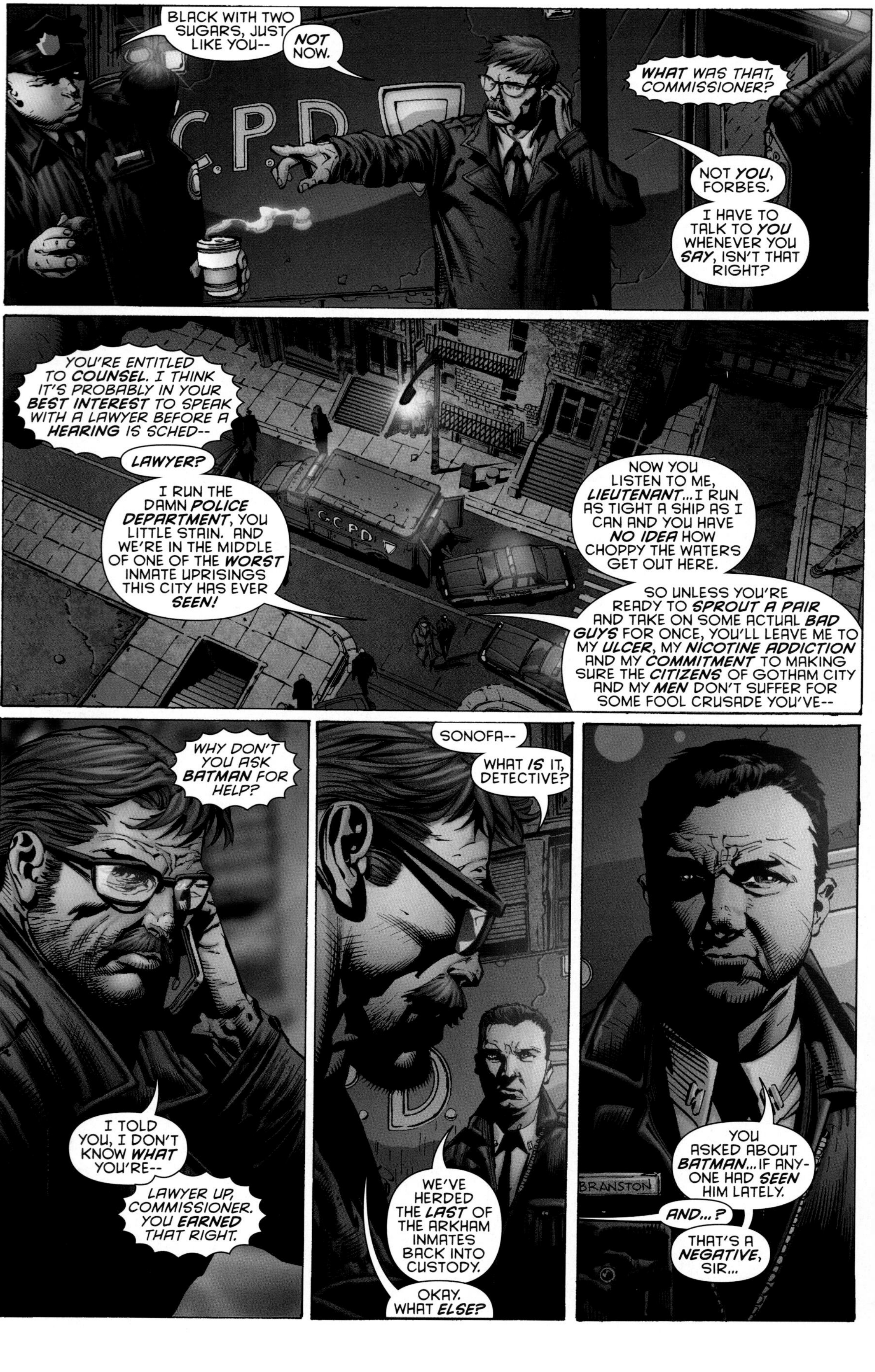
BLACK WITH TWO SUGARS, JUST LIKE YOU--
NOT NOW.
WHAT WAS THAT, COMMISSIONER?
NOT YOU, FORBES.
I HAVE TO TALK TO YOU WHENEVER YOU SAY, ISN'T THAT RIGHT?
YOU'RE ENTITLED TO COUNSEL. I THINK IT'S PROBABLY IN YOUR BEST INTEREST TO SPEAK WITH A LAWYER BEFORE A HEARING IS SCHED--
LAWYER?
I RUN THE DAMN POLICE DEPARTMENT, YOU LITTLE STAIN. AND WE'RE IN THE MIDDLE OF ONE OF THE WORST INMATE UPRISINGS THIS CITY HAS EVER SEEN!
NOW YOU LISTEN TO ME, LIEUTENANT... I RUN AS TIGHT A SHIP AS I CAN AND YOU HAVE NO IDEA HOW CHOPPY THE WATERS GET OUT HERE.
SO UNLESS YOU'RE READY TO SPROUT A PAIR AND TAKE ON SOME ACTUAL BAD GUYS FOR ONCE, YOU'LL LEAVE ME TO MY ULCER, MY NICOTINE ADDICTION AND MY COMMITMENT TO MAKING SURE THE CITIZENS OF GOTHAM CITY AND MY MEN DON'T SUFFER FOR SOME FOOL CRUSADE YOU'VE--
WHY DON'T YOU ASK BATMAN FOR HELP?
I TOLD YOU, I DON'T KNOW WHAT YOU'RE--
LAWYER UP, COMMISSIONER. YOU EARNED THAT RIGHT.
SONOFA--
WHAT IS IT, DETECTIVE?
WE'VE HERDED THE LAST OF THE ARKHAM INMATES BACK INTO CUSTODY.
OKAY. WHAT ELSE?
BRANSTON
YOU ASKED ABOUT BATMAN... IF ANYONE HAD SEEN HIM LATELY.
AND...?
THAT'S A NEGATIVE, SIR...

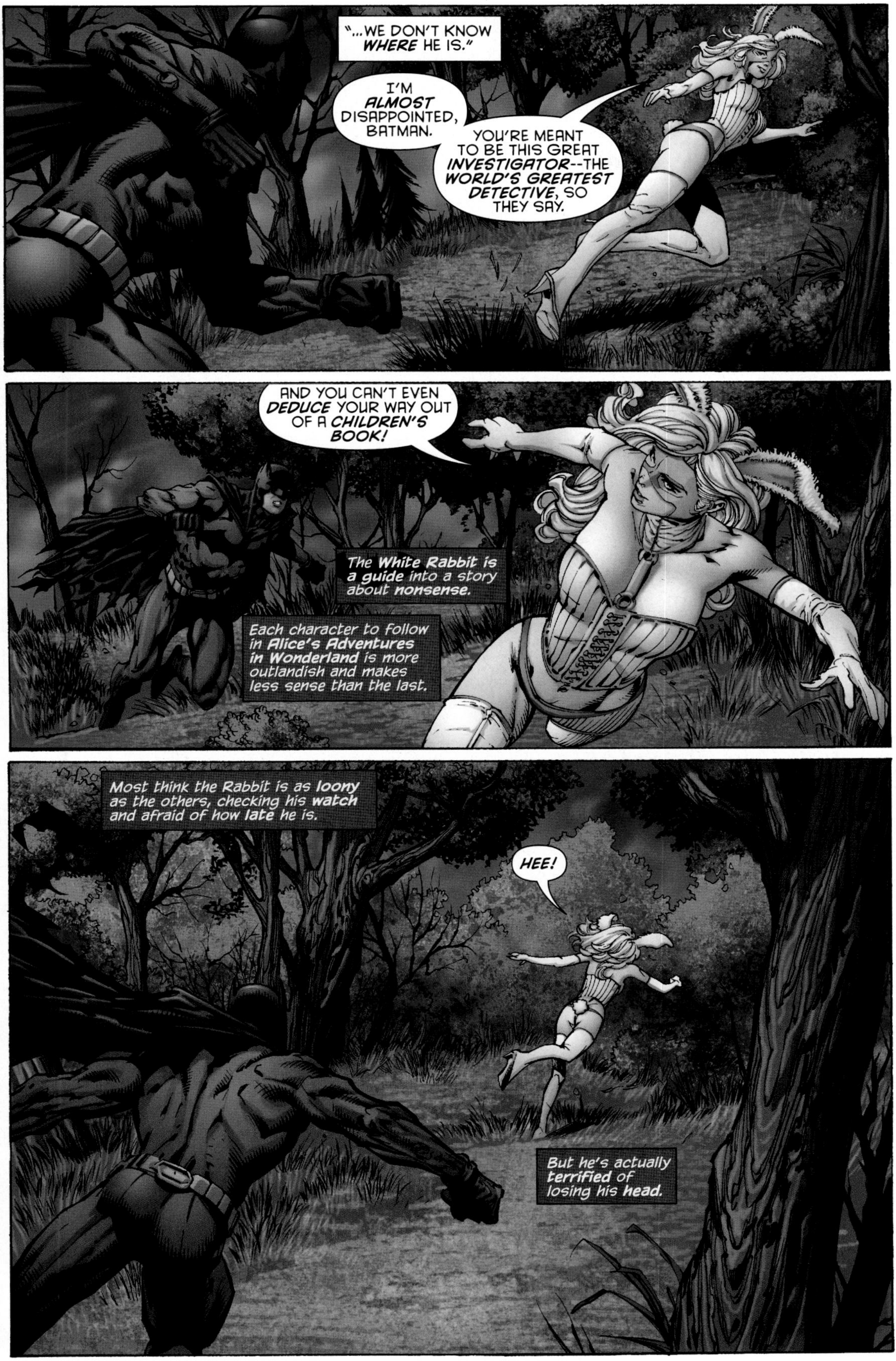
"...WE DON'T KNOW WHERE HE IS."
I'M ALMOST DISAPPOINTED, BATMAN.
YOU'RE MEANT TO BE THIS GREAT INVESTIGATOR--THE WORLD'S GREATEST DETECTIVE, SO THEY SAY.
AND YOU CAN'T EVEN DEDUCE YOUR WAY OUT OF A CHILDREN'S BOOK!
The White Rabbit is a guide into a story about nonsense.
Each character to follow in Alice's Adventures in Wonderland is more outlandish and makes less sense than the last.
Most think the Rabbit is as loony as the others, checking his watch and afraid of how late he is.
HEE!
But he's actually terrified of losing his head.

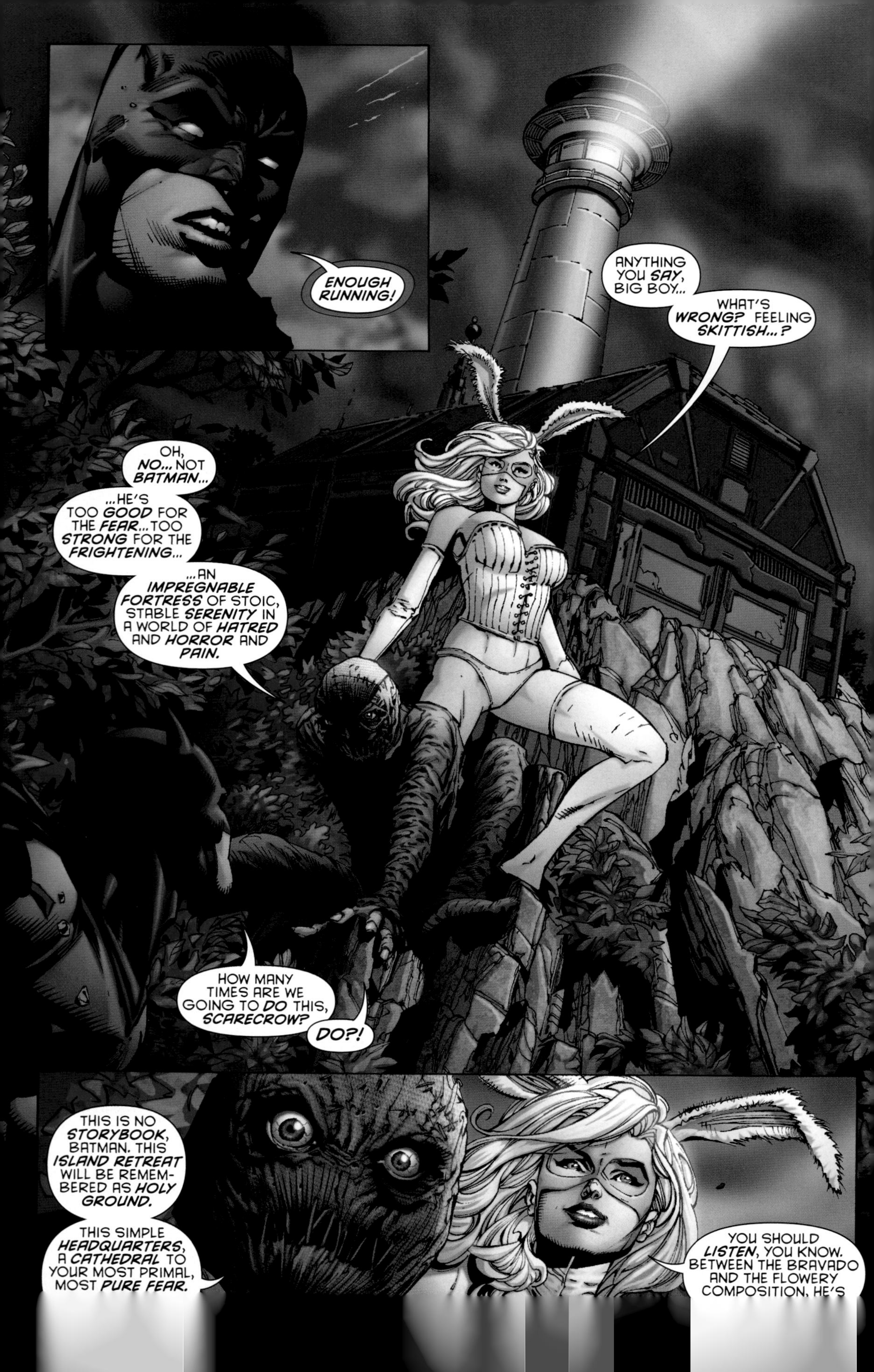
ENOUGH RUNNING!
ANYTHING YOU SAY, BIG BOY...
WHAT'S WRONG? FEELING SKITTISH...?
OH, NO... NOT BATMAN...
...HE'S TOO GOOD FOR THE FEAR...TOO STRONG FOR THE FRIGHTENING...
...AN IMPREGNABLE FORTRESS OF STOIC, STABLE SERENITY IN A WORLD OF HATRED AND HORROR AND PAIN.
HOW MANY TIMES ARE WE GOING TO DO THIS, SCARECROW?
DO?!
THIS IS NO STORYBOOK, BATMAN. THIS ISLAND RETREAT WILL BE REMEMBERED AS HOLY GROUND.
THIS SIMPLE HEADQUARTERS, A CATHEDRAL TO YOUR MOST PRIMAL, MOST PURE FEAR.
YOU SHOULD LISTEN, YOU KNOW. BETWEEN THE BRAVADO AND THE FLOWERY COMPOSITION, HE'S

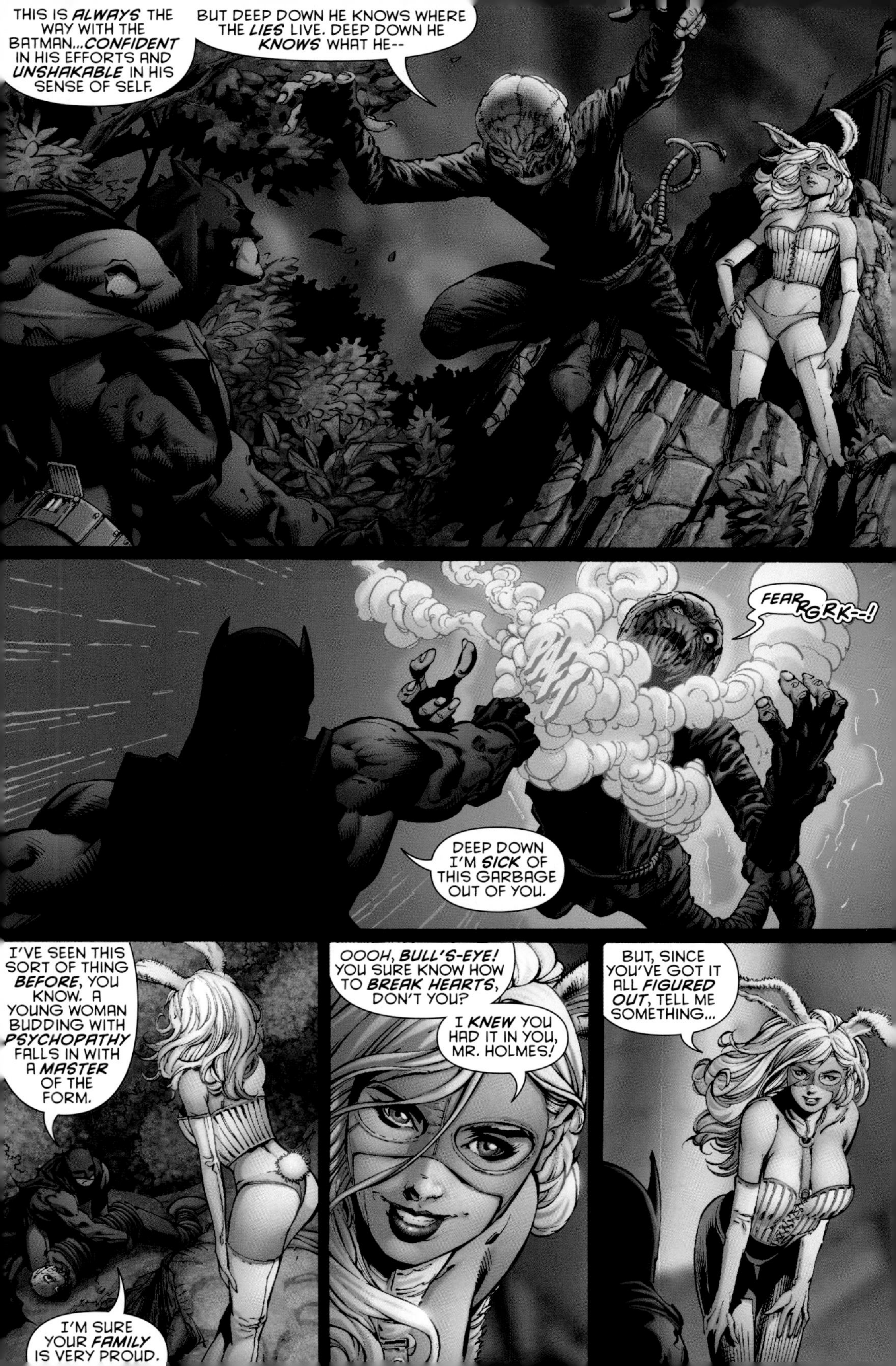

THIS IS ALWAYS THE WAY WITH THE BATMAN...CONFIDENT IN HIS EFFORTS AND UNSHAKABLE IN HIS SENSE OF SELF.
BUT DEEP DOWN HE KNOWS WHERE THE LIES LIVE. DEEP DOWN HE KNOWS WHAT HE--
FEARRGRK--!
DEEP DOWN I'M SICK OF THIS GARBAGE OUT OF YOU.
I'VE SEEN THIS SORT OF THING BEFORE, YOU KNOW. A YOUNG WOMAN BUDDING WITH PSYCHOPATHY FALLS IN WITH A MASTER OF THE FORM.
I'M SURE YOUR FAMILY IS VERY PROUD.
OOOH, BULL'S-EYE! YOU SURE KNOW HOW TO BREAK HEARTS, DON'T YOU?
I KNEW YOU HAD IT IN YOU, MR. HOLMES!
BUT, SINCE YOU'VE GOT IT ALL FIGURED OUT, TELL ME SOMETHING...

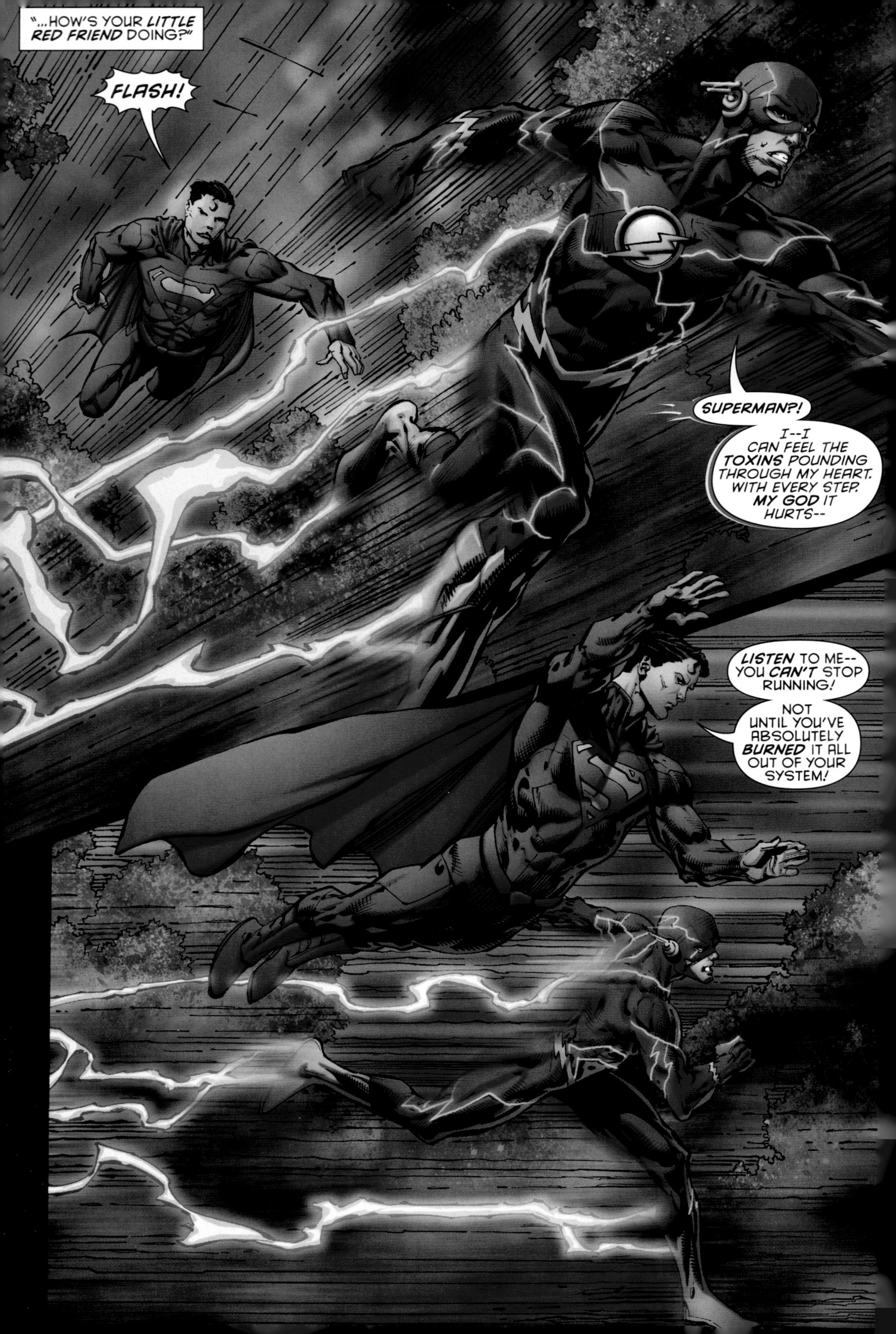
"...HOW'S YOUR LITTLE RED FRIEND DOING?"
FLASH!
SUPERMAN?!
I--I CAN FEEL THE TOXINS POUNDING THROUGH MY HEART. WITH EVERY STEP. MY GOD IT HURTS--
LISTEN TO ME-- YOU CAN'T STOP RUNNING!
NOT UNTIL YOU'VE ABSOLUTELY BURNED IT ALL OUT OF YOUR SYSTEM!

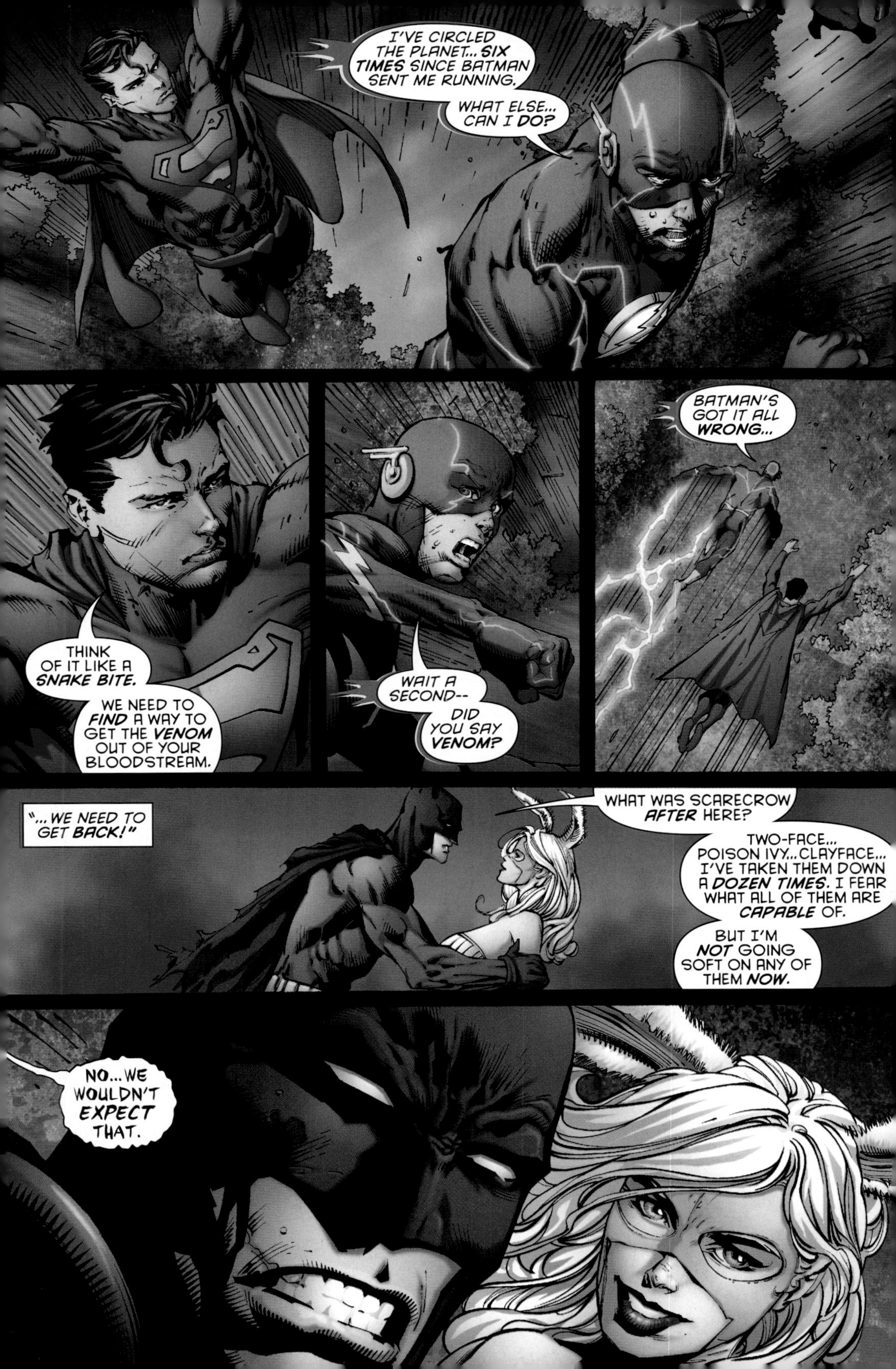
I'VE CIRCLED THE PLANET... SIX TIMES SINCE BATMAN SENT ME RUNNING.
WHAT ELSE... CAN I DO?
THINK OF IT LIKE A SNAKE BITE.
WE NEED TO FIND A WAY TO GET THE VENOM OUT OF YOUR BLOODSTREAM.
WAIT A SECOND--
DID YOU SAY VENOM?
BATMAN'S GOT IT ALL WRONG...
"...WE NEED TO GET BACK!"
WHAT WAS SCARECROW AFTER HERE?
TWO-FACE... POISON IVY...CLAYFACE... I'VE TAKEN THEM DOWN A DOZEN TIMES. I FEAR WHAT ALL OF THEM ARE CAPABLE OF.
BUT I'M NOT GOING SOFT ON ANY OF THEM NOW.
NO...WE WOULDN'T EXPECT THAT.

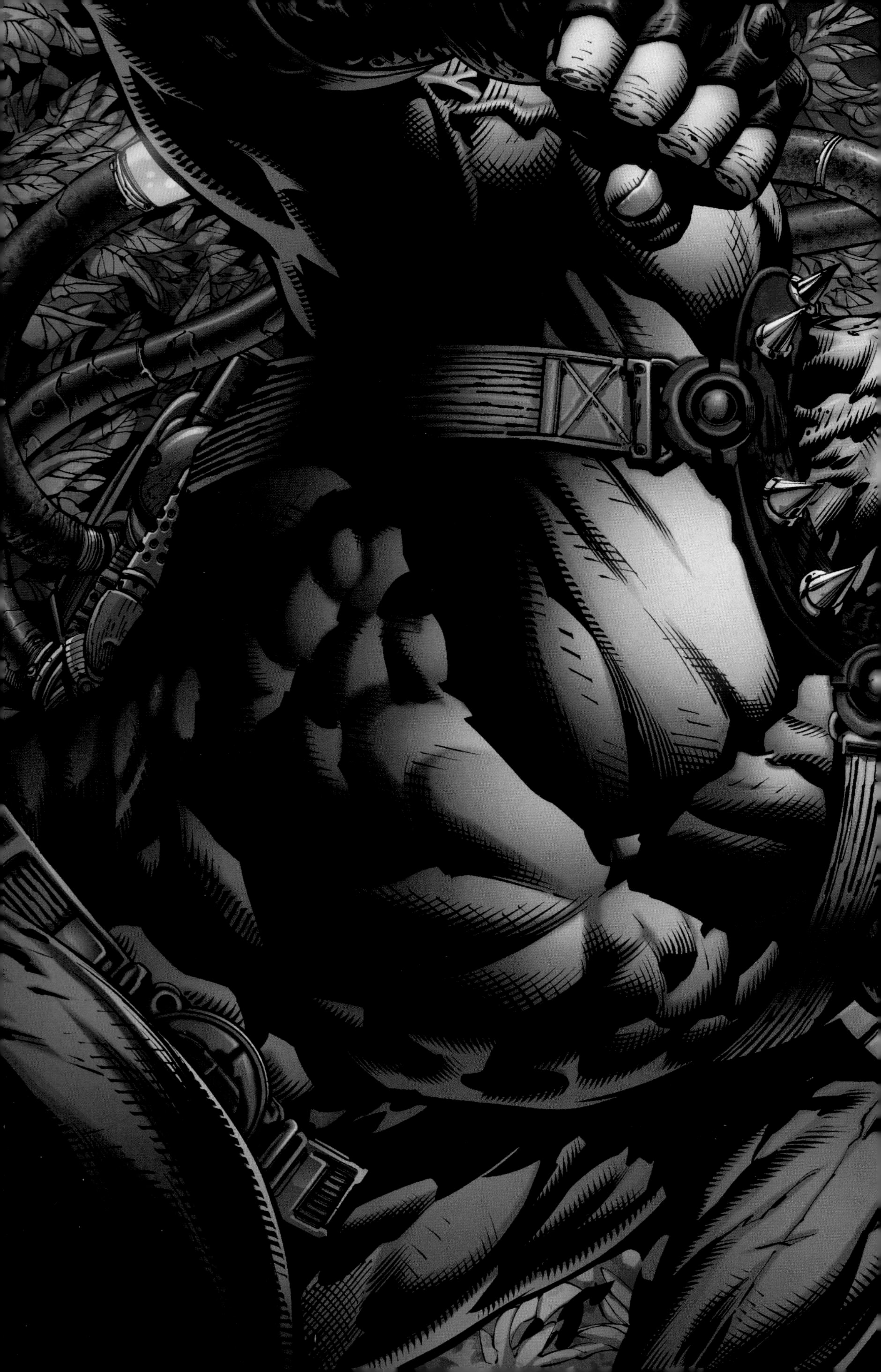

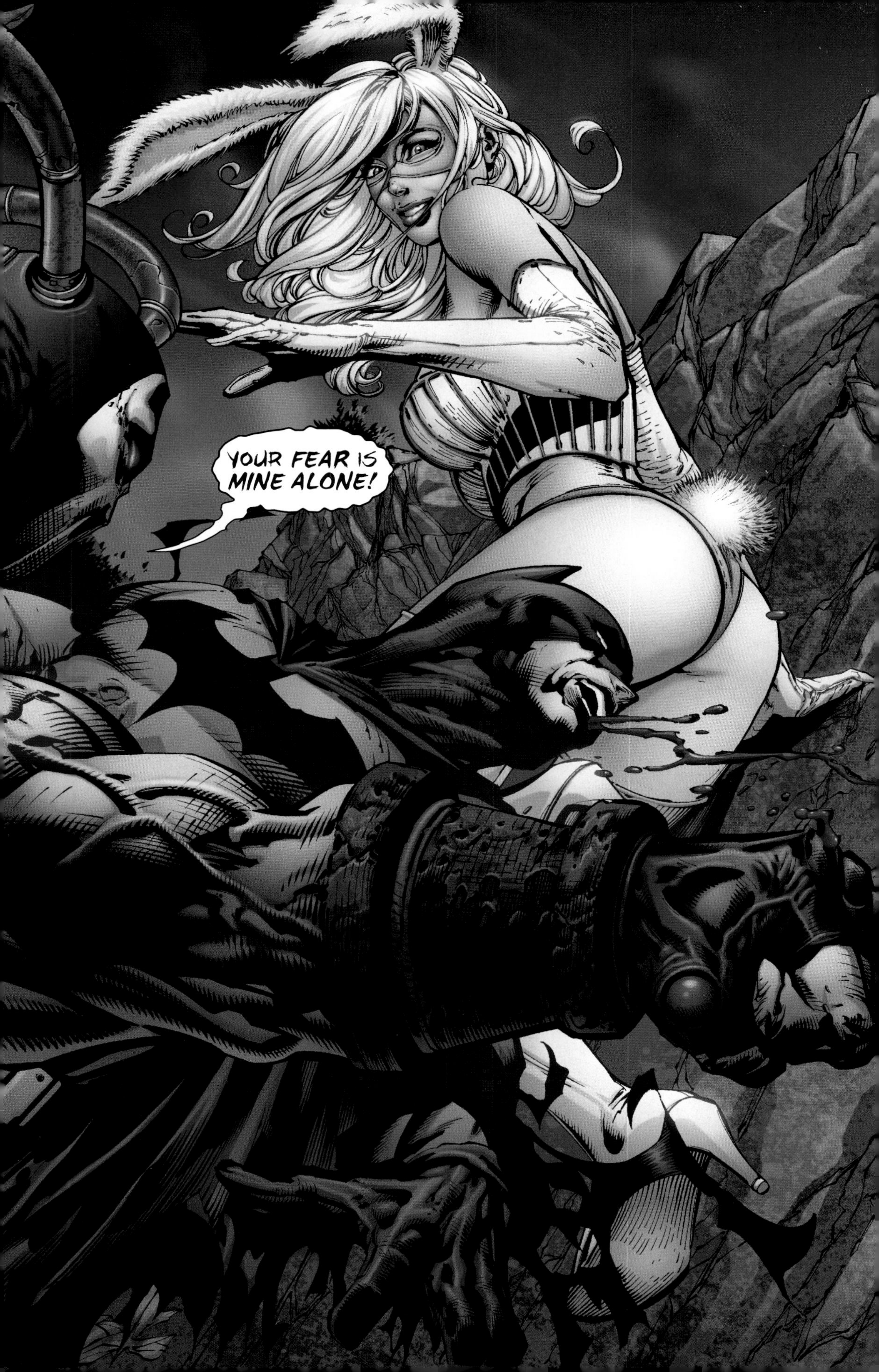
YOUR FEAR IS MINE ALONE!

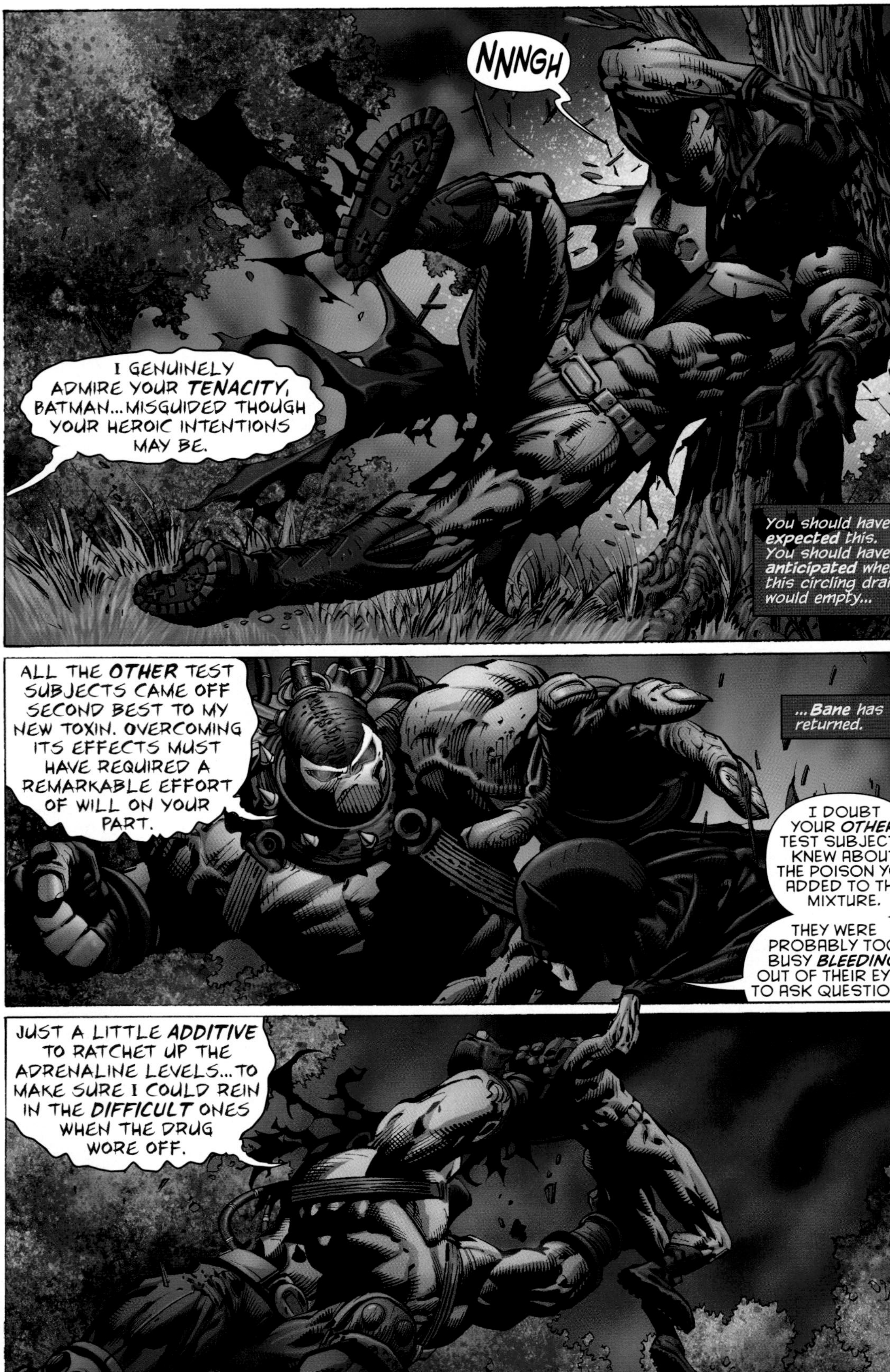
NNNGH
I GENUINELY ADMIRE YOUR TENACITY, BATMAN...MISGUIDED THOUGH YOUR HEROIC INTENTIONS MAY BE.
You should have expected this. You should have anticipated where this circling drain would empty...
ALL THE OTHER TEST SUBJECTS CAME OFF SECOND BEST TO MY NEW TOXIN. OVERCOMING ITS EFFECTS MUST HAVE REQUIRED A REMARKABLE EFFORT OF WILL ON YOUR PART.
...Bane has returned.
I DOUBT YOUR OTHER TEST SUBJECTS KNEW ABOUT THE POISON YOU ADDED TO THE MIXTURE.
THEY WERE PROBABLY TOO BUSY BLEEDING OUT OF THEIR EYES TO ASK QUESTIONS.
JUST A LITTLE ADDITIVE TO RATCHET UP THE ADRENALINE LEVELS...TO MAKE SURE I COULD REIN IN THE DIFFICULT ONES WHEN THE DRUG WORE OFF.

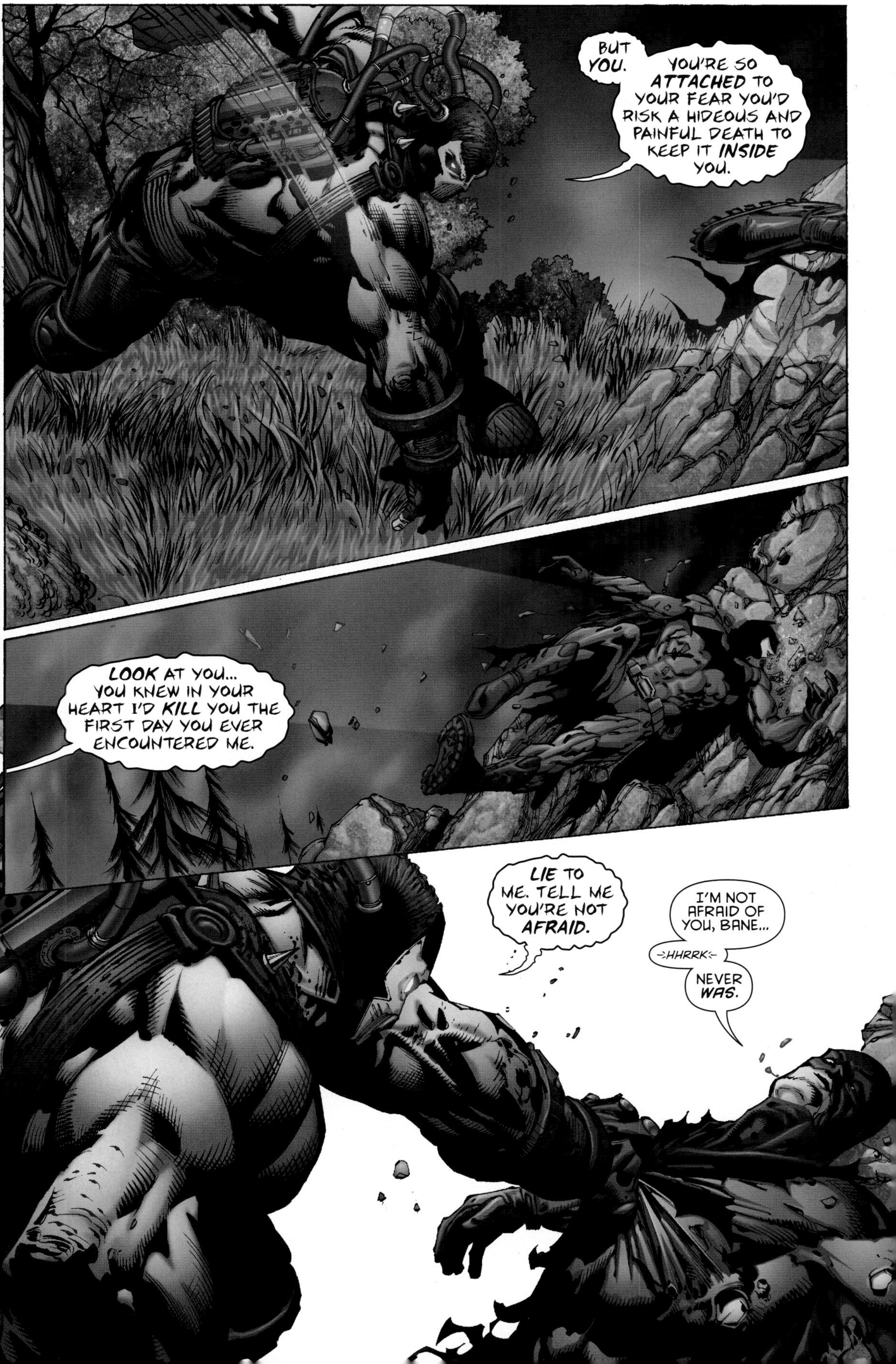
BUT YOU.
YOU'RE SO ATTACHED TO YOUR FEAR YOU'D RISK A HIDEOUS AND PAINFUL DEATH TO KEEP IT INSIDE YOU.
LOOK AT YOU... YOU KNEW IN YOUR HEART I'D KILL YOU THE FIRST DAY YOU EVER ENCOUNTERED ME.
LIE TO ME. TELL ME YOU'RE NOT AFRAID.
I'M NOT AFRAID OF YOU, BANE...
HHRRK
NEVER WAS.

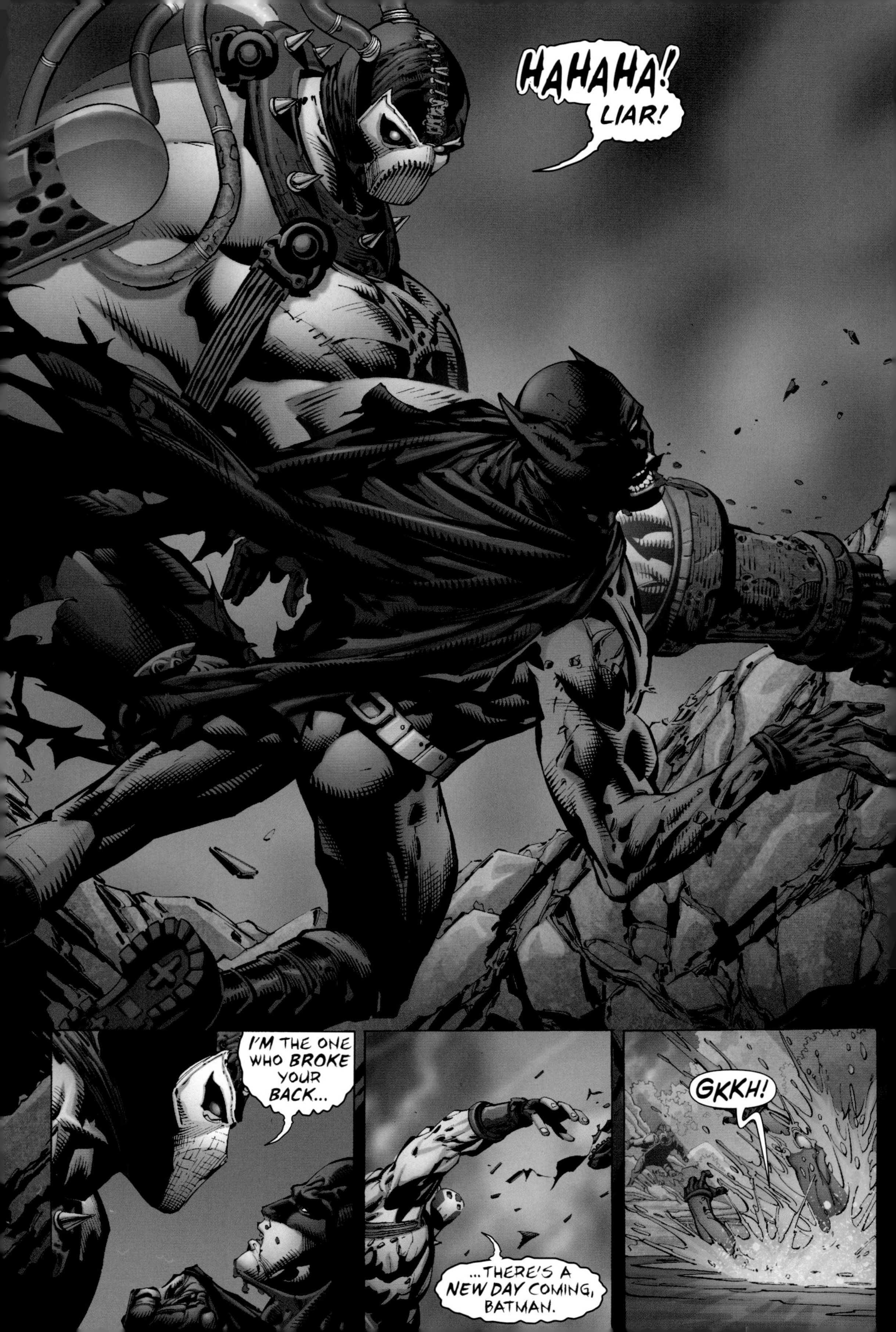
HAHAHA! LIAR!
I'M THE ONE WHO BROKE YOUR BACK...
...THERE'S A NEW DAY COMING, BATMAN.
GKKH!

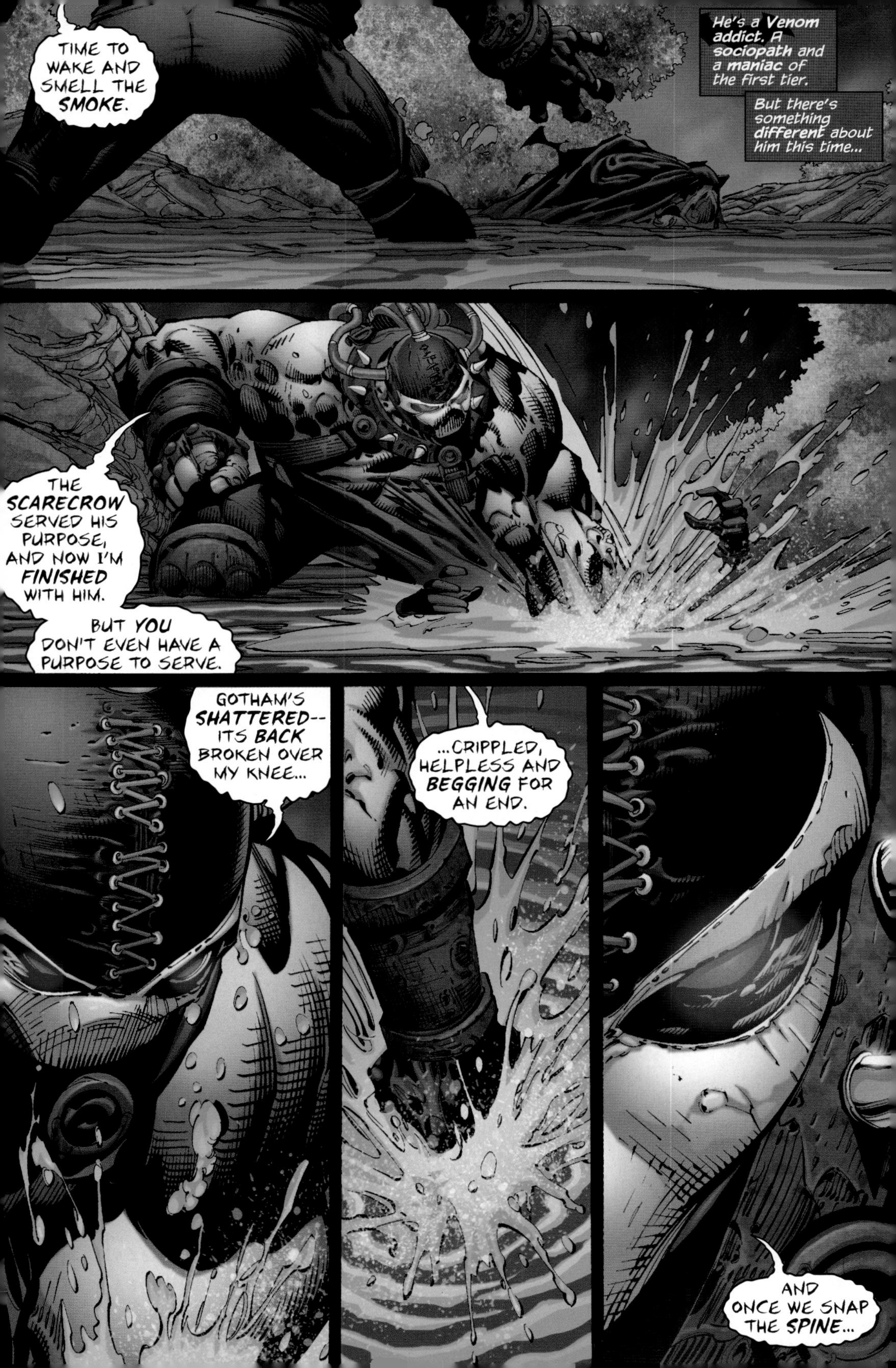
TIME TO WAKE AND SMELL THE SMOKE.
He's a Venom addict. A sociopath and a maniac of the first tier.
But there's something different about him this time...
THE SCARECROW SERVED HIS PURPOSE, AND NOW I'M FINISHED WITH HIM.
BUT YOU DON'T EVEN HAVE A PURPOSE TO SERVE.
GOTHAM'S SHATTERED-- ITS BACK BROKEN OVER MY KNEE...
...CRIPPLED, HELPLESS AND BEGGING FOR AN END.
AND ONCE WE SNAP THE SPINE...

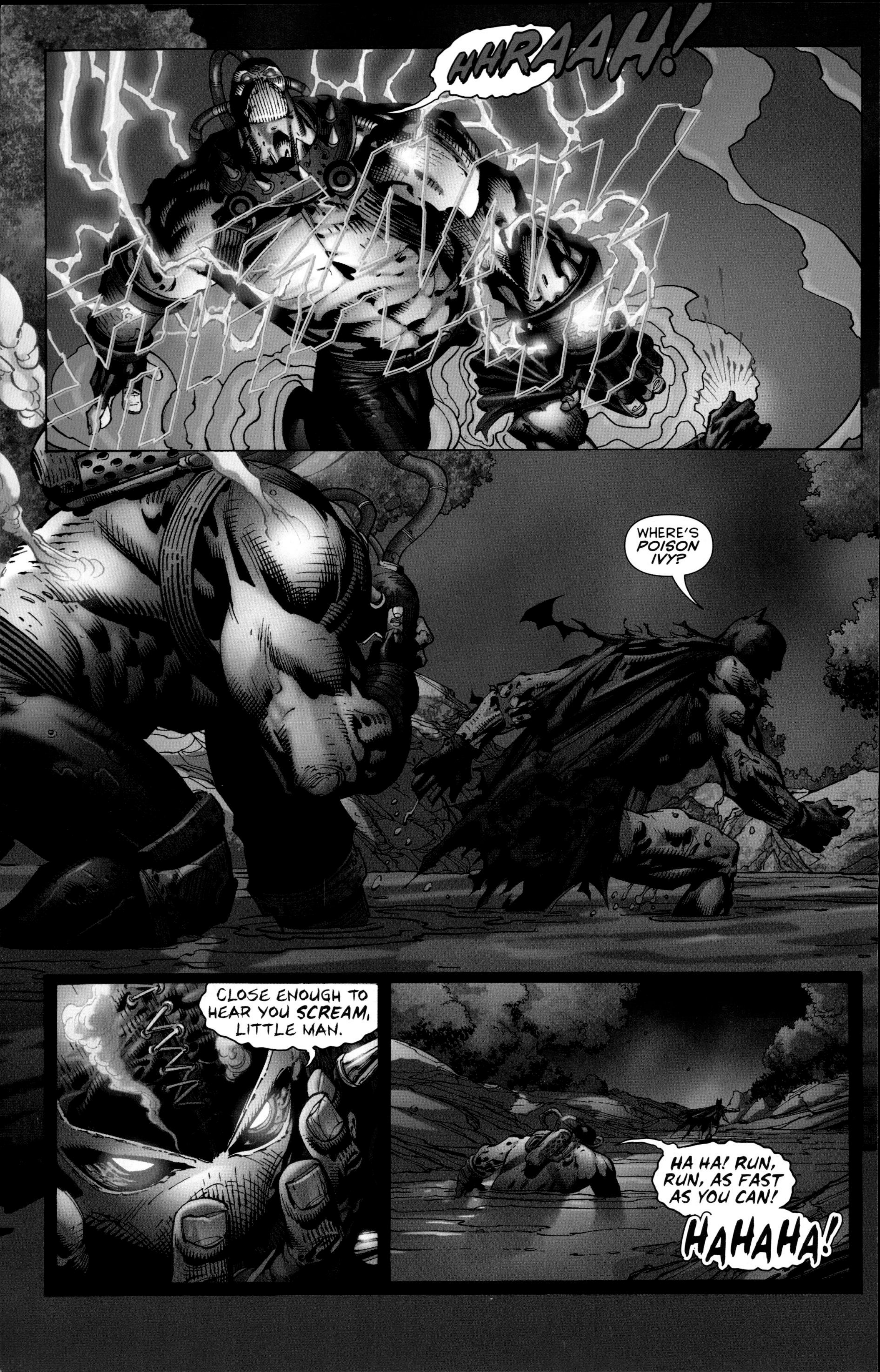
HHRAAH!
ZZZAKK
WHERE'S POISON IVY?
CLOSE ENOUGH TO HEAR YOU SCREAM, LITTLE MAN.
HA HA! RUN, RUN, AS FAST AS YOU CAN!
HAHAHA!

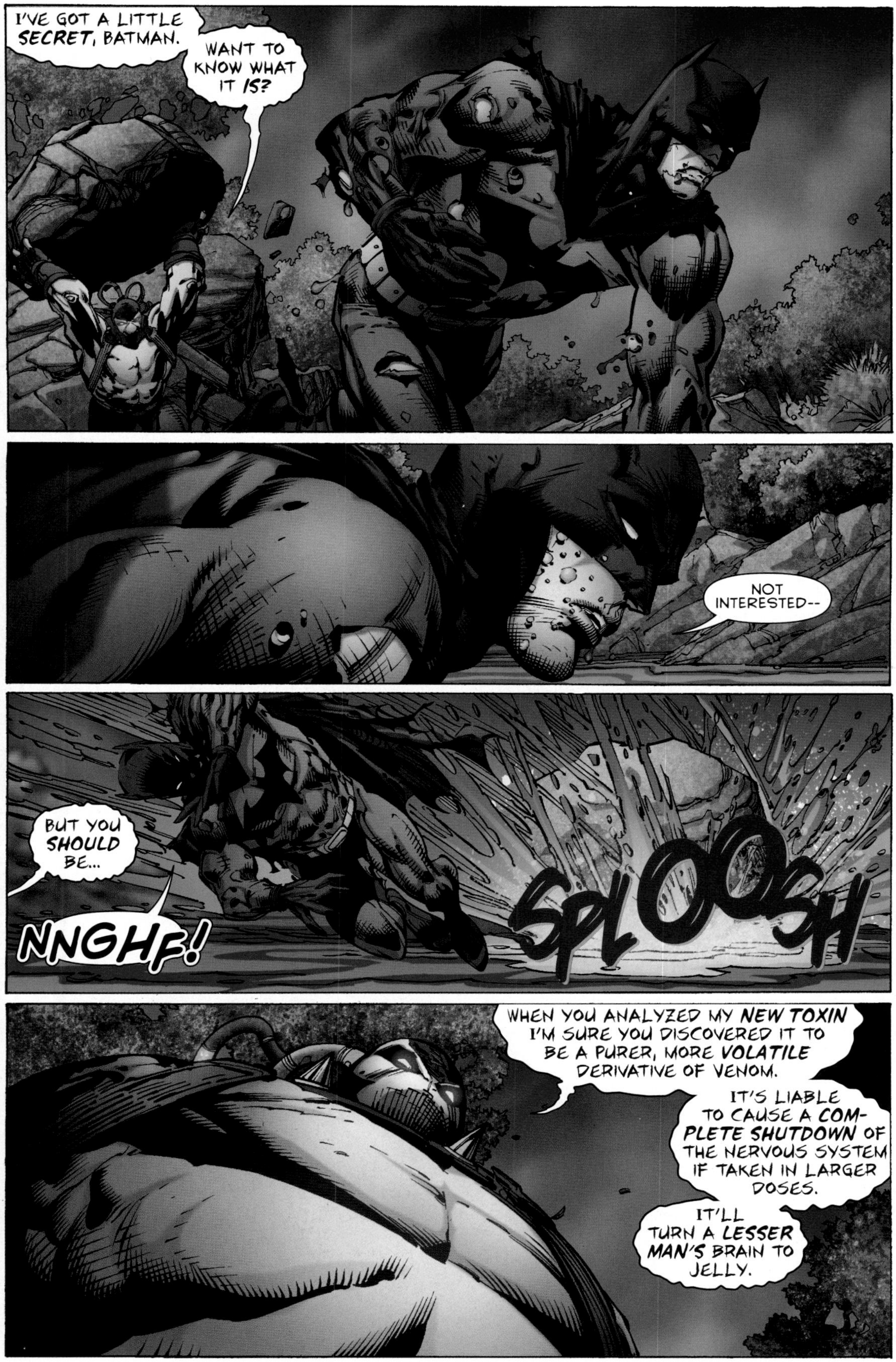
I'VE GOT A LITTLE SECRET, BATMAN.
WANT TO KNOW WHAT IT IS?
NOT INTERESTED--
BUT YOU SHOULD BE...
NNGHF!
SPLOOSH
WHEN YOU ANALYZED MY NEW TOXIN I'M SURE YOU DISCOVERED IT TO BE A PURER, MORE VOLATILE DERIVATIVE OF VENOM.
IT'S LIABLE TO CAUSE A COMPLETE SHUTDOWN OF THE NERVOUS SYSTEM IF TAKEN IN LARGER DOSES.
IT'LL TURN A LESSER MAN'S BRAIN TO JELLY.

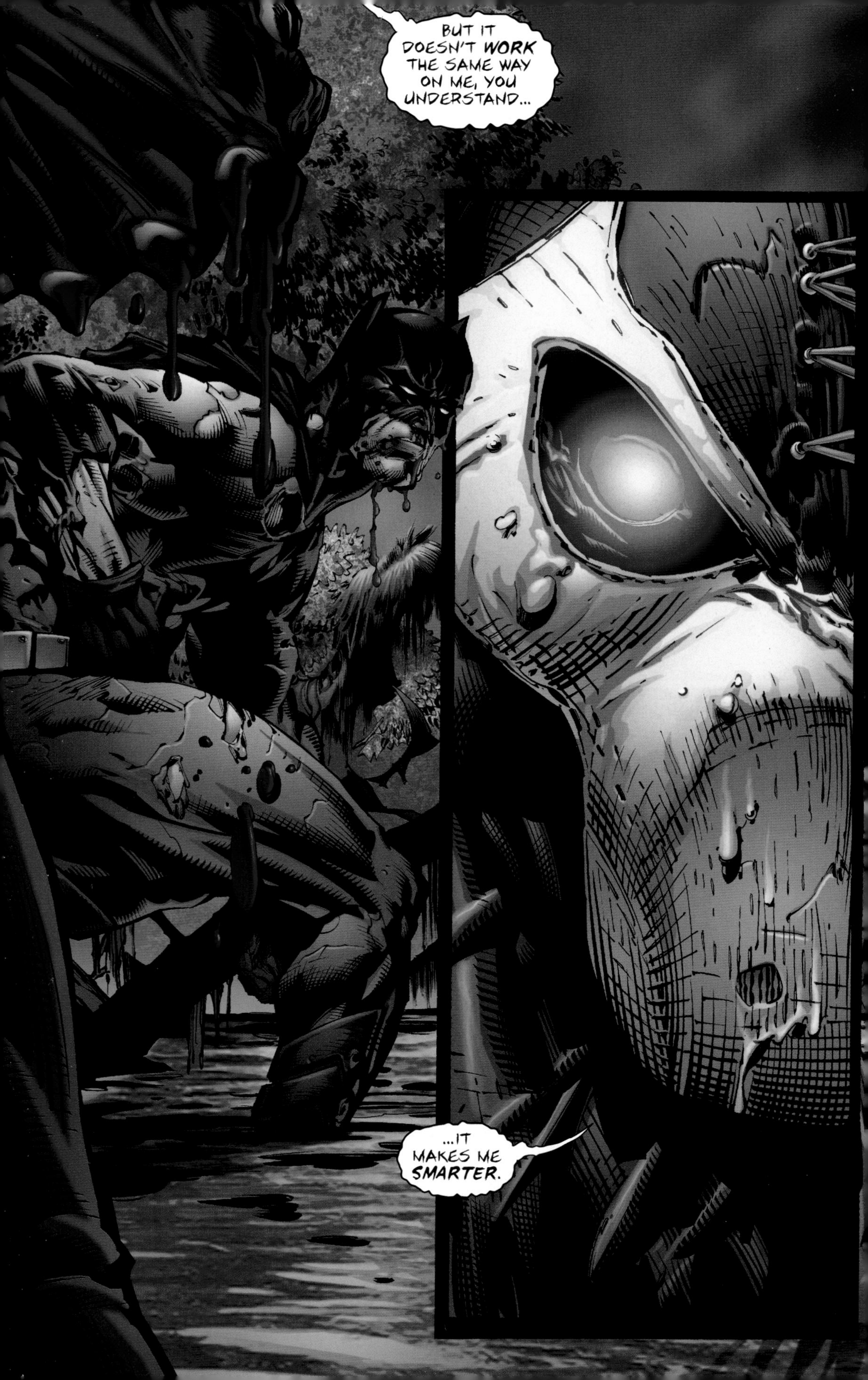
BUT IT DOESN'T **WORK** THE SAME WAY ON ME, YOU UNDERSTAND...
...IT MAKES ME **SMARTER**.

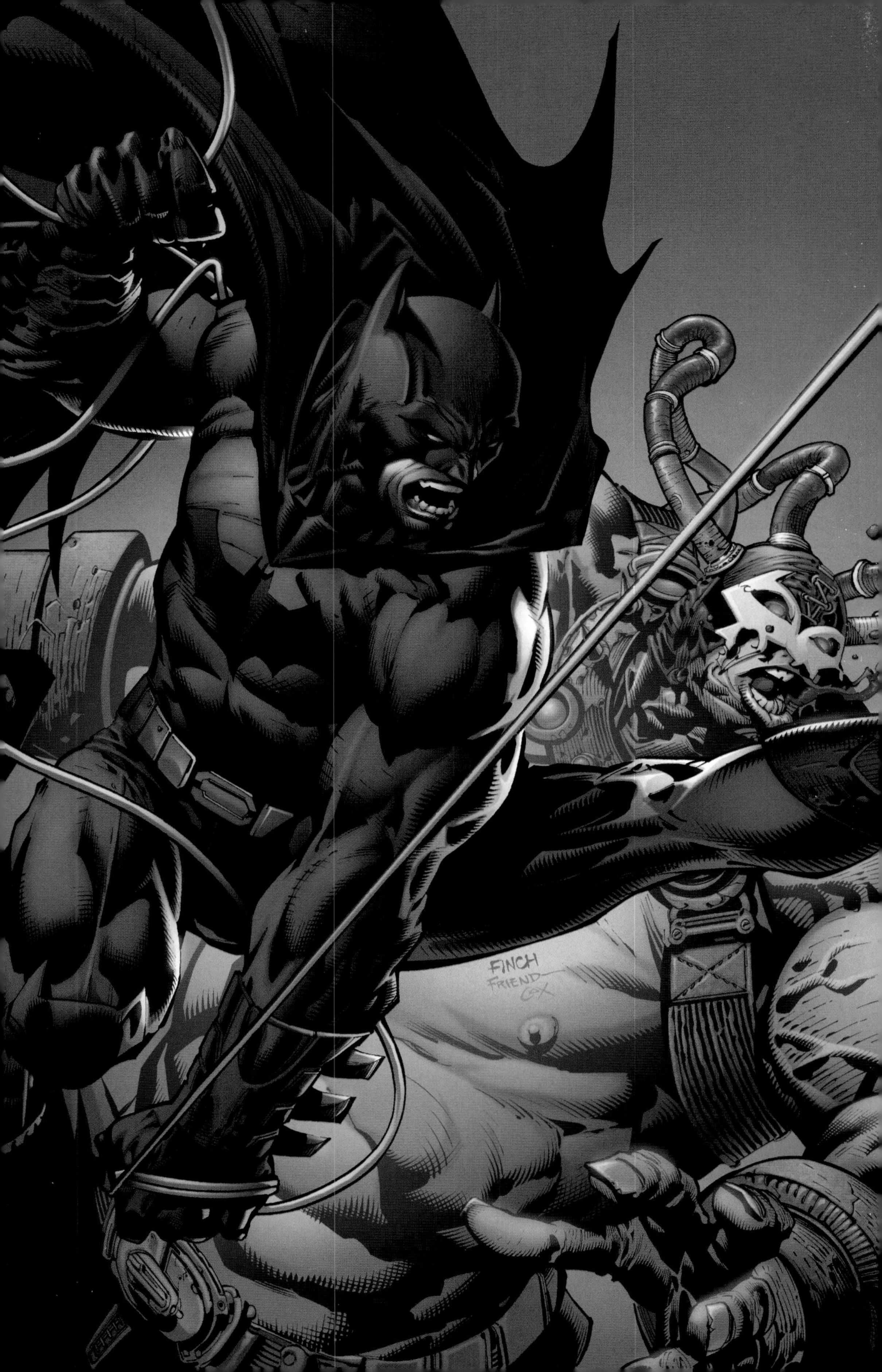
FINCH
FRIEND
COX

THE FINAL CURTAIN

PAUL JENKINS writer/co-plotter DAVID FINCH penciller/co-plotter RICHARD FRIEND inker
cover art by DAVID FINCH, RICHARD FRIEND & JEROMY COX

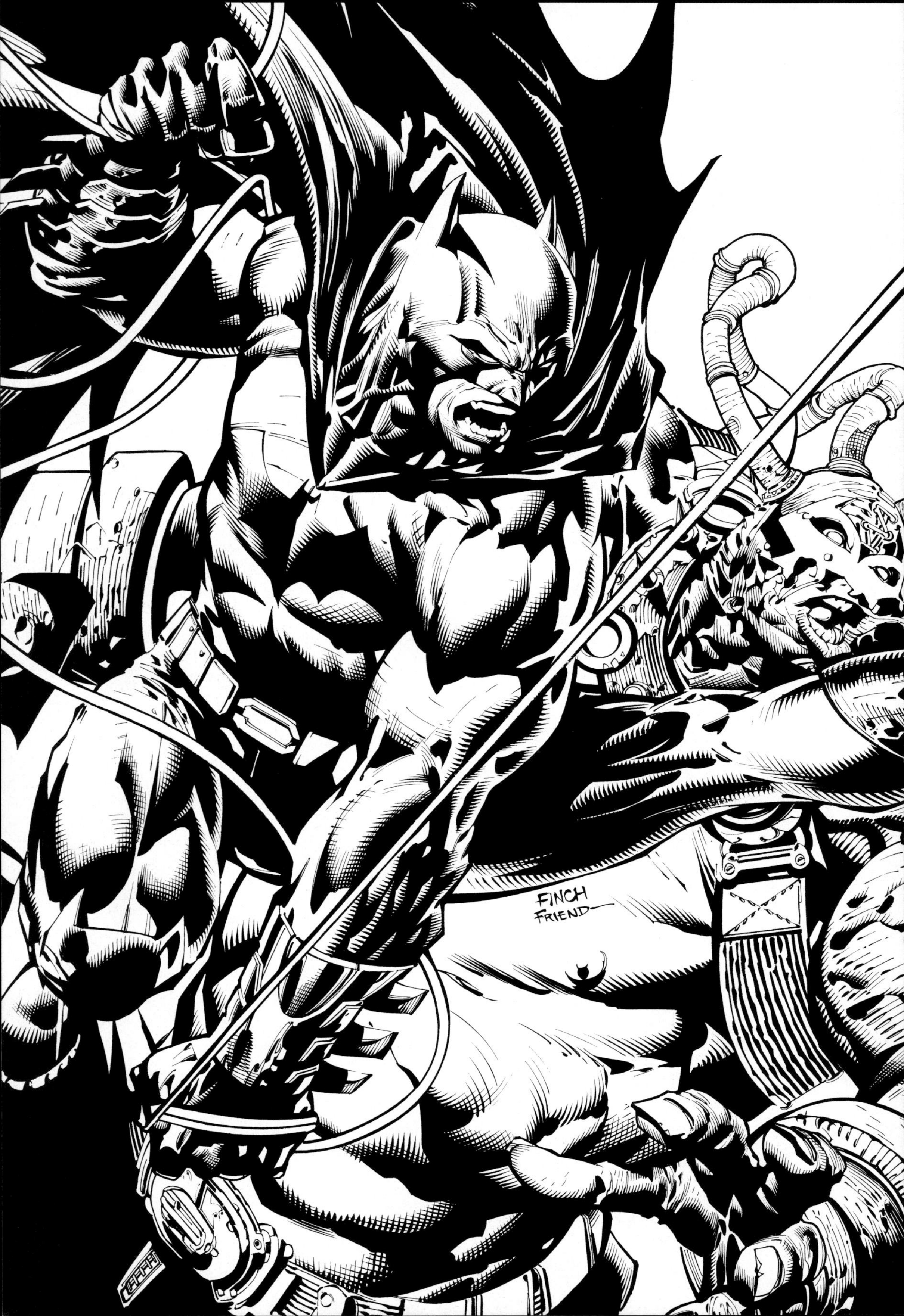
FINCH
FRIEND

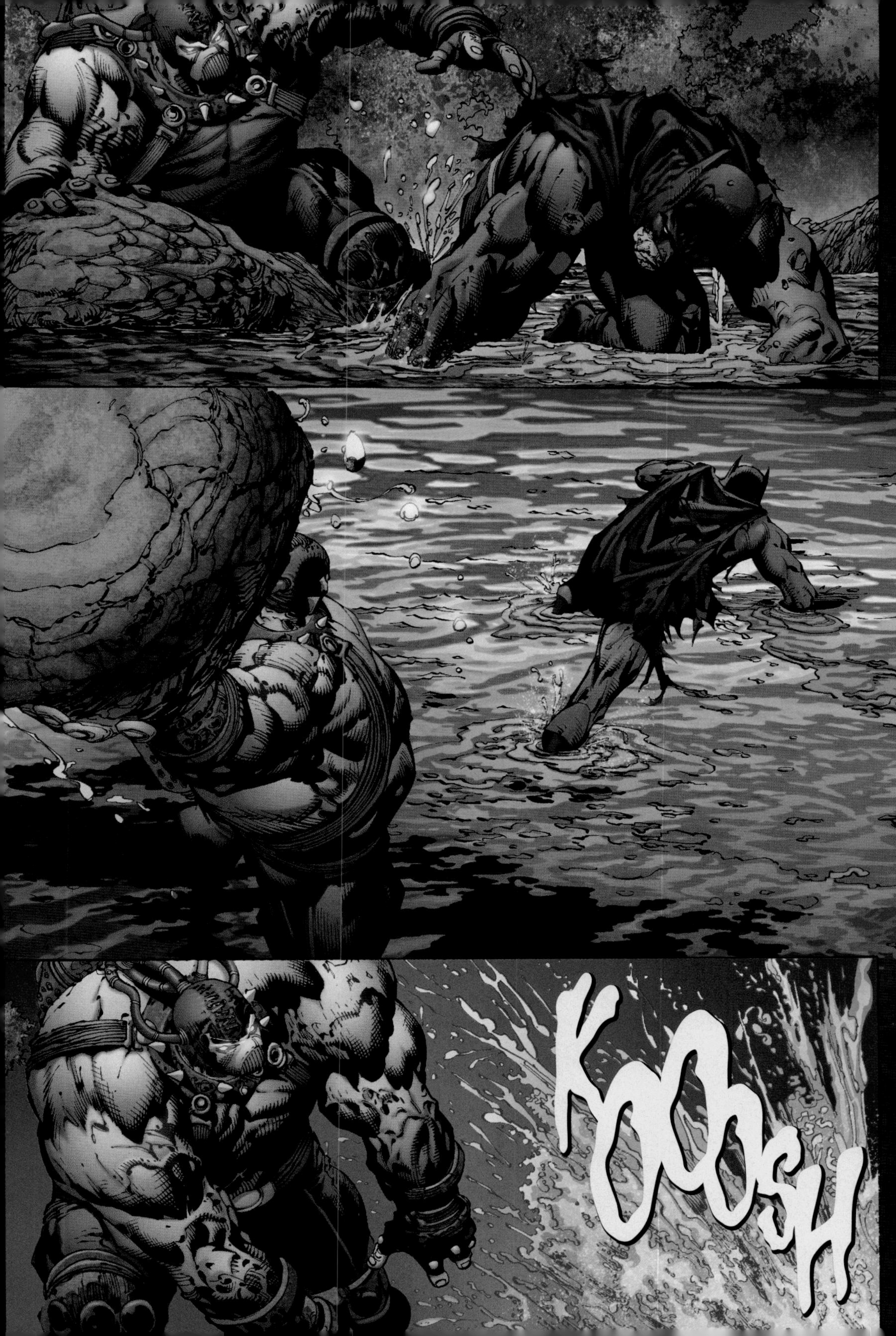
KOOOSH

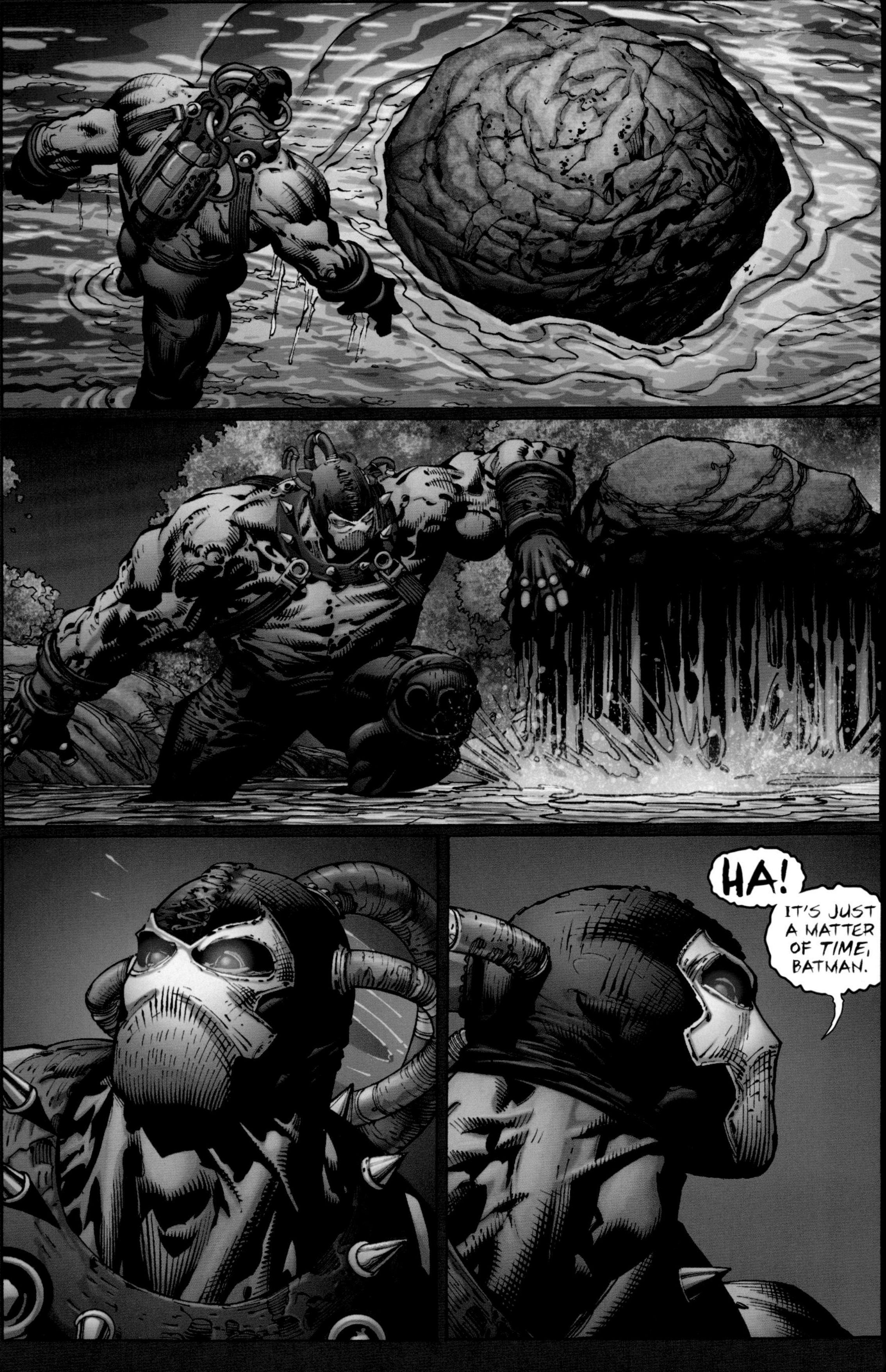
HA!
IT'S JUST A MATTER OF TIME, BATMAN.

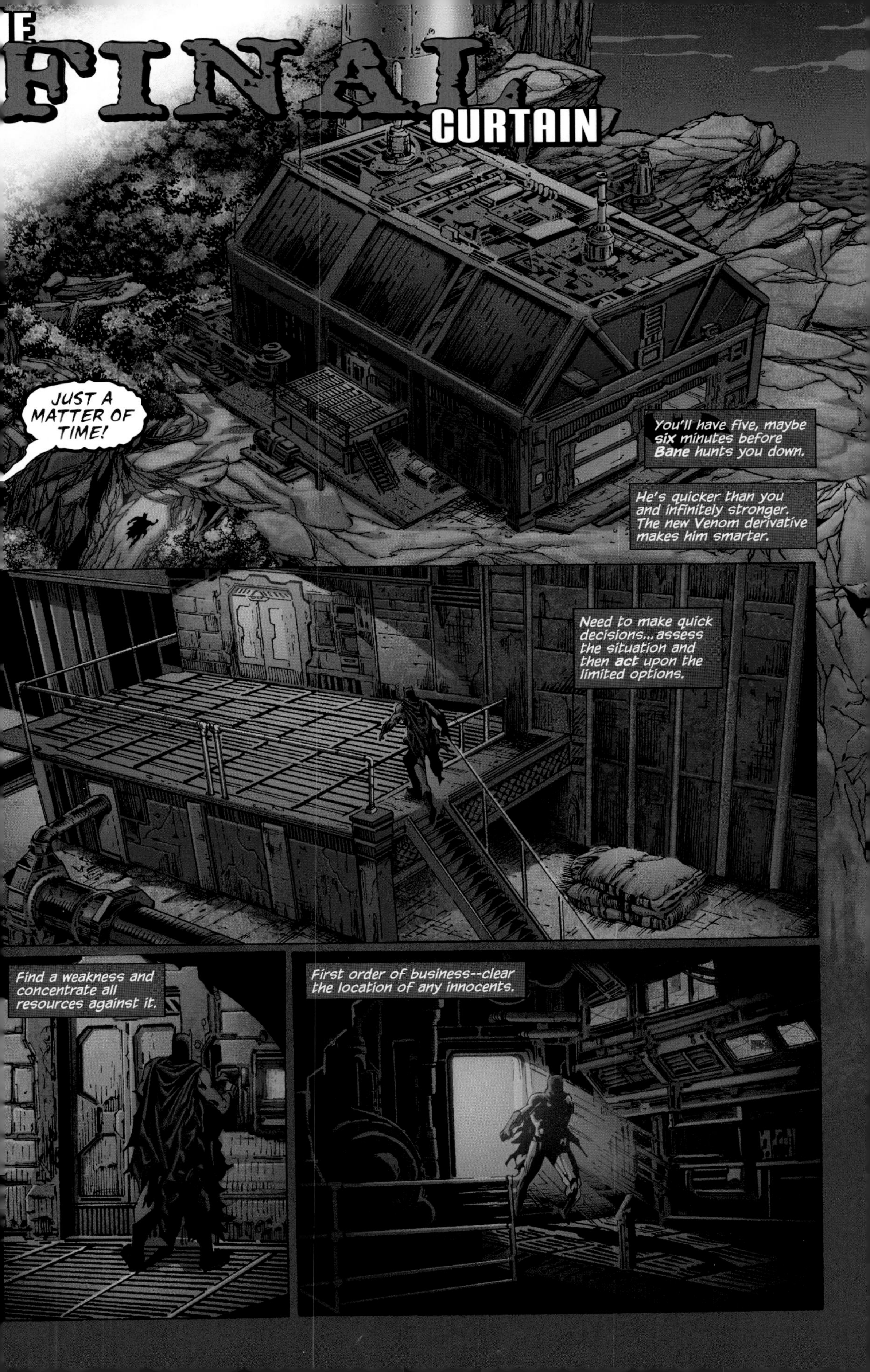

[TH]E FINAL CURTAIN
JUST A MATTER OF TIME!
You'll have five, maybe six minutes before Bane hunts you down.
He's quicker than you and infinitely stronger. The new Venom derivative makes him smarter.
Need to make quick decisions... assess the situation and then act upon the limited options.
Find a weakness and concentrate all resources against it.
First order of business--clear the location of any innocents.

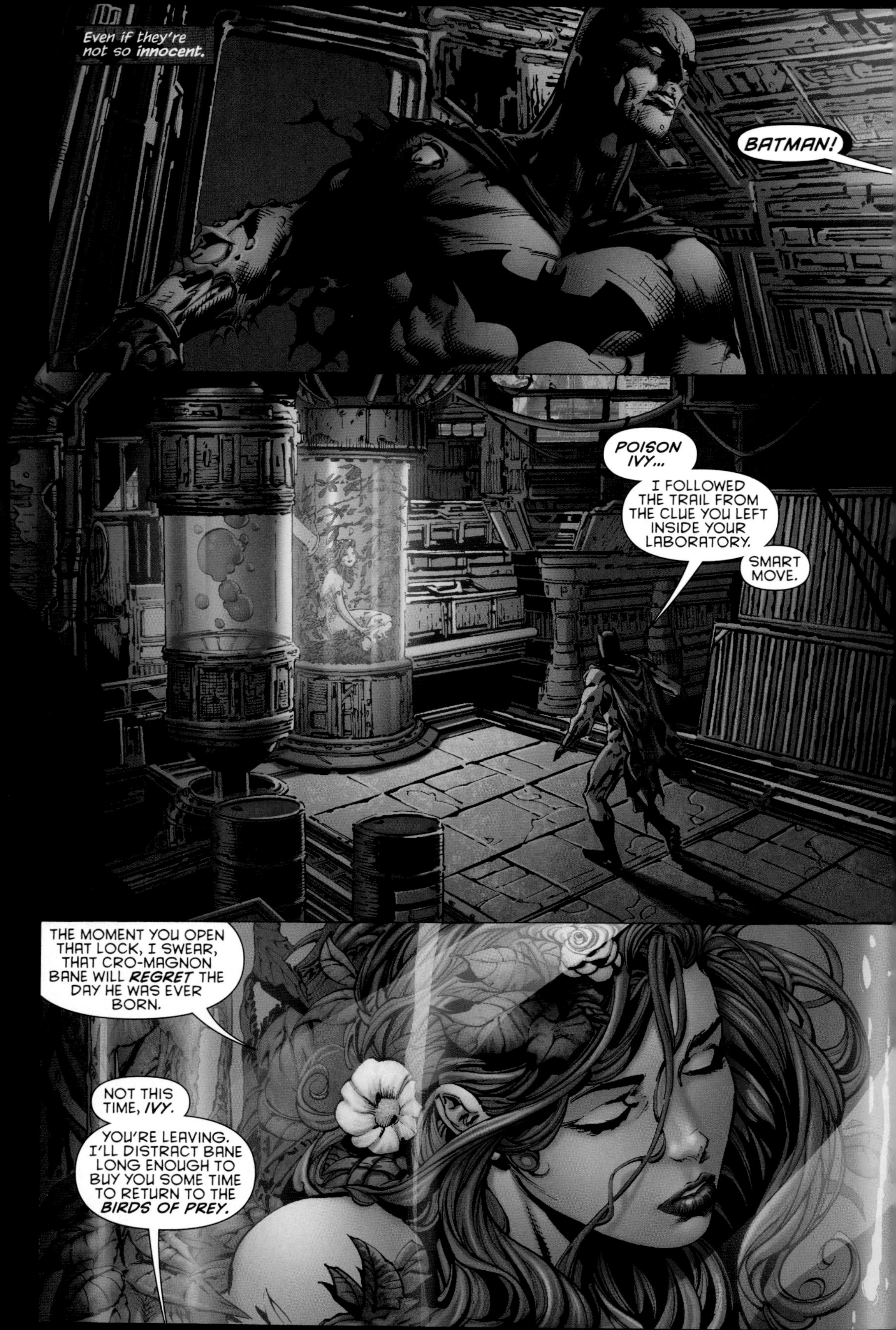
Even if they're not so innocent.
BATMAN!
POISON IVY...
I FOLLOWED THE TRAIL FROM THE CLUE YOU LEFT INSIDE YOUR LABORATORY.
SMART MOVE.
THE MOMENT YOU OPEN THAT LOCK, I SWEAR, THAT CRO-MAGNON BANE WILL REGRET THE DAY HE WAS EVER BORN.
NOT THIS TIME, IVY.
YOU'RE LEAVING. I'LL DISTRACT BANE LONG ENOUGH TO BUY YOU SOME TIME TO RETURN TO THE BIRDS OF PREY.

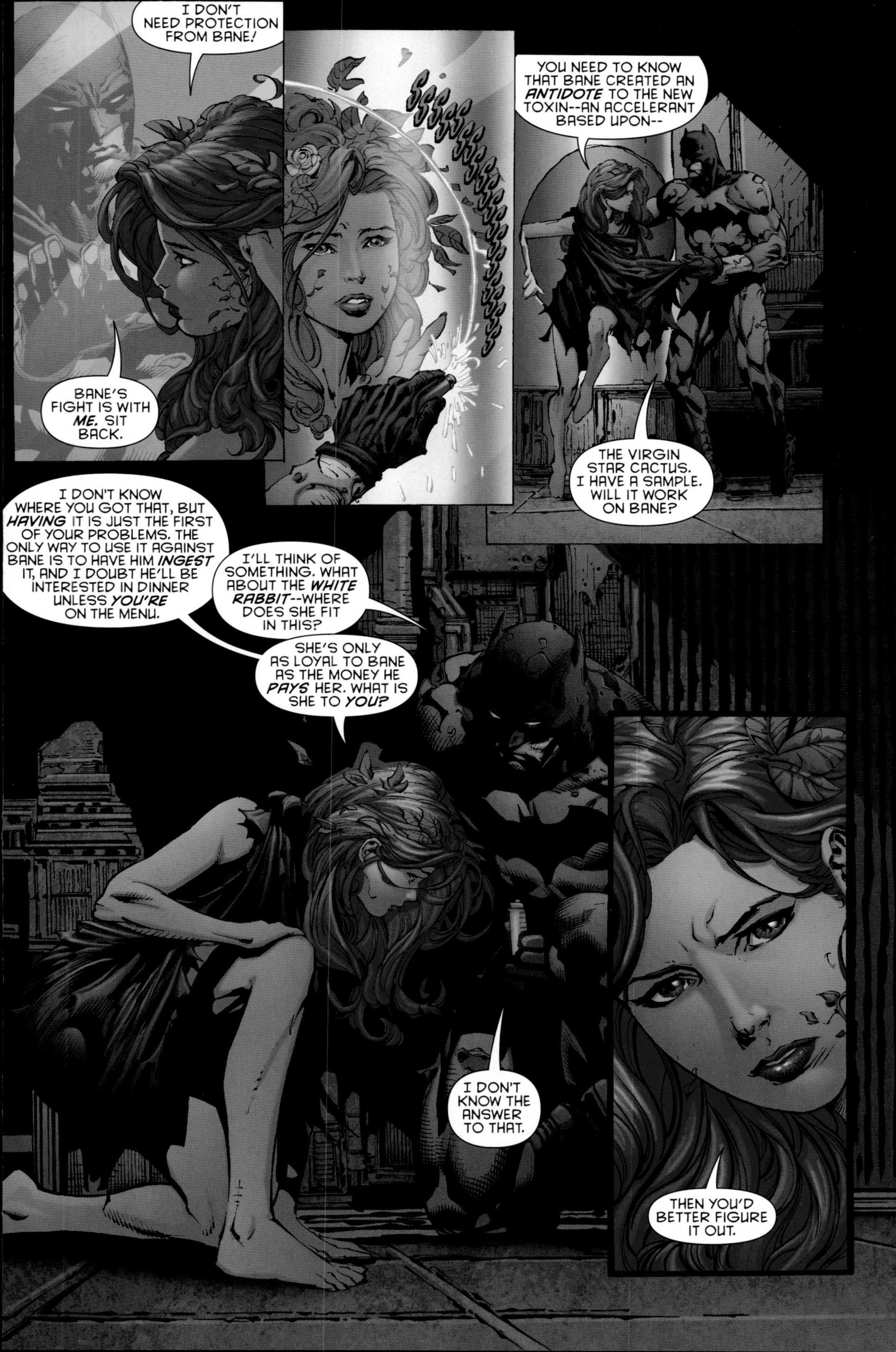
I DON'T NEED PROTECTION FROM BANE!
BANE'S FIGHT IS WITH ME. SIT BACK.
SSSSSSSSSSSSSSSSSSSSS
YOU NEED TO KNOW THAT BANE CREATED AN ANTIDOTE TO THE NEW TOXIN--AN ACCELERANT BASED UPON--
THE VIRGIN STAR CACTUS. I HAVE A SAMPLE. WILL IT WORK ON BANE?
I DON'T KNOW WHERE YOU GOT THAT, BUT HAVING IT IS JUST THE FIRST OF YOUR PROBLEMS. THE ONLY WAY TO USE IT AGAINST BANE IS TO HAVE HIM INGEST IT, AND I DOUBT HE'LL BE INTERESTED IN DINNER UNLESS YOU'RE ON THE MENU.
I'LL THINK OF SOMETHING. WHAT ABOUT THE WHITE RABBIT--WHERE DOES SHE FIT IN THIS?
SHE'S ONLY AS LOYAL TO BANE AS THE MONEY HE PAYS HER. WHAT IS SHE TO YOU?
I DON'T KNOW THE ANSWER TO THAT.
THEN YOU'D BETTER FIGURE IT OUT.

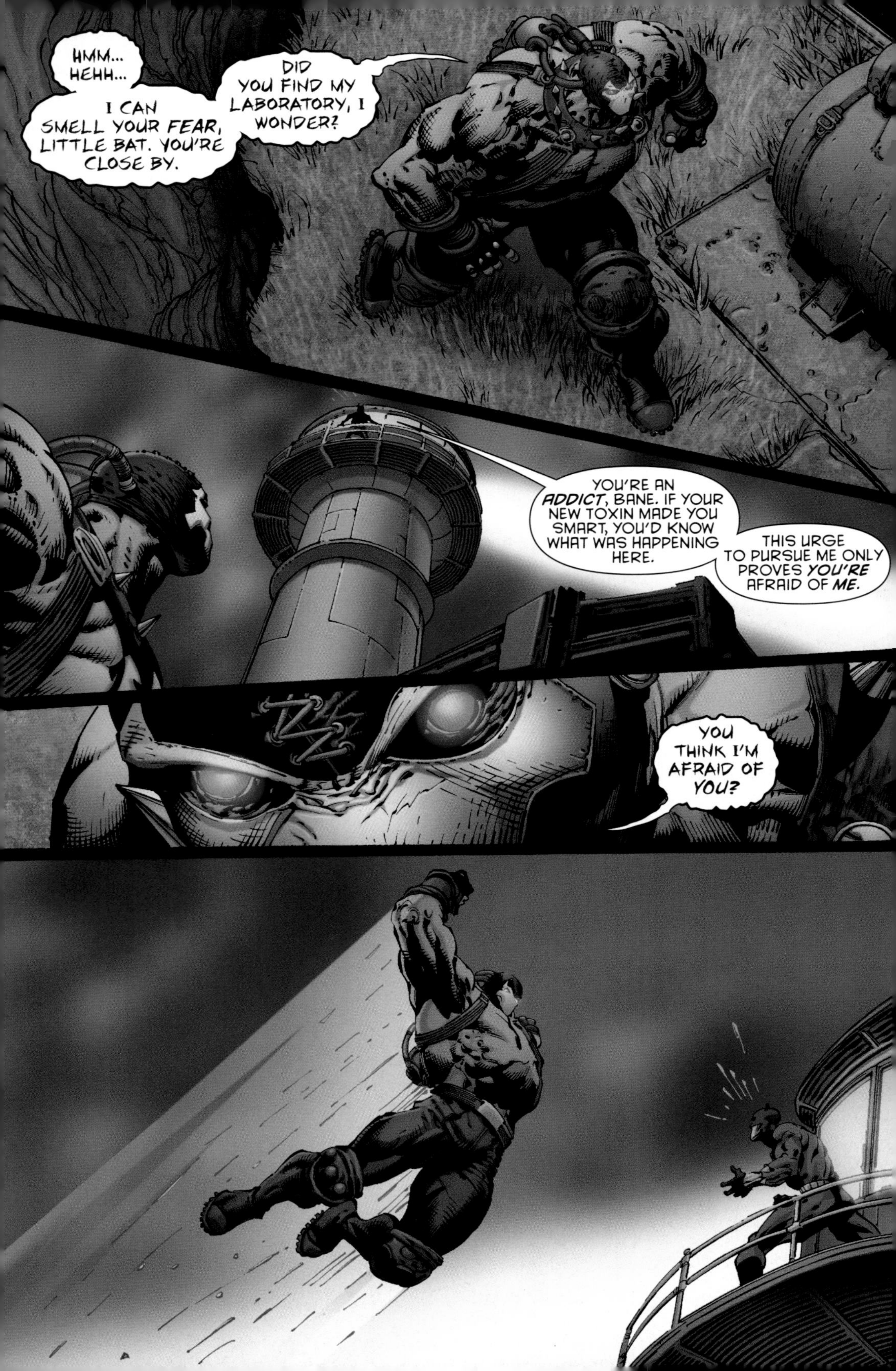
HMM... HEHH...
I CAN SMELL YOUR FEAR, LITTLE BAT. YOU'RE CLOSE BY.
DID YOU FIND MY LABORATORY, I WONDER?
YOU'RE AN ADDICT, BANE. IF YOUR NEW TOXIN MADE YOU SMART, YOU'D KNOW WHAT WAS HAPPENING HERE.
THIS URGE TO PURSUE ME ONLY PROVES YOU'RE AFRAID OF ME.
YOU THINK I'M AFRAID OF YOU?

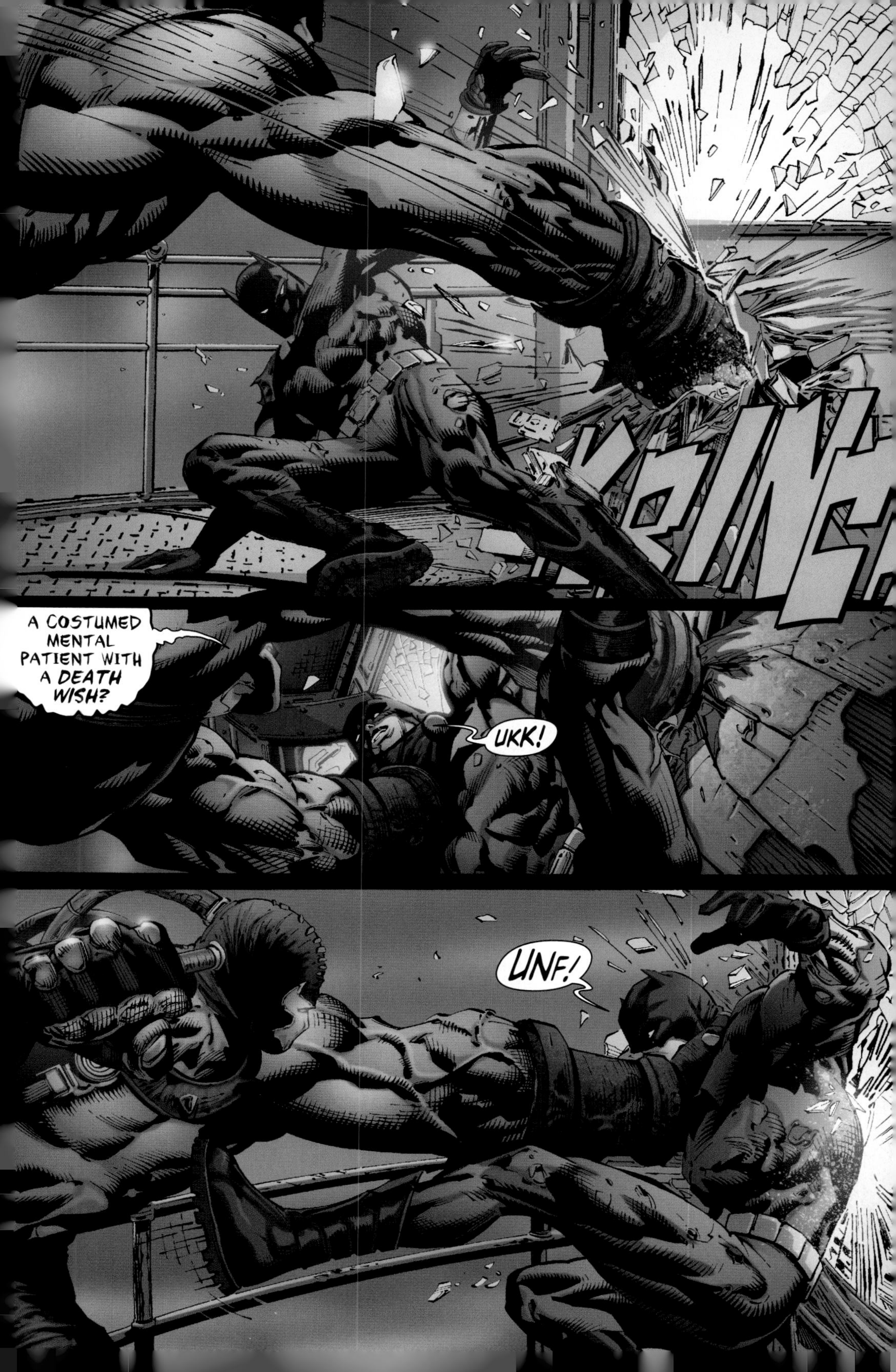

KRANG!
A COSTUMED MENTAL PATIENT WITH A DEATH WISH?
UKK!
UNF!

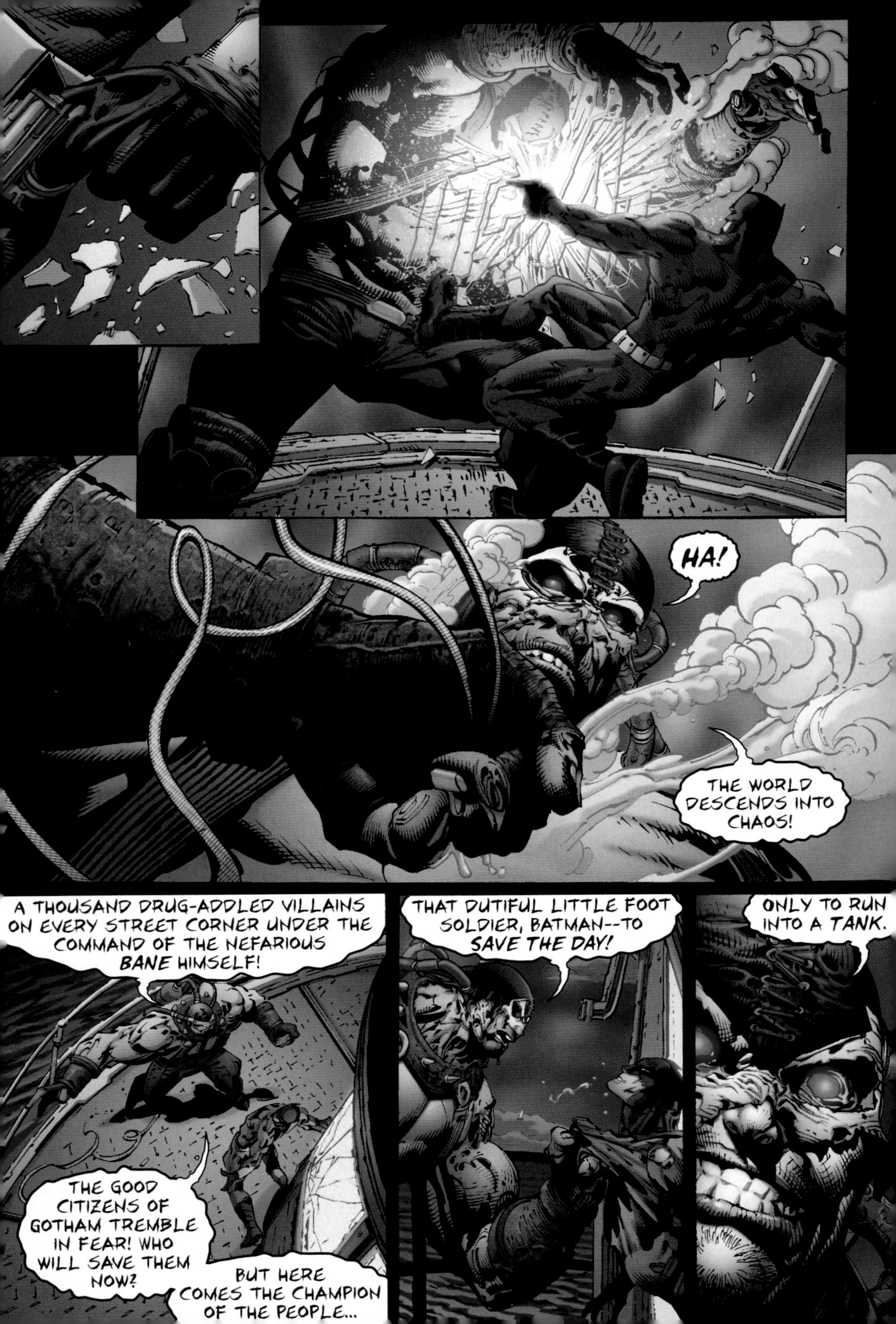
HA!
THE WORLD DESCENDS INTO CHAOS!
A THOUSAND DRUG-ADDLED VILLAINS ON EVERY STREET CORNER UNDER THE COMMAND OF THE NEFARIOUS BANE HIMSELF!
THE GOOD CITIZENS OF GOTHAM TREMBLE IN FEAR! WHO WILL SAVE THEM NOW?
BUT HERE COMES THE CHAMPION OF THE PEOPLE...
THAT DUTIFUL LITTLE FOOT SOLDIER, BATMAN--TO SAVE THE DAY!
ONLY TO RUN INTO A TANK.

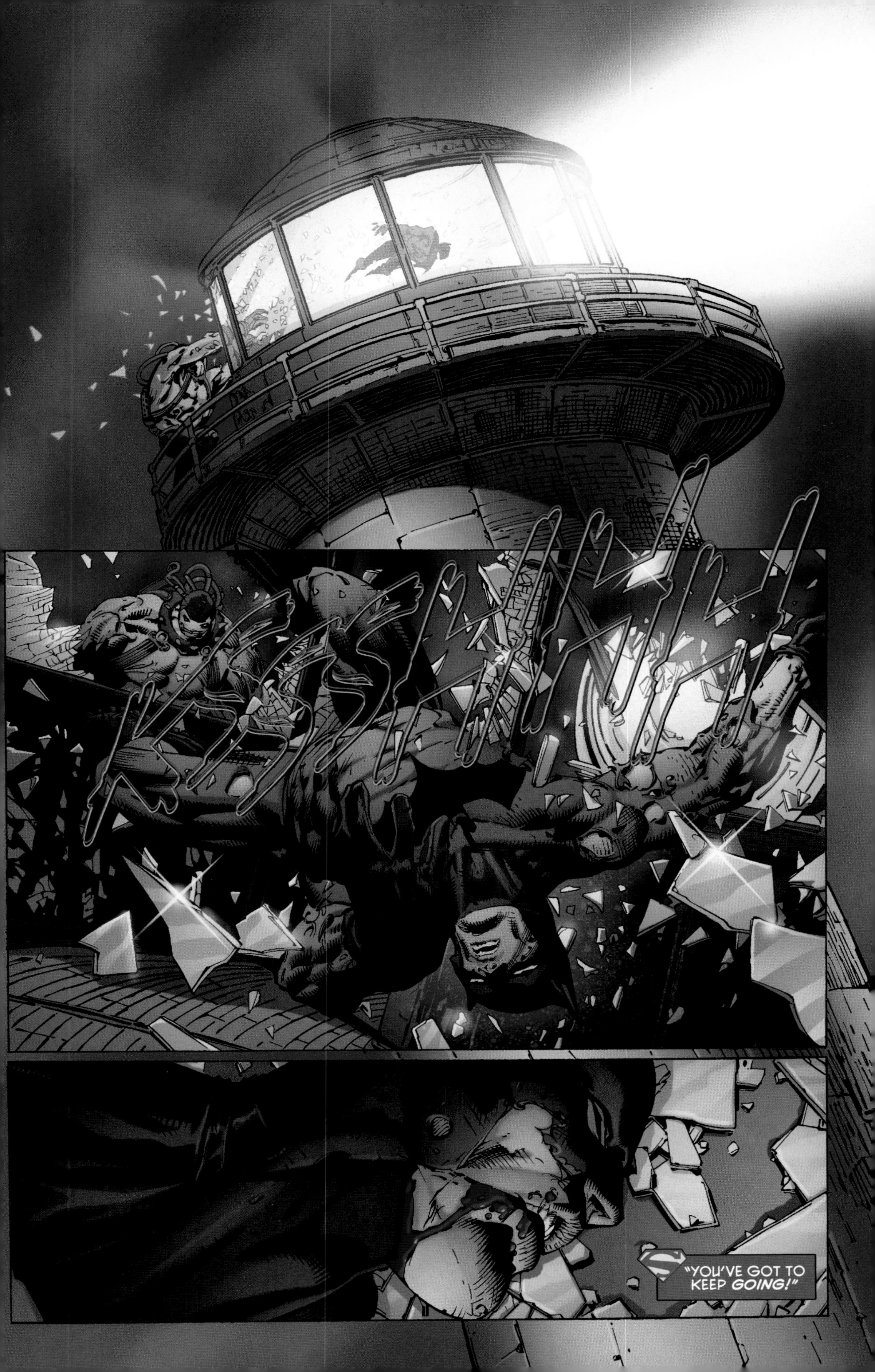
"YOU'VE GOT TO KEEP GOING!"

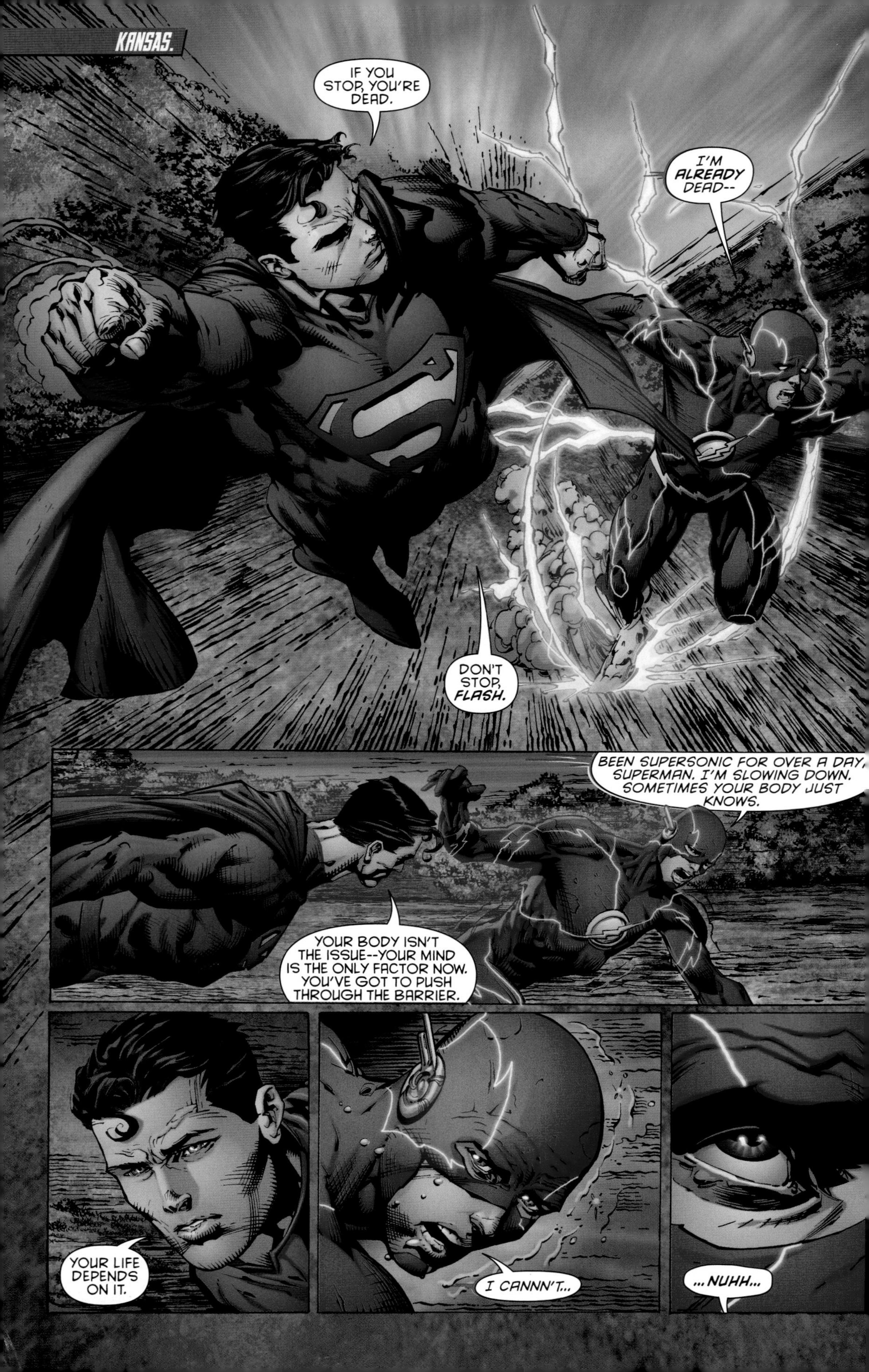
KANSAS.
IF YOU STOP, YOU'RE DEAD.
I'M ALREADY DEAD--
DON'T STOP, FLASH.
BEEN SUPERSONIC FOR OVER A DAY, SUPERMAN. I'M SLOWING DOWN. SOMETIMES YOUR BODY JUST KNOWS.
YOUR BODY ISN'T THE ISSUE--YOUR MIND IS THE ONLY FACTOR NOW. YOU'VE GOT TO PUSH THROUGH THE BARRIER.
YOUR LIFE DEPENDS ON IT.
I CANNN'T...
...NUHH...

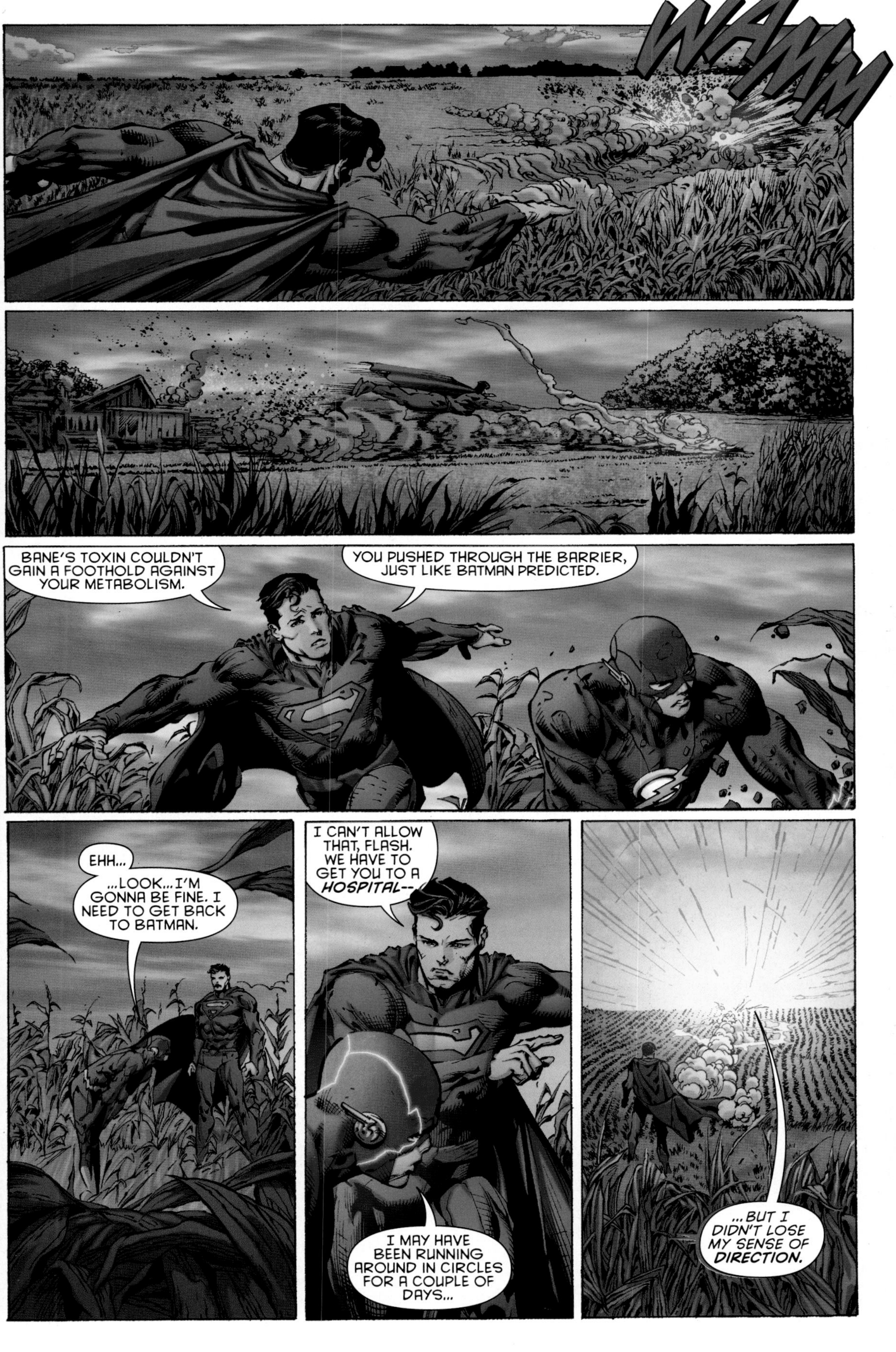
WAMM
BANE'S TOXIN COULDN'T GAIN A FOOTHOLD AGAINST YOUR METABOLISM.
YOU PUSHED THROUGH THE BARRIER, JUST LIKE BATMAN PREDICTED.
EHH...
...LOOK...I'M GONNA BE FINE. I NEED TO GET BACK TO BATMAN.
I CAN'T ALLOW THAT, FLASH. WE HAVE TO GET YOU TO A HOSPITAL--
I MAY HAVE BEEN RUNNING AROUND IN CIRCLES FOR A COUPLE OF DAYS...
...BUT I DIDN'T LOSE MY SENSE OF DIRECTION.

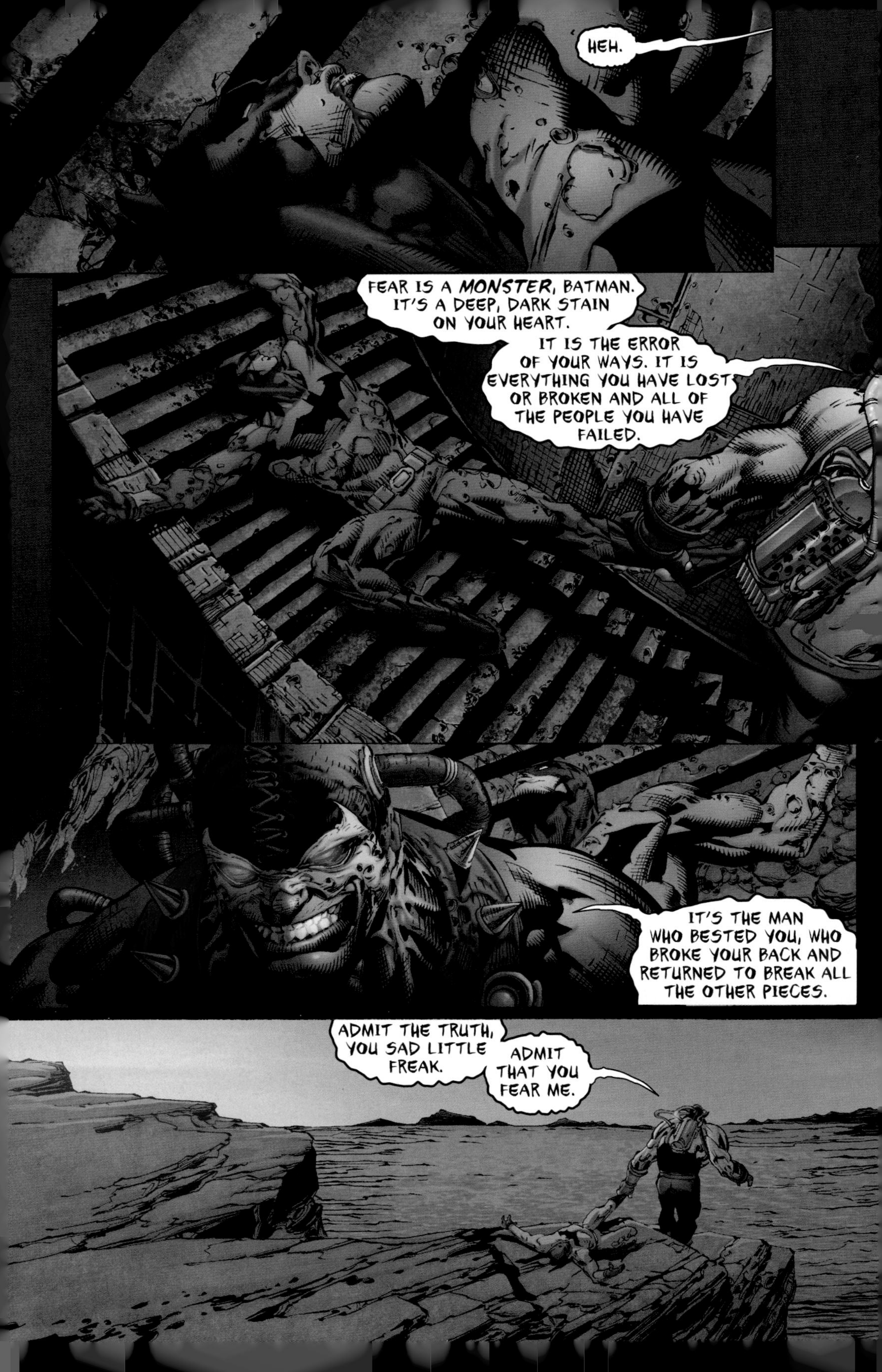
HEH.
FEAR IS A *MONSTER*, BATMAN. IT'S A DEEP, DARK STAIN ON YOUR HEART.
IT IS THE ERROR OF YOUR WAYS. IT IS EVERYTHING YOU HAVE LOST OR BROKEN AND ALL OF THE PEOPLE YOU HAVE FAILED.
IT'S THE MAN WHO BESTED YOU, WHO BROKE YOUR BACK AND RETURNED TO BREAK ALL THE OTHER PIECES.
ADMIT THE TRUTH, YOU SAD LITTLE FREAK.
ADMIT THAT YOU FEAR ME.

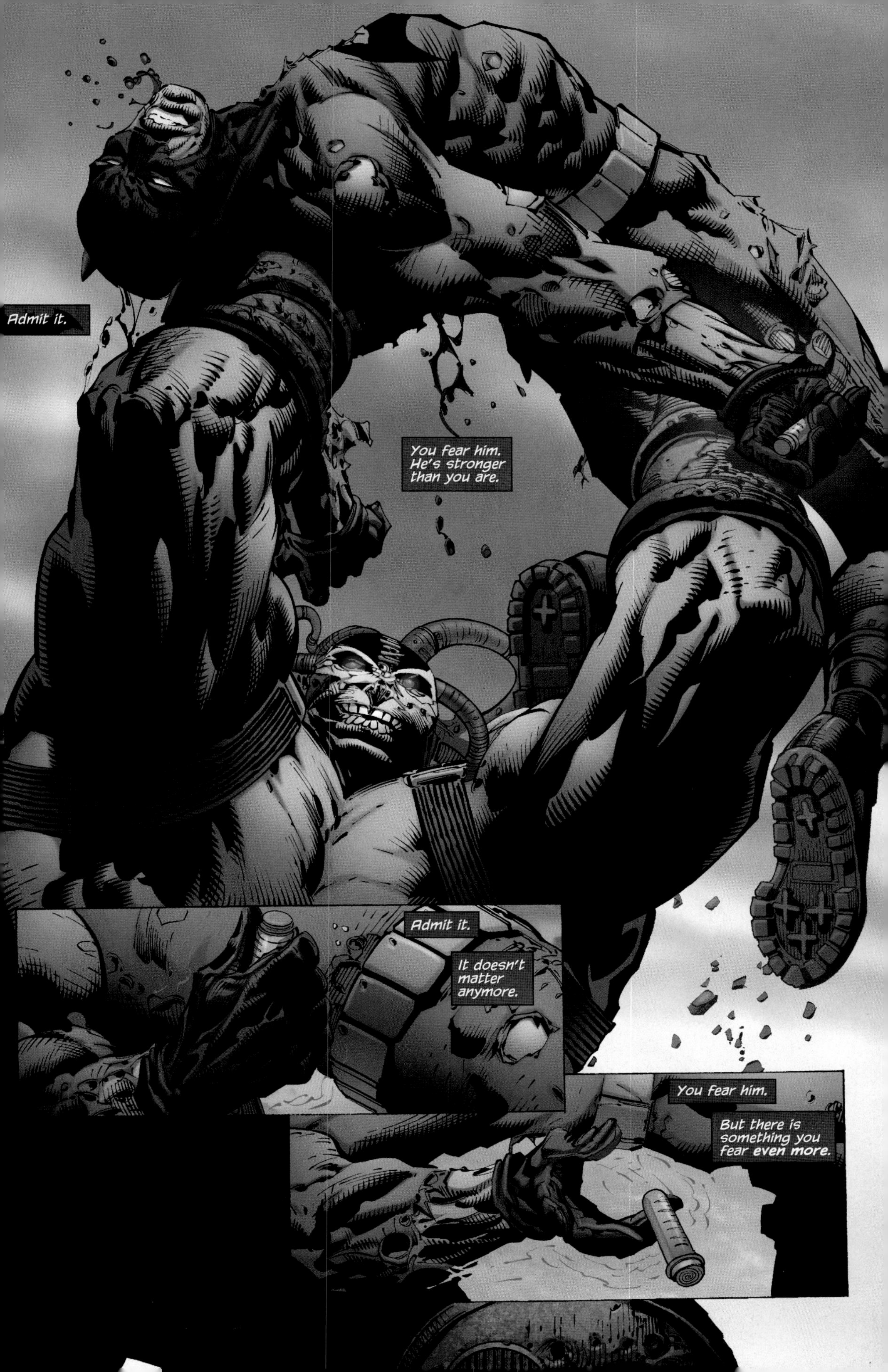
Admit it.
You fear him. He's stronger than you are.
Admit it.
It doesn't matter anymore.
You fear him.
But there is something you fear **even more**.

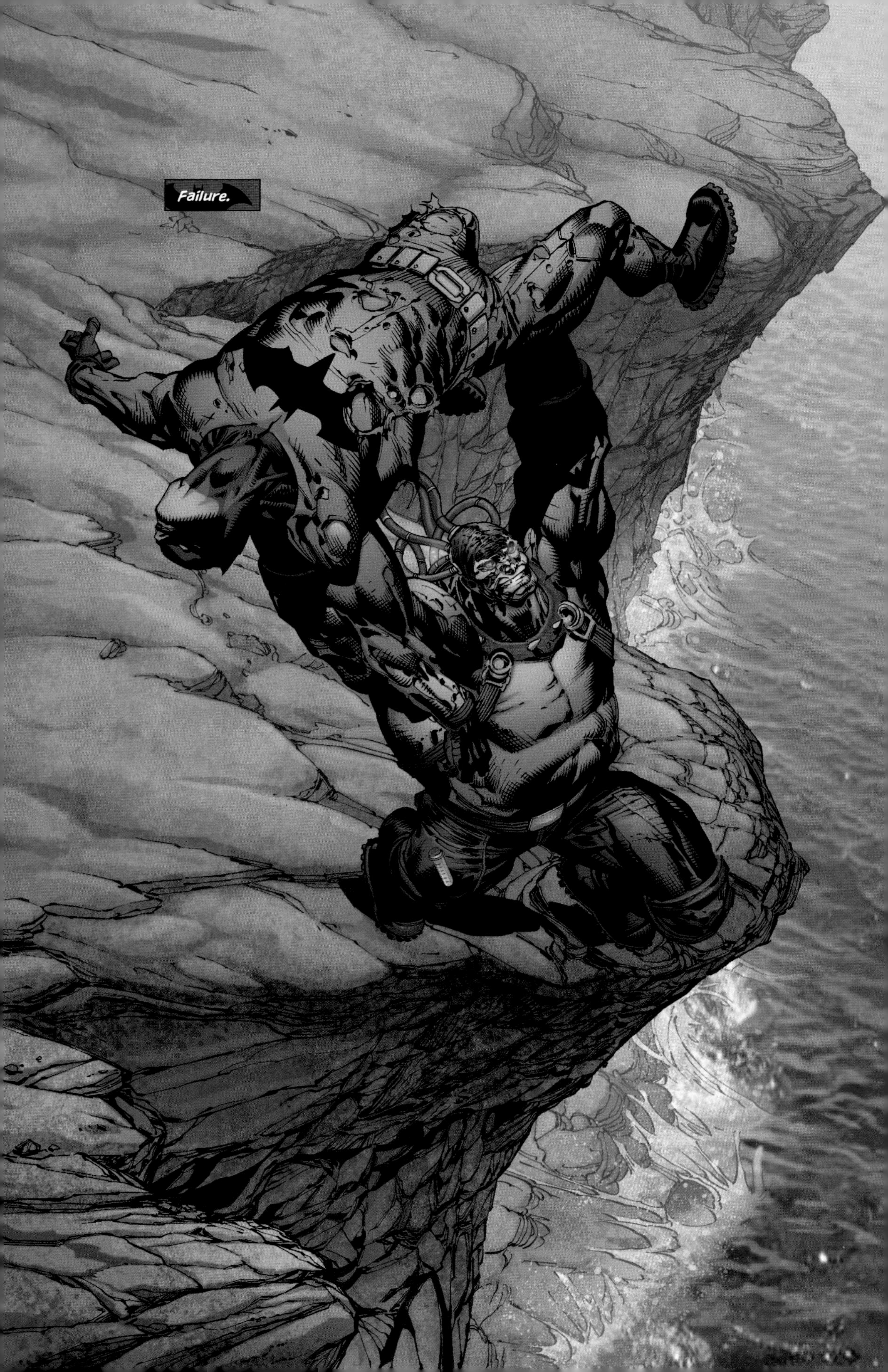
Failure.

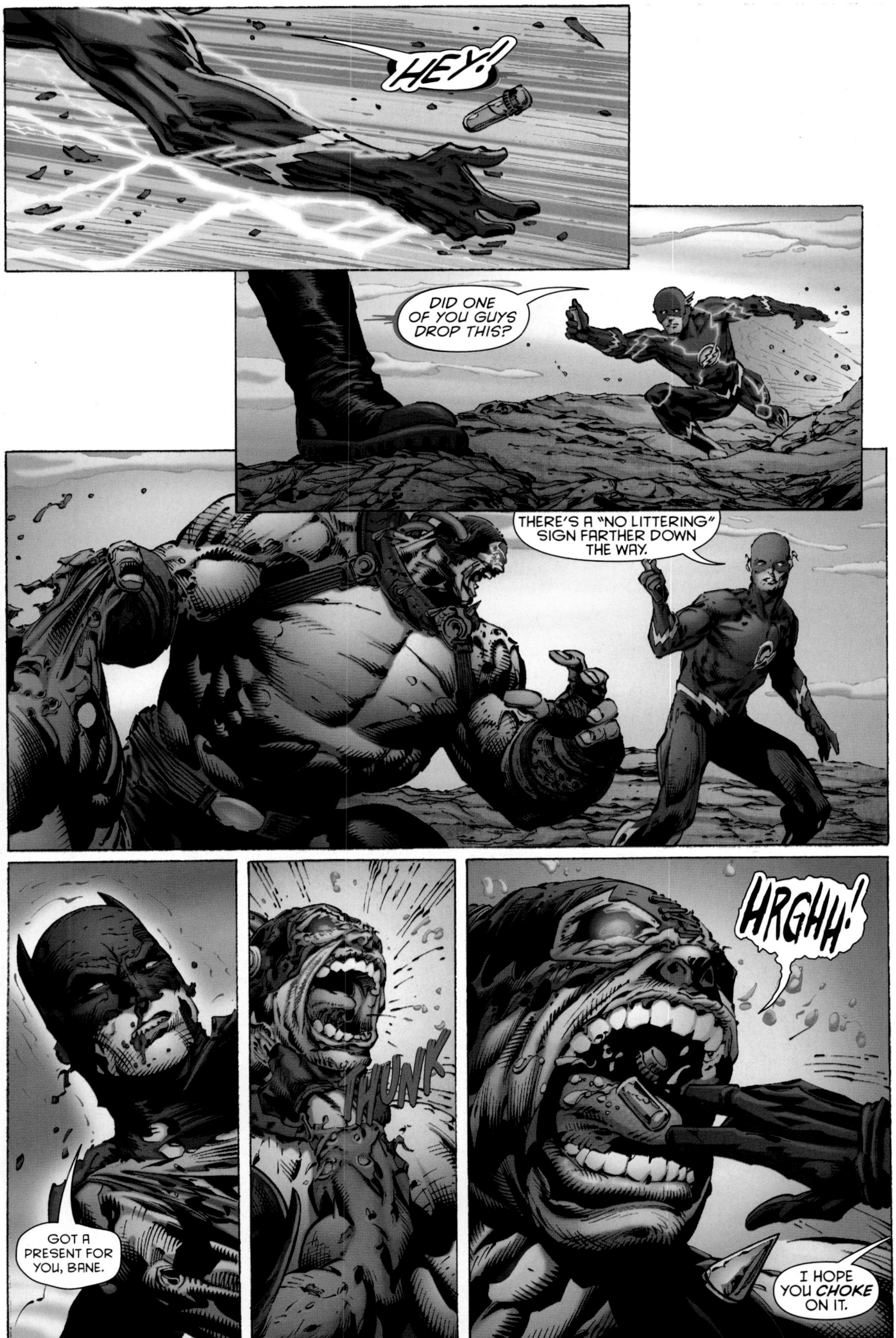
HEY!
DID ONE OF YOU GUYS DROP THIS?
THERE'S A "NO LITTERING" SIGN FARTHER DOWN THE WAY.
GOT A PRESENT FOR YOU, BANE.
THUNK
HRGHH!
I HOPE YOU CHOKE ON IT.

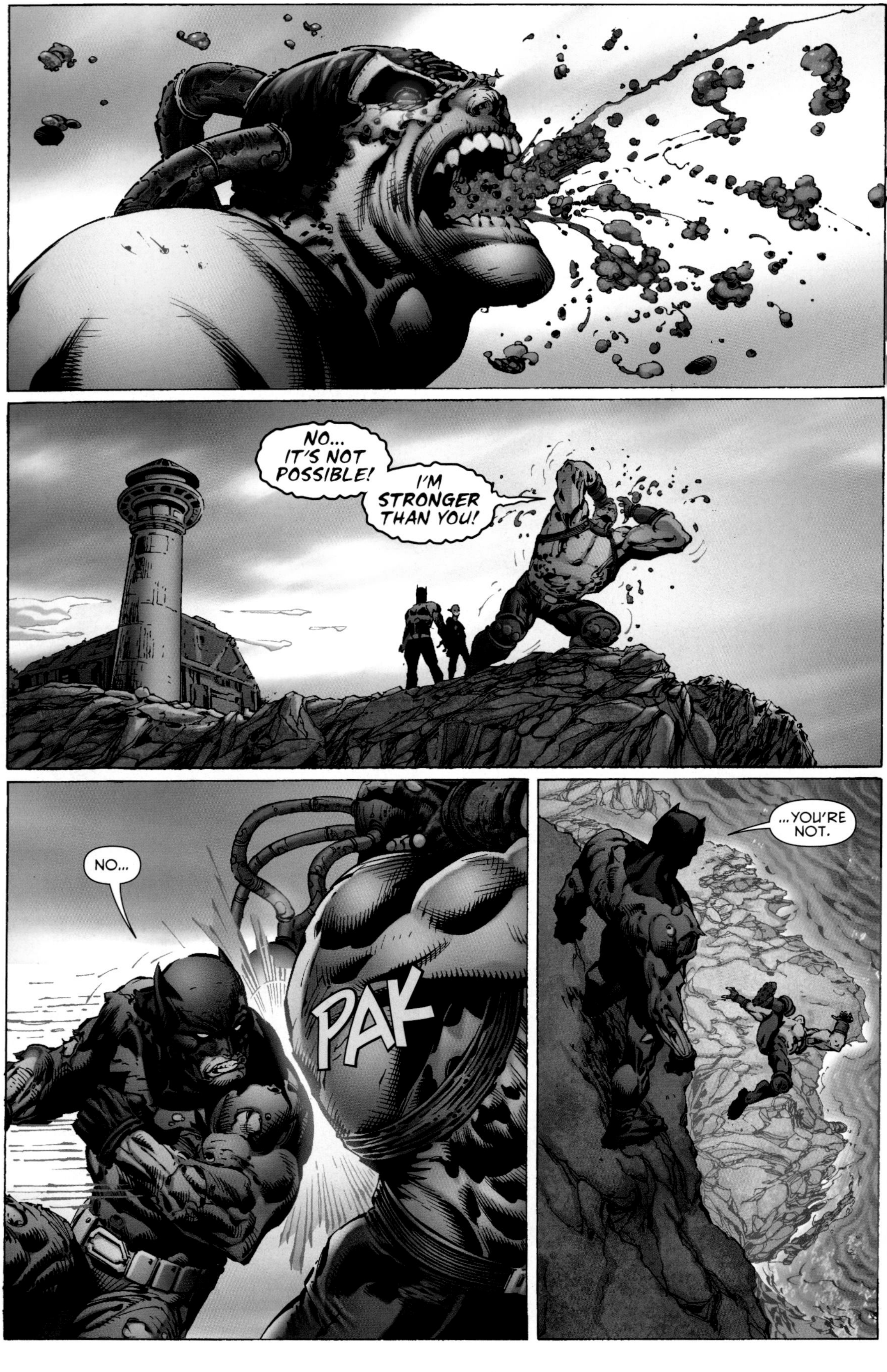
NO... IT'S NOT POSSIBLE!
I'M STRONGER THAN YOU!
NO...
PAK
...YOU'RE NOT.

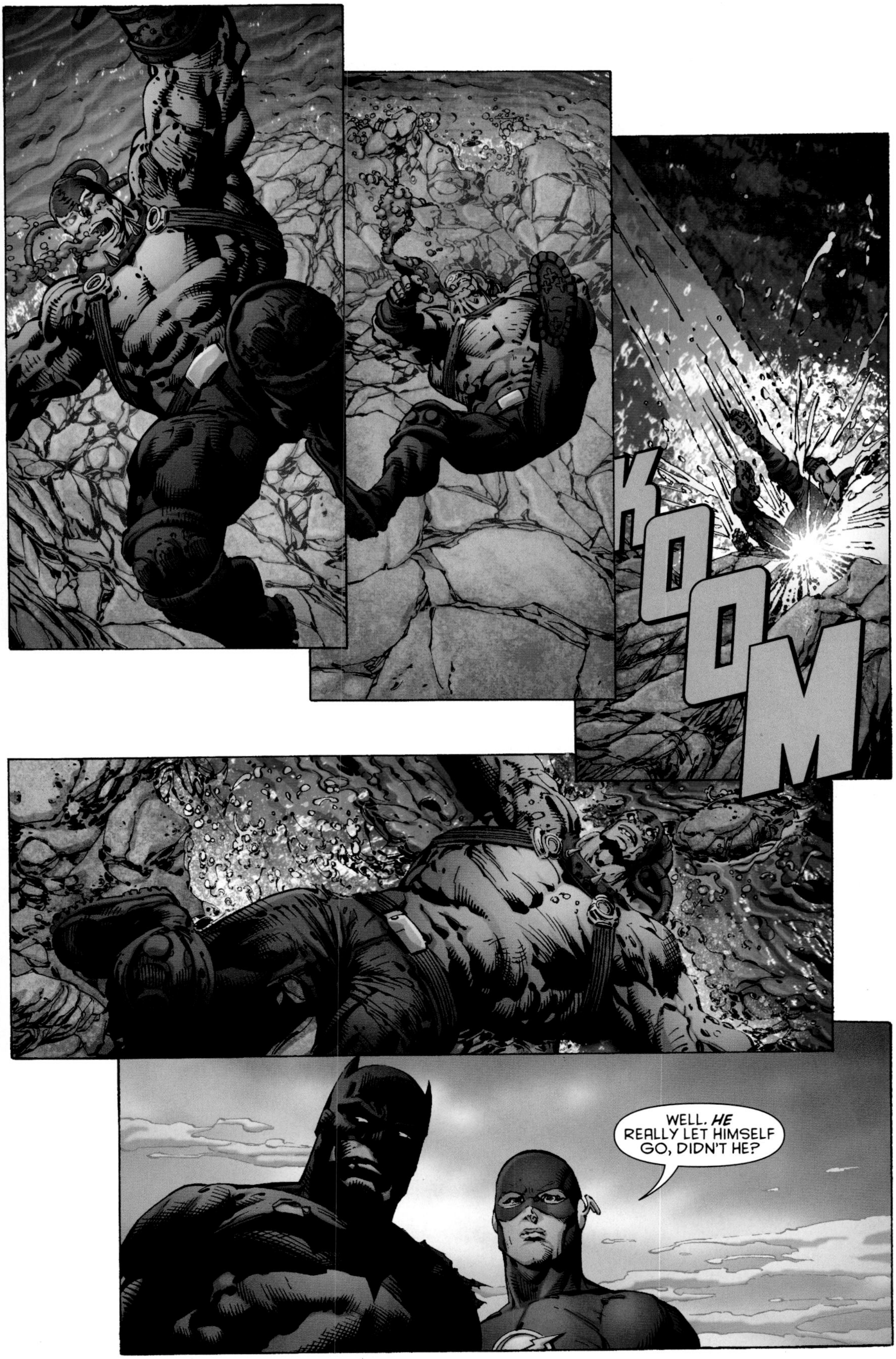
KOOM
WELL. HE REALLY LET HIMSELF GO, DIDN'T HE?

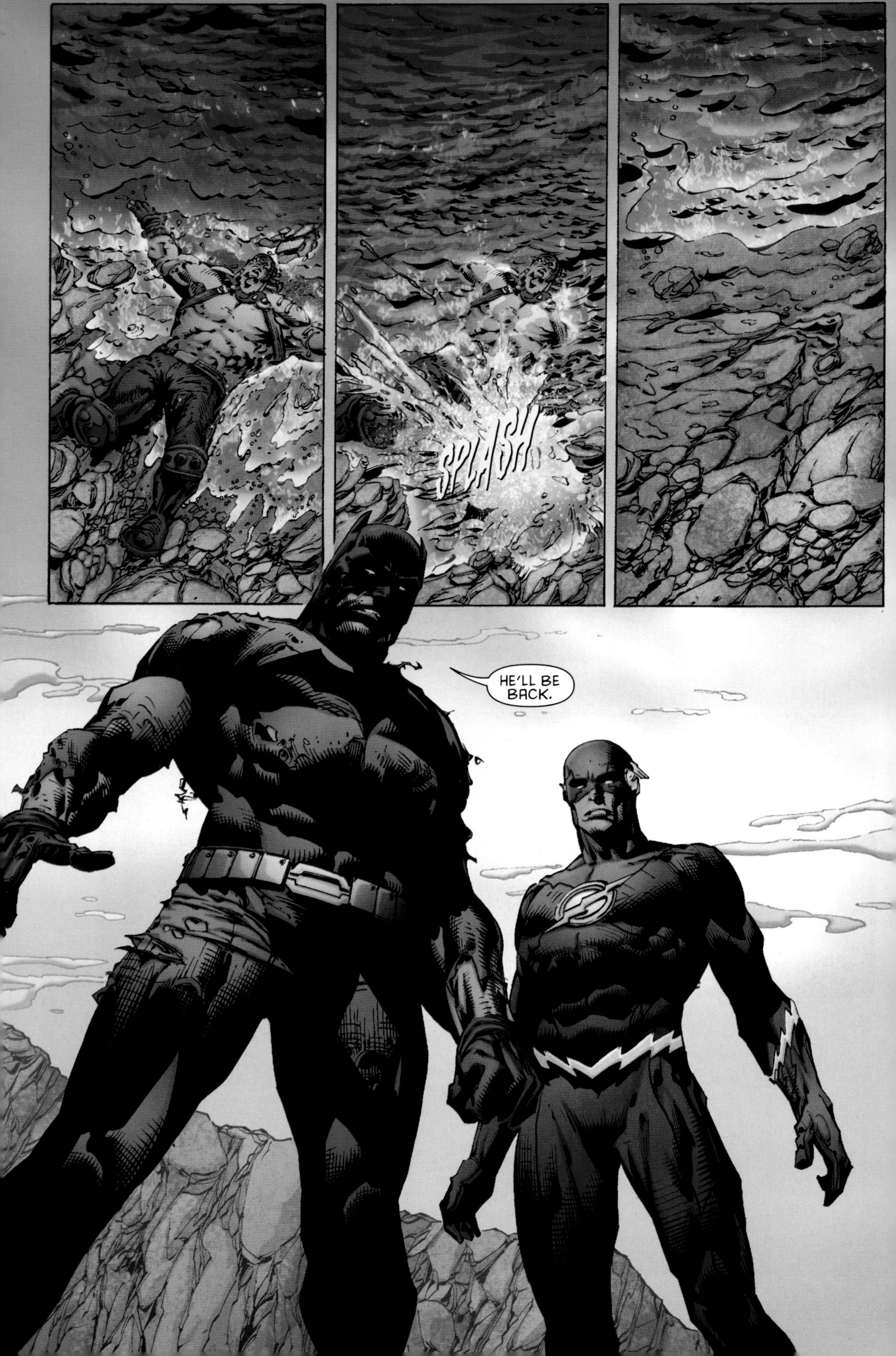
SPLASH
HE'LL BE BACK.

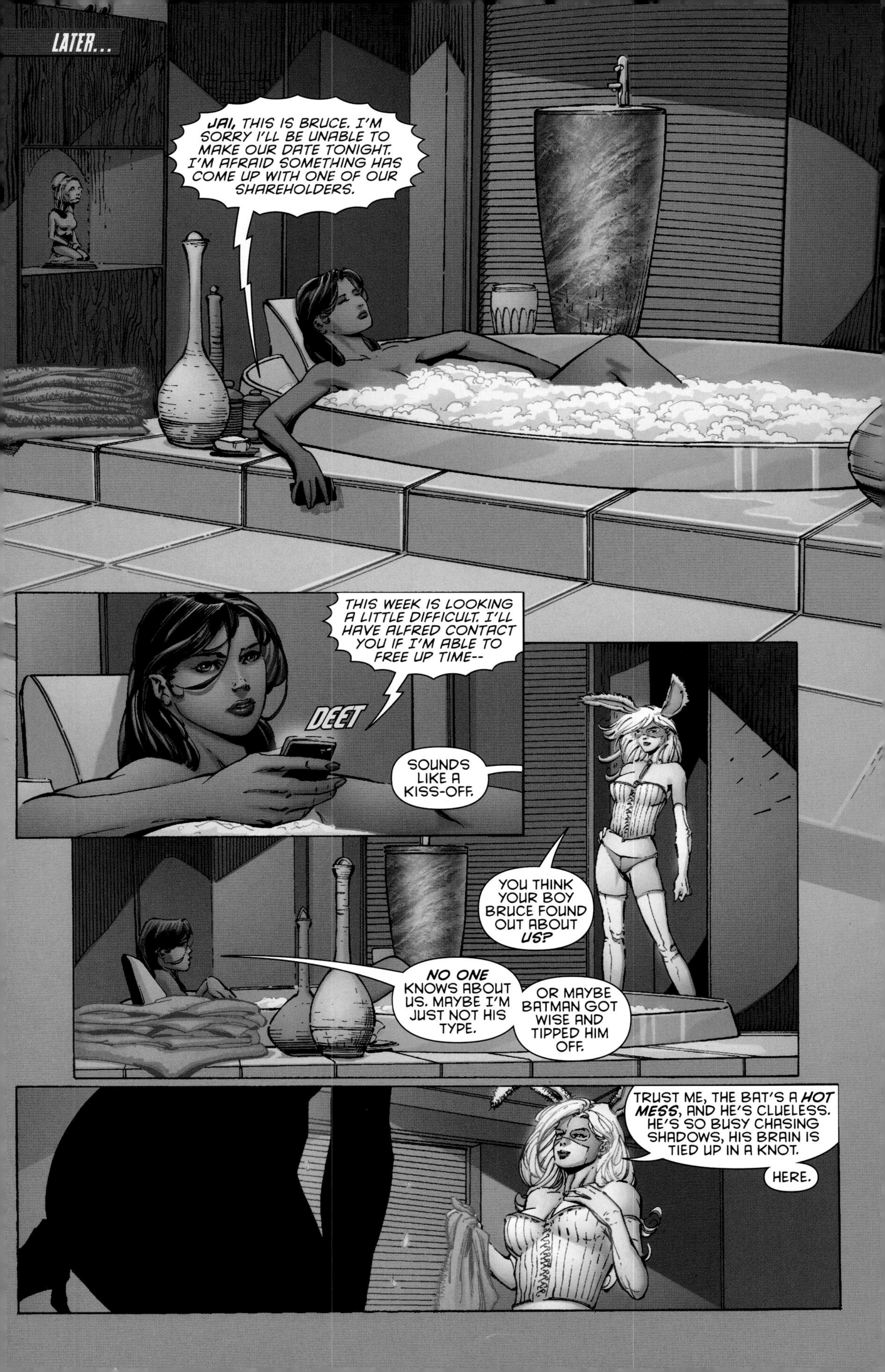
LATER...
JAI, THIS IS BRUCE. I'M SORRY I'LL BE UNABLE TO MAKE OUR DATE TONIGHT. I'M AFRAID SOMETHING HAS COME UP WITH ONE OF OUR SHAREHOLDERS.
THIS WEEK IS LOOKING A LITTLE DIFFICULT. I'LL HAVE ALFRED CONTACT YOU IF I'M ABLE TO FREE UP TIME--
DEET
SOUNDS LIKE A KISS-OFF.
YOU THINK YOUR BOY BRUCE FOUND OUT ABOUT US?
NO ONE KNOWS ABOUT US. MAYBE I'M JUST NOT HIS TYPE.
OR MAYBE BATMAN GOT WISE AND TIPPED HIM OFF.
TRUST ME, THE BAT'S A HOT MESS, AND HE'S CLUELESS. HE'S SO BUSY CHASING SHADOWS, HIS BRAIN IS TIED UP IN A KNOT.
HERE.

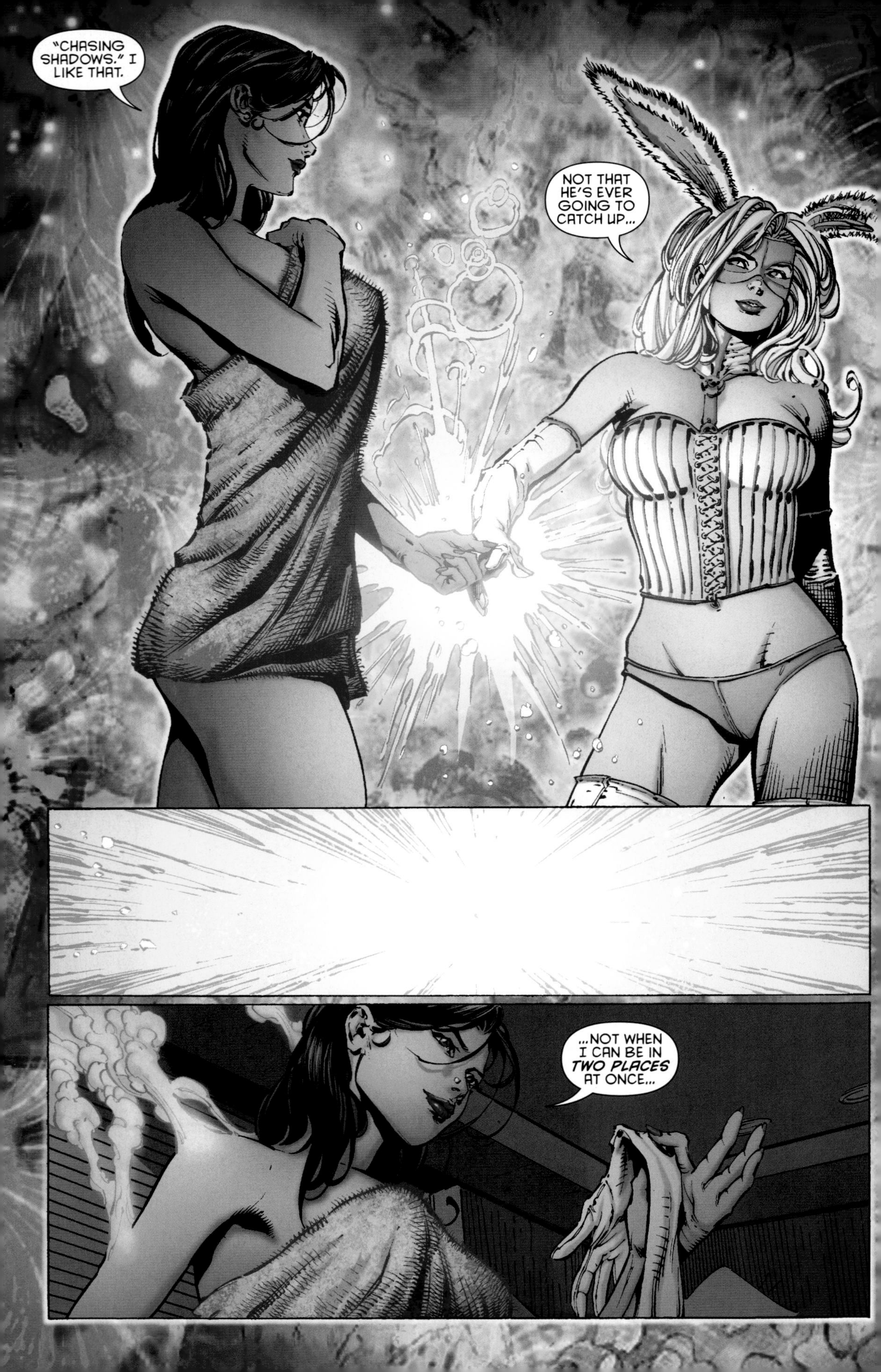
"CHASING SHADOWS." I LIKE THAT.
NOT THAT HE'S EVER GOING TO CATCH UP...
...NOT WHEN I CAN BE IN *TWO PLACES* AT ONCE...

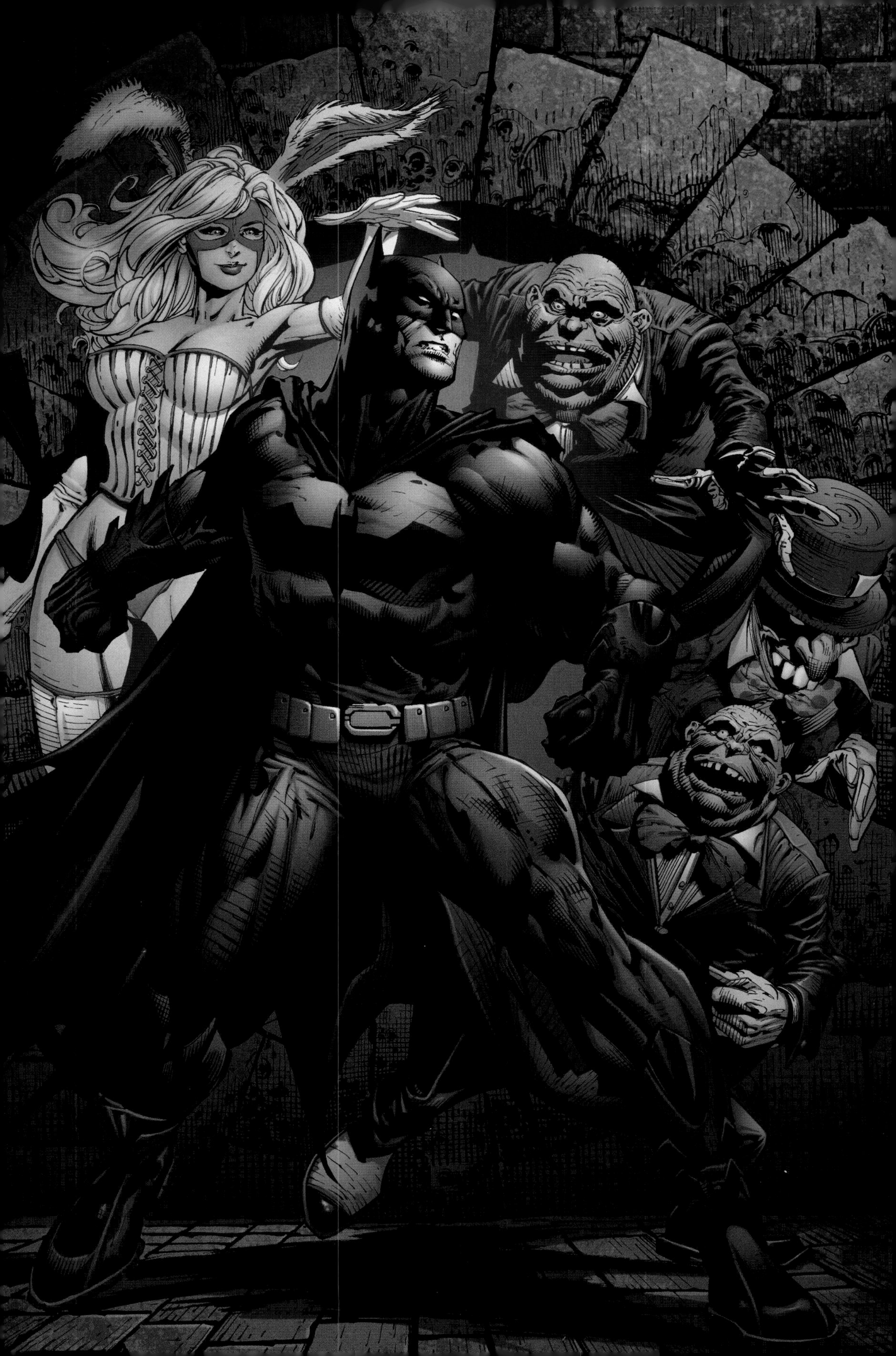

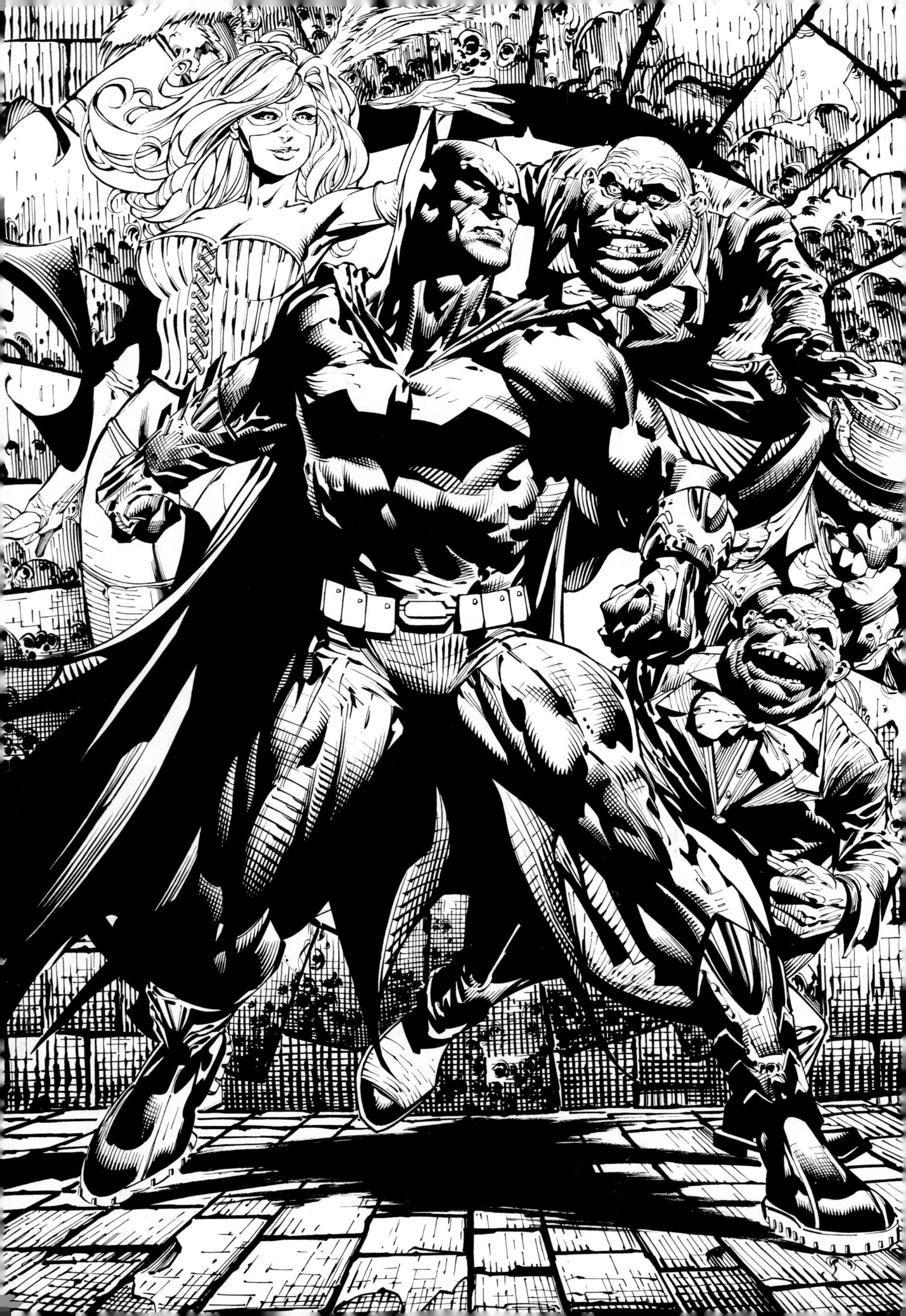

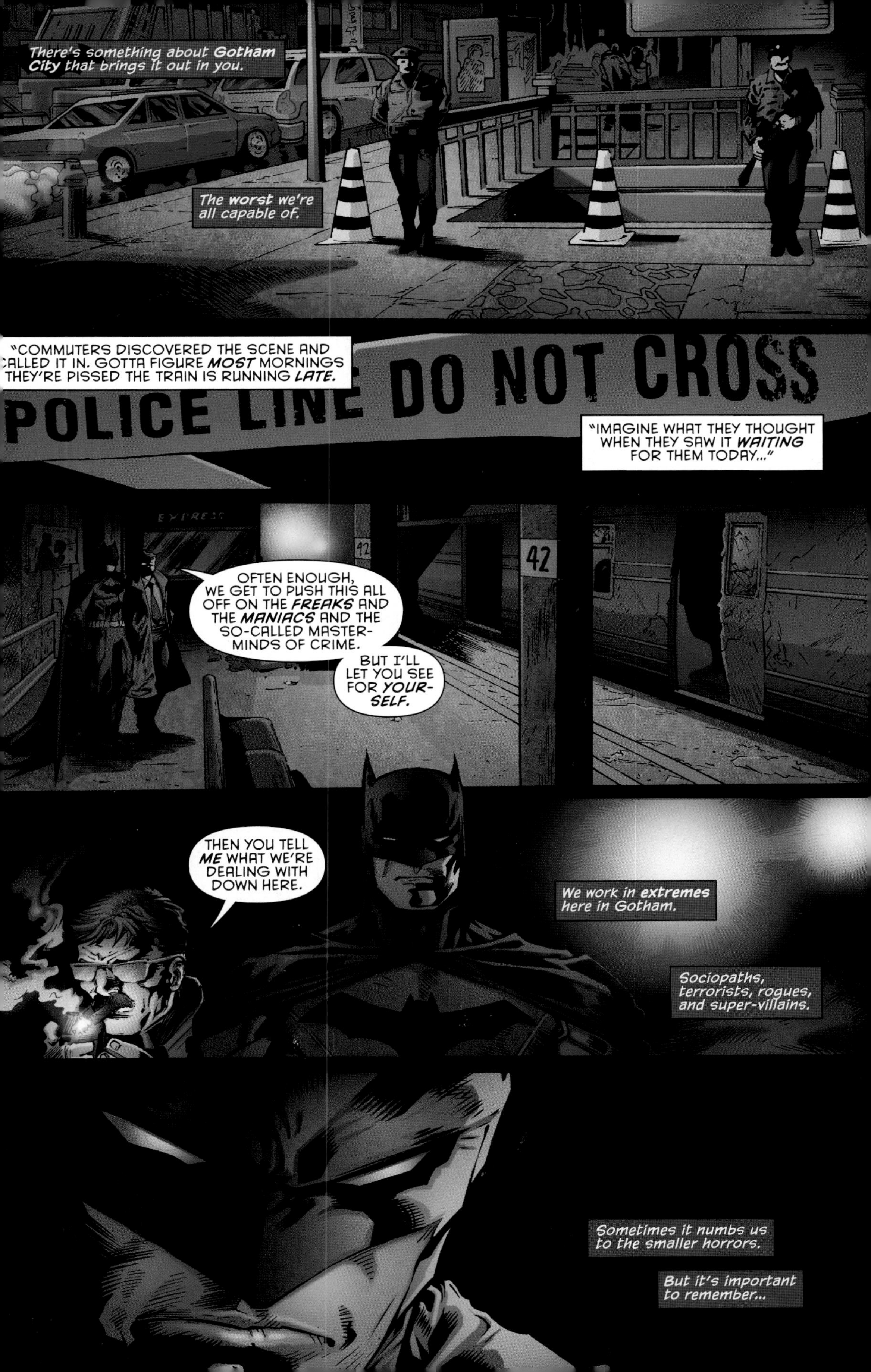
There's something about Gotham City that brings it out in you.
The worst we're all capable of.
"COMMUTERS DISCOVERED THE SCENE AND CALLED IT IN. GOTTA FIGURE MOST MORNINGS THEY'RE PISSED THE TRAIN IS RUNNING LATE.
POLICE LINE DO NOT CROSS
"IMAGINE WHAT THEY THOUGHT WHEN THEY SAW IT WAITING FOR THEM TODAY..."
EXPRESS
42
42
OFTEN ENOUGH, WE GET TO PUSH THIS ALL OFF ON THE FREAKS AND THE MANIACS AND THE SO-CALLED MASTER-MINDS OF CRIME.
BUT I'LL LET YOU SEE FOR YOUR-SELF.
THEN YOU TELL ME WHAT WE'RE DEALING WITH DOWN HERE.
We work in extremes here in Gotham.
Sociopaths, terrorists, rogues, and super-villains.
Sometimes it numbs us to the smaller horrors.
But it's important to remember...

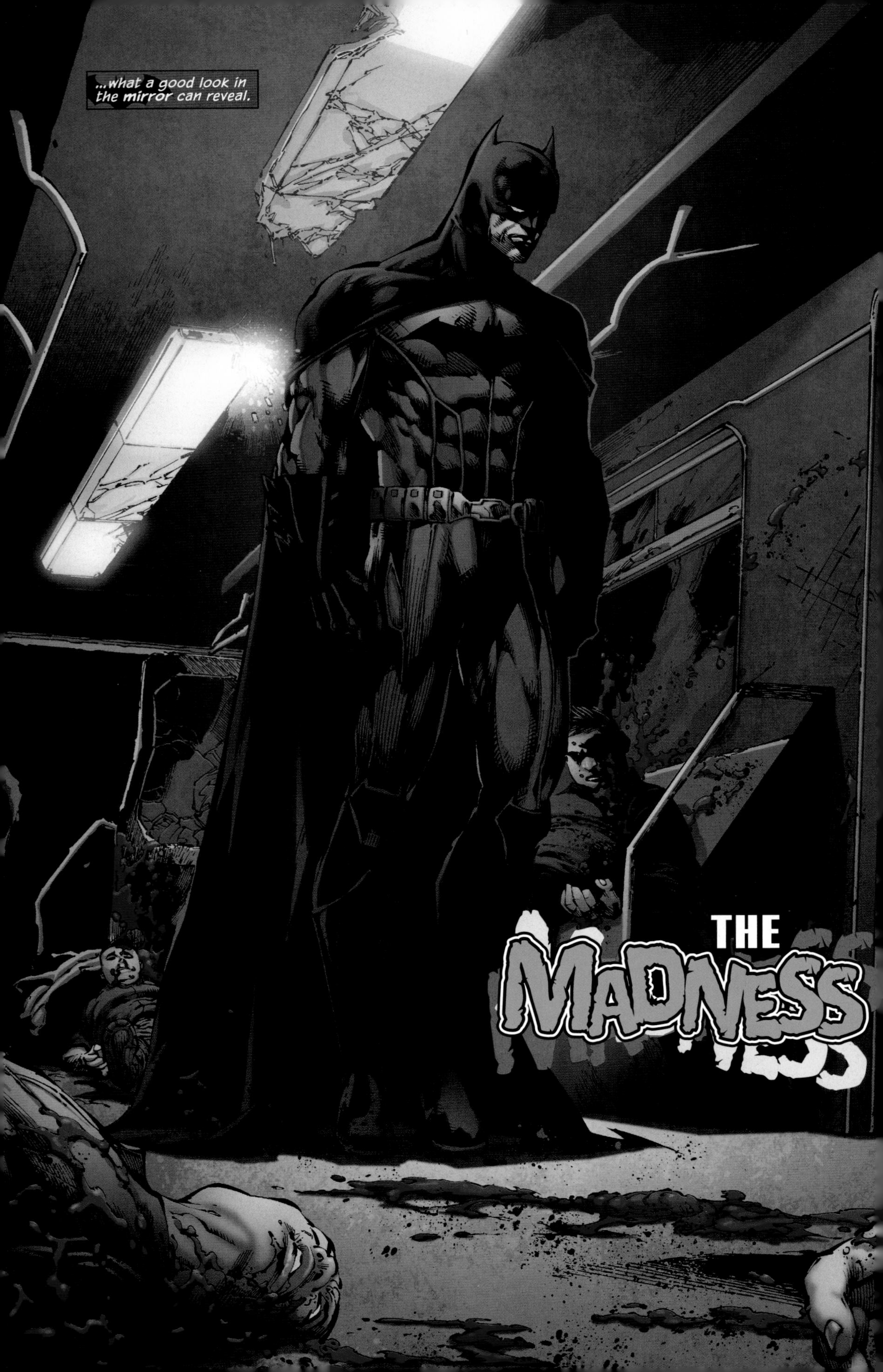
...what a good look in the mirror can reveal.
THE MADNESS

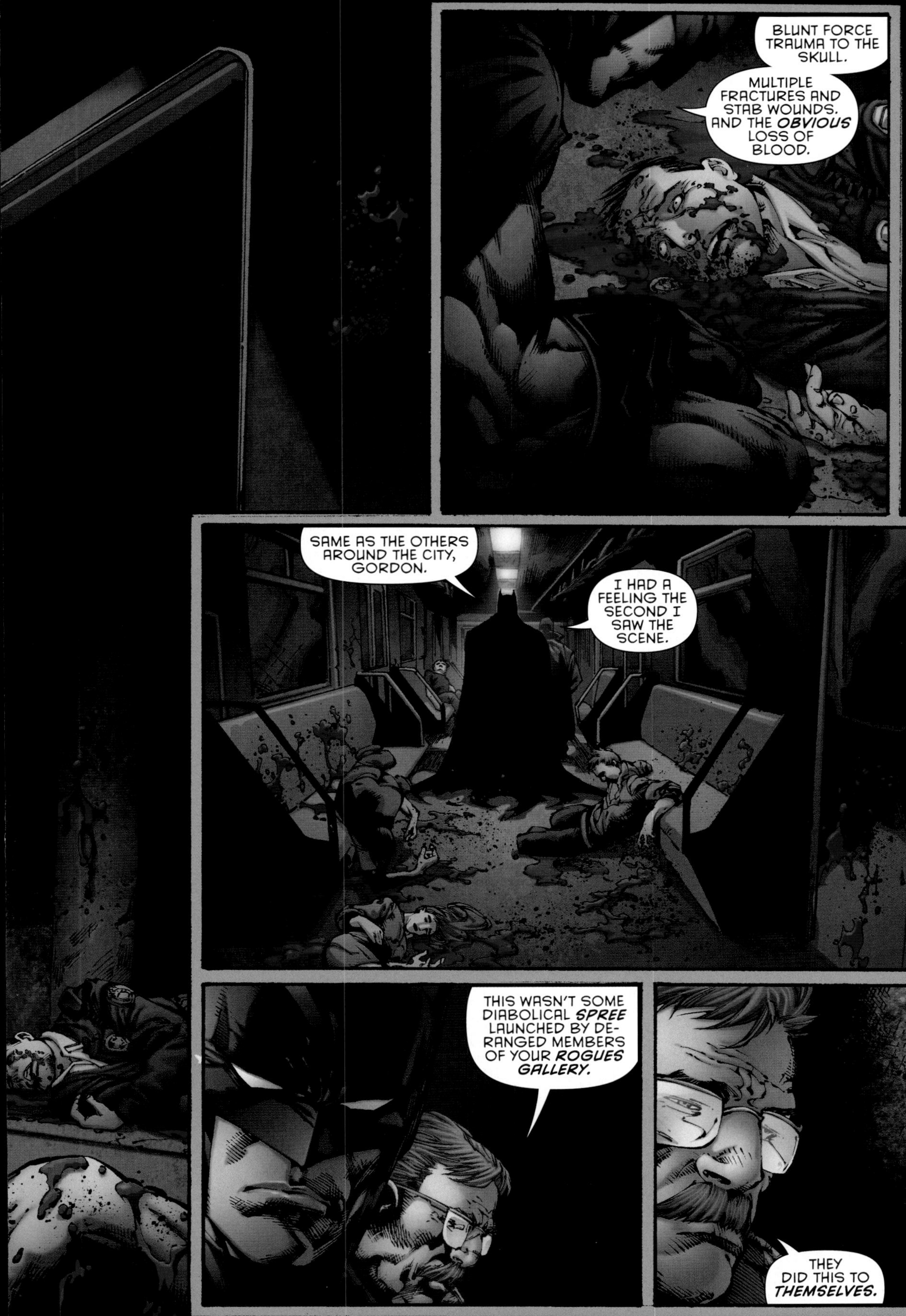
BLUNT FORCE TRAUMA TO THE SKULL.
MULTIPLE FRACTURES AND STAB WOUNDS. AND THE *OBVIOUS* LOSS OF BLOOD.
SAME AS THE OTHERS AROUND THE CITY, GORDON.
I HAD A FEELING THE SECOND I SAW THE SCENE.
THIS WASN'T SOME DIABOLICAL *SPREE* LAUNCHED BY DE-RANGED MEMBERS OF YOUR *ROGUES GALLERY.*
THEY DID THIS TO *THEMSELVES.*

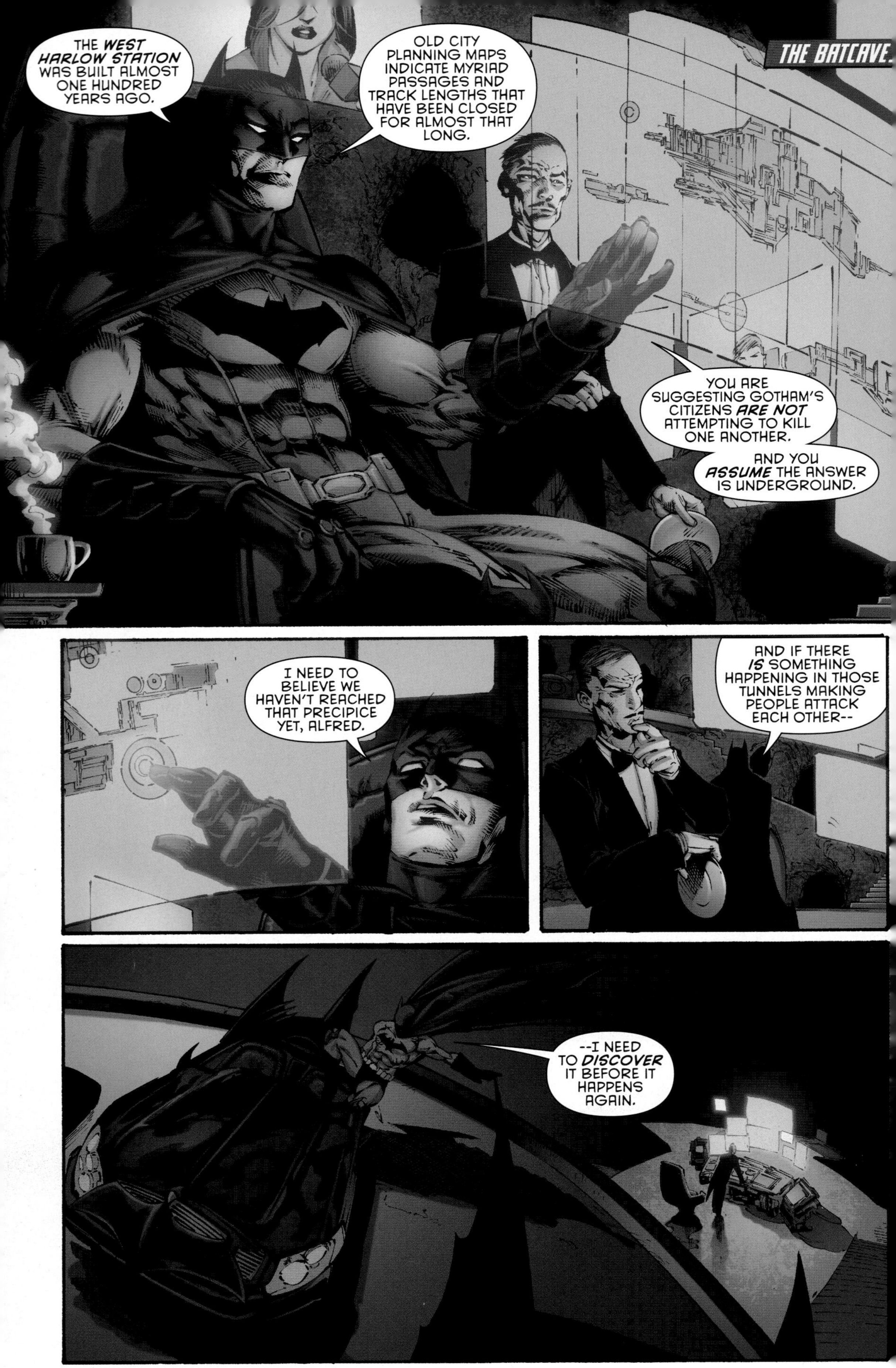
THE BATCAVE.
THE WEST HARLOW STATION WAS BUILT ALMOST ONE HUNDRED YEARS AGO.
OLD CITY PLANNING MAPS INDICATE MYRIAD PASSAGES AND TRACK LENGTHS THAT HAVE BEEN CLOSED FOR ALMOST THAT LONG.
YOU ARE SUGGESTING GOTHAM'S CITIZENS ARE NOT ATTEMPTING TO KILL ONE ANOTHER.
AND YOU ASSUME THE ANSWER IS UNDERGROUND.
I NEED TO BELIEVE WE HAVEN'T REACHED THAT PRECIPICE YET, ALFRED.
AND IF THERE IS SOMETHING HAPPENING IN THOSE TUNNELS MAKING PEOPLE ATTACK EACH OTHER--
--I NEED TO DISCOVER IT BEFORE IT HAPPENS AGAIN.

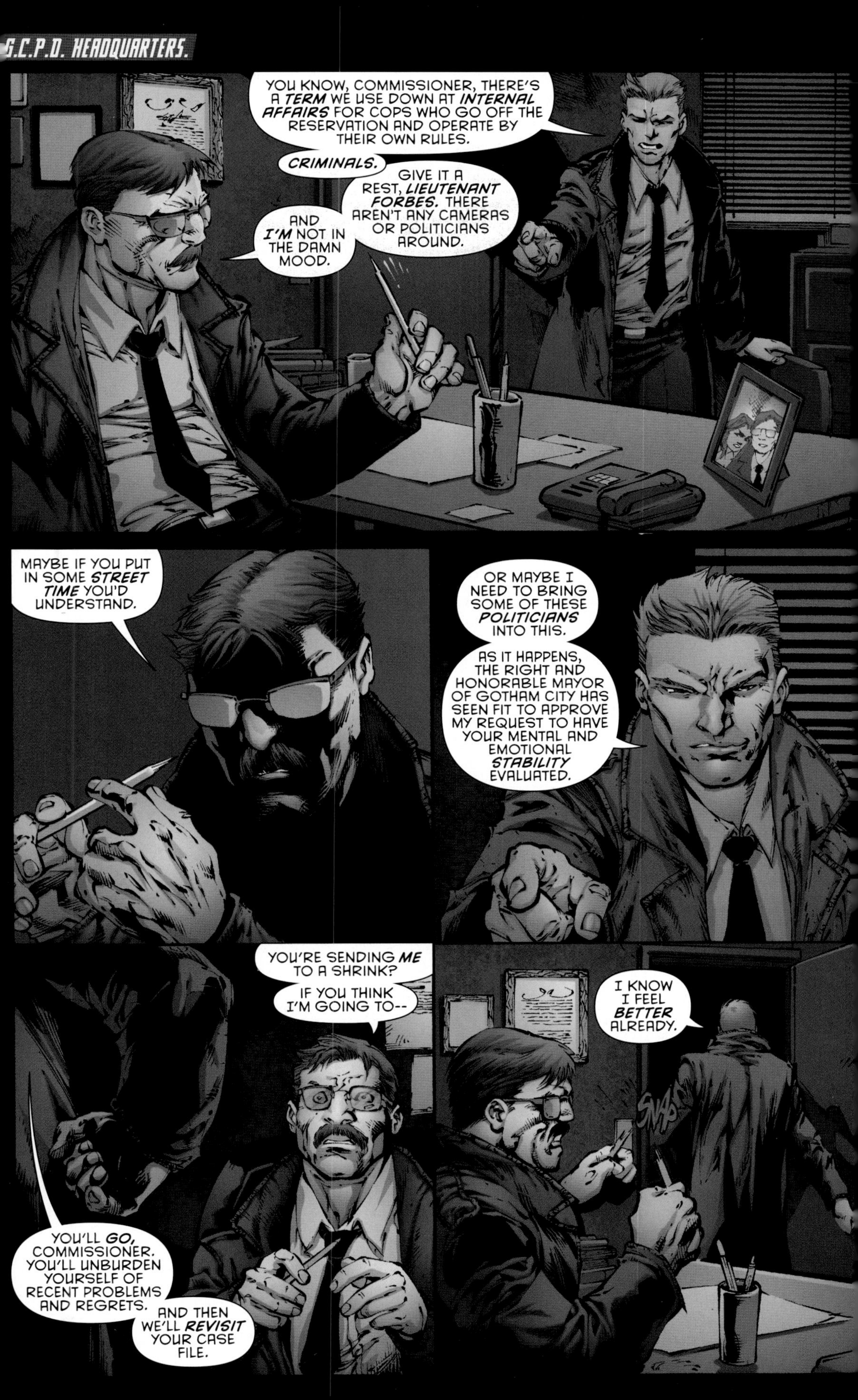

G.C.P.D. HEADQUARTERS.
YOU KNOW, COMMISSIONER, THERE'S A TERM WE USE DOWN AT INTERNAL AFFAIRS FOR COPS WHO GO OFF THE RESERVATION AND OPERATE BY THEIR OWN RULES.
CRIMINALS.
GIVE IT A REST, LIEUTENANT FORBES. THERE AREN'T ANY CAMERAS OR POLITICIANS AROUND.
AND I'M NOT IN THE DAMN MOOD.
MAYBE IF YOU PUT IN SOME STREET TIME YOU'D UNDERSTAND.
OR MAYBE I NEED TO BRING SOME OF THESE POLITICIANS INTO THIS.
AS IT HAPPENS, THE RIGHT AND HONORABLE MAYOR OF GOTHAM CITY HAS SEEN FIT TO APPROVE MY REQUEST TO HAVE YOUR MENTAL AND EMOTIONAL STABILITY EVALUATED.
YOU'RE SENDING ME TO A SHRINK?
IF YOU THINK I'M GOING TO--
YOU'LL GO, COMMISSIONER. YOU'LL UNBURDEN YOURSELF OF RECENT PROBLEMS AND REGRETS.
AND THEN WE'LL REVISIT YOUR CASE FILE.
SNAP
I KNOW I FEEL BETTER ALREADY.

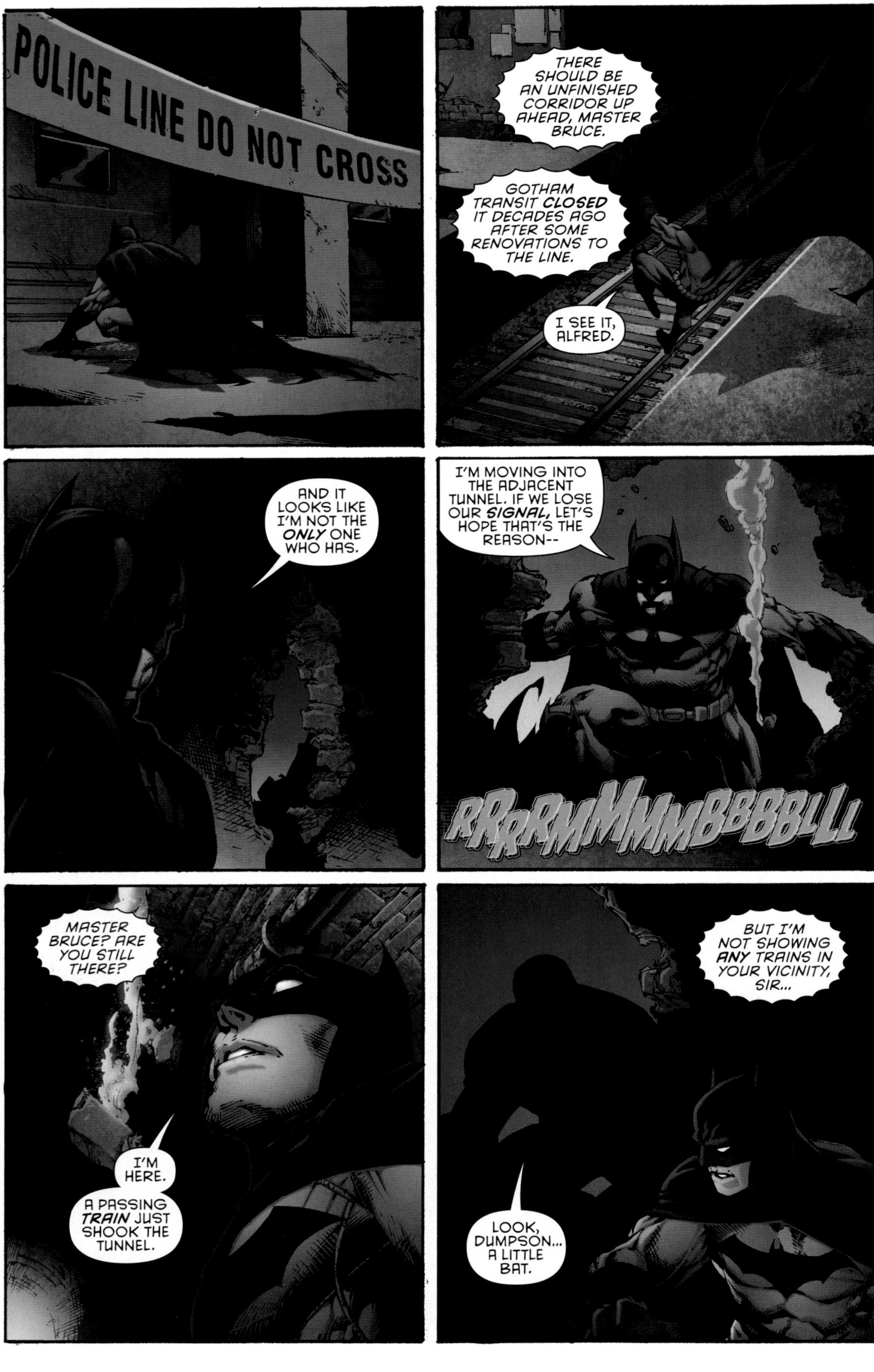
POLICE LINE DO NOT CROSS
THERE SHOULD BE AN UNFINISHED CORRIDOR UP AHEAD, MASTER BRUCE.
GOTHAM TRANSIT CLOSED IT DECADES AGO AFTER SOME RENOVATIONS TO THE LINE.
I SEE IT, ALFRED.
AND IT LOOKS LIKE I'M NOT THE ONLY ONE WHO HAS.
I'M MOVING INTO THE ADJACENT TUNNEL. IF WE LOSE OUR SIGNAL, LET'S HOPE THAT'S THE REASON--
RRRRMMMMMBBBBLLL
MASTER BRUCE? ARE YOU STILL THERE?
I'M HERE.
A PASSING TRAIN JUST SHOOK THE TUNNEL.
BUT I'M NOT SHOWING ANY TRAINS IN YOUR VICINITY, SIR...
LOOK, DUMPSON... A LITTLE BAT.

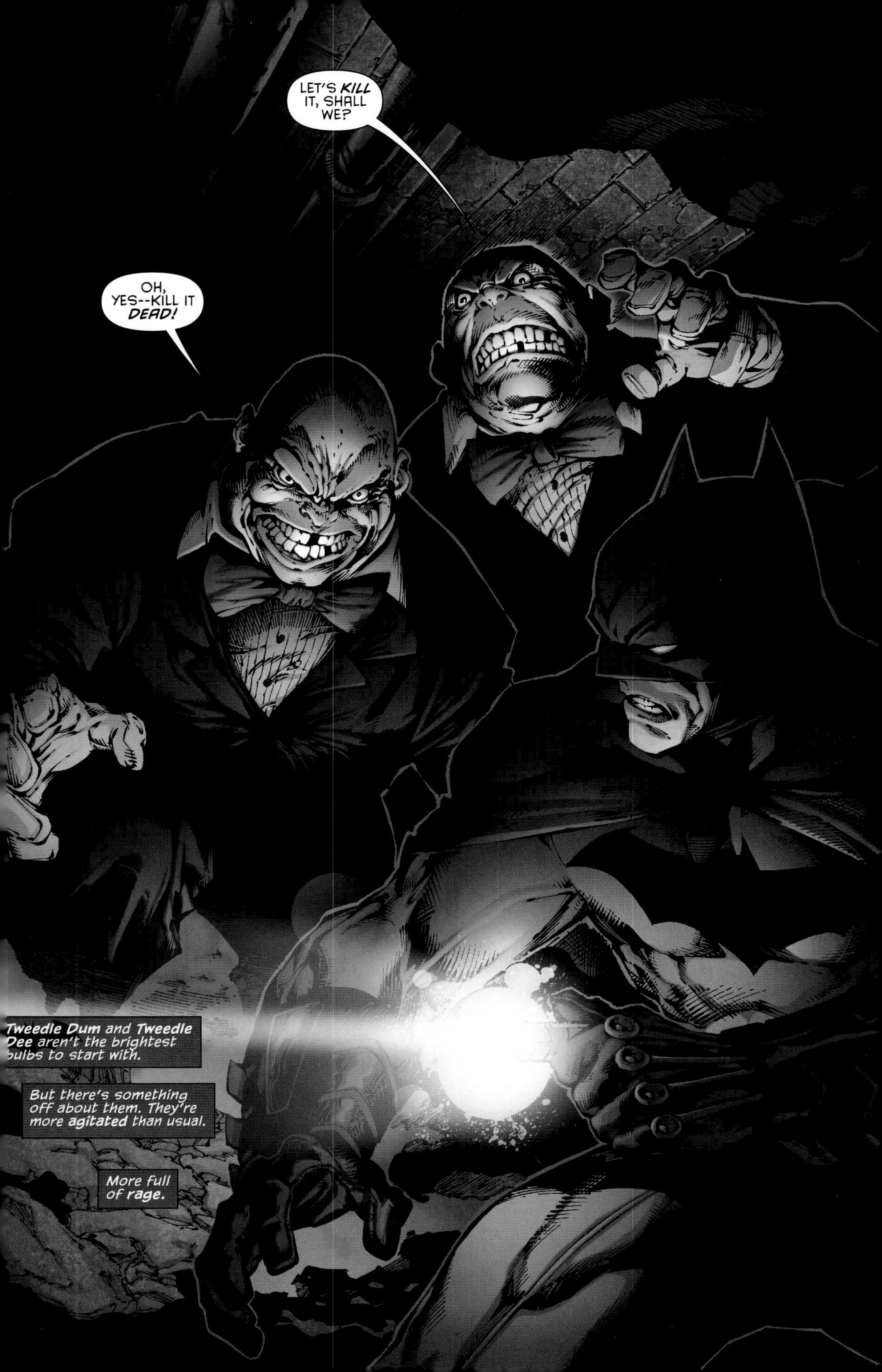
LET'S KILL IT, SHALL WE?
OH, YES--KILL IT DEAD!
Tweedle Dum and Tweedle Dee aren't the brightest bulbs to start with.
But there's something off about them. They're more agitated than usual.
More full of rage.

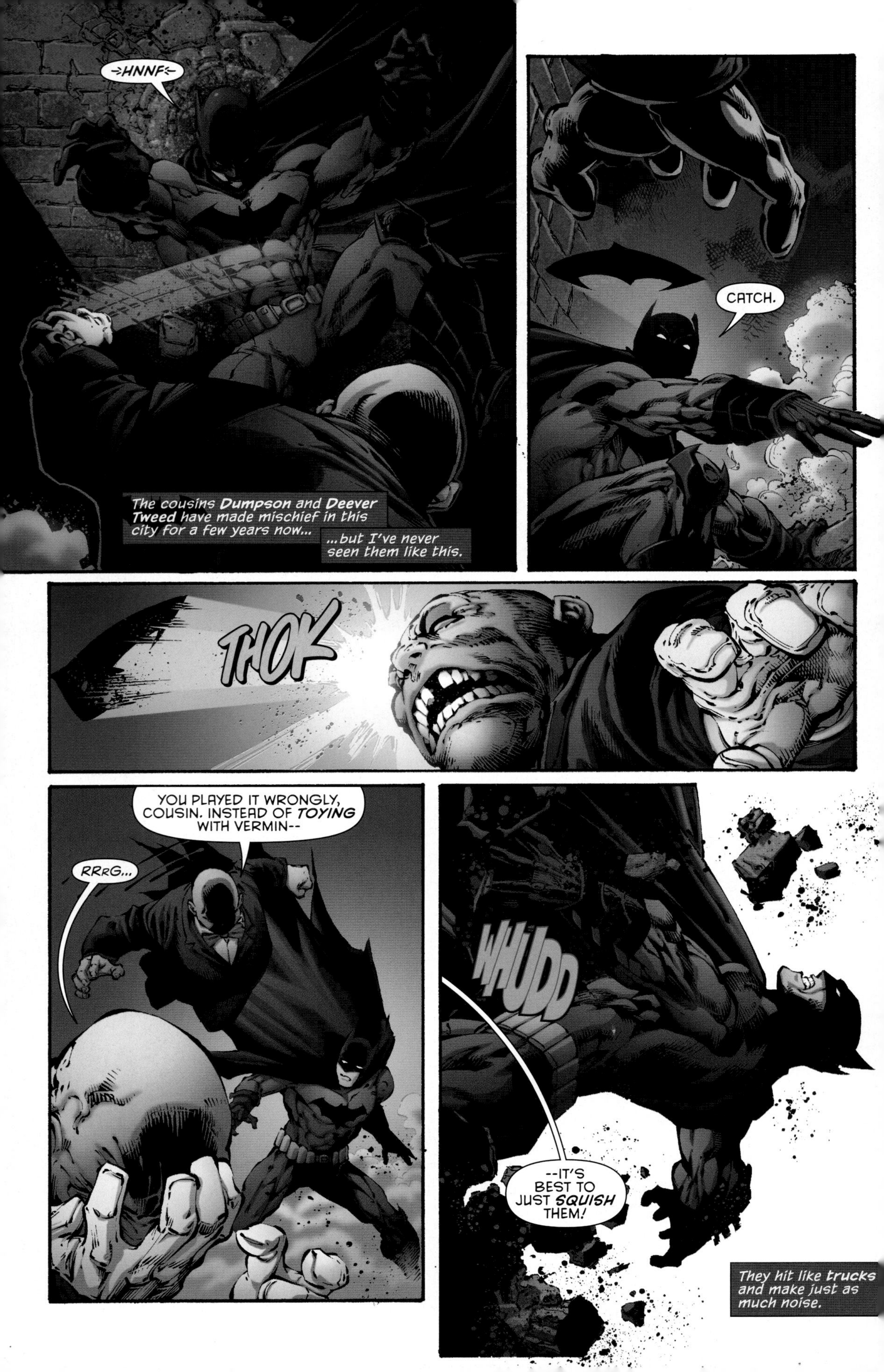

-HNNF-
The cousins Dumpson and Deever Tweed have made mischief in this city for a few years now...
...but I've never seen them like this.
CATCH.
THOK
YOU PLAYED IT WRONGLY, COUSIN. INSTEAD OF TOYING WITH VERMIN--
RRRG...
WHUDD
--IT'S BEST TO JUST SQUISH THEM!
They hit like trucks and make just as much noise.

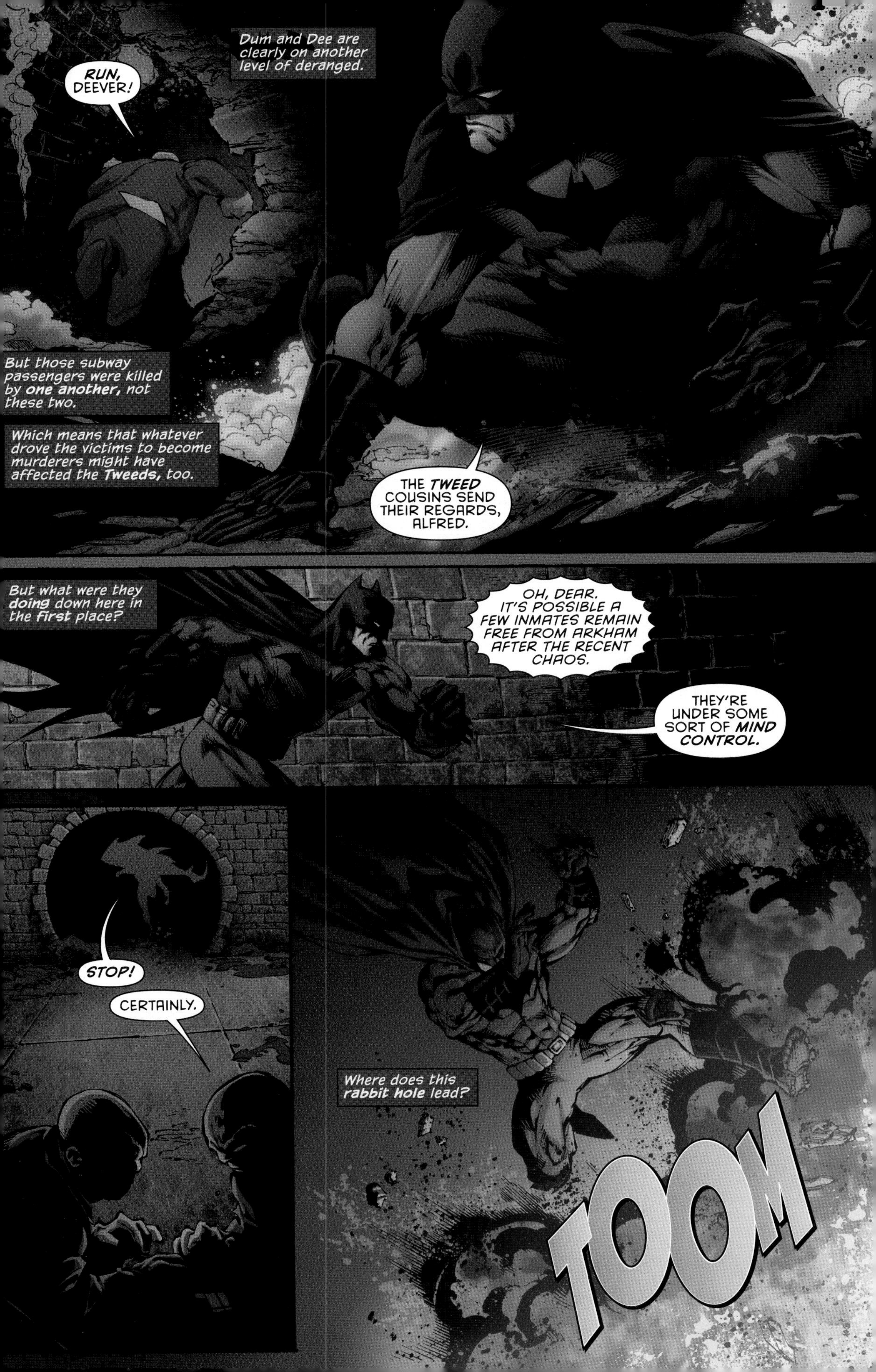
Dum and Dee are clearly on another level of deranged.
RUN, DEEVER!
But those subway passengers were killed by one another, not these two.
Which means that whatever drove the victims to become murderers might have affected the Tweeds, too.
THE TWEED COUSINS SEND THEIR REGARDS, ALFRED.
But what were they doing down here in the first place?
OH, DEAR. IT'S POSSIBLE A FEW INMATES REMAIN FREE FROM ARKHAM AFTER THE RECENT CHAOS.
THEY'RE UNDER SOME SORT OF MIND CONTROL.
STOP!
CERTAINLY.
Where does this rabbit hole lead?
TOOM

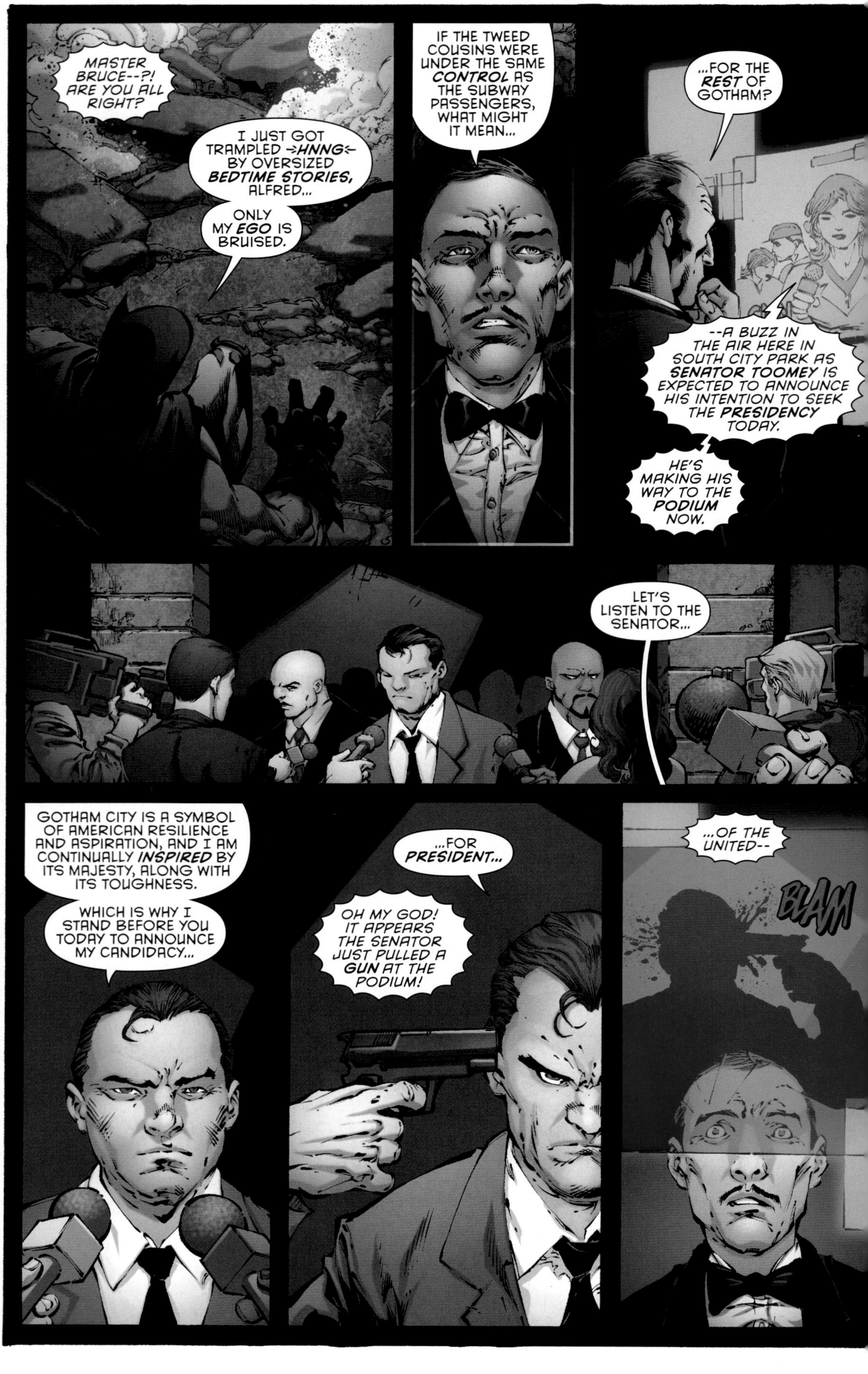
MASTER BRUCE--?! ARE YOU ALL RIGHT?
I JUST GOT TRAMPLED ⇒HNNG⇐ BY OVERSIZED BEDTIME STORIES, ALFRED...
ONLY MY EGO IS BRUISED.
IF THE TWEED COUSINS WERE UNDER THE SAME CONTROL AS THE SUBWAY PASSENGERS, WHAT MIGHT IT MEAN...
...FOR THE REST OF GOTHAM?
--A BUZZ IN THE AIR HERE IN SOUTH CITY PARK AS SENATOR TOOMEY IS EXPECTED TO ANNOUNCE HIS INTENTION TO SEEK THE PRESIDENCY TODAY.
HE'S MAKING HIS WAY TO THE PODIUM NOW.
LET'S LISTEN TO THE SENATOR...
GOTHAM CITY IS A SYMBOL OF AMERICAN RESILIENCE AND ASPIRATION, AND I AM CONTINUALLY INSPIRED BY ITS MAJESTY, ALONG WITH ITS TOUGHNESS.
WHICH IS WHY I STAND BEFORE YOU TODAY TO ANNOUNCE MY CANDIDACY...
...FOR PRESIDENT...
OH MY GOD! IT APPEARS THE SENATOR JUST PULLED A GUN AT THE PODIUM!
...OF THE UNITED--
BLAM

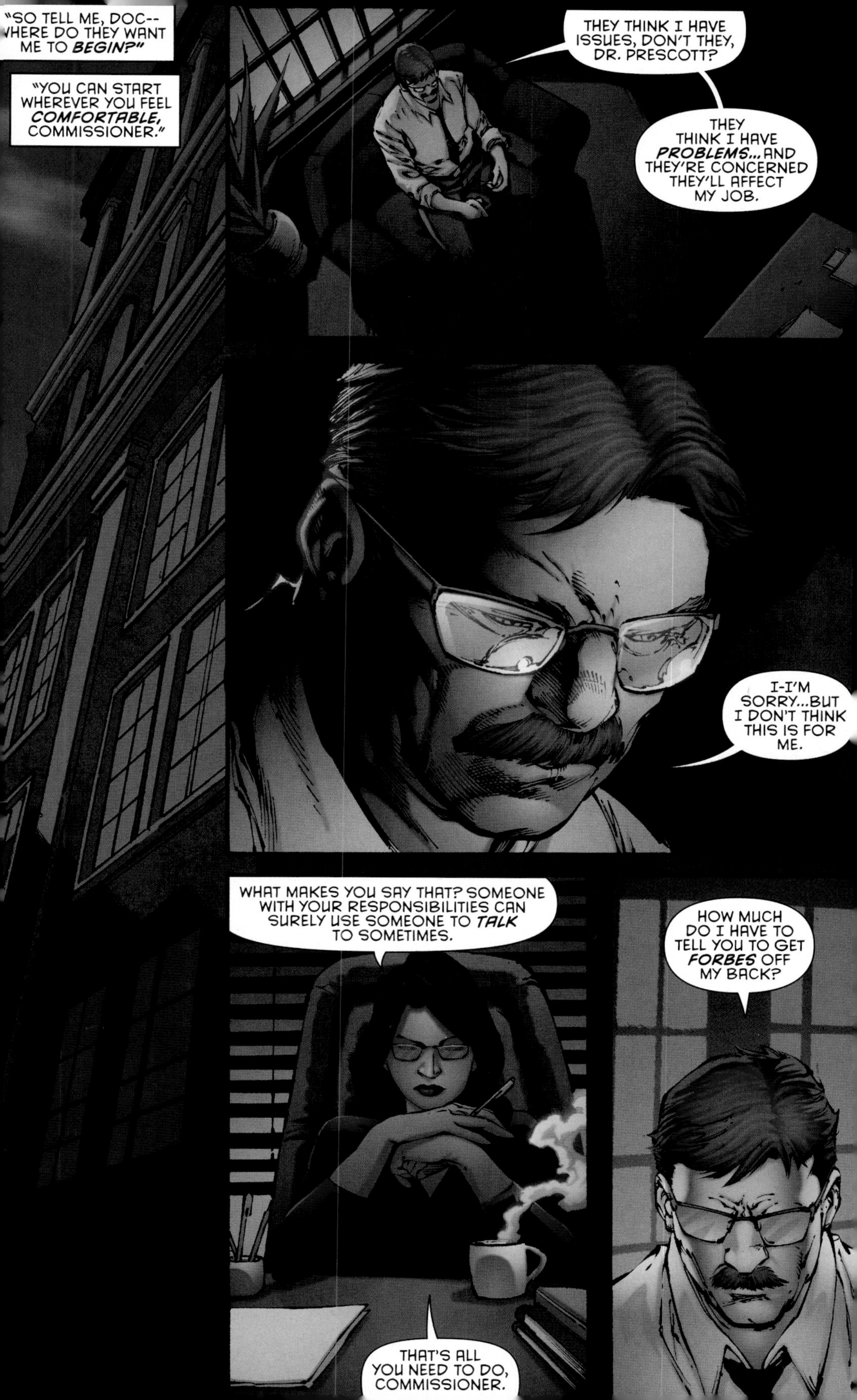
"SO TELL ME, DOC--WHERE DO THEY WANT ME TO BEGIN?"
"YOU CAN START WHEREVER YOU FEEL COMFORTABLE, COMMISSIONER."
THEY THINK I HAVE ISSUES, DON'T THEY, DR. PRESCOTT?
THEY THINK I HAVE PROBLEMS...AND THEY'RE CONCERNED THEY'LL AFFECT MY JOB.
I-I'M SORRY...BUT I DON'T THINK THIS IS FOR ME.
WHAT MAKES YOU SAY THAT? SOMEONE WITH YOUR RESPONSIBILITIES CAN SURELY USE SOMEONE TO TALK TO SOMETIMES.
THAT'S ALL YOU NEED TO DO, COMMISSIONER.
HOW MUCH DO I HAVE TO TELL YOU TO GET FORBES OFF MY BACK?

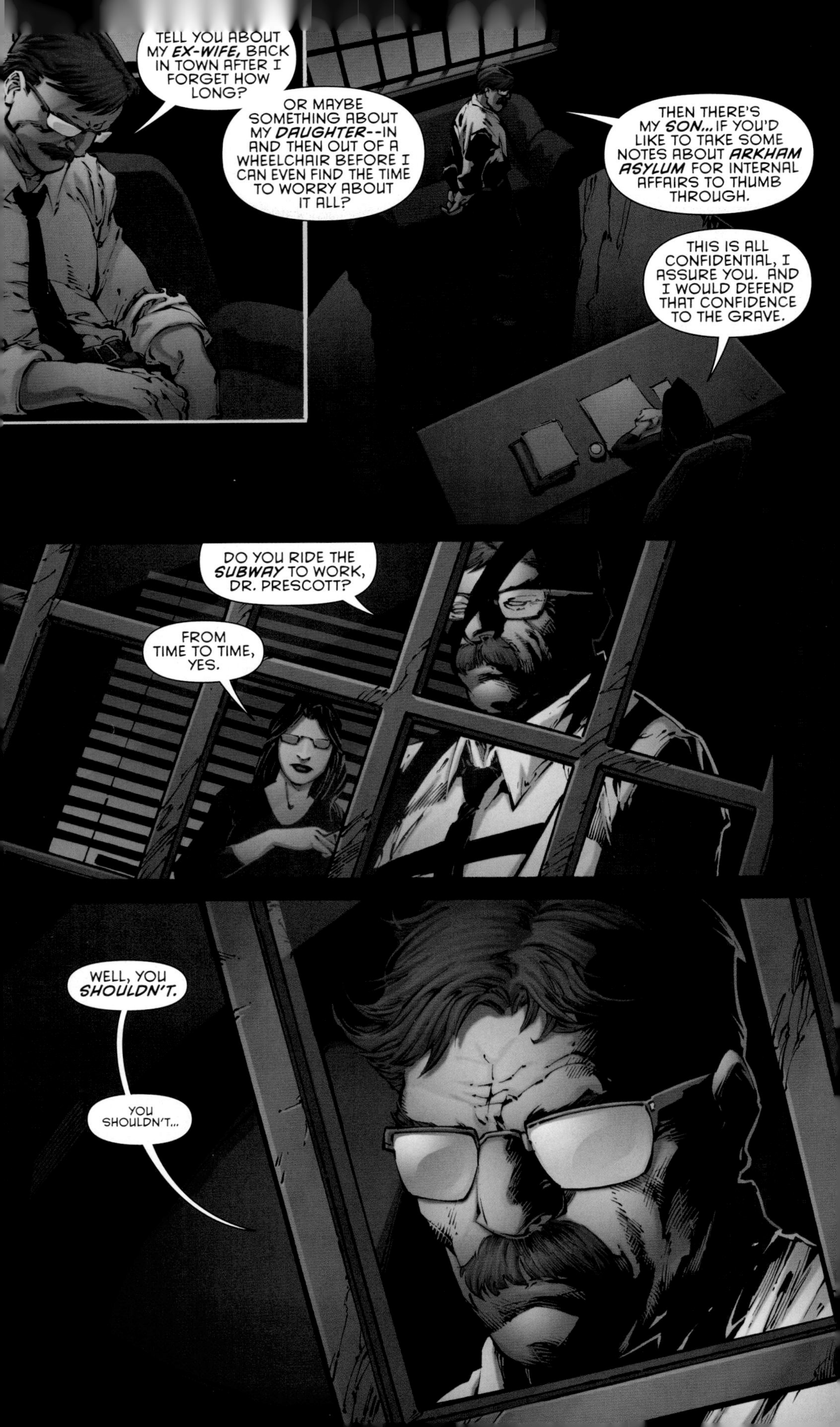
TELL YOU ABOUT MY EX-WIFE, BACK IN TOWN AFTER I FORGET HOW LONG?
OR MAYBE SOMETHING ABOUT MY DAUGHTER--IN AND THEN OUT OF A WHEELCHAIR BEFORE I CAN EVEN FIND THE TIME TO WORRY ABOUT IT ALL?
THEN THERE'S MY SON... IF YOU'D LIKE TO TAKE SOME NOTES ABOUT ARKHAM ASYLUM FOR INTERNAL AFFAIRS TO THUMB THROUGH.
THIS IS ALL CONFIDENTIAL, I ASSURE YOU. AND I WOULD DEFEND THAT CONFIDENCE TO THE GRAVE.
DO YOU RIDE THE SUBWAY TO WORK, DR. PRESCOTT?
FROM TIME TO TIME, YES.
WELL, YOU SHOULDN'T.
YOU SHOULDN'T...

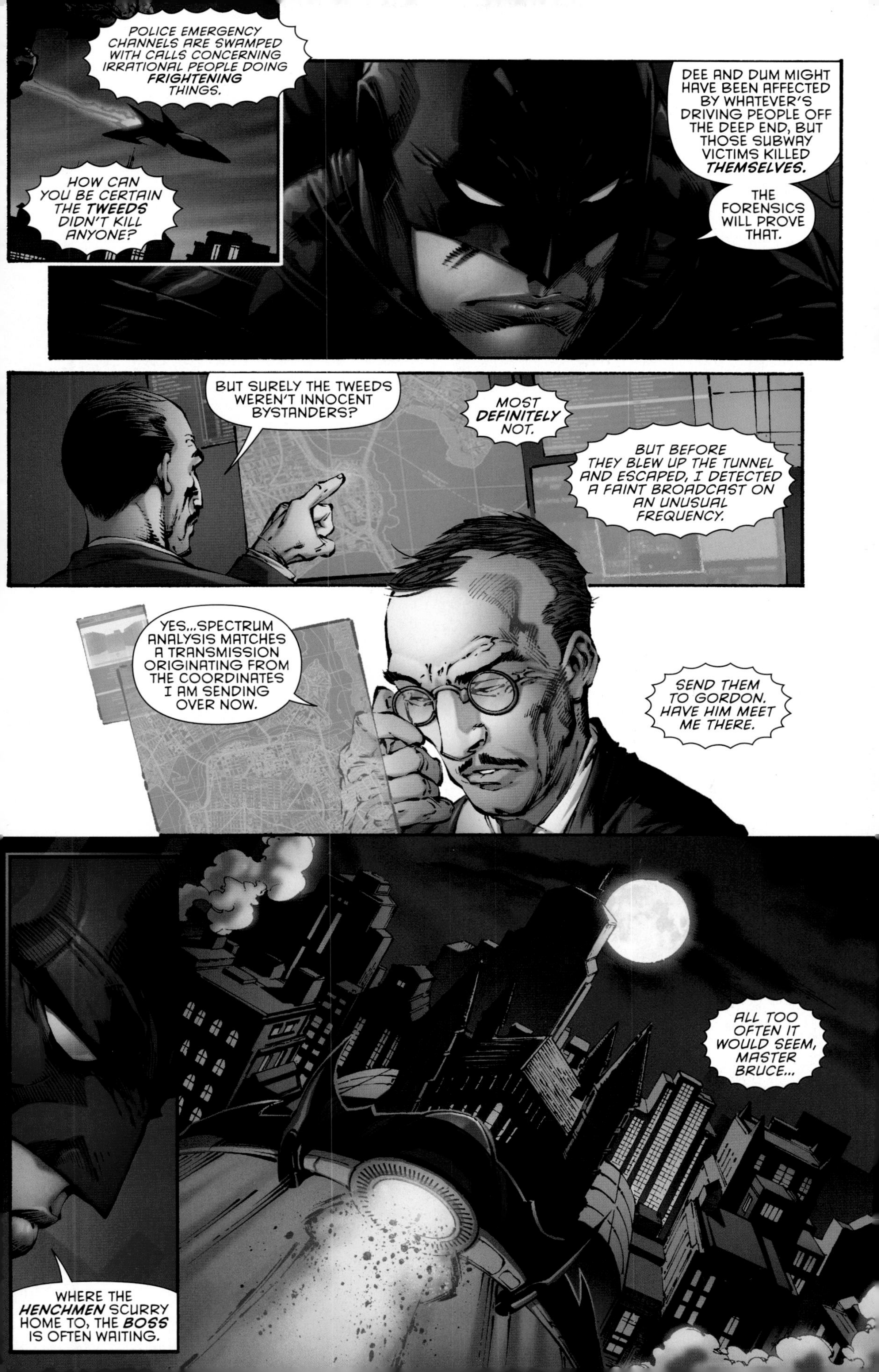
POLICE EMERGENCY CHANNELS ARE SWAMPED WITH CALLS CONCERNING IRRATIONAL PEOPLE DOING FRIGHTENING THINGS.
HOW CAN YOU BE CERTAIN THE TWEEDS DIDN'T KILL ANYONE?
DEE AND DUM MIGHT HAVE BEEN AFFECTED BY WHATEVER'S DRIVING PEOPLE OFF THE DEEP END, BUT THOSE SUBWAY VICTIMS KILLED THEMSELVES.
THE FORENSICS WILL PROVE THAT.
BUT SURELY THE TWEEDS WEREN'T INNOCENT BYSTANDERS?
MOST DEFINITELY NOT.
BUT BEFORE THEY BLEW UP THE TUNNEL AND ESCAPED, I DETECTED A FAINT BROADCAST ON AN UNUSUAL FREQUENCY.
YES...SPECTRUM ANALYSIS MATCHES A TRANSMISSION ORIGINATING FROM THE COORDINATES I AM SENDING OVER NOW.
SEND THEM TO GORDON. HAVE HIM MEET ME THERE.
WHERE THE HENCHMEN SCURRY HOME TO, THE BOSS IS OFTEN WAITING.
ALL TOO OFTEN IT WOULD SEEM, MASTER BRUCE...

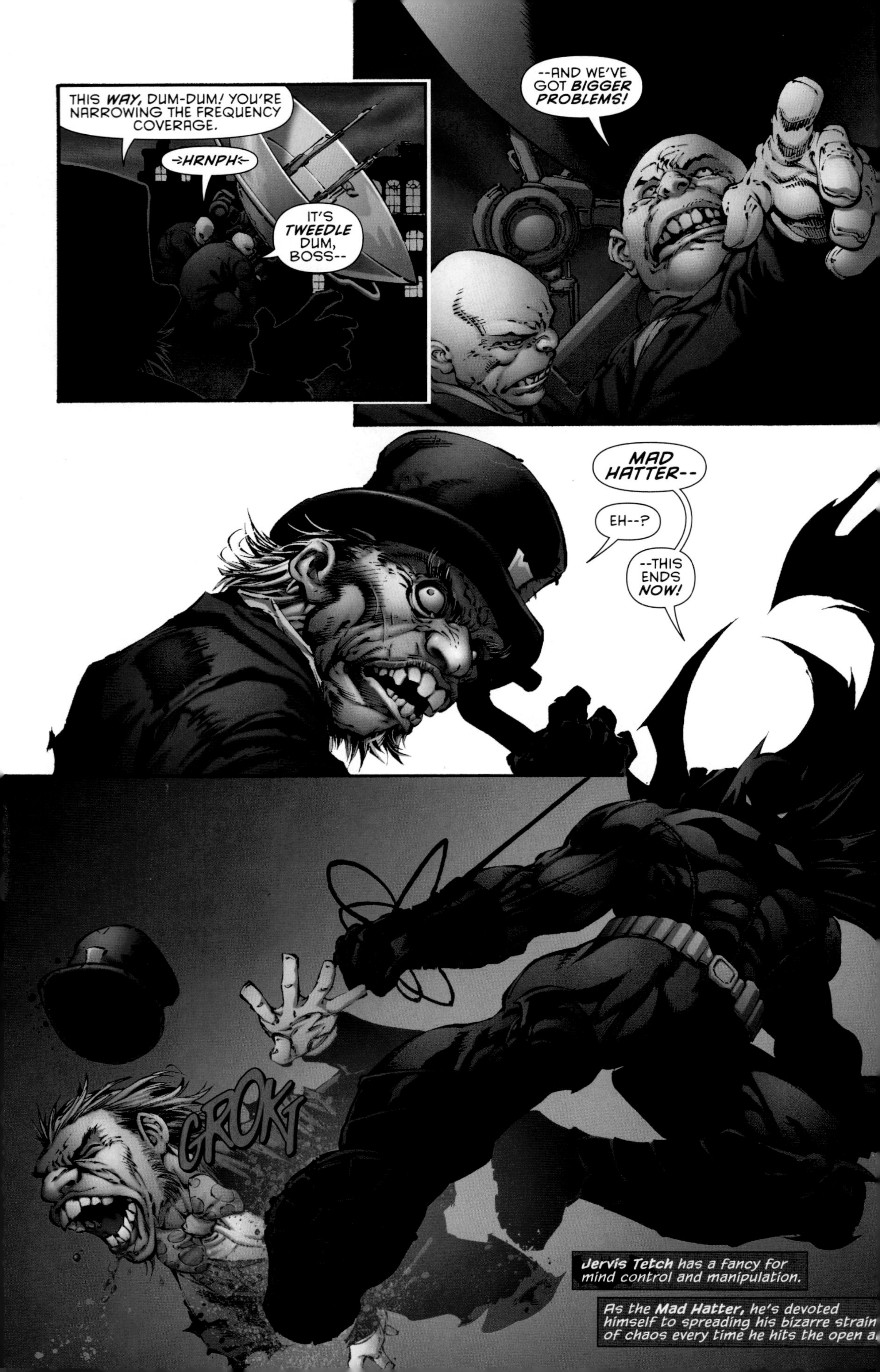
THIS WAY, DUM-DUM! YOU'RE NARROWING THE FREQUENCY COVERAGE.
HRNPH
IT'S TWEEDLE DUM, BOSS--
--AND WE'VE GOT BIGGER PROBLEMS!
MAD HATTER--
EH--?
--THIS ENDS NOW!
GROK!
Jervis Tetch has a fancy for mind control and manipulation.
As the Mad Hatter, he's devoted himself to spreading his bizarre strain of chaos every time he hits the open a

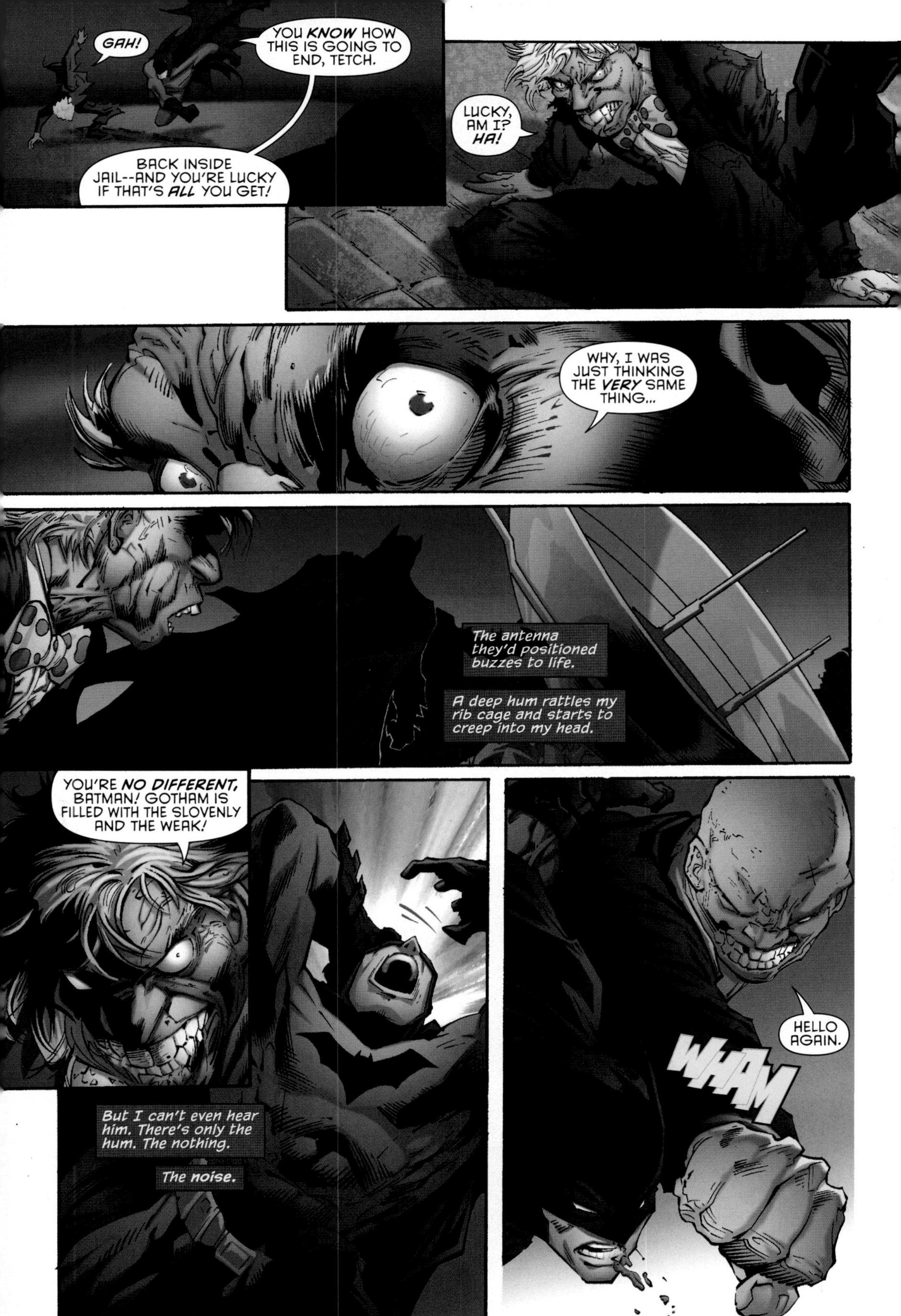
GAH!
YOU KNOW HOW THIS IS GOING TO END, TETCH.
BACK INSIDE JAIL--AND YOU'RE LUCKY IF THAT'S ALL YOU GET!
LUCKY, AM I? HA!
WHY, I WAS JUST THINKING THE VERY SAME THING...
The antenna they'd positioned buzzes to life.
A deep hum rattles my rib cage and starts to creep into my head.
YOU'RE NO DIFFERENT, BATMAN! GOTHAM IS FILLED WITH THE SLOVENLY AND THE WEAK!
But I can't even hear him. There's only the hum. The nothing.
The noise.
HELLO AGAIN.
WHAM

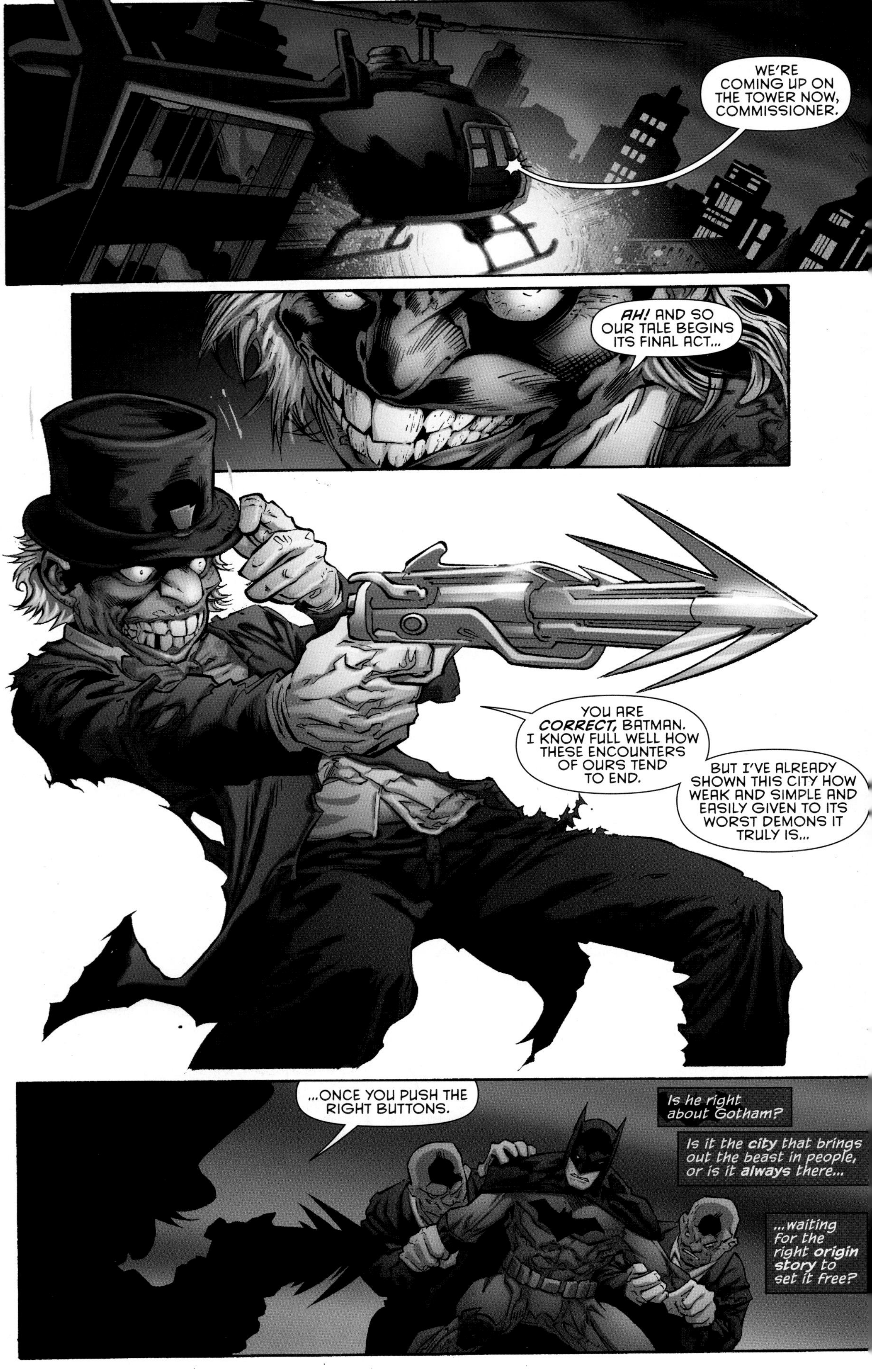
WE'RE COMING UP ON THE TOWER NOW, COMMISSIONER.
AH! AND SO OUR TALE BEGINS ITS FINAL ACT...
YOU ARE CORRECT, BATMAN. I KNOW FULL WELL HOW THESE ENCOUNTERS OF OURS TEND TO END.
BUT I'VE ALREADY SHOWN THIS CITY HOW WEAK AND SIMPLE AND EASILY GIVEN TO ITS WORST DEMONS IT TRULY IS...
...ONCE YOU PUSH THE RIGHT BUTTONS.
Is he right about Gotham?
Is it the city that brings out the beast in people, or is it always there...
...waiting for the right origin story to set it free?

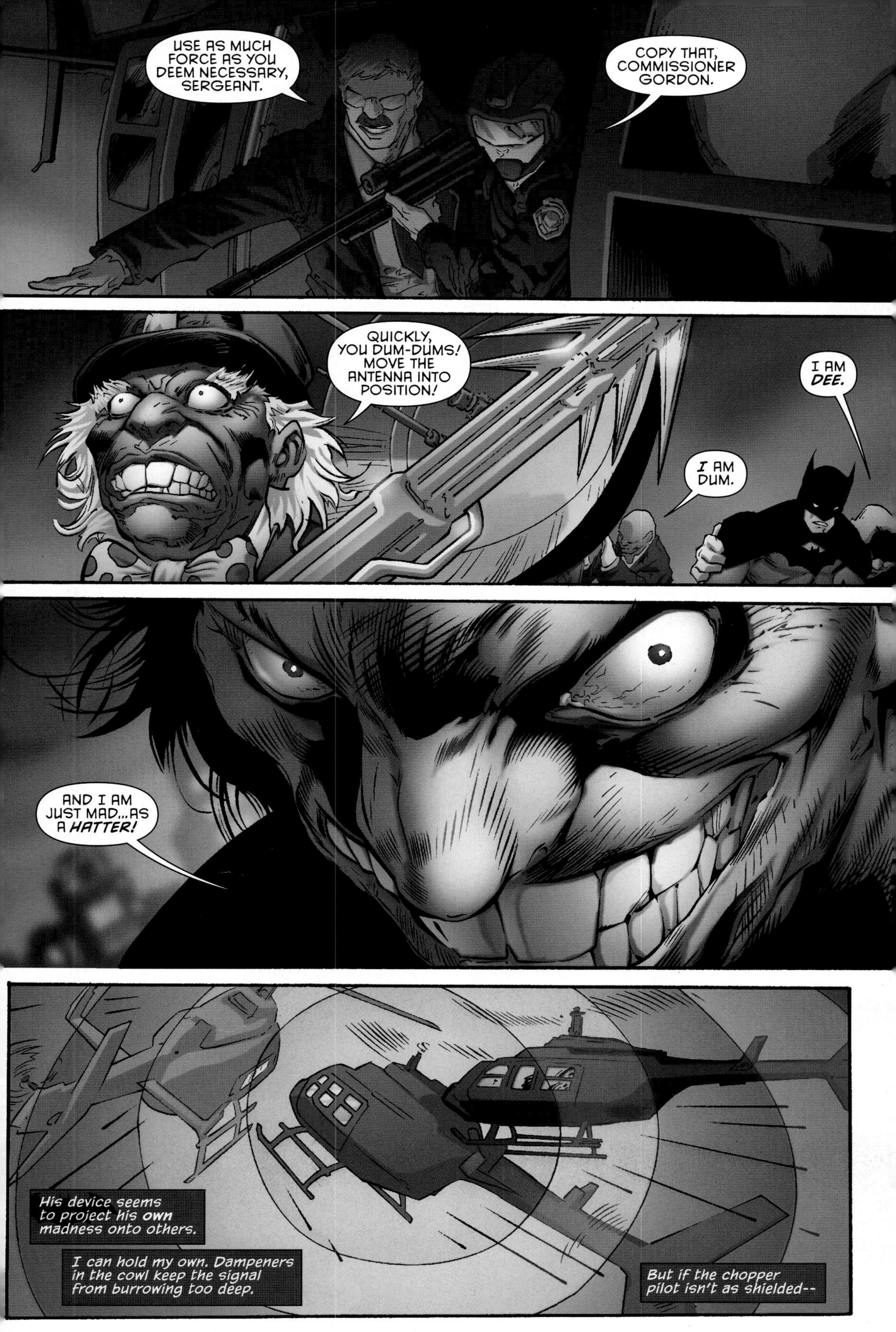
USE AS MUCH FORCE AS YOU DEEM NECESSARY, SERGEANT.
COPY THAT, COMMISSIONER GORDON.
QUICKLY, YOU DUM-DUMS! MOVE THE ANTENNA INTO POSITION!
I AM DEE.
I AM DUM.
AND I AM JUST MAD...AS A HATTER!
His device seems to project his own madness onto others.
I can hold my own. Dampeners in the cowl keep the signal from burrowing too deep.
But if the chopper pilot isn't as shielded--

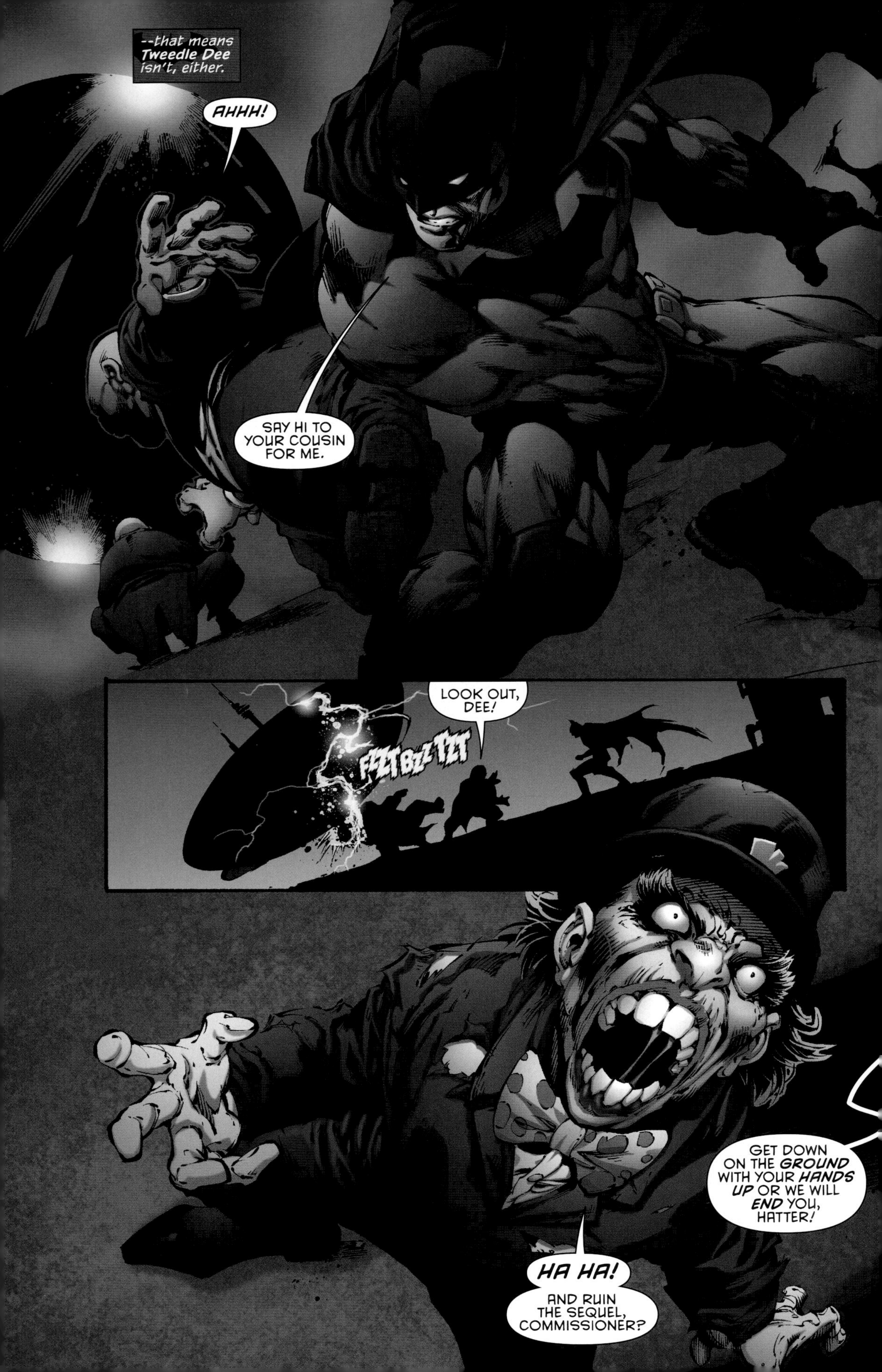
--that means Tweedle Dee isn't, either.
AHHH!
SAY HI TO YOUR COUSIN FOR ME.
LOOK OUT, DEE!
FZZT BZZ TZT
GET DOWN ON THE GROUND WITH YOUR HANDS UP OR WE WILL END YOU, HATTER!
HA HA!
AND RUIN THE SEQUEL, COMMISSIONER?

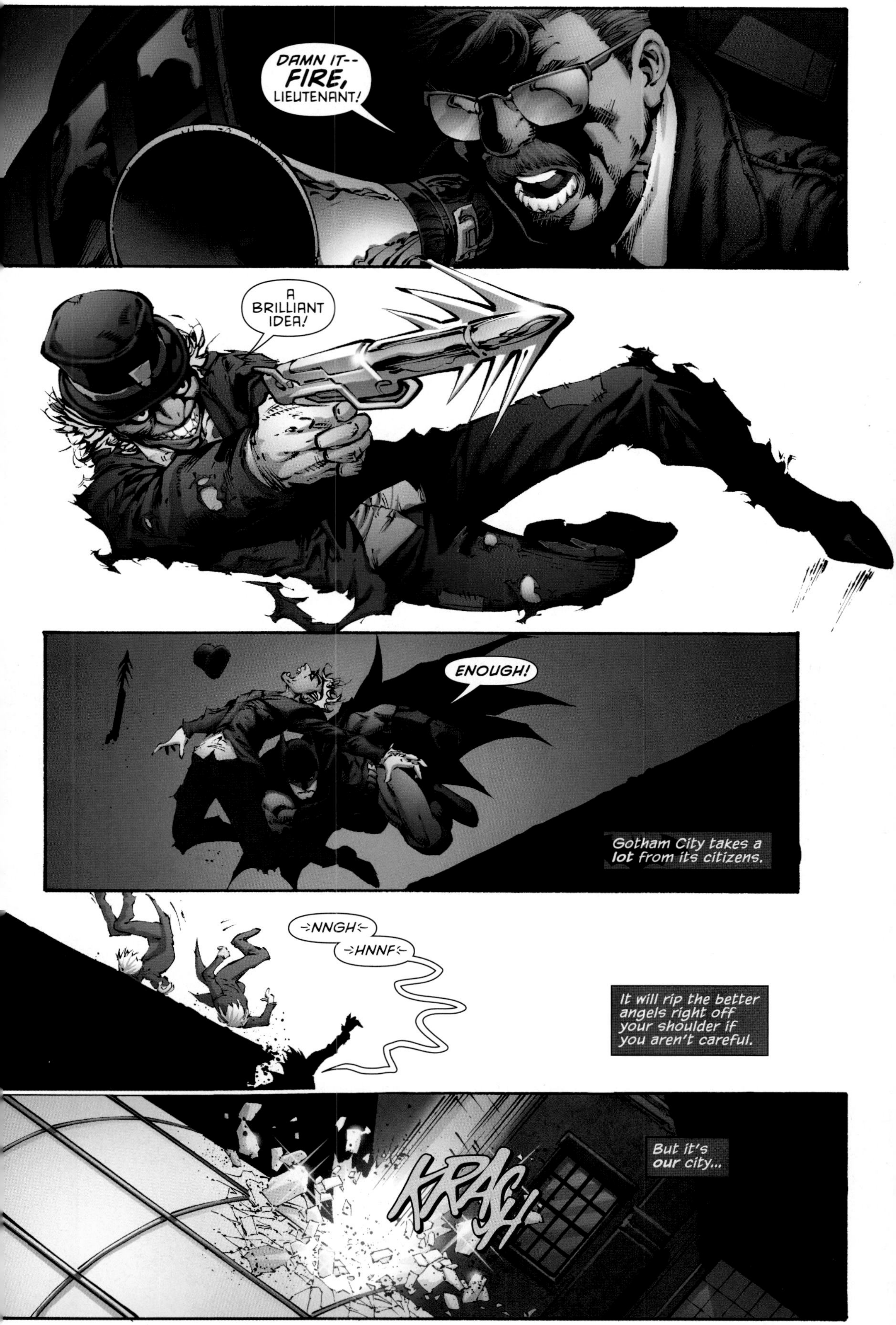
DAMN IT-- FIRE, LIEUTENANT!
A BRILLIANT IDEA!
ENOUGH!
Gotham City takes a lot from its citizens.
-NNGH-
-HNNF-
It will rip the better angels right off your shoulder if you aren't careful.
But it's our city...

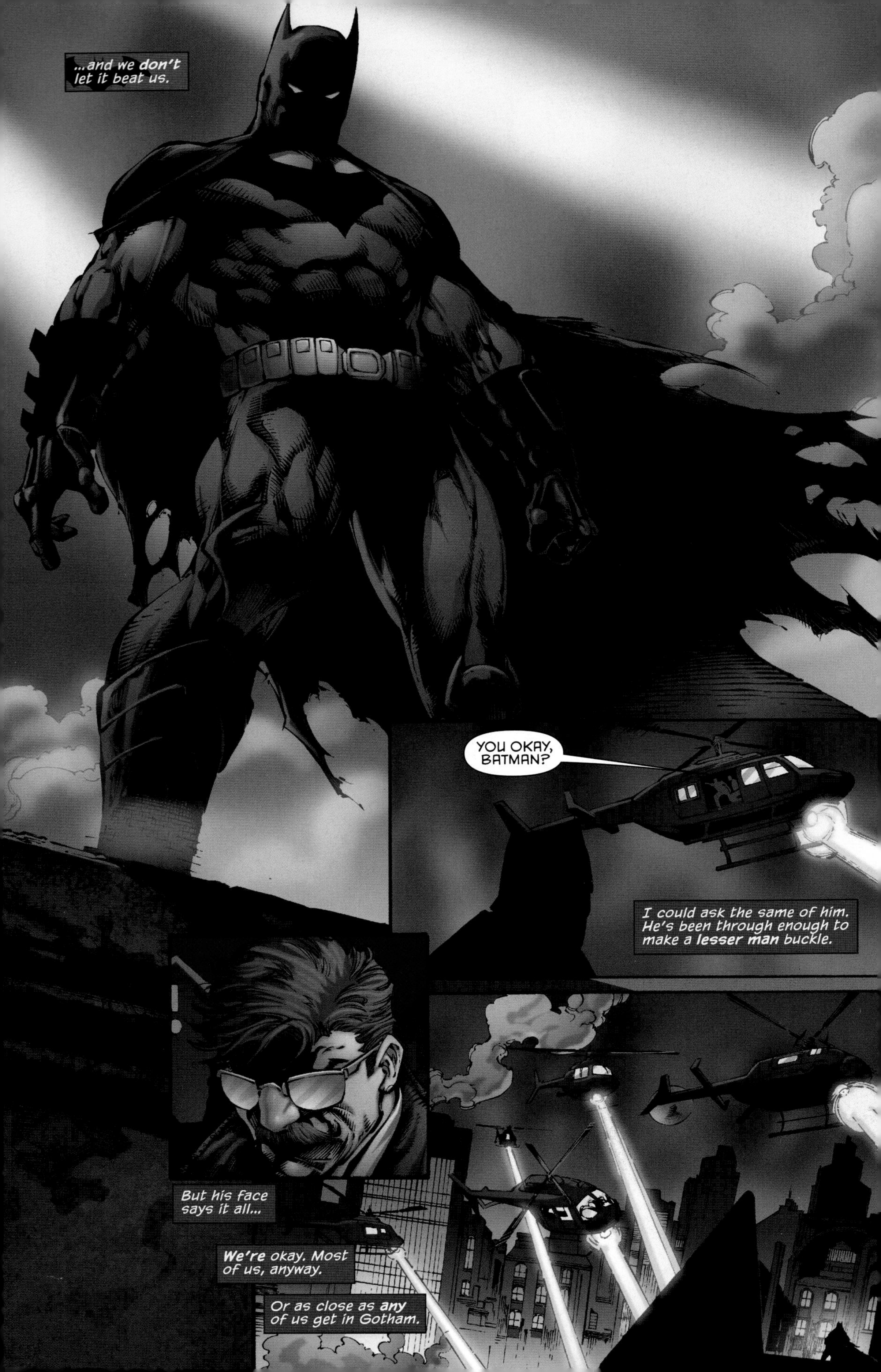
...and we don't let it beat us.
YOU OKAY, BATMAN?
I could ask the same of him. He's been through enough to make a lesser man buckle.
But his face says it all...
We're okay. Most of us, anyway.
Or as close as any of us get in Gotham.

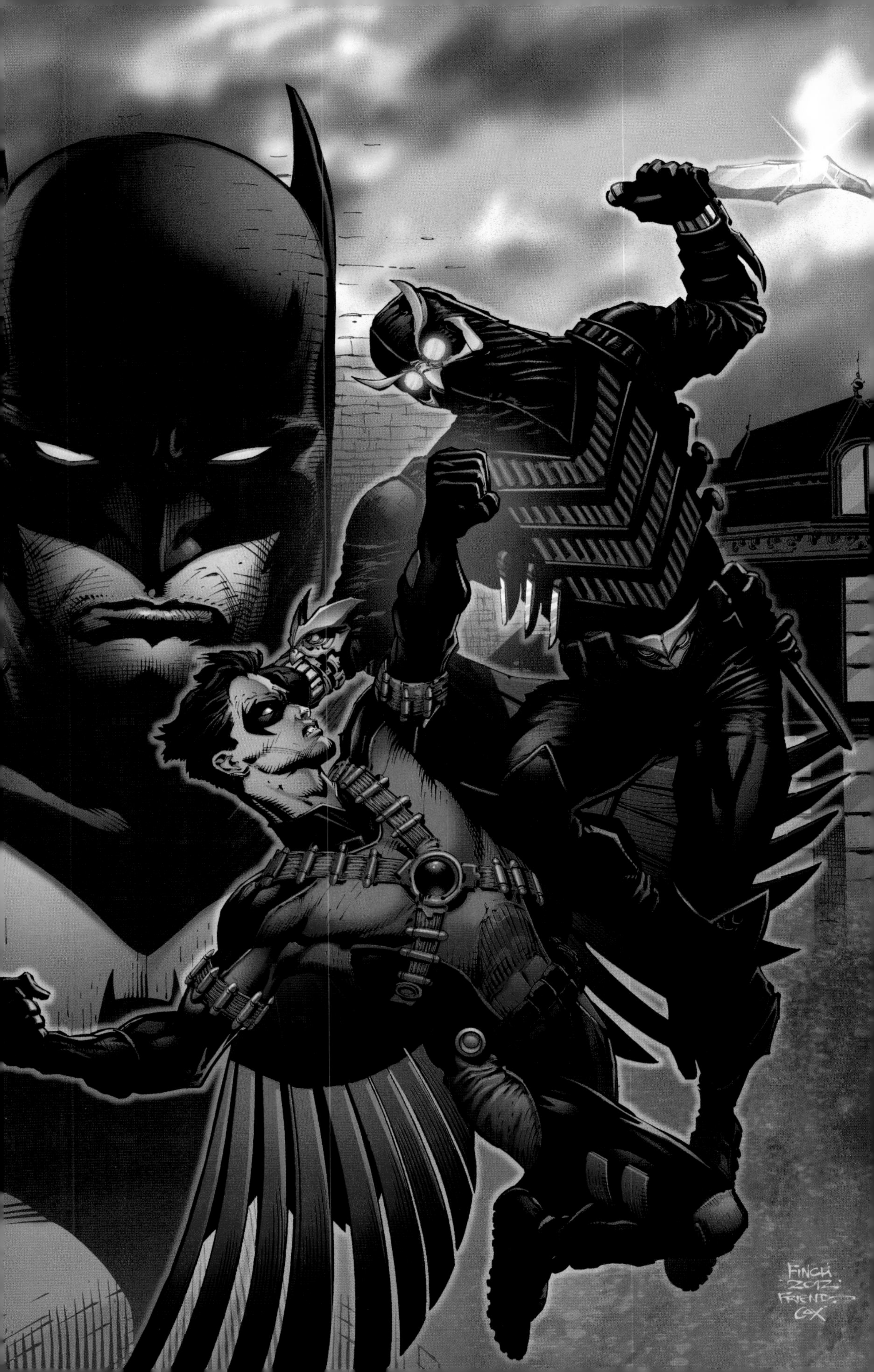
FINCH
2012
FRIEND
COX

"I CAN NO LONGER BE BROKEN"
JUDD WINICK writer **DAVID FINCH** penciller **RICHARD FRIEND** inker
cover art by **DAVID FINCH, RICHARD FRIEND & JEROMY COX**

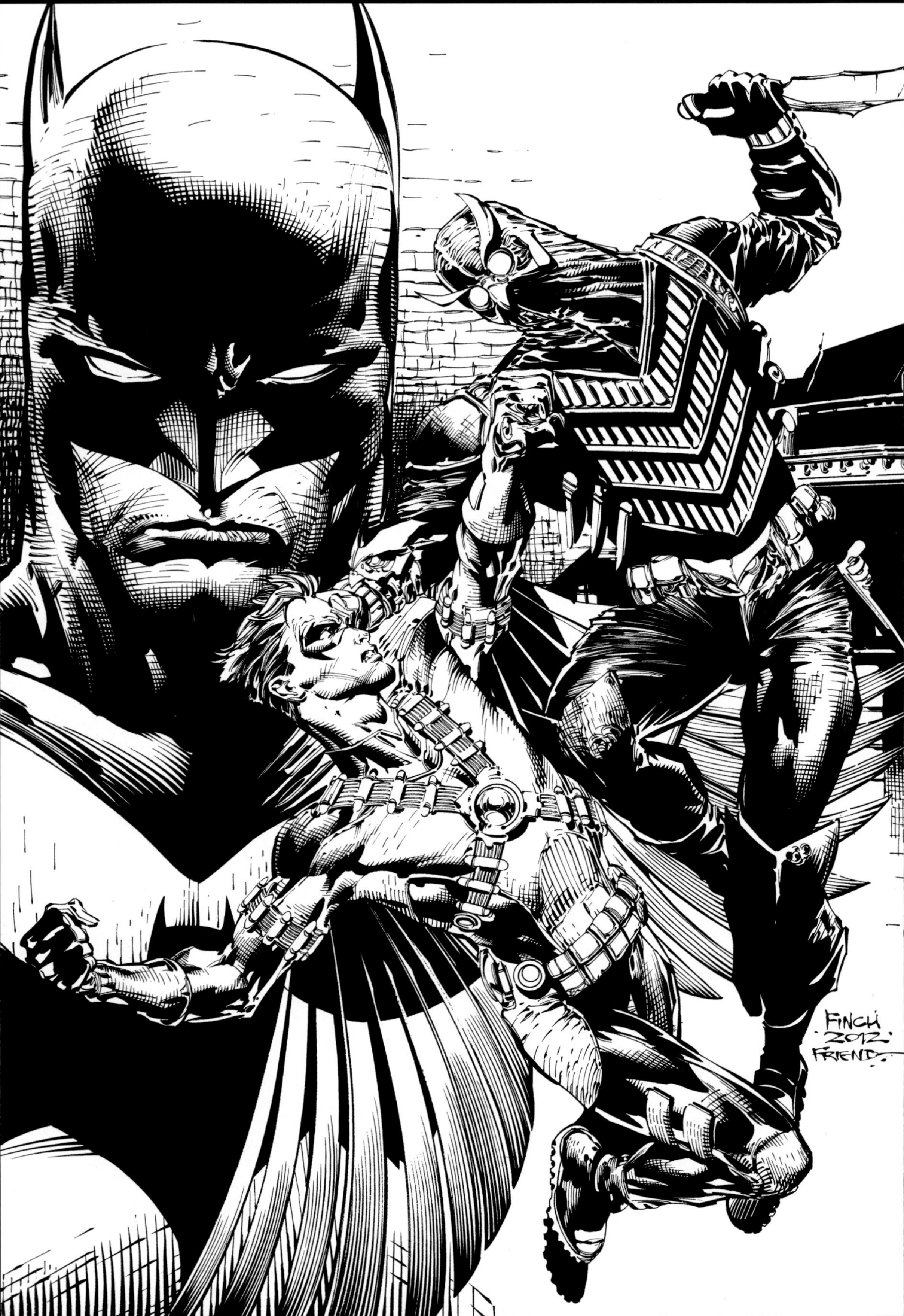
FINCH
2012
FRIEND

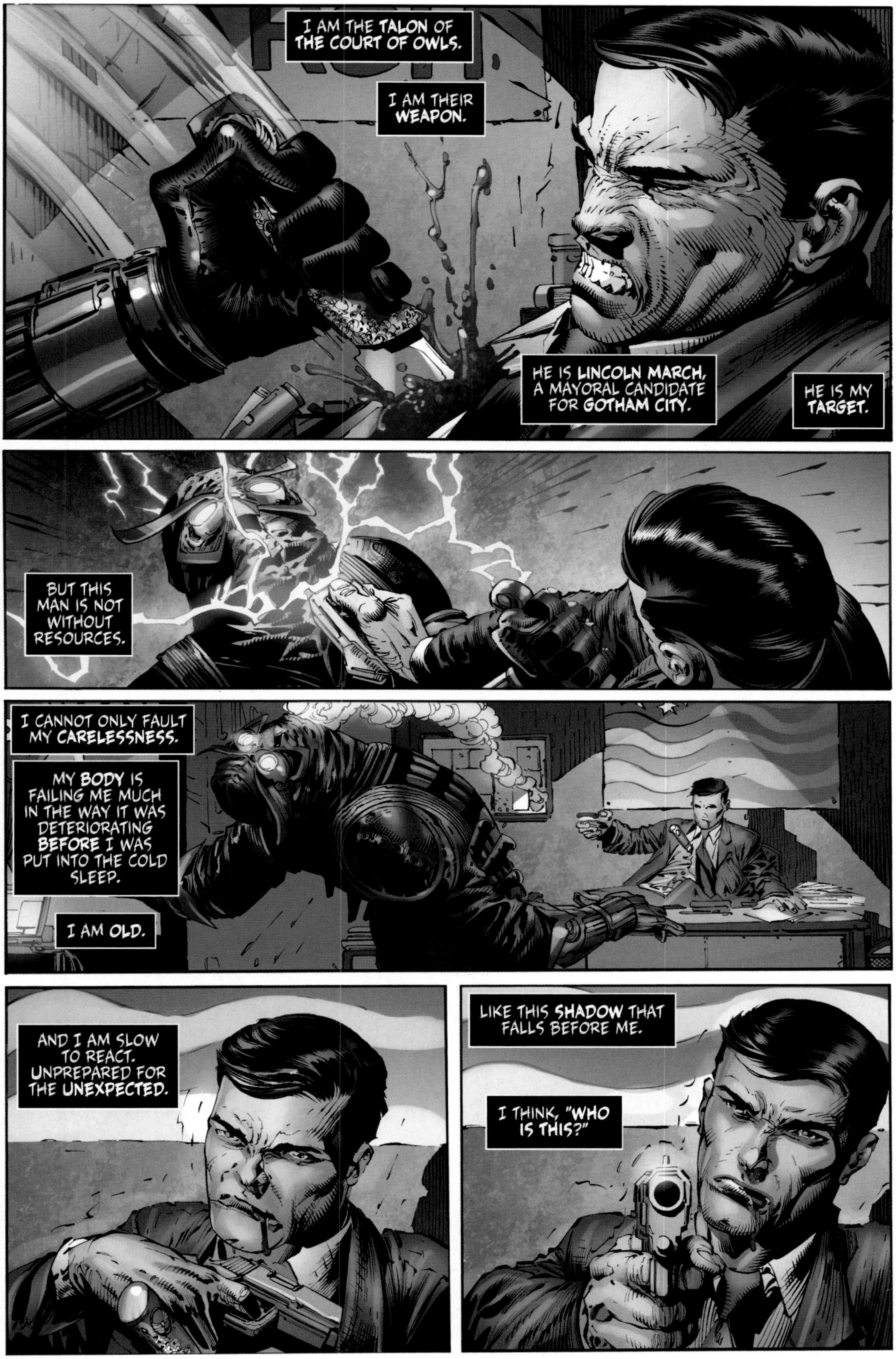
I AM THE TALON OF THE COURT OF OWLS.
I AM THEIR WEAPON.
HE IS LINCOLN MARCH, A MAYORAL CANDIDATE FOR GOTHAM CITY.
HE IS MY TARGET.
BUT THIS MAN IS NOT WITHOUT RESOURCES.
I CANNOT ONLY FAULT MY CARELESSNESS.
MY BODY IS FAILING ME MUCH IN THE WAY IT WAS DETERIORATING BEFORE I WAS PUT INTO THE COLD SLEEP.
I AM OLD.
AND I AM SLOW TO REACT. UNPREPARED FOR THE UNEXPECTED.
LIKE THIS SHADOW THAT FALLS BEFORE ME.
I THINK, "WHO IS THIS?"

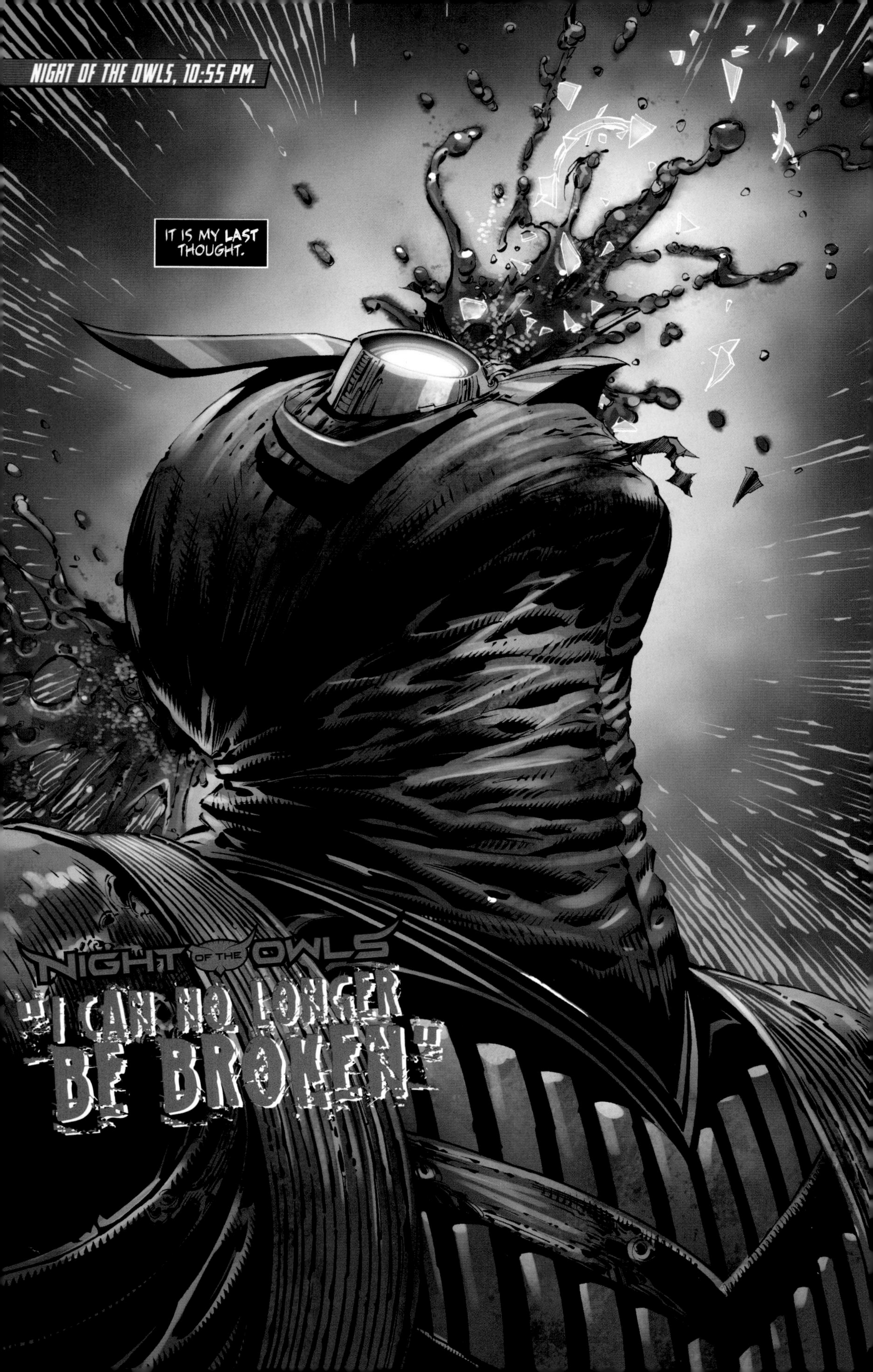
NIGHT OF THE OWLS, 10:55 PM.
IT IS MY LAST THOUGHT.
NIGHT OF THE OWLS
"I CAN NO LONGER BE BROKEN"

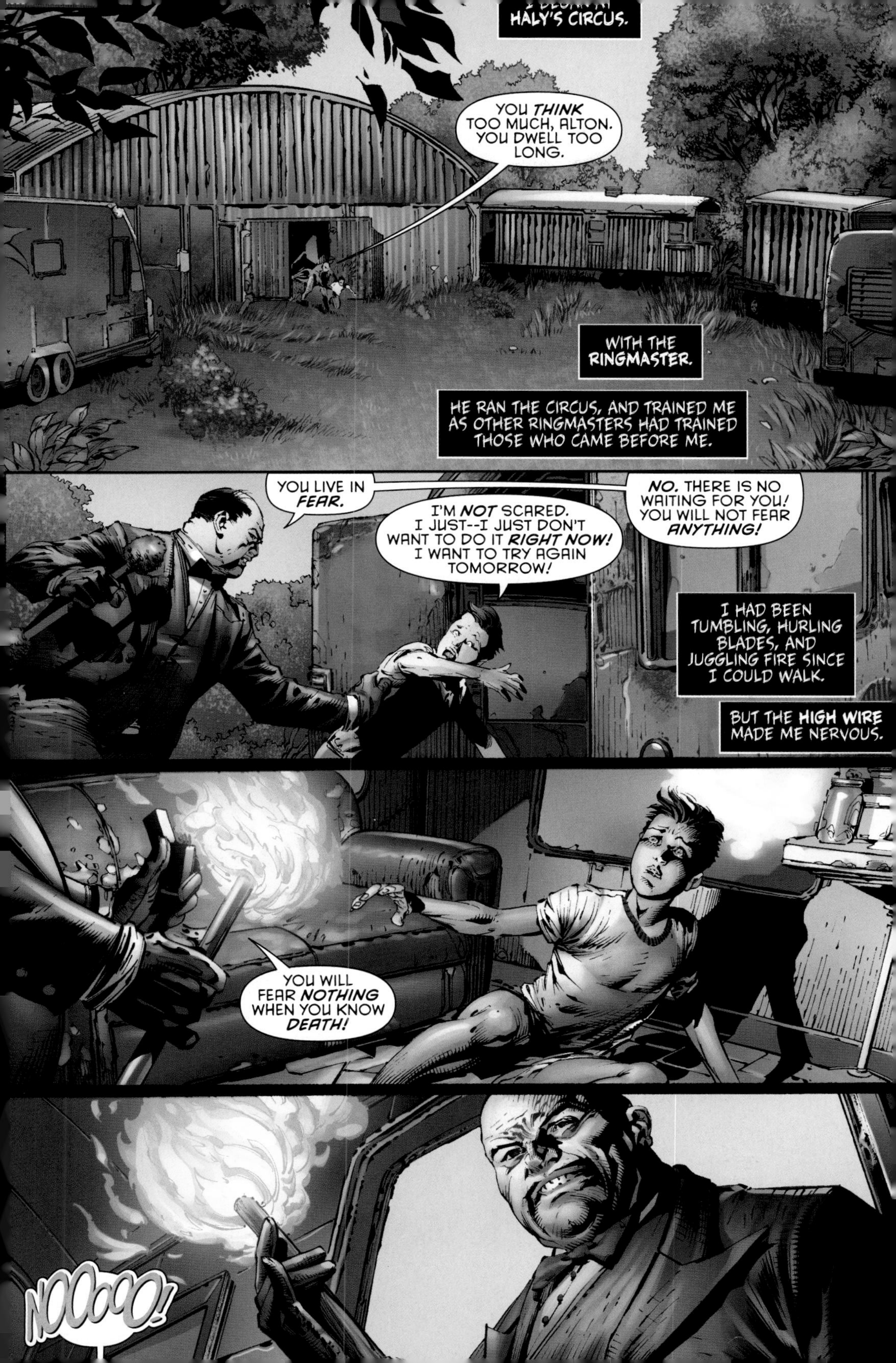
HALY'S CIRCUS.
YOU *THINK* TOO MUCH, ALTON. YOU DWELL TOO LONG.
WITH THE **RINGMASTER.**
HE RAN THE CIRCUS, AND TRAINED ME AS OTHER RINGMASTERS HAD TRAINED THOSE WHO CAME BEFORE ME.
YOU LIVE IN *FEAR.*
I'M *NOT* SCARED. I JUST--I JUST DON'T WANT TO DO IT *RIGHT NOW!* I WANT TO TRY AGAIN TOMORROW!
NO. THERE IS NO WAITING FOR YOU! YOU WILL NOT FEAR *ANYTHING!*
I HAD BEEN TUMBLING, HURLING BLADES, AND JUGGLING FIRE SINCE I COULD WALK.
BUT THE **HIGH WIRE** MADE ME NERVOUS.
YOU WILL FEAR *NOTHING* WHEN YOU KNOW *DEATH!*
NOOOOO!

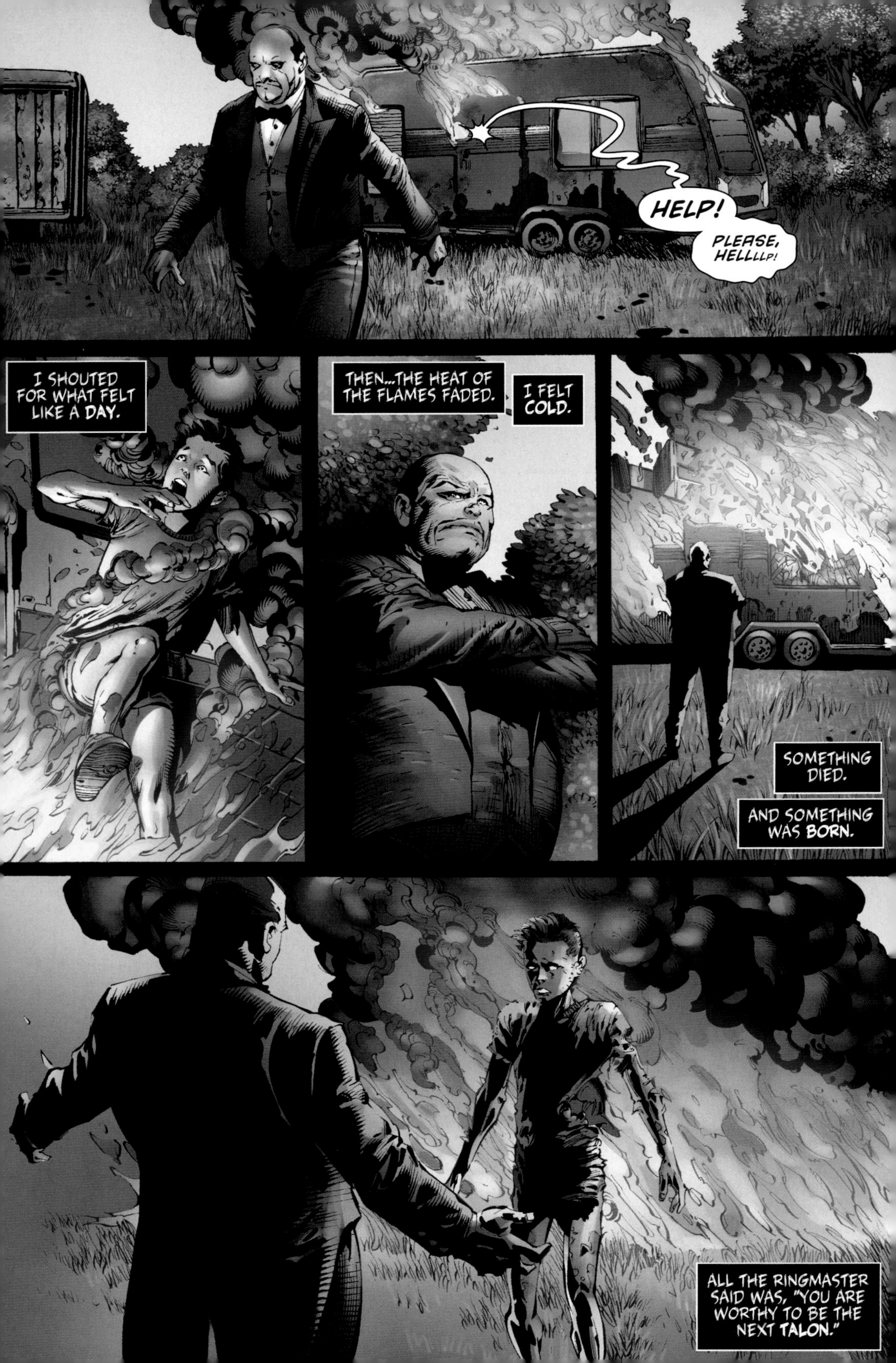
HELP!
PLEASE, HELLLLP!
I SHOUTED FOR WHAT FELT LIKE A DAY.
THEN...THE HEAT OF THE FLAMES FADED.
I FELT COLD.
SOMETHING DIED.
AND SOMETHING WAS BORN.
ALL THE RINGMASTER SAID WAS, "YOU ARE WORTHY TO BE THE NEXT TALON."

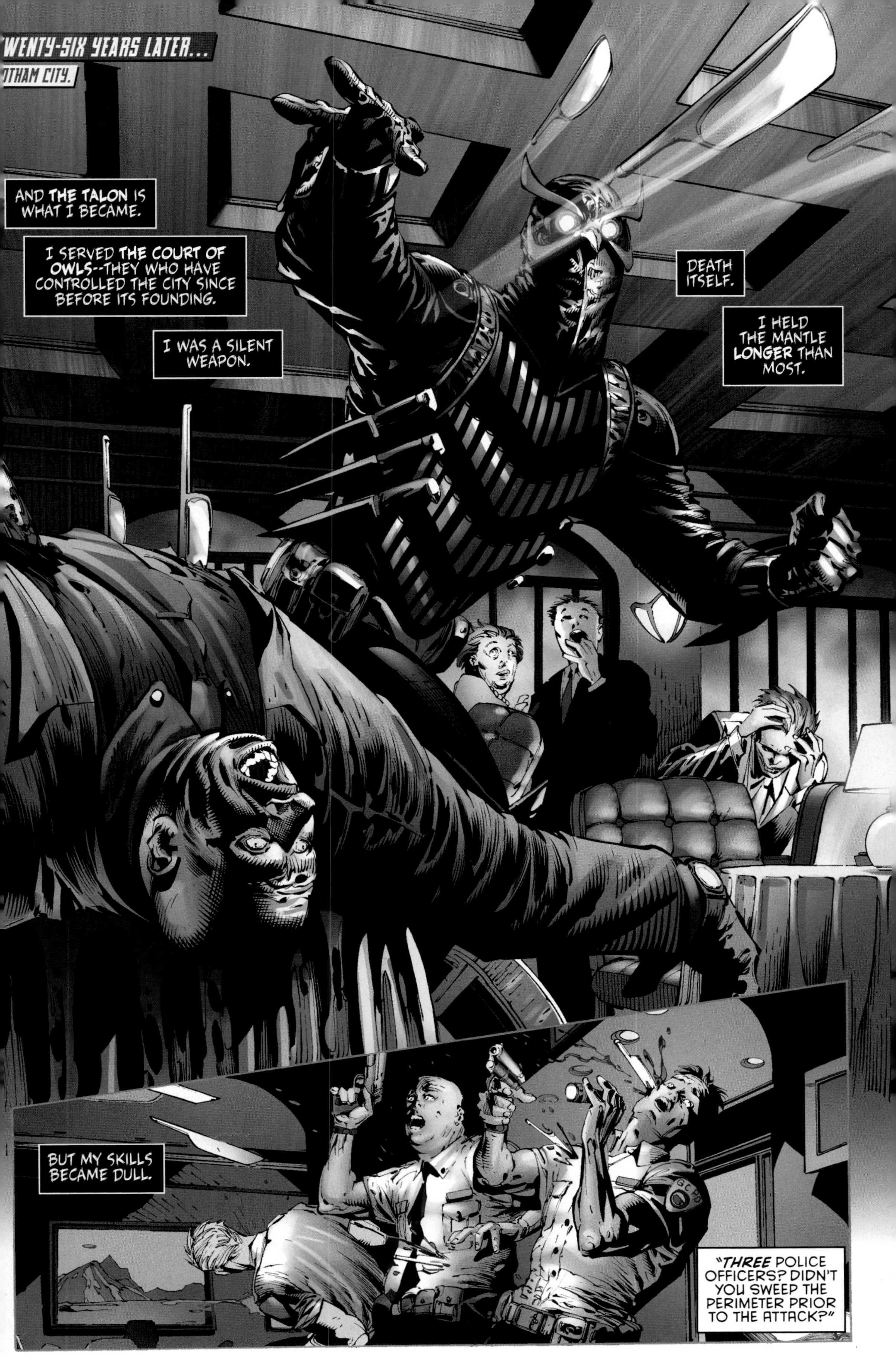

WENTY-SIX YEARS LATER...
OTHAM CITY.
AND THE TALON IS WHAT I BECAME.
I SERVED THE COURT OF OWLS--THEY WHO HAVE CONTROLLED THE CITY SINCE BEFORE ITS FOUNDING.
I WAS A SILENT WEAPON.
DEATH ITSELF.
I HELD THE MANTLE LONGER THAN MOST.
BUT MY SKILLS BECAME DULL.
"THREE POLICE OFFICERS? DIDN'T YOU SWEEP THE PERIMETER PRIOR TO THE ATTACK?"

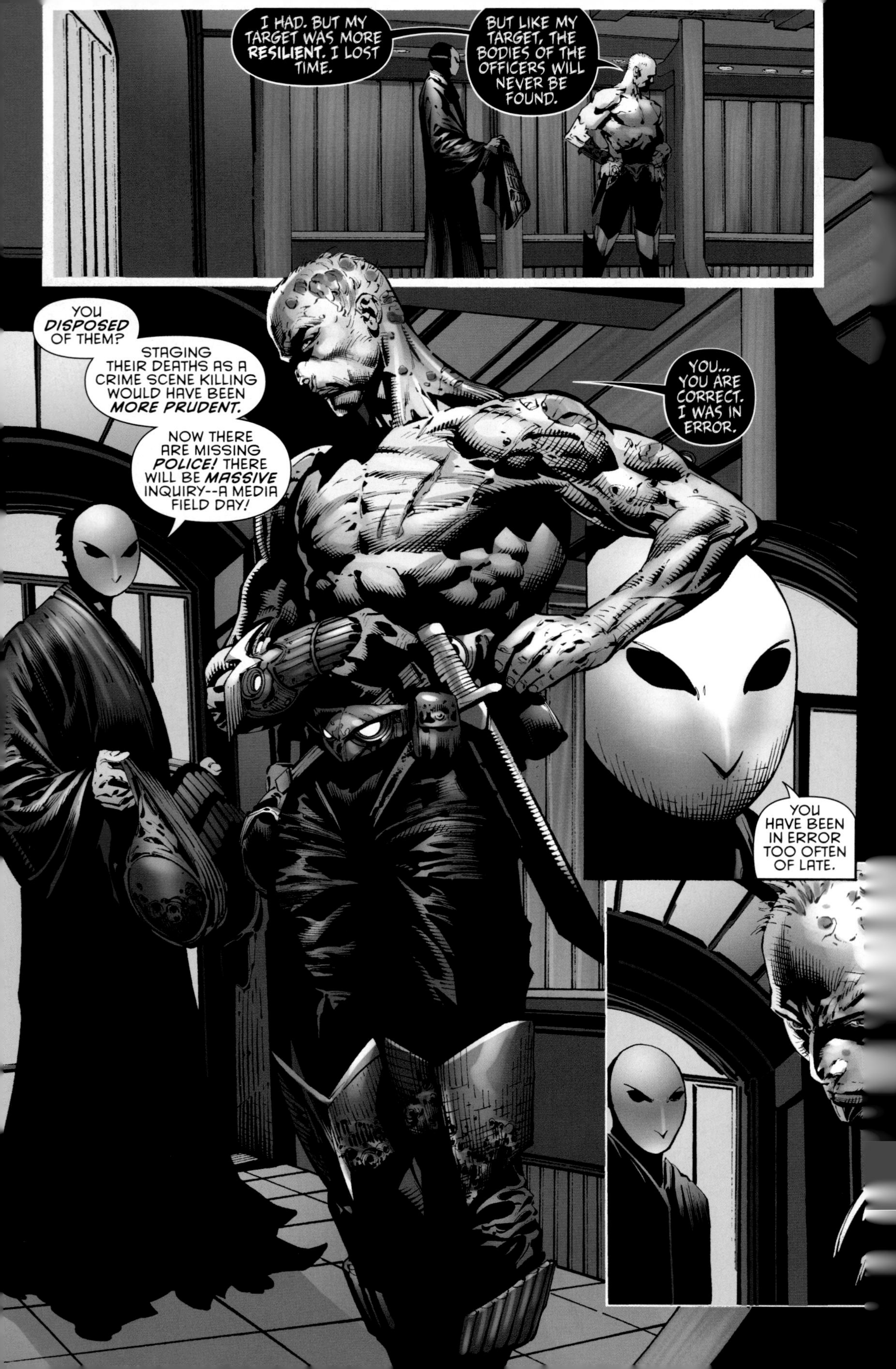
I HAD. BUT MY TARGET WAS MORE RESILIENT. I LOST TIME.
BUT LIKE MY TARGET, THE BODIES OF THE OFFICERS WILL NEVER BE FOUND.
YOU DISPOSED OF THEM?
STAGING THEIR DEATHS AS A CRIME SCENE KILLING WOULD HAVE BEEN MORE PRUDENT.
NOW THERE ARE MISSING POLICE! THERE WILL BE MASSIVE INQUIRY--A MEDIA FIELD DAY!
YOU... YOU ARE CORRECT. I WAS IN ERROR.
YOU HAVE BEEN IN ERROR TOO OFTEN OF LATE.

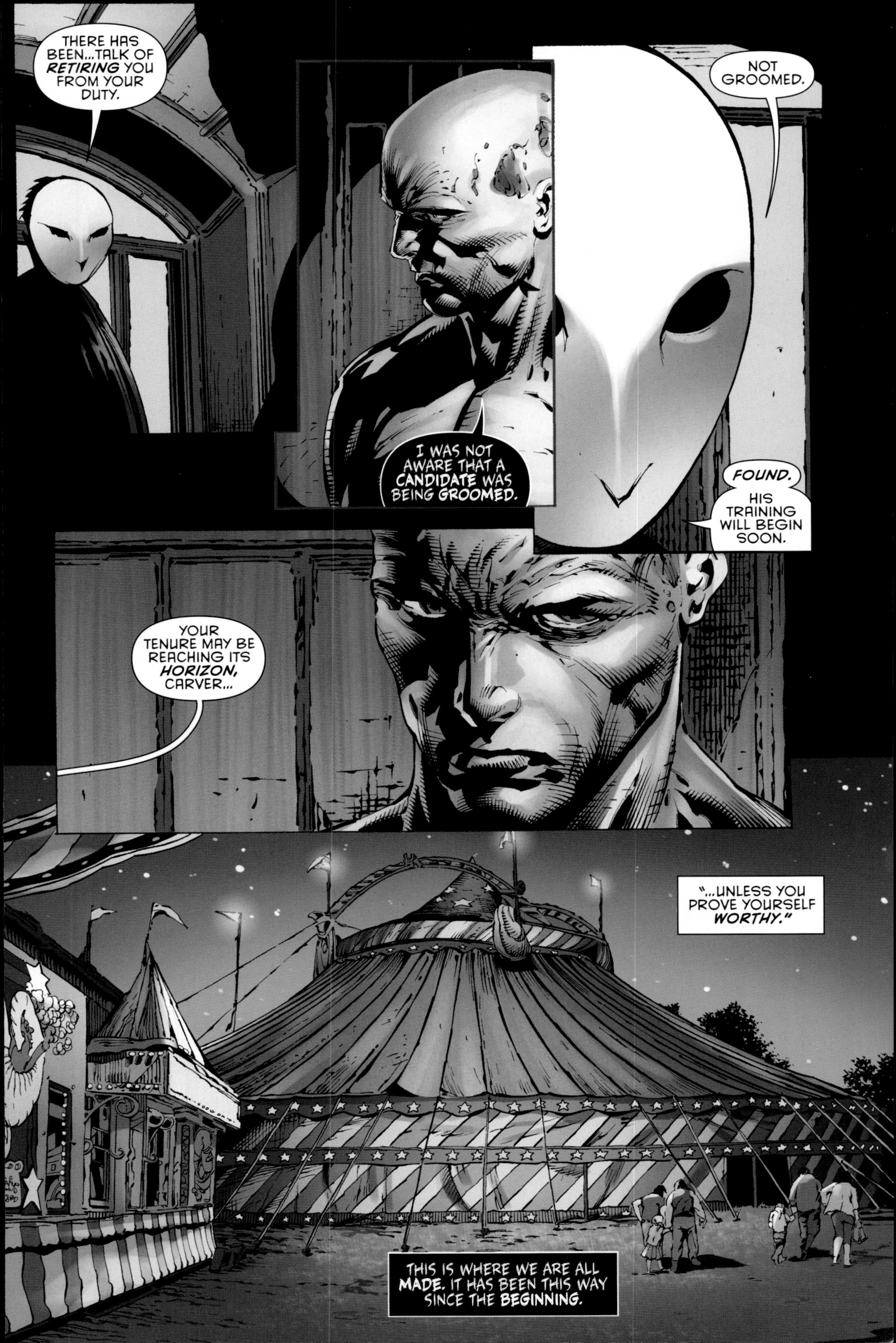
THERE HAS BEEN...TALK OF RETIRING YOU FROM YOUR DUTY.
I WAS NOT AWARE THAT A CANDIDATE WAS BEING GROOMED.
NOT GROOMED.
FOUND.
HIS TRAINING WILL BEGIN SOON.
YOUR TENURE MAY BE REACHING ITS HORIZON, CARVER...
"...UNLESS YOU PROVE YOURSELF WORTHY."
THIS IS WHERE WE ARE ALL MADE. IT HAS BEEN THIS WAY SINCE THE BEGINNING.

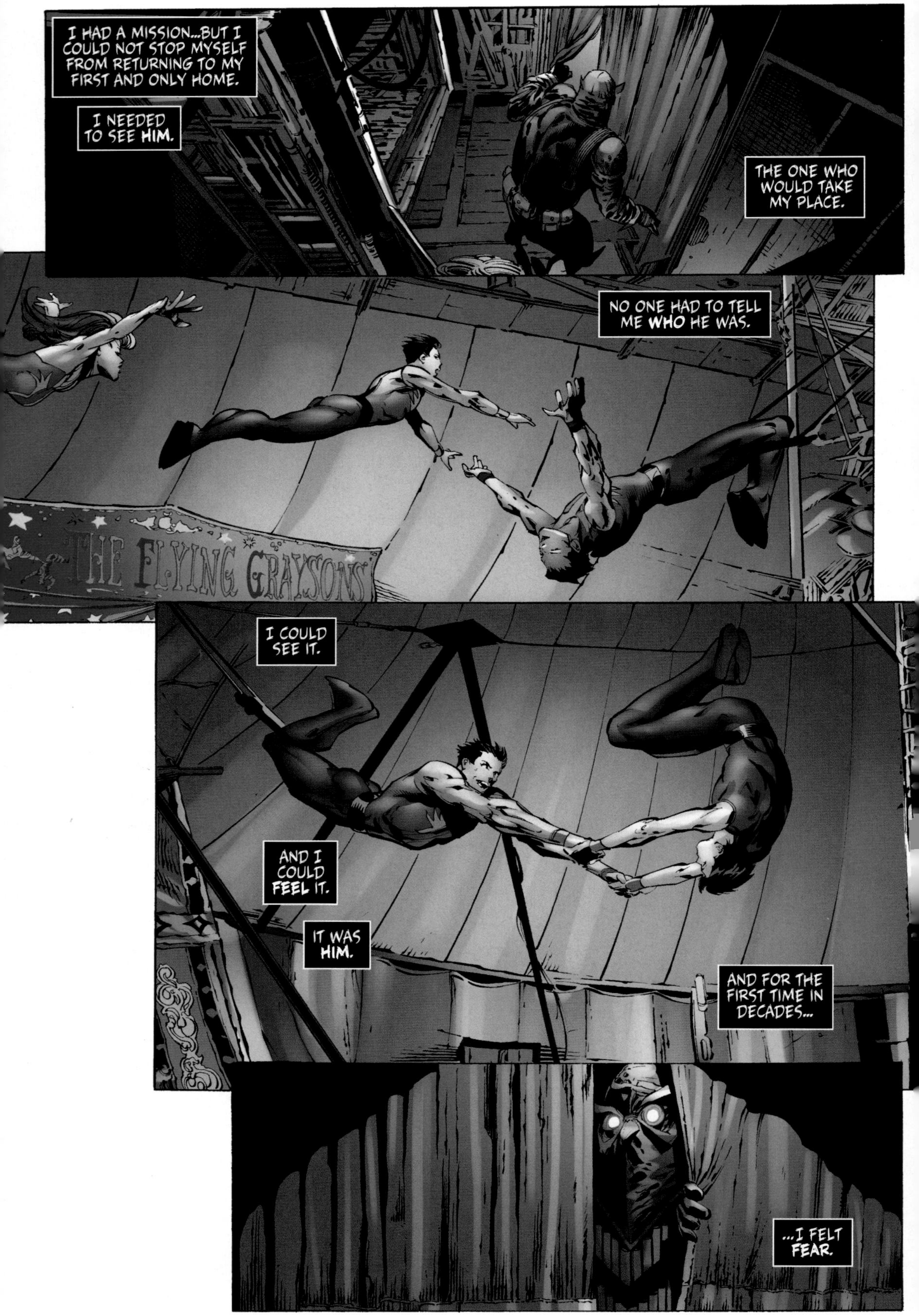
I HAD A MISSION...BUT I COULD NOT STOP MYSELF FROM RETURNING TO MY FIRST AND ONLY HOME.
I NEEDED TO SEE HIM.
THE ONE WHO WOULD TAKE MY PLACE.
NO ONE HAD TO TELL ME WHO HE WAS.
THE FLYING GRAYSONS
I COULD SEE IT.
AND I COULD FEEL IT.
IT WAS HIM.
AND FOR THE FIRST TIME IN DECADES...
...I FELT FEAR.

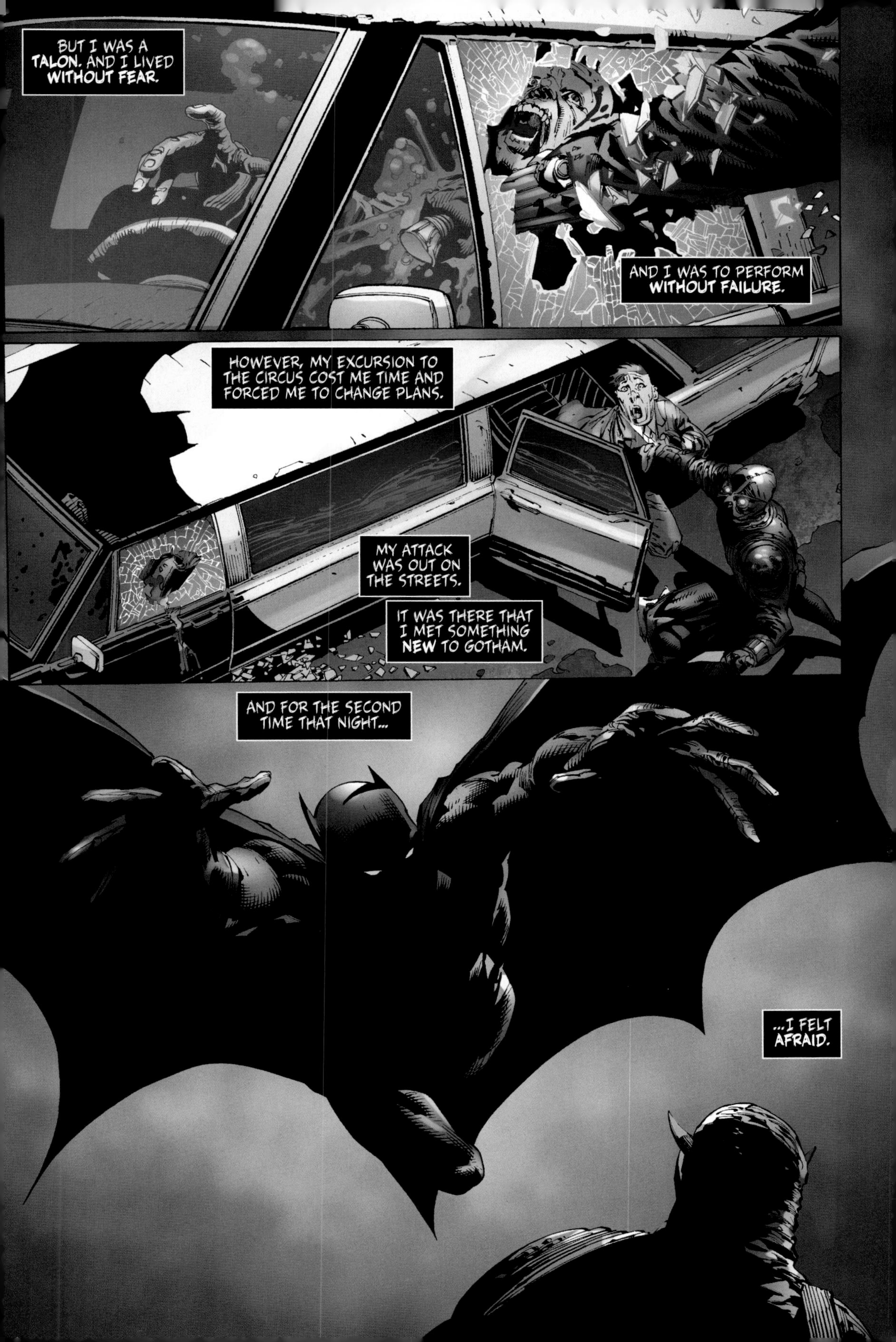
BUT I WAS A TALON. AND I LIVED WITHOUT FEAR.
AND I WAS TO PERFORM WITHOUT FAILURE.
HOWEVER, MY EXCURSION TO THE CIRCUS COST ME TIME AND FORCED ME TO CHANGE PLANS.
MY ATTACK WAS OUT ON THE STREETS.
IT WAS THERE THAT I MET SOMETHING NEW TO GOTHAM.
AND FOR THE SECOND TIME THAT NIGHT...
...I FELT AFRAID.

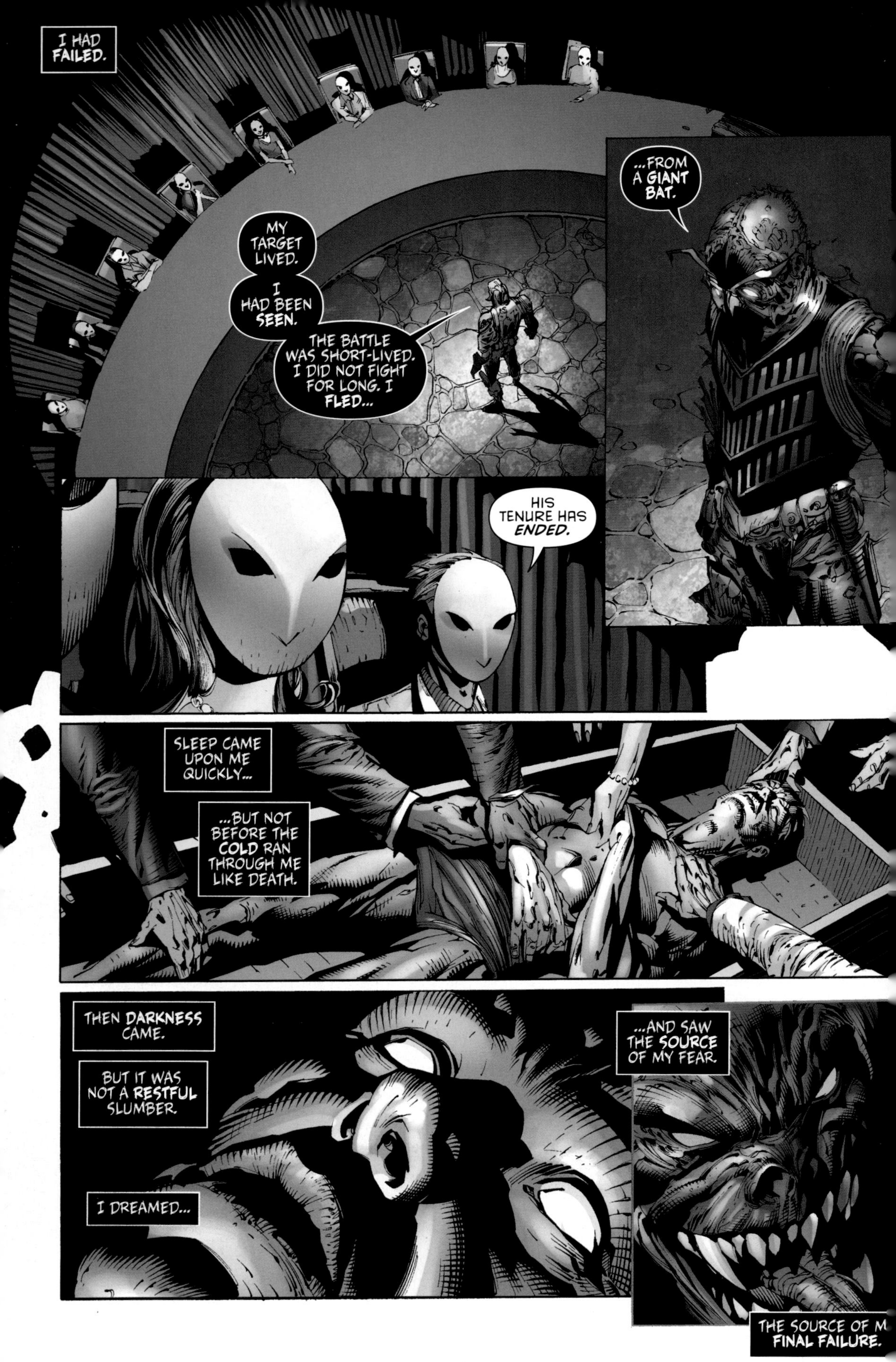
I HAD FAILED.
MY TARGET LIVED.
I HAD BEEN SEEN.
THE BATTLE WAS SHORT-LIVED. I DID NOT FIGHT FOR LONG. I FLED...
...FROM A GIANT BAT.
HIS TENURE HAS ENDED.
SLEEP CAME UPON ME QUICKLY...
...BUT NOT BEFORE THE COLD RAN THROUGH ME LIKE DEATH.
THEN DARKNESS CAME.
BUT IT WAS NOT A RESTFUL SLUMBER.
I DREAMED...
...AND SAW THE SOURCE OF MY FEAR.
THE SOURCE OF M
FINAL FAILURE.

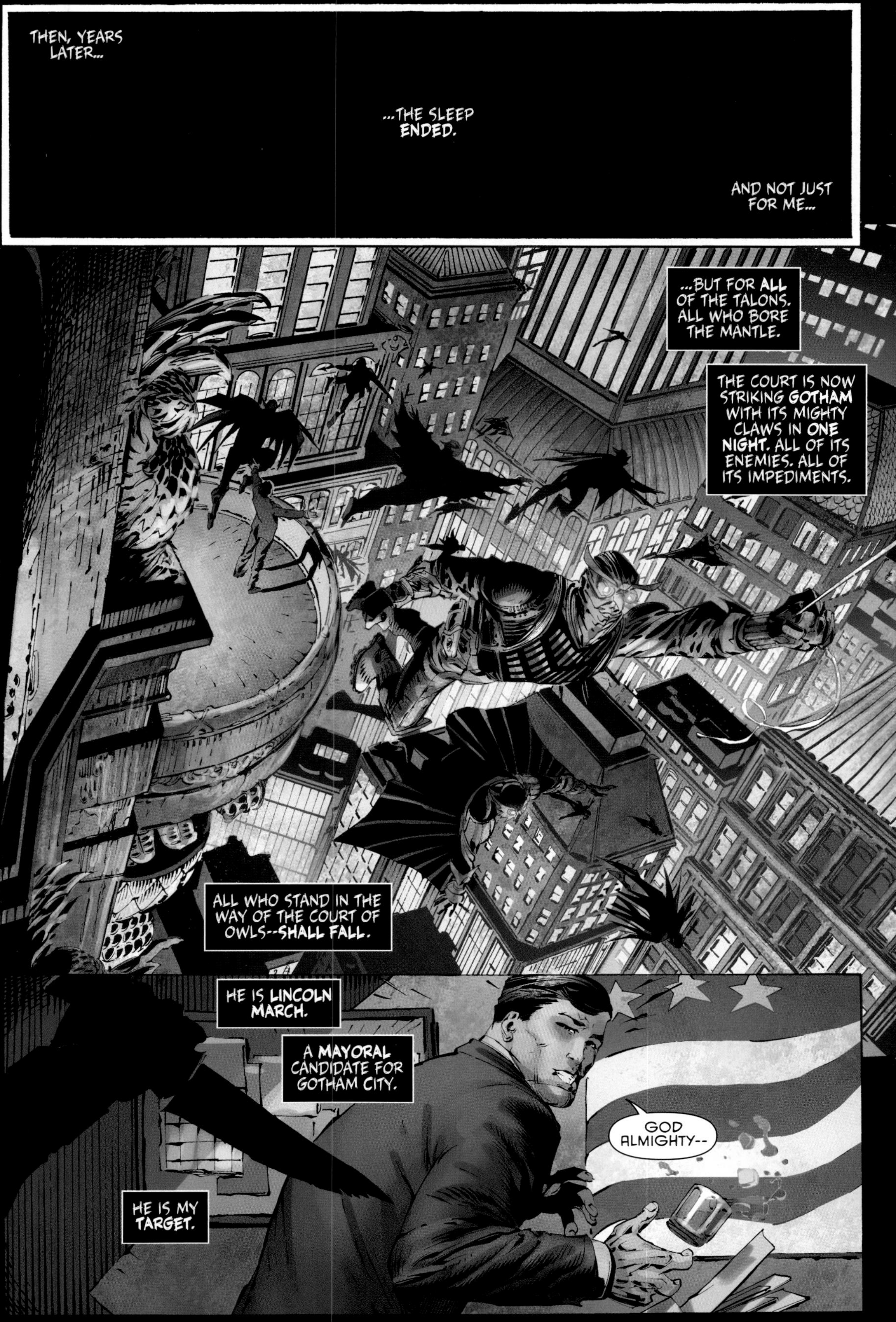
THEN, YEARS LATER...
...THE SLEEP ENDED.
AND NOT JUST FOR ME...
...BUT FOR ALL OF THE TALONS. ALL WHO BORE THE MANTLE.
THE COURT IS NOW STRIKING GOTHAM WITH ITS MIGHTY CLAWS IN ONE NIGHT. ALL OF ITS ENEMIES. ALL OF ITS IMPEDIMENTS.
ALL WHO STAND IN THE WAY OF THE COURT OF OWLS--SHALL FALL.
HE IS LINCOLN MARCH.
A MAYORAL CANDIDATE FOR GOTHAM CITY.
GOD ALMIGHTY--
HE IS MY TARGET.

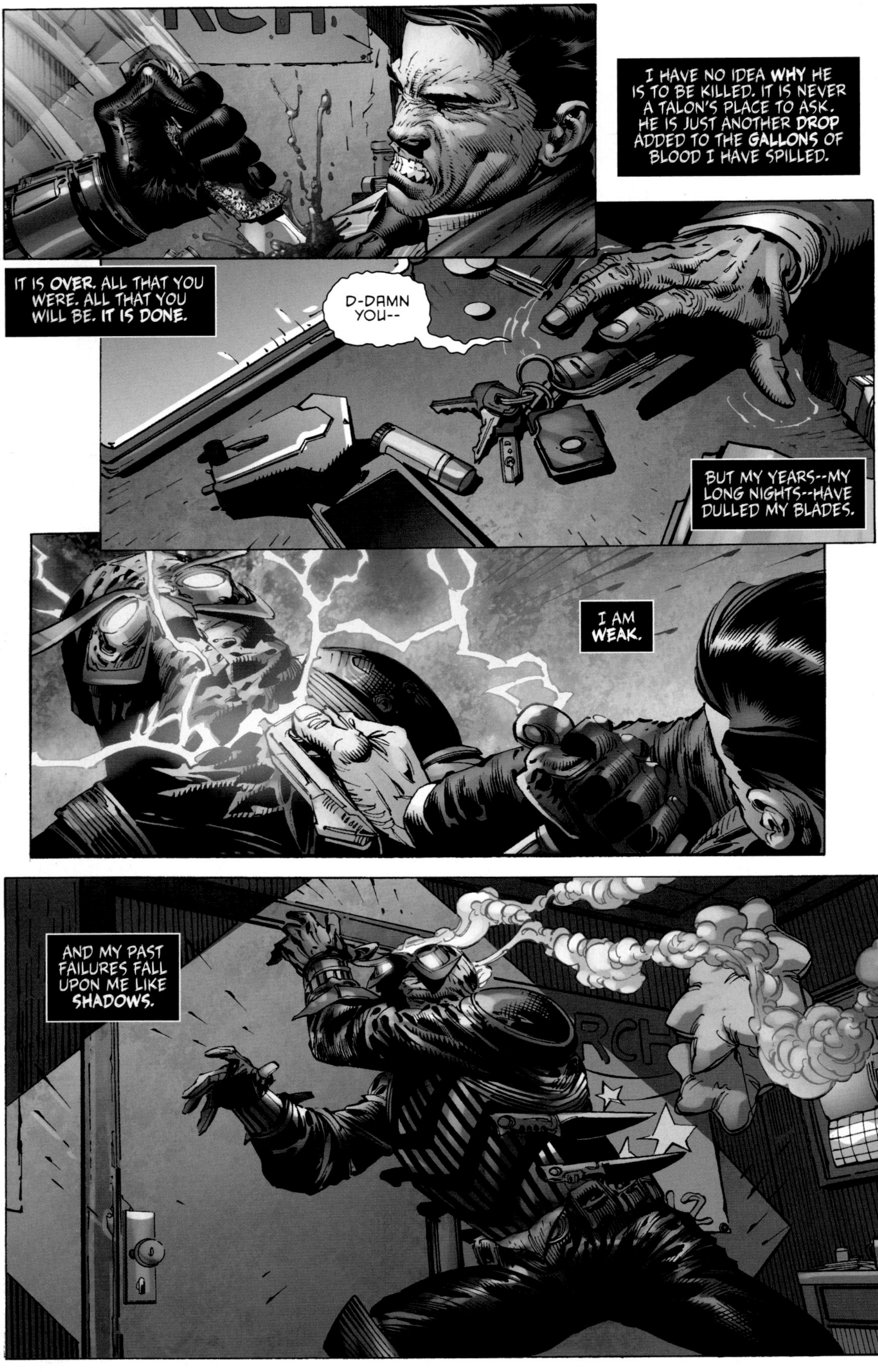
I HAVE NO IDEA WHY HE IS TO BE KILLED. IT IS NEVER A TALON'S PLACE TO ASK. HE IS JUST ANOTHER DROP ADDED TO THE GALLONS OF BLOOD I HAVE SPILLED.
IT IS OVER. ALL THAT YOU WERE. ALL THAT YOU WILL BE. IT IS DONE.
D-DAMN YOU--
BUT MY YEARS--MY LONG NIGHTS--HAVE DULLED MY BLADES.
I AM WEAK.
AND MY PAST FAILURES FALL UPON ME LIKE SHADOWS.

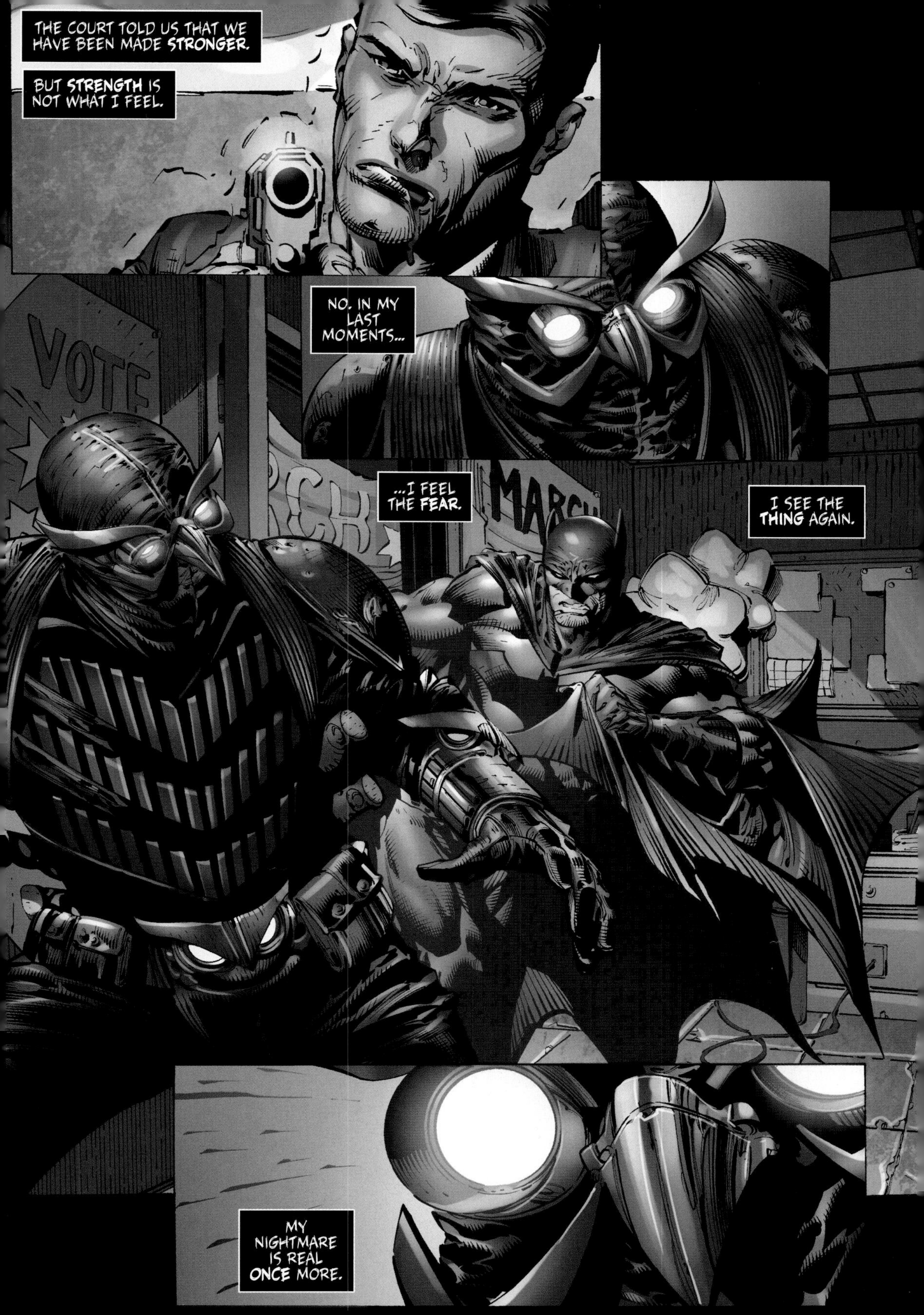
THE COURT TOLD US THAT WE HAVE BEEN MADE STRONGER.
BUT STRENGTH IS NOT WHAT I FEEL.
NO. IN MY LAST MOMENTS...
...I FEEL THE FEAR.
I SEE THE THING AGAIN.
MY NIGHTMARE IS REAL ONCE MORE.
VOTE
MARCH

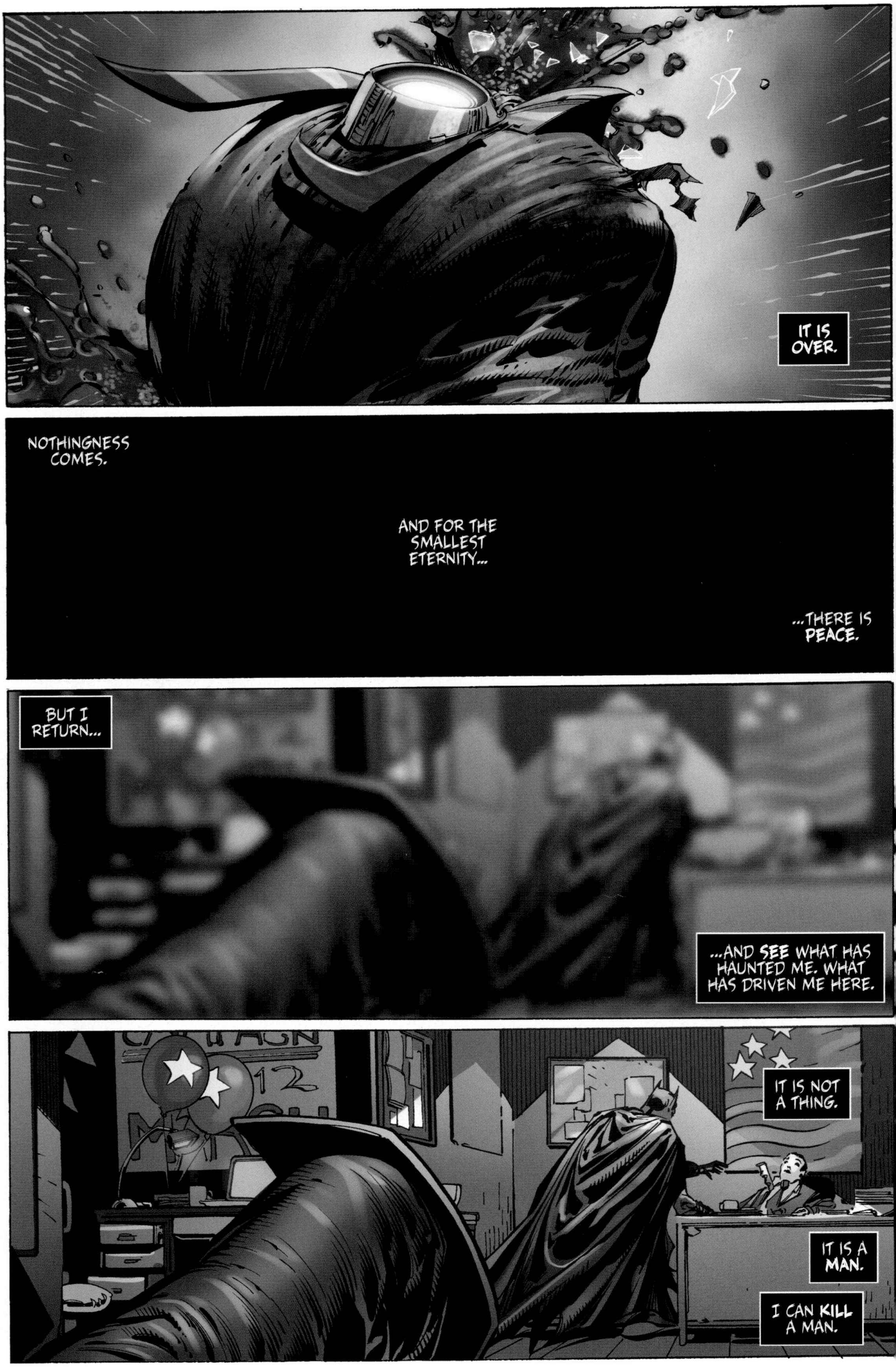
IT IS OVER.
NOTHINGNESS COMES.
AND FOR THE SMALLEST ETERNITY...
...THERE IS PEACE.
BUT I RETURN...
...AND SEE WHAT HAS HAUNTED ME. WHAT HAS DRIVEN ME HERE.
IT IS NOT A THING.
IT IS A MAN.
I CAN KILL A MAN.

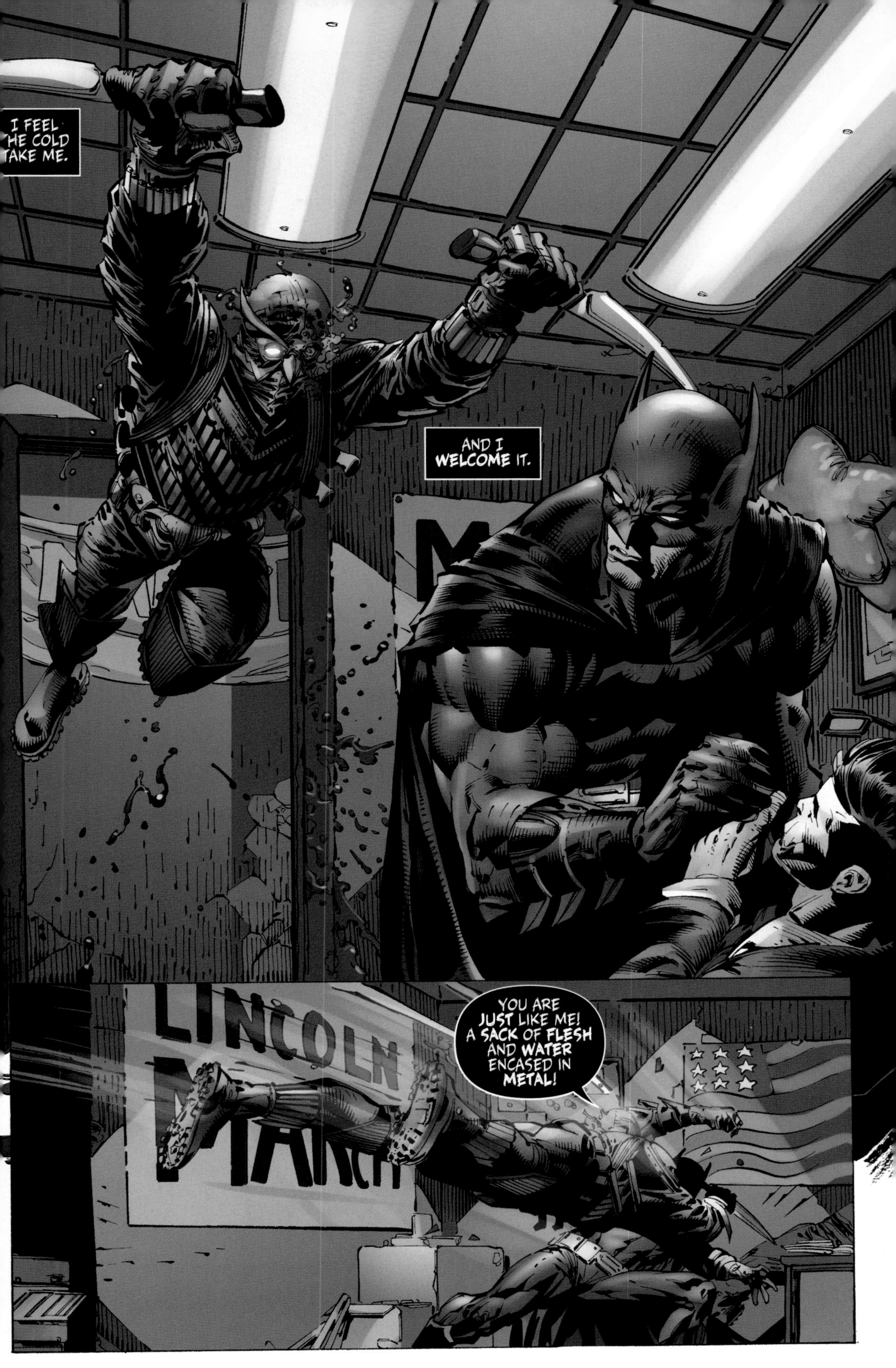
I FEEL HE COLD AKE ME.
AND I WELCOME IT.
LINCOLN
YOU ARE JUST LIKE ME! A SACK OF FLESH AND WATER ENCASED IN METAL!

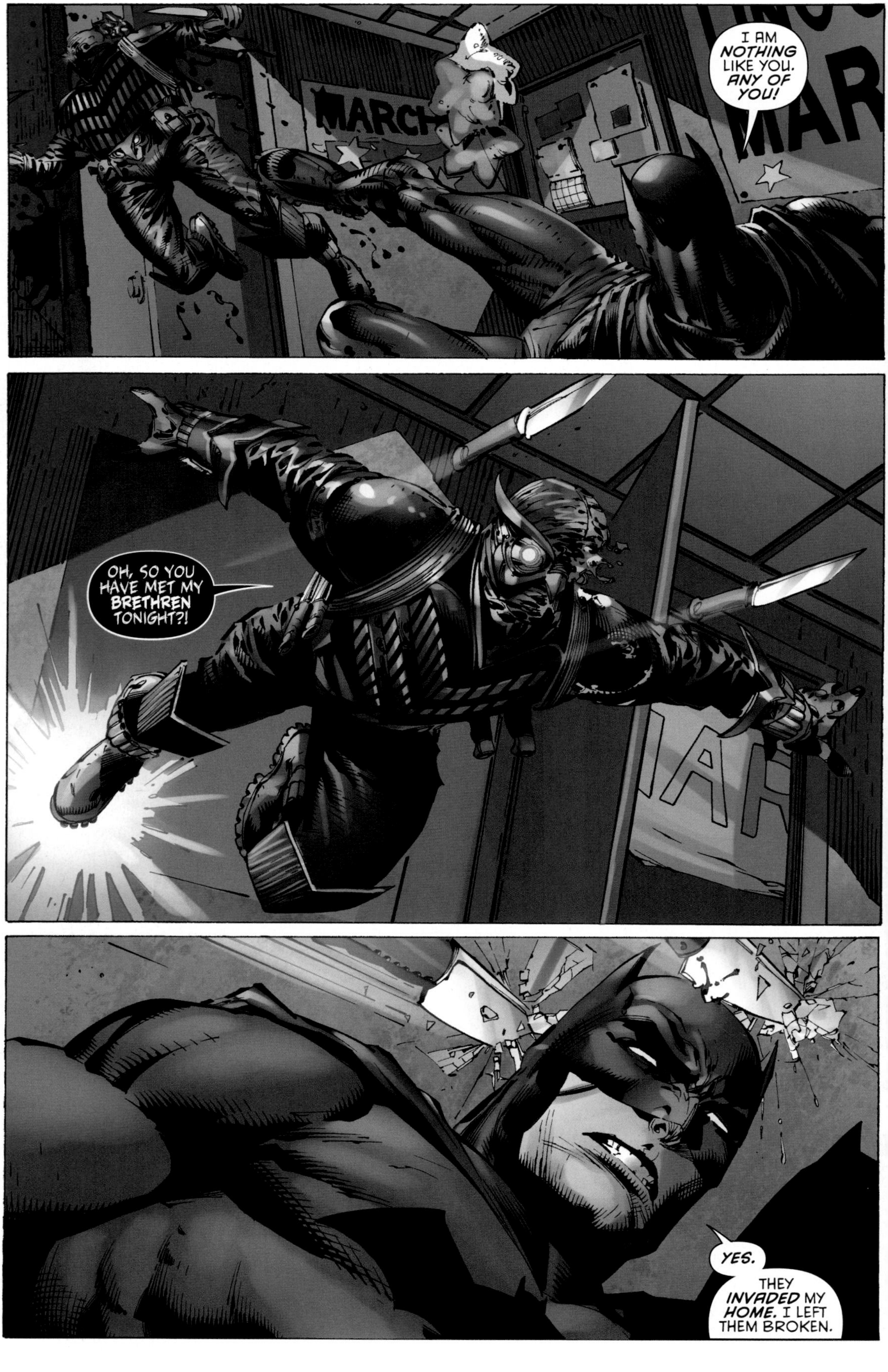
MARCH
I AM NOTHING LIKE YOU. ANY OF YOU!
OH, SO YOU HAVE MET MY BRETHREN TONIGHT?!
YES.
THEY INVADED MY HOME. I LEFT THEM BROKEN.

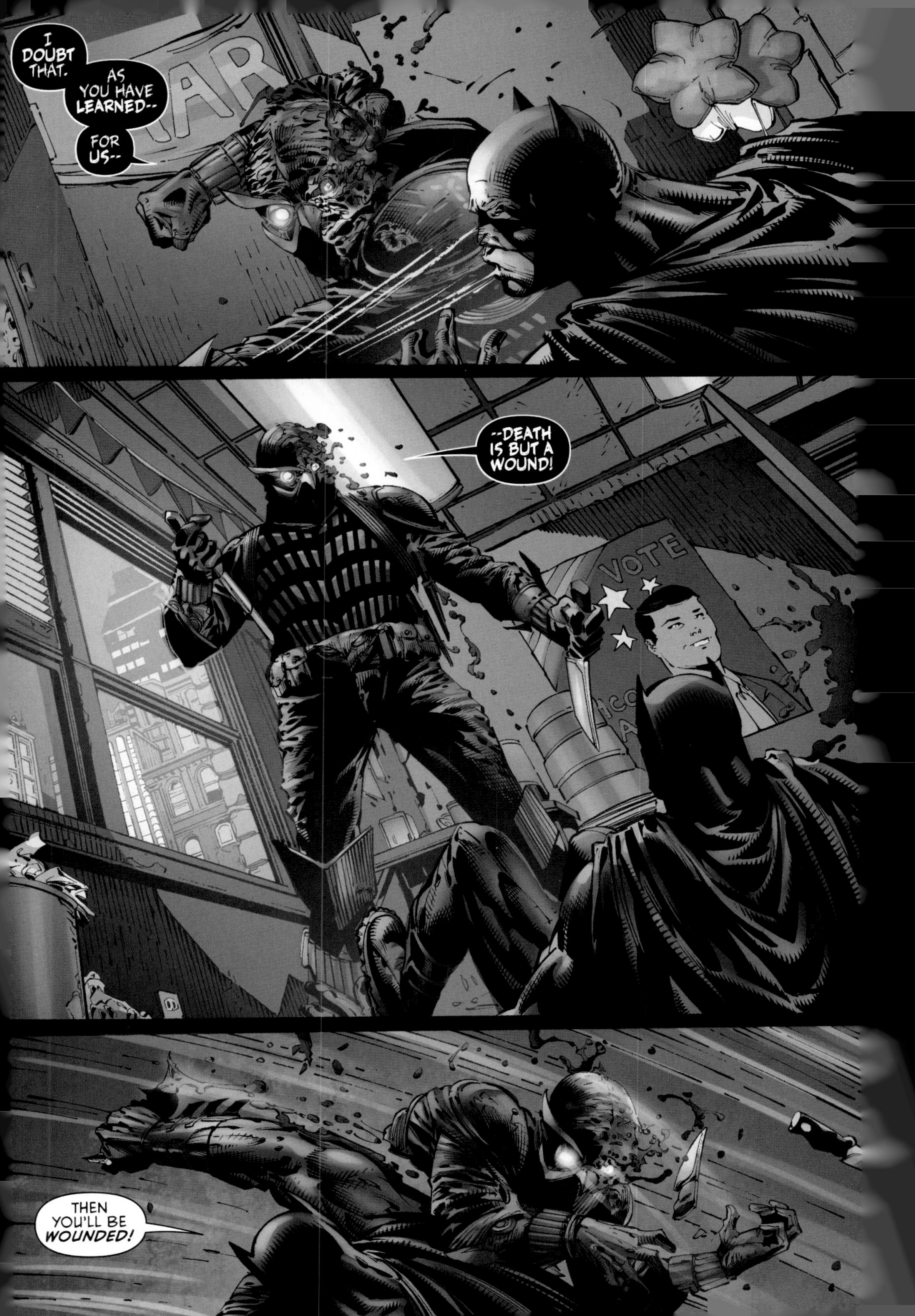
I DOUBT THAT.
AS YOU HAVE LEARNED--
FOR US--
--DEATH IS BUT A WOUND!
VOTE
THEN YOU'LL BE *WOUNDED!*

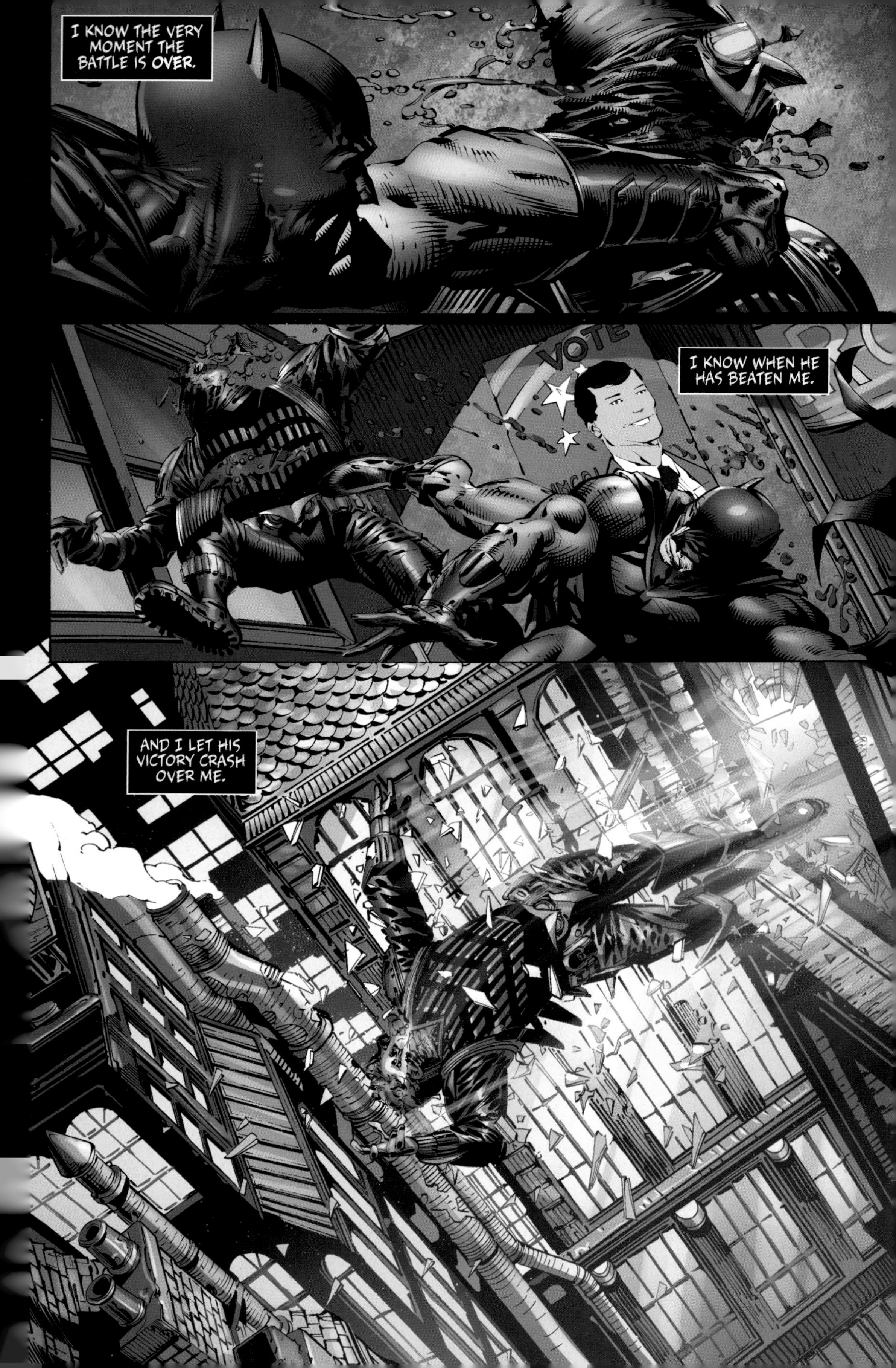
I KNOW THE VERY MOMENT THE BATTLE IS OVER.
VOTE
I KNOW WHEN HE HAS BEATEN ME.
AND I LET HIS VICTORY CRASH OVER ME.

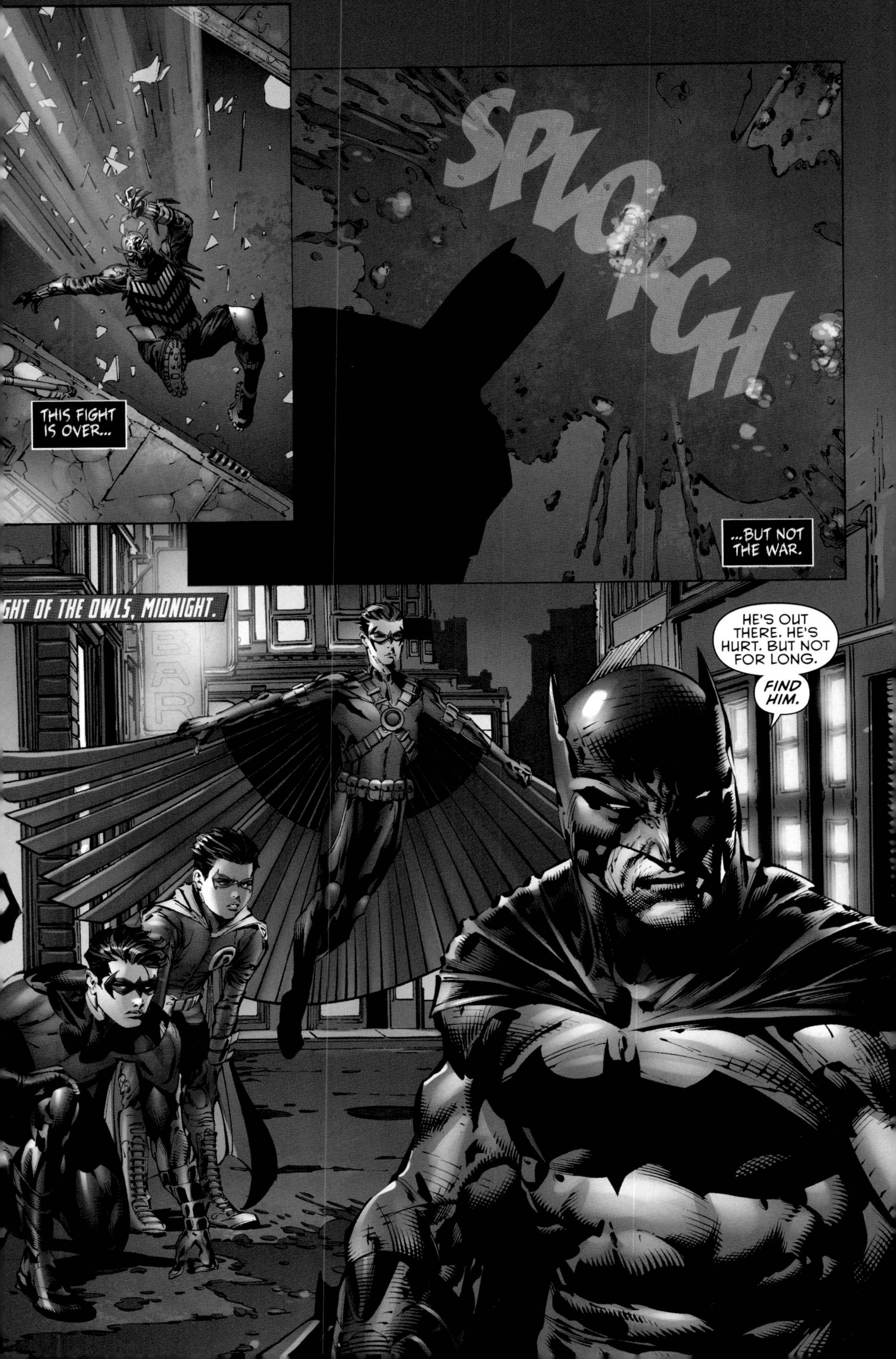
THIS FIGHT IS OVER...
SPLORCH
...BUT NOT THE WAR.
GHT OF THE OWLS, MIDNIGHT.
BAR
HE'S OUT THERE. HE'S HURT. BUT NOT FOR LONG.
FIND HIM.

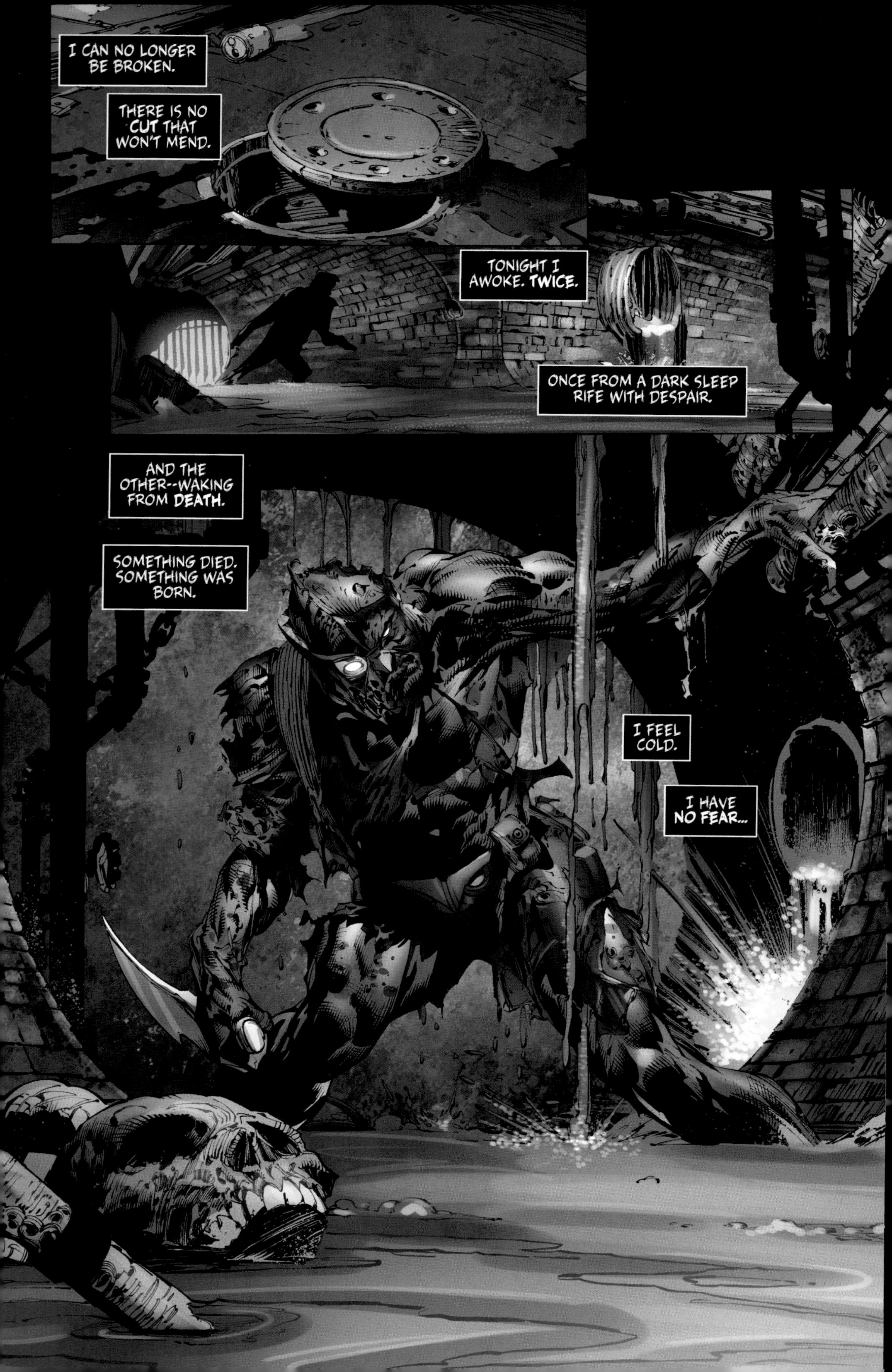
I CAN NO LONGER BE BROKEN.
THERE IS NO **CUT** THAT WON'T MEND.
TONIGHT I AWOKE. **TWICE.**
ONCE FROM A DARK SLEEP RIFE WITH DESPAIR.
AND THE OTHER--WAKING FROM **DEATH.**
SOMETHING DIED. SOMETHING WAS BORN.
I FEEL COLD.
I HAVE **NO FEAR...**

PENC[redacted]H

PENCILLER INKER PAGE# 20

TITLE ISSUE # 2 MONTH

INTERIORS

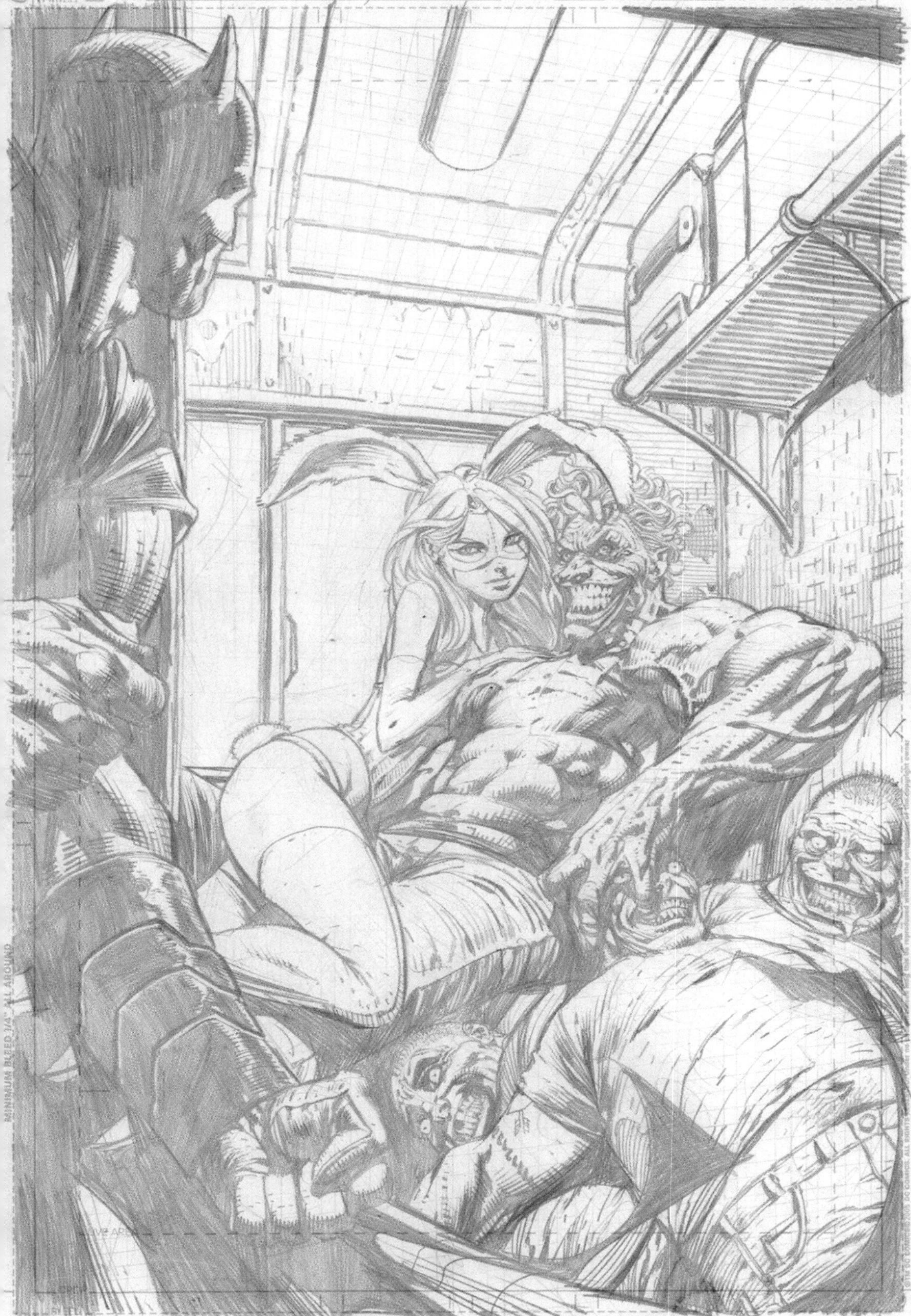

MINIMUM BLEED 1/4" ALL AROUND

← CUT RIGHT-HAND PAGE AT THIS LINE

DOUBLE PAGE SPREAD: CUT AS SHOWN, ABUT PAGE EDGES, TAPE ON BACK, DO NOT OVERLAP

CUT LEFT HAND PAGE AT THIS LINE →

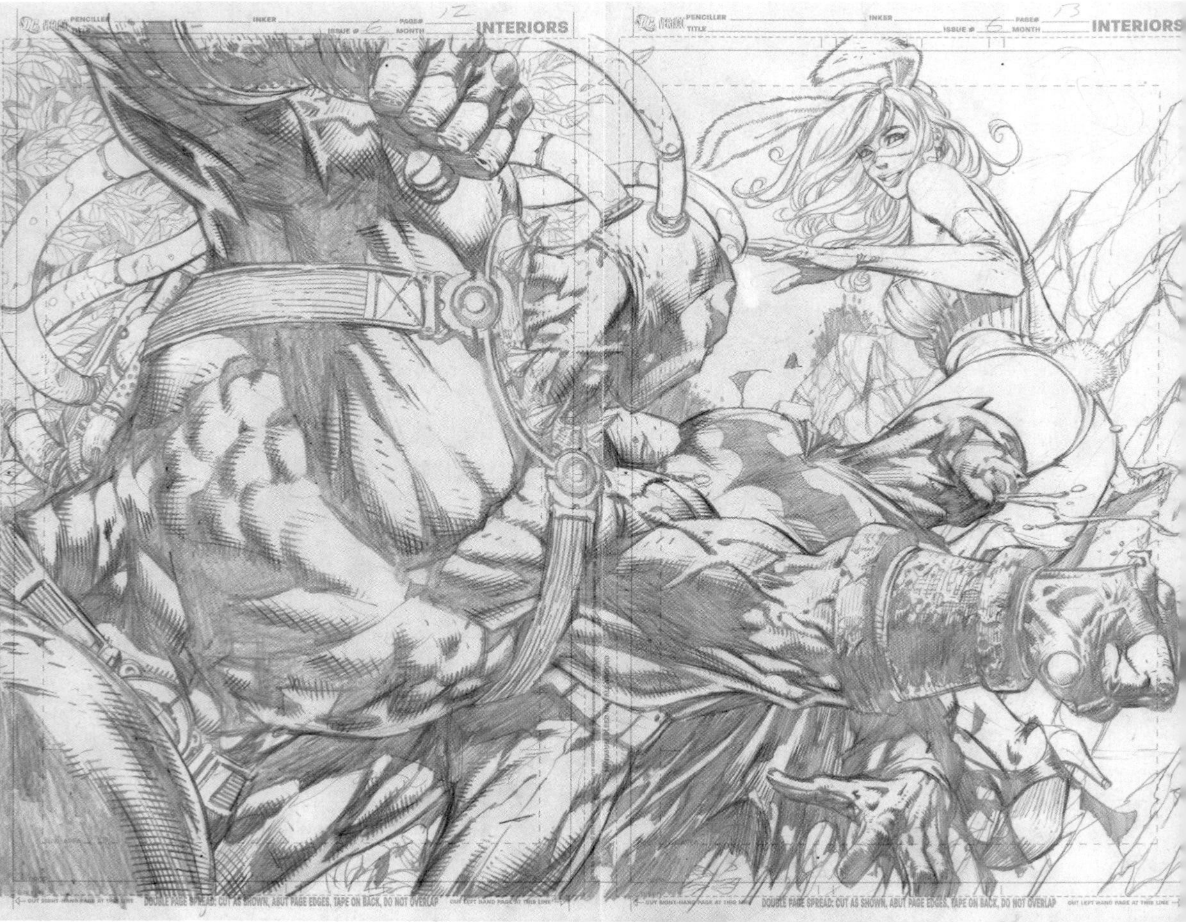
PENCILLER
INKER
PAGE# 12
ISSUE # 6
MONTH
INTERIORS
DOUBLE PAGE SPREAD: CUT AS SHOWN, ABUT PAGE EDGES, TAPE ON BACK, DO NOT OVERLAP
PENCILLER
TITLE
INKER
PAGE# 13
ISSUE # 6
MONTH
INTERIORS
DOUBLE PAGE SPREAD: CUT AS SHOWN, ABUT PAGE EDGES, TAPE ON BACK, DO NOT OVERLAP

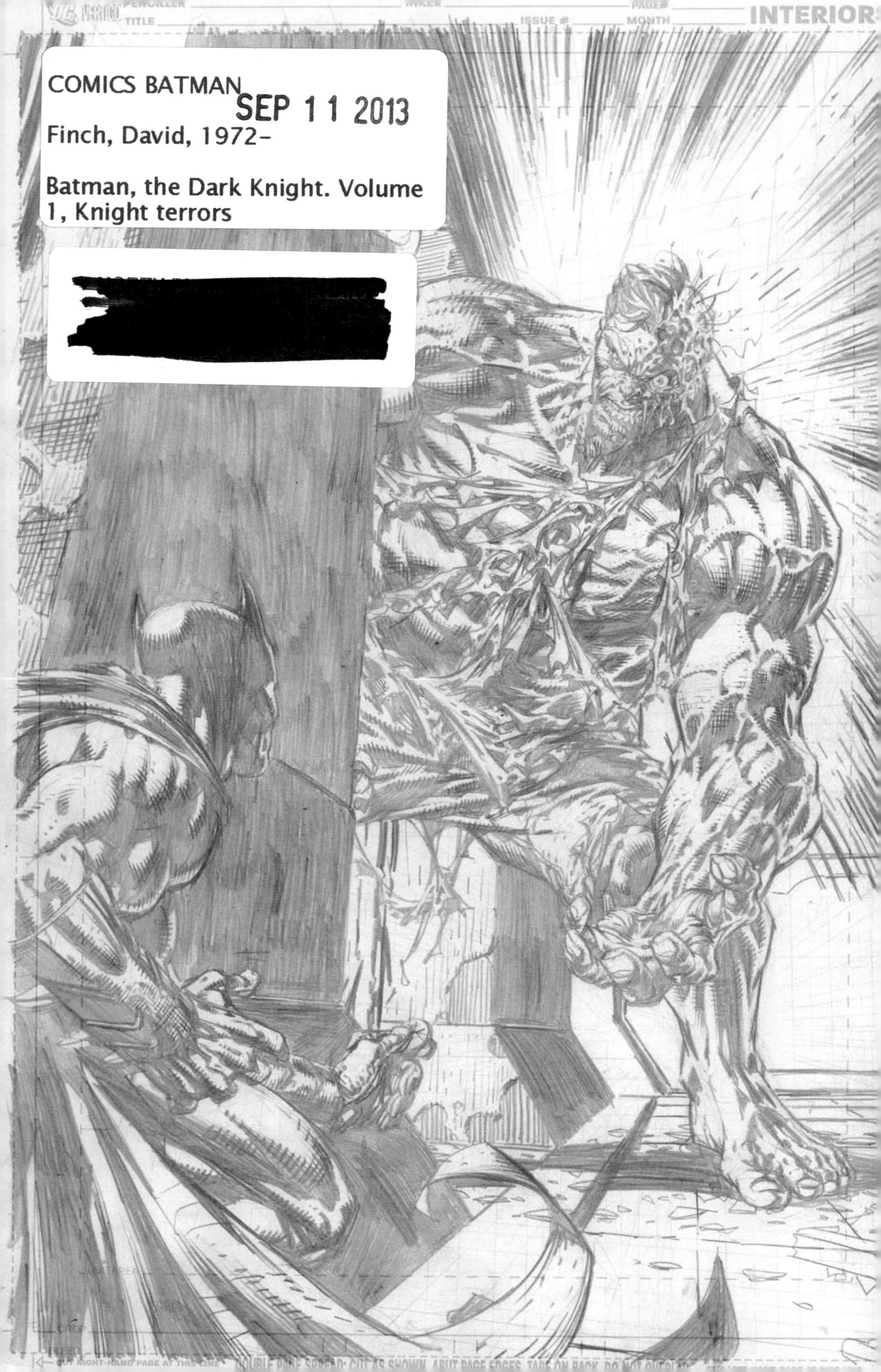
TITLE
ISSUE #
MONTH
INTERIOR